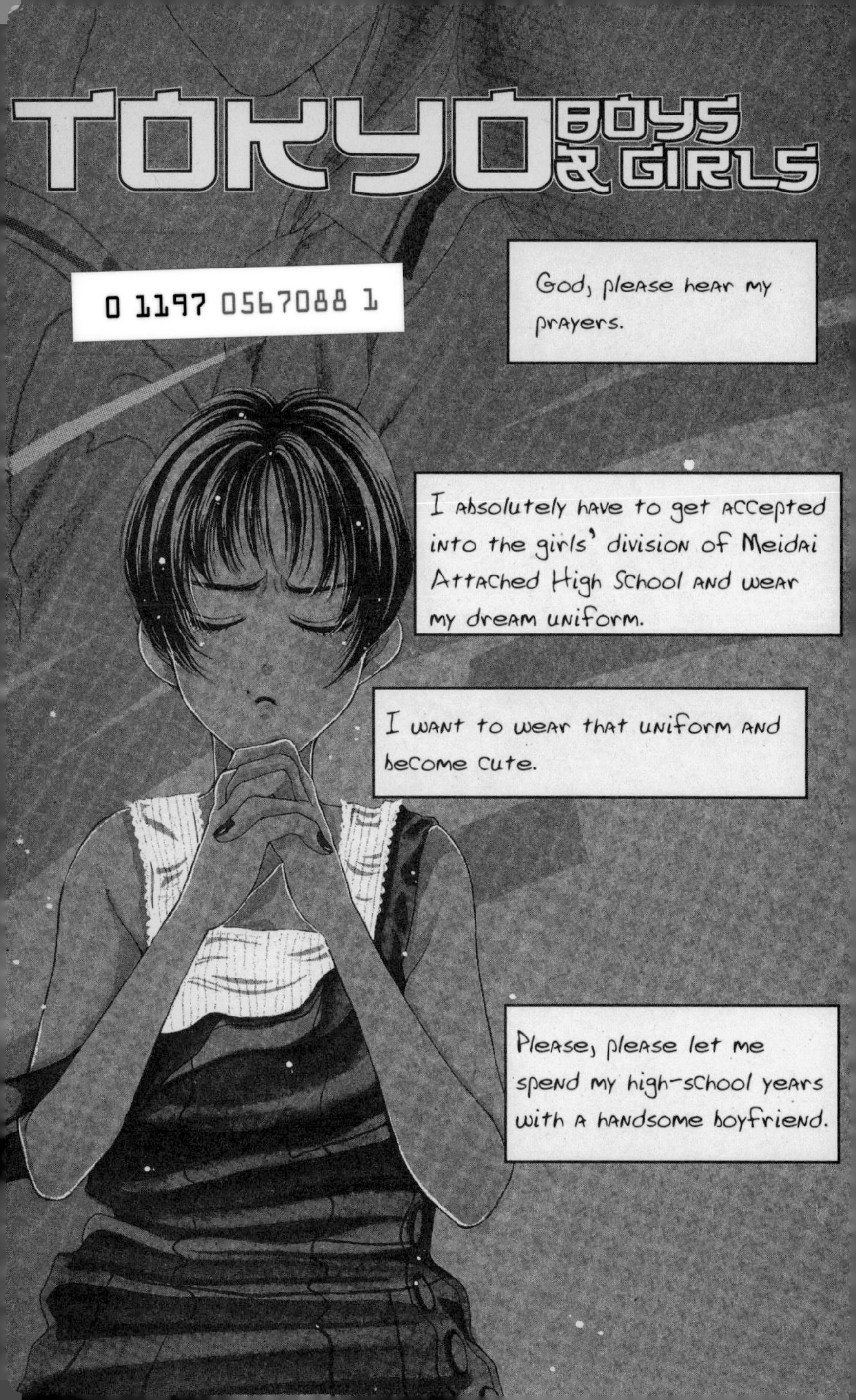
TOKYO BOYS & GIRLS
0 1197 0567088 1
God, please hear my prayers.
I absolutely have to get accepted into the girls' division of Meidai Attached High School and wear my dream uniform.
I want to wear that uniform and become cute.
Please, please let me spend my high-school years with a handsome boyfriend.

Shojo Beat

東京
少年少女

1

TOKYO BOYS & GIRLS™
Story & Art by Miki Aihara

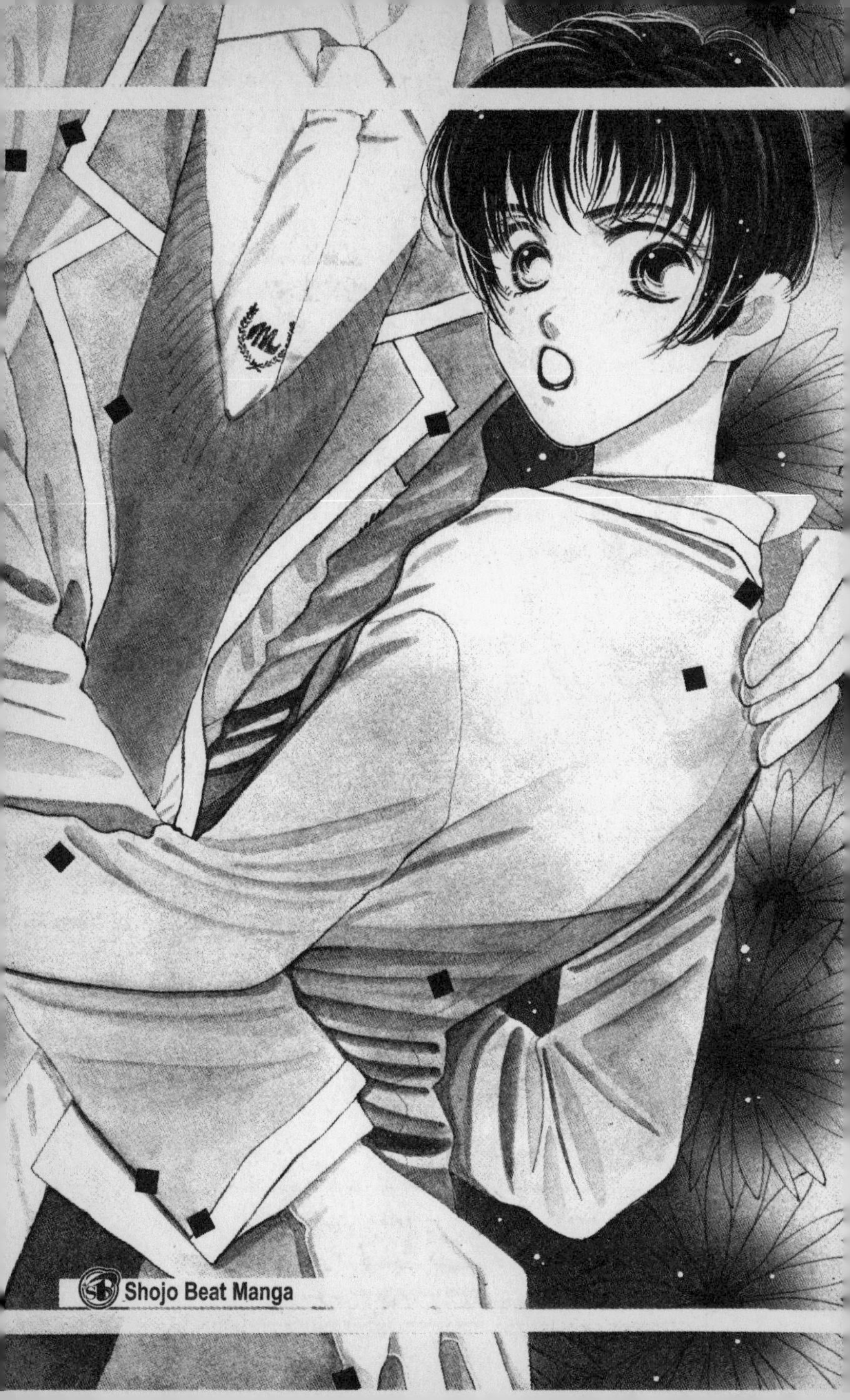
Shojo Beat Manga

TOKYO BOYS & GIRLS

CONTENTS

Shojo Beat Manga

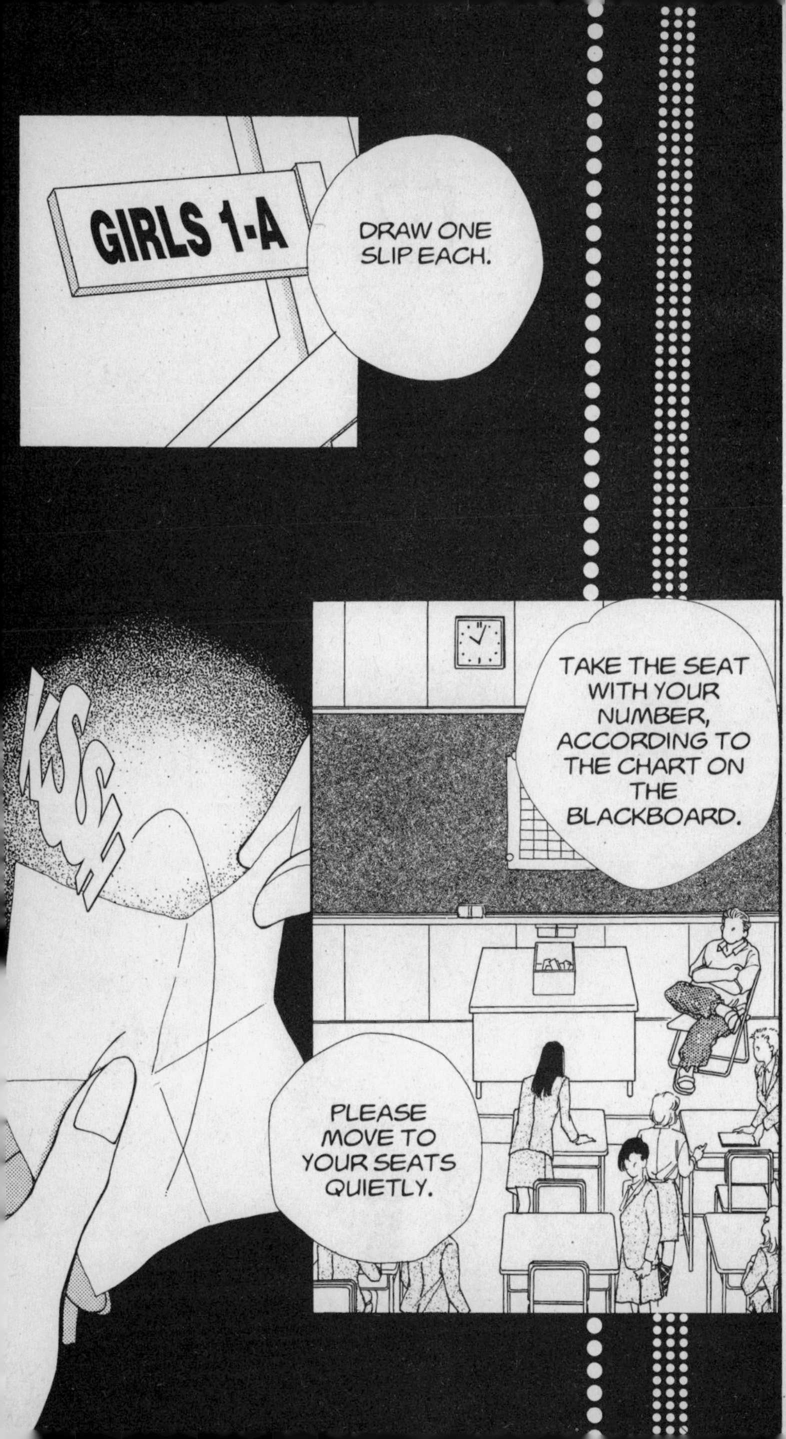
GIRLS 1-A
DRAW ONE SLIP EACH.
TAKE THE SEAT WITH YOUR NUMBER, ACCORDING TO THE CHART ON THE BLACKBOARD.
PLEASE MOVE TO YOUR SEATS QUIETLY.
KSSH

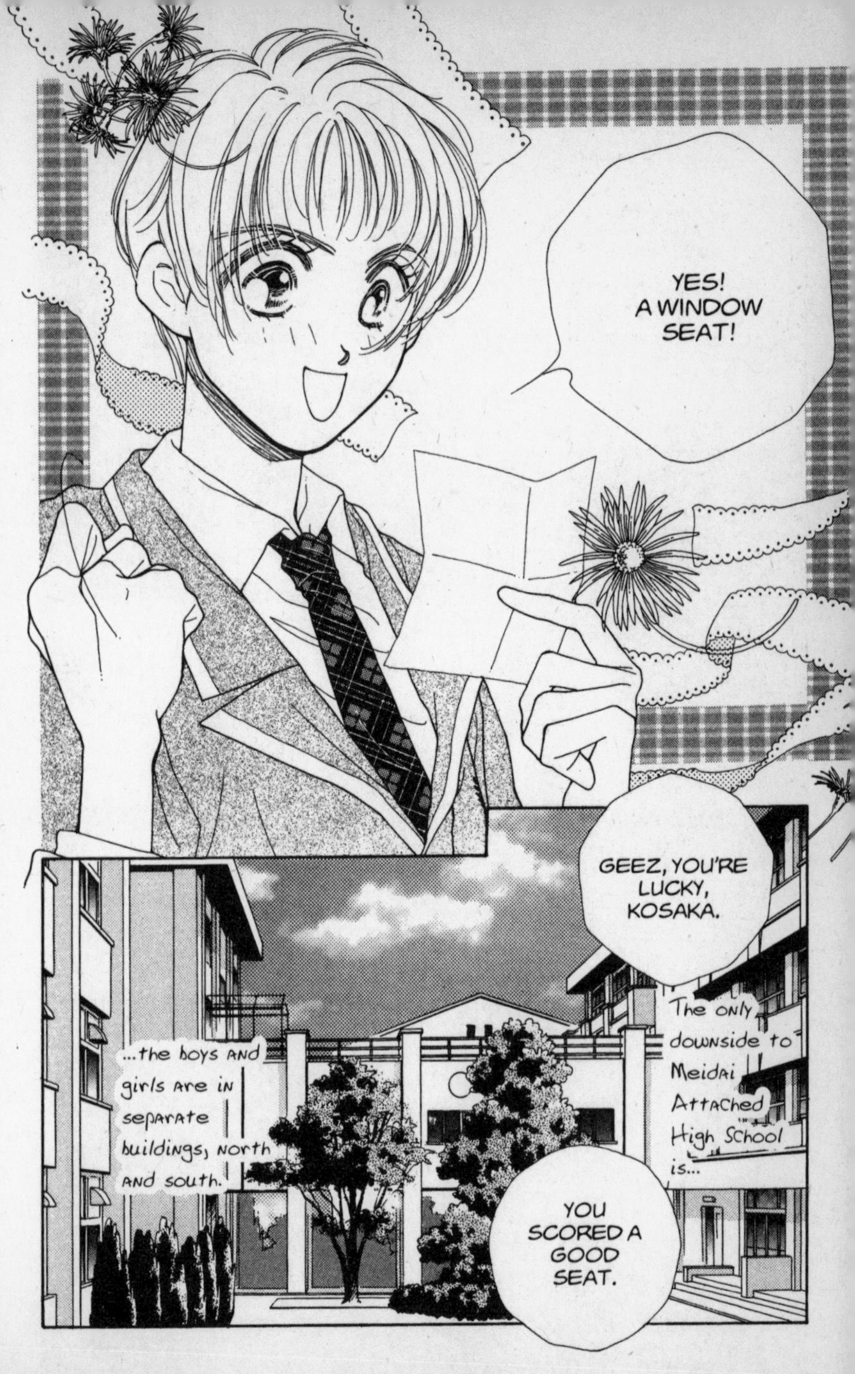
YES! A WINDOW SEAT!
GEEZ, YOU'RE LUCKY, KOSAKA.
The only downside to Meidai Attached High School is...
YOU SCORED A GOOD SEAT.
...the boys and girls are in separate buildings, north and south.

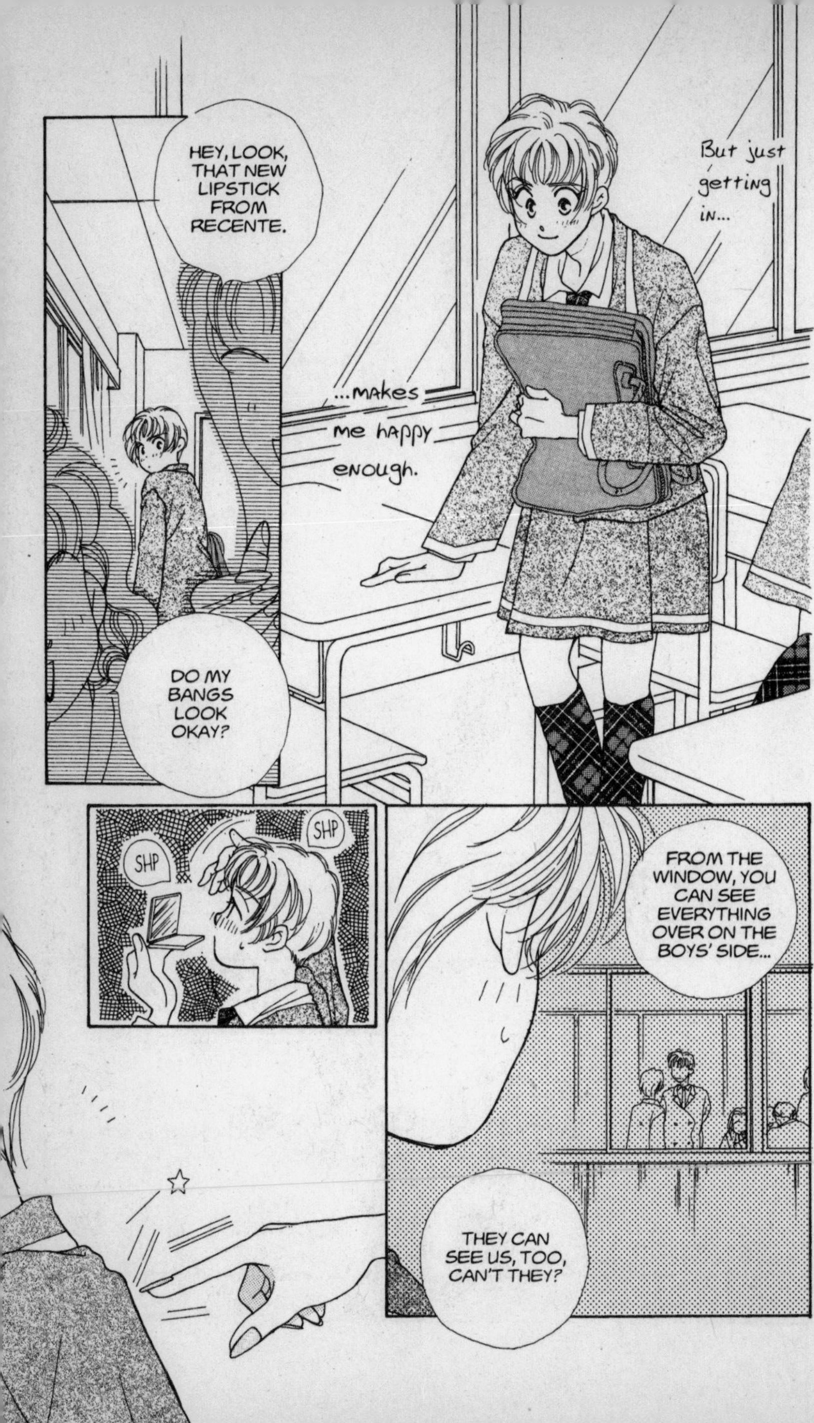
But just getting in...
...makes me happy enough.
HEY, LOOK, THAT NEW LIPSTICK FROM RECENTE.
DO MY BANGS LOOK OKAY?
FROM THE WINDOW, YOU CAN SEE EVERYTHING OVER ON THE BOYS' SIDE...
THEY CAN SEE US, TOO, CAN'T THEY?
SHP
SHP

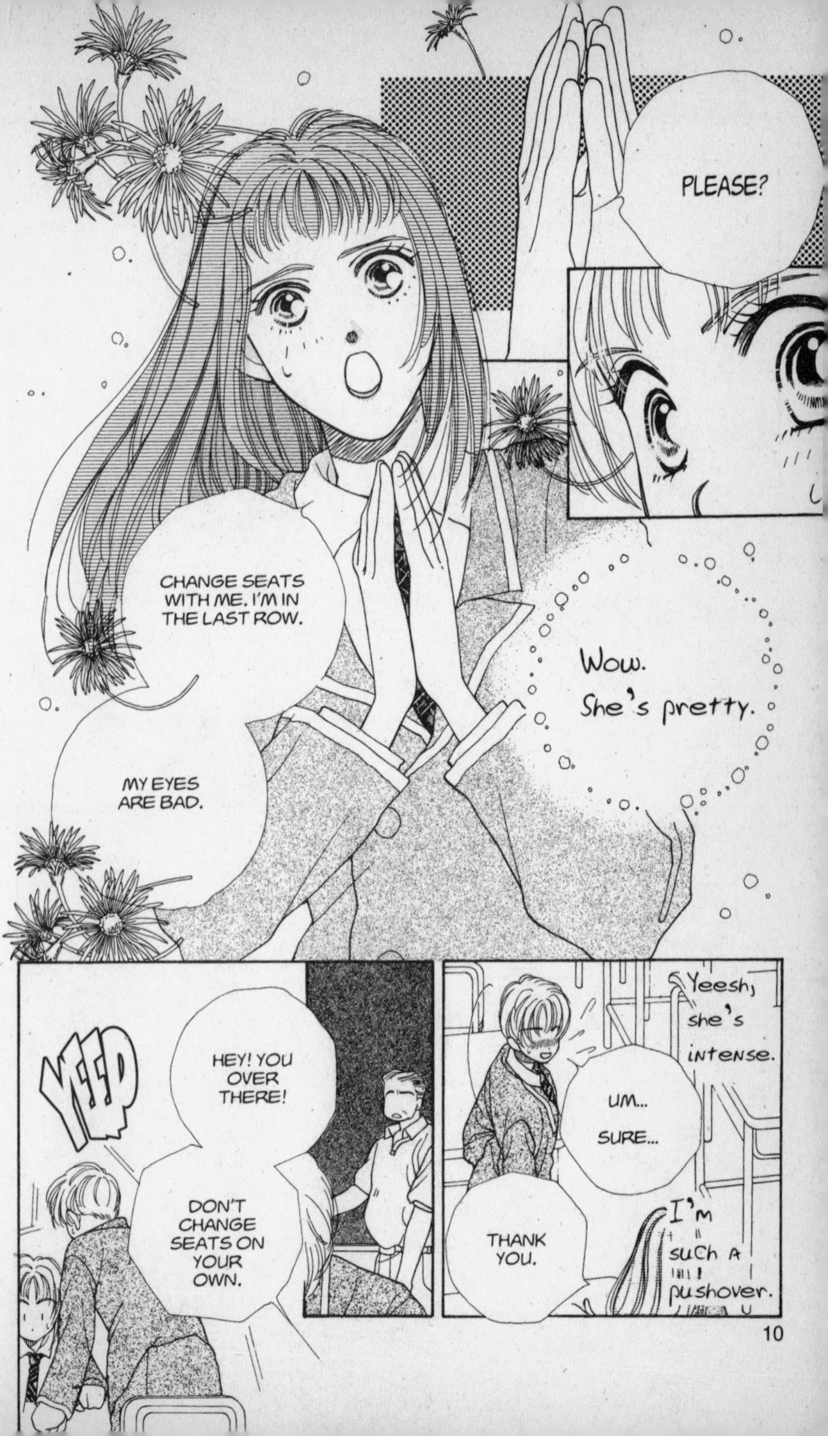
PLEASE?
CHANGE SEATS WITH ME. I'M IN THE LAST ROW.
MY EYES ARE BAD.
Wow. She's pretty.
Yeesh, she's intense.
UM... SURE...
THANK YOU.
I'm such a pushover.
HEY! YOU OVER THERE!
DON'T CHANGE SEATS ON YOUR OWN.

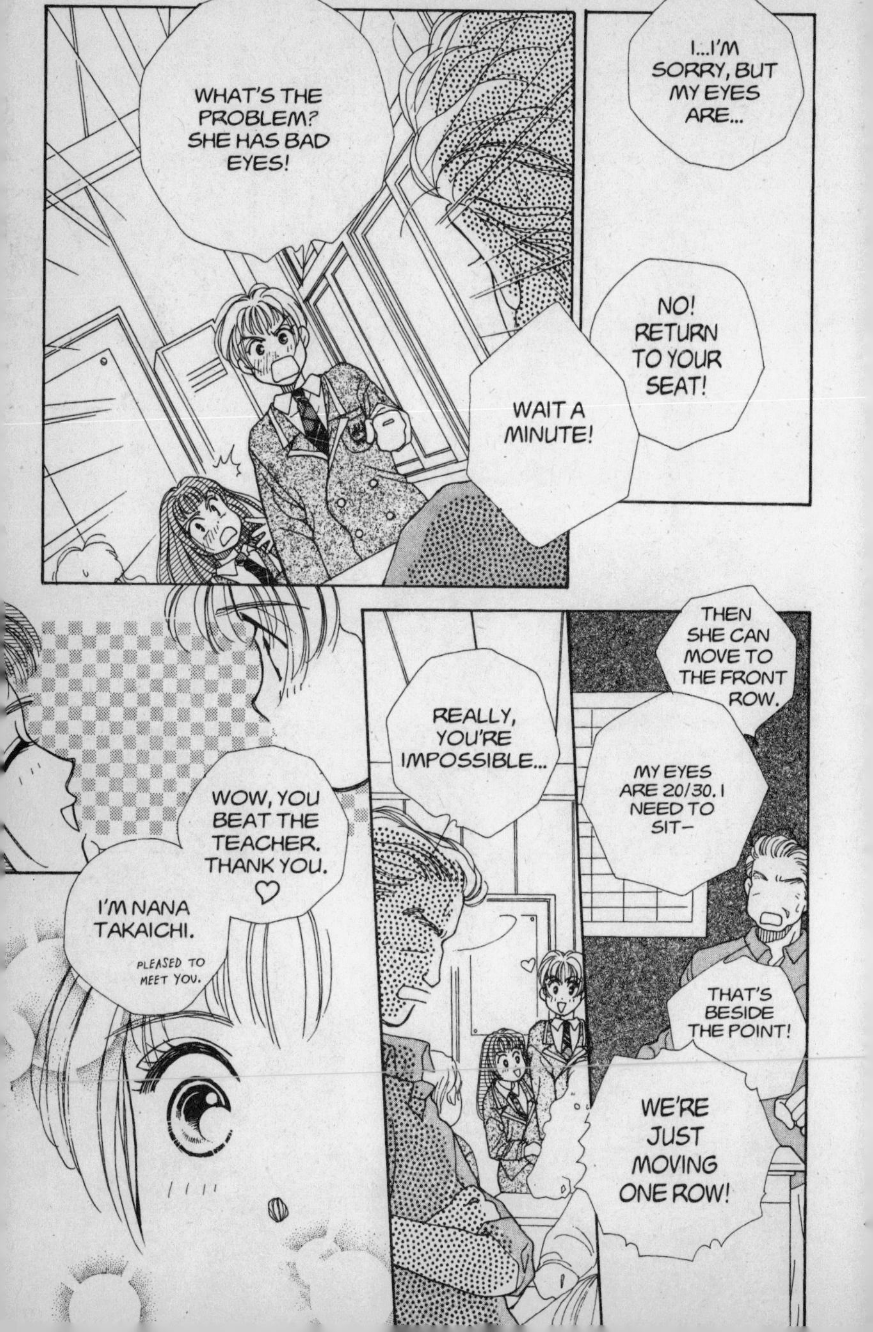
I...I'M SORRY, BUT MY EYES ARE...
NO! RETURN TO YOUR SEAT!
WAIT A MINUTE!
WHAT'S THE PROBLEM? SHE HAS BAD EYES!
THEN SHE CAN MOVE TO THE FRONT ROW.
MY EYES ARE 20/30. I NEED TO SIT–
REALLY, YOU'RE IMPOSSIBLE...
THAT'S BESIDE THE POINT!
WE'RE JUST MOVING ONE ROW!
WOW, YOU BEAT THE TEACHER. THANK YOU. ♡
I'M NANA TAKAICHI.
PLEASED TO MEET YOU.

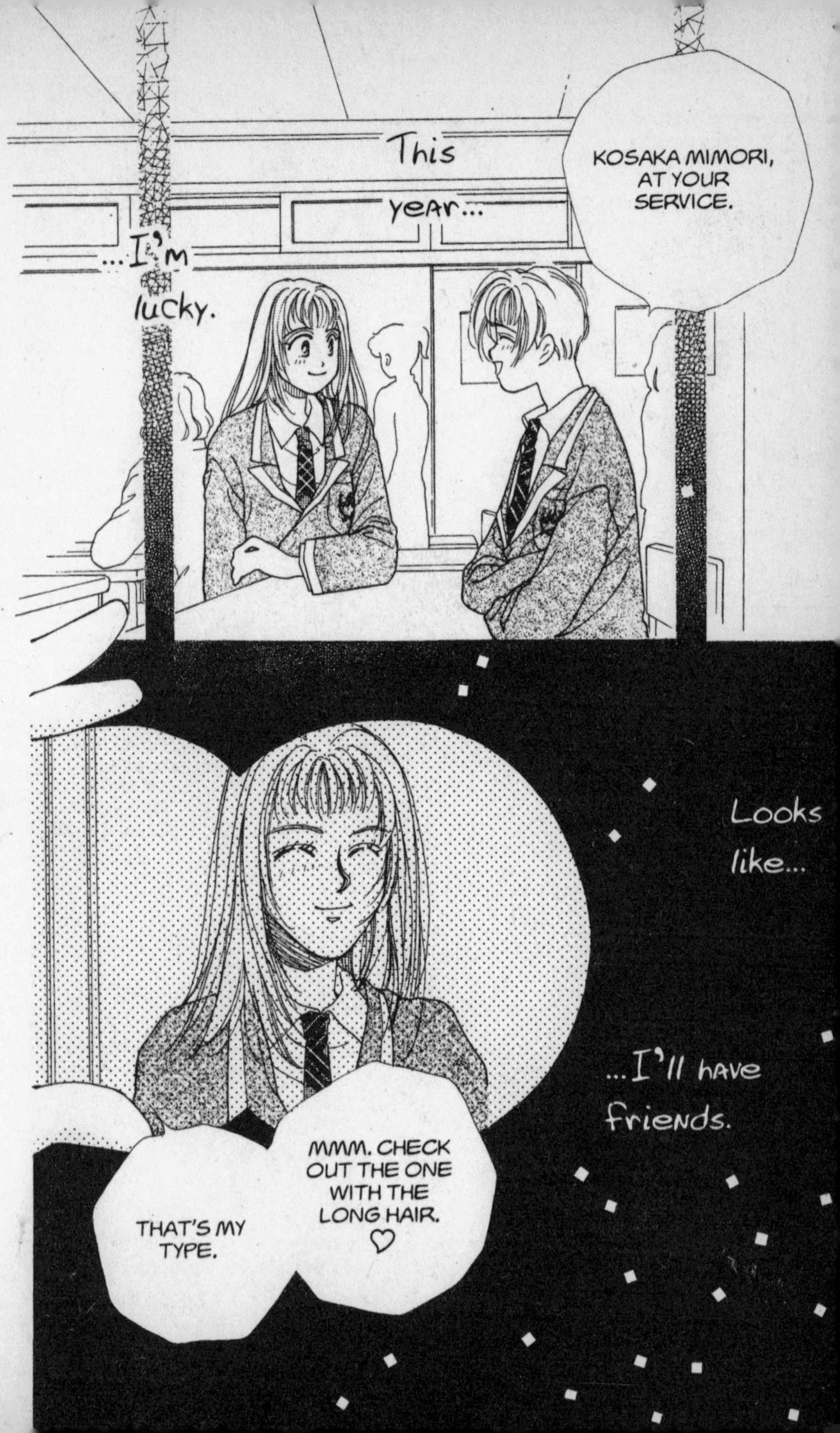
KOSAKA MIMORI, AT YOUR SERVICE.
This year...
...I'm lucky.
Looks like...
...I'll have friends.
MMM. CHECK OUT THE ONE WITH THE LONG HAIR. ♡
THAT'S MY TYPE.

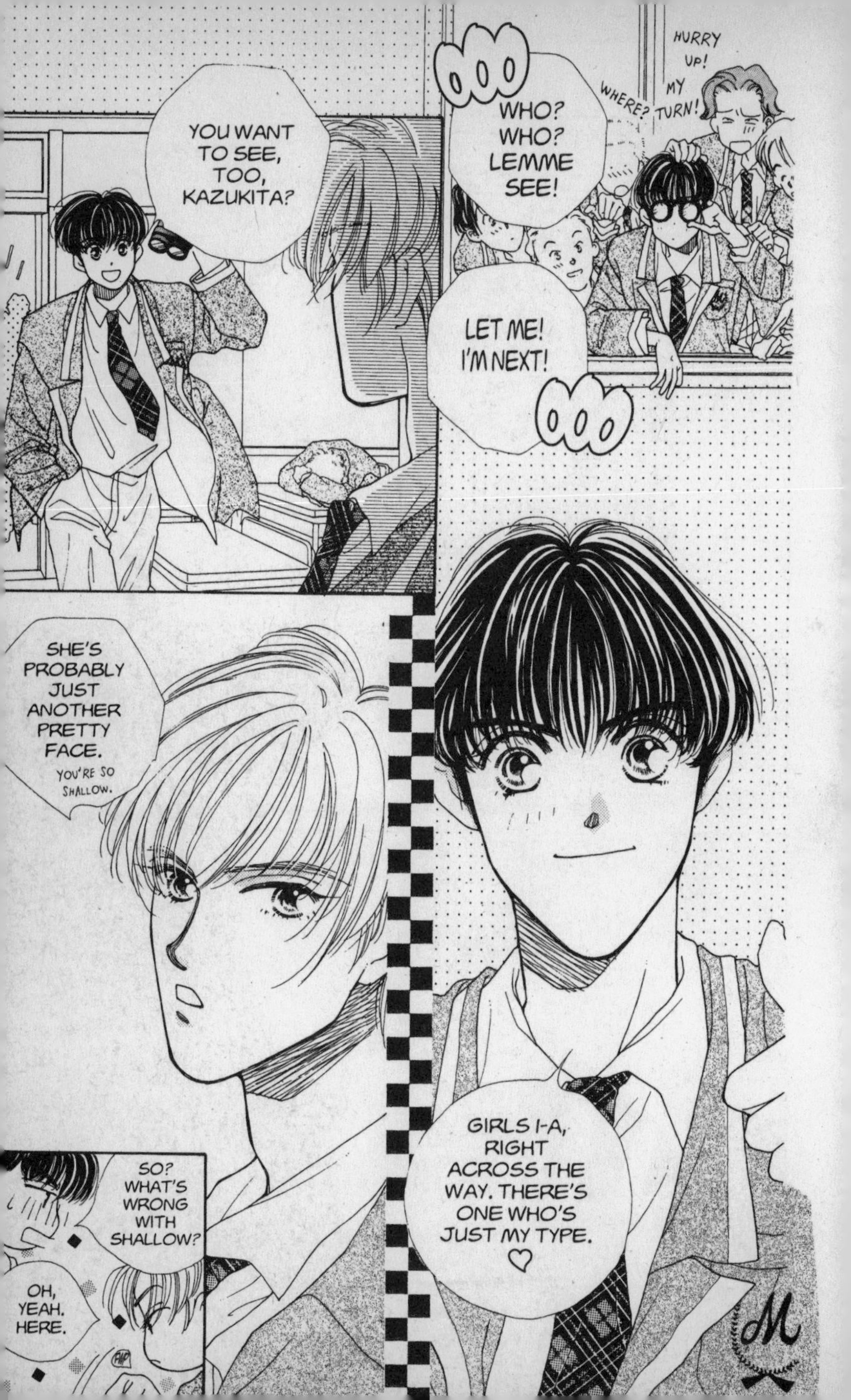
HURRY UP!
MY TURN!
WHERE?
WHO? WHO? LEMME SEE!
LET ME! I'M NEXT!
YOU WANT TO SEE, TOO, KAZUKITA?
GIRLS I-A, RIGHT ACROSS THE WAY. THERE'S ONE WHO'S JUST MY TYPE. ♡
SHE'S PROBABLY JUST ANOTHER PRETTY FACE.
YOU'RE SO SHALLOW.
SO? WHAT'S WRONG WITH SHALLOW?
OH, YEAH. HERE.

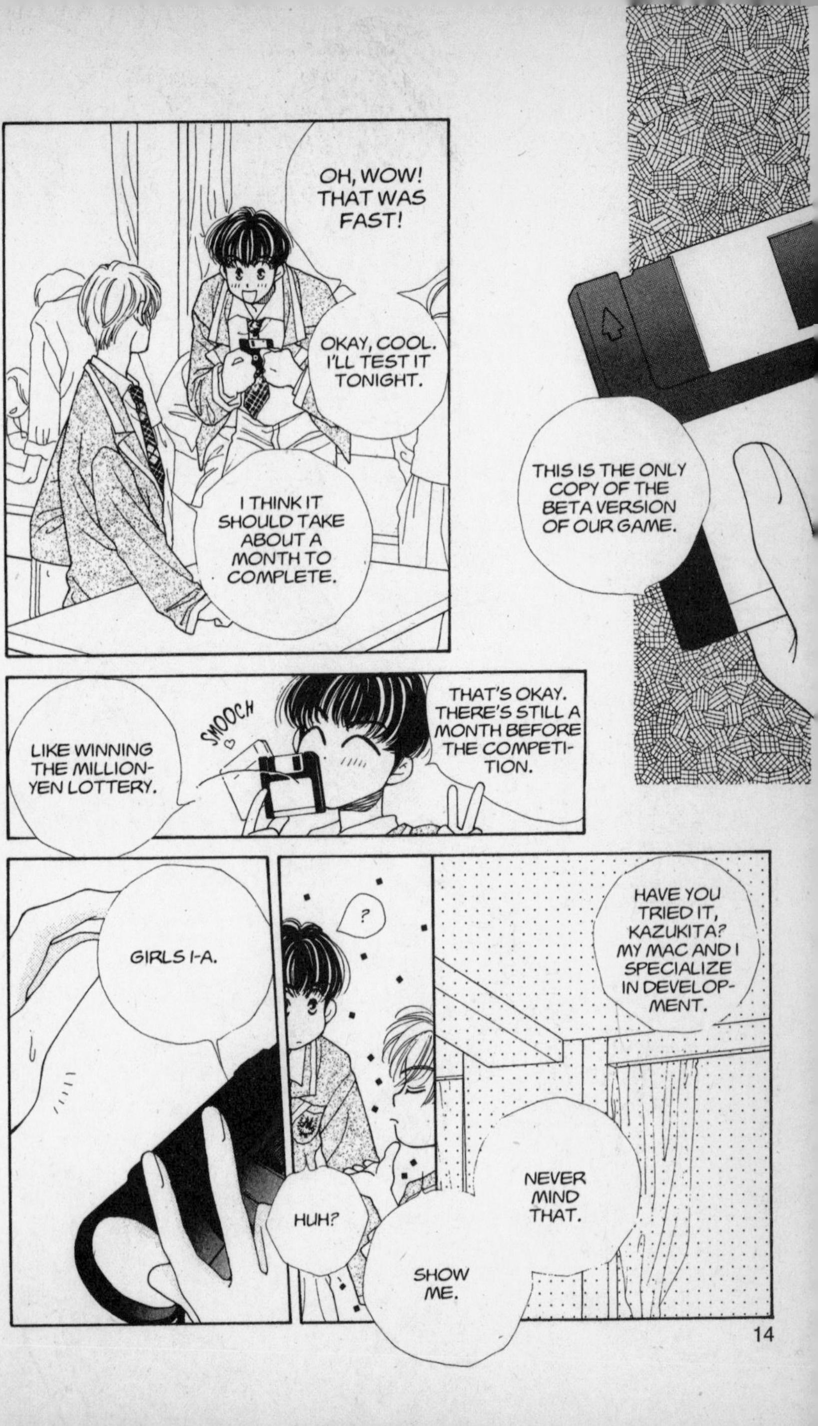
THIS IS THE ONLY COPY OF THE BETA VERSION OF OUR GAME.
OH, WOW! THAT WAS FAST!
OKAY, COOL. I'LL TEST IT TONIGHT.
I THINK IT SHOULD TAKE ABOUT A MONTH TO COMPLETE.
THAT'S OKAY. THERE'S STILL A MONTH BEFORE THE COMPETI- TION.
SMOOCH
LIKE WINNING THE MILLION- YEN LOTTERY.
HAVE YOU TRIED IT, KAZUKITA? MY MAC AND I SPECIALIZE IN DEVELOP- MENT.
?
NEVER MIND THAT.
HUH?
SHOW ME.
GIRLS I-A.

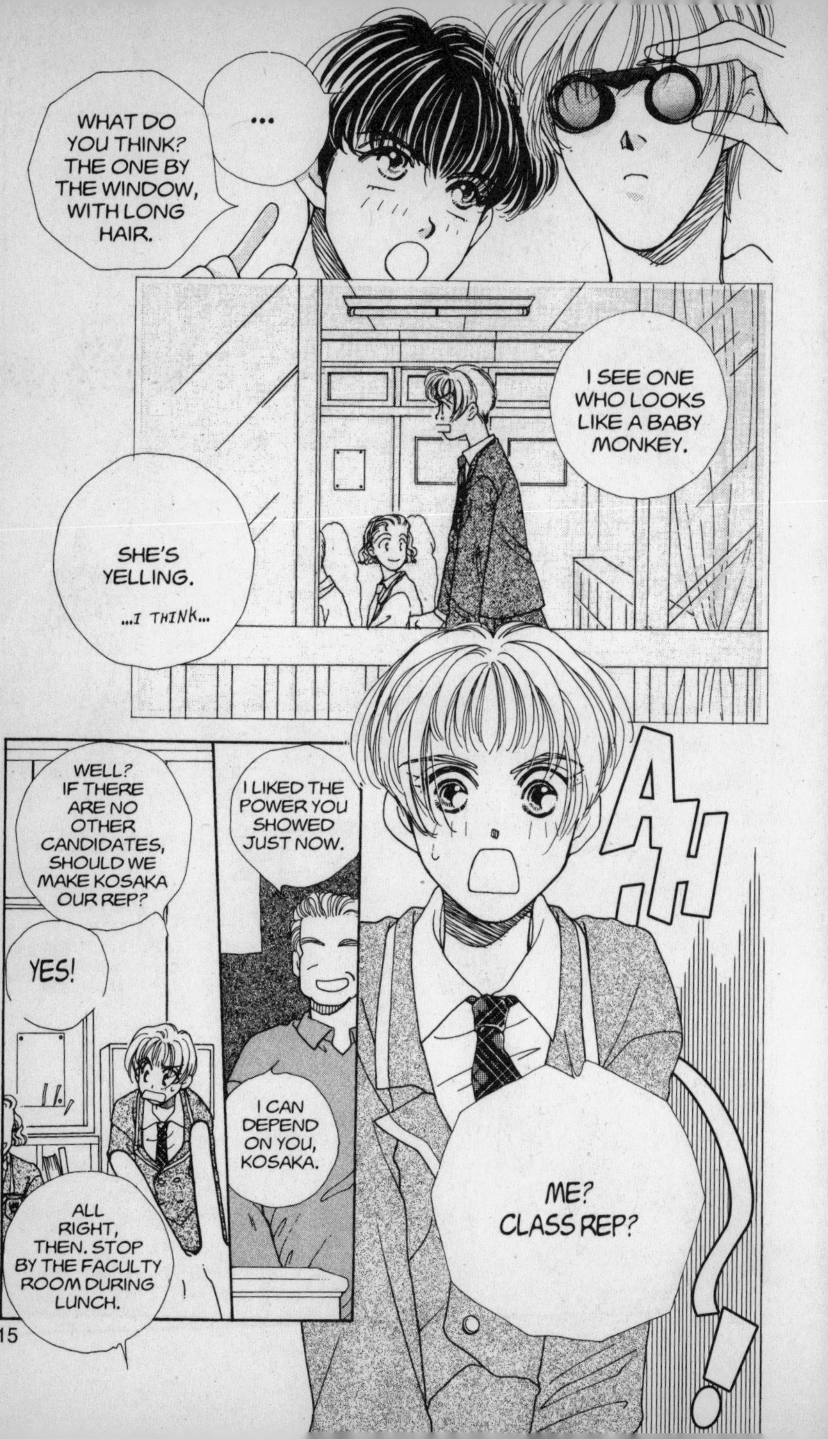
...
WHAT DO YOU THINK? THE ONE BY THE WINDOW, WITH LONG HAIR.
I SEE ONE WHO LOOKS LIKE A BABY MONKEY.
SHE'S YELLING.
...I THINK...
AH
ME? CLASS REP?
!
I LIKED THE POWER YOU SHOWED JUST NOW.
I CAN DEPEND ON YOU, KOSAKA.
WELL? IF THERE ARE NO OTHER CANDIDATES, SHOULD WE MAKE KOSAKA OUR REP?
YES!
ALL RIGHT, THEN. STOP BY THE FACULTY ROOM DURING LUNCH.

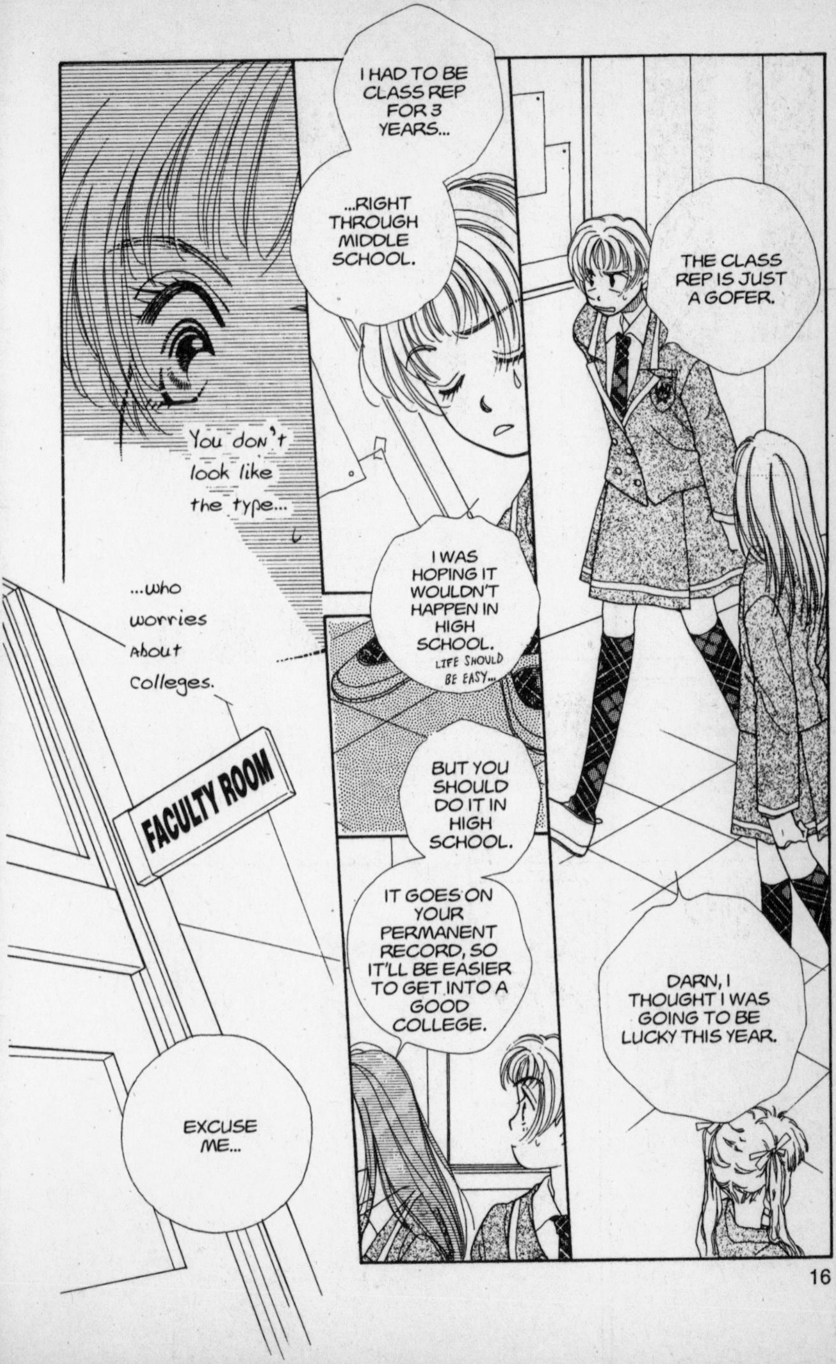
THE CLASS REP IS JUST A GOFER.
DARN, I THOUGHT I WAS GOING TO BE LUCKY THIS YEAR.
I HAD TO BE CLASS REP FOR 3 YEARS...
...RIGHT THROUGH MIDDLE SCHOOL.
I WAS HOPING IT WOULDN'T HAPPEN IN HIGH SCHOOL.
LIFE SHOULD BE EASY...
BUT YOU SHOULD DO IT IN HIGH SCHOOL.
IT GOES ON YOUR PERMANENT RECORD, SO IT'LL BE EASIER TO GET INTO A GOOD COLLEGE.
You don't look like the type...
...who worries about colleges.
FACULTY ROOM
EXCUSE ME...

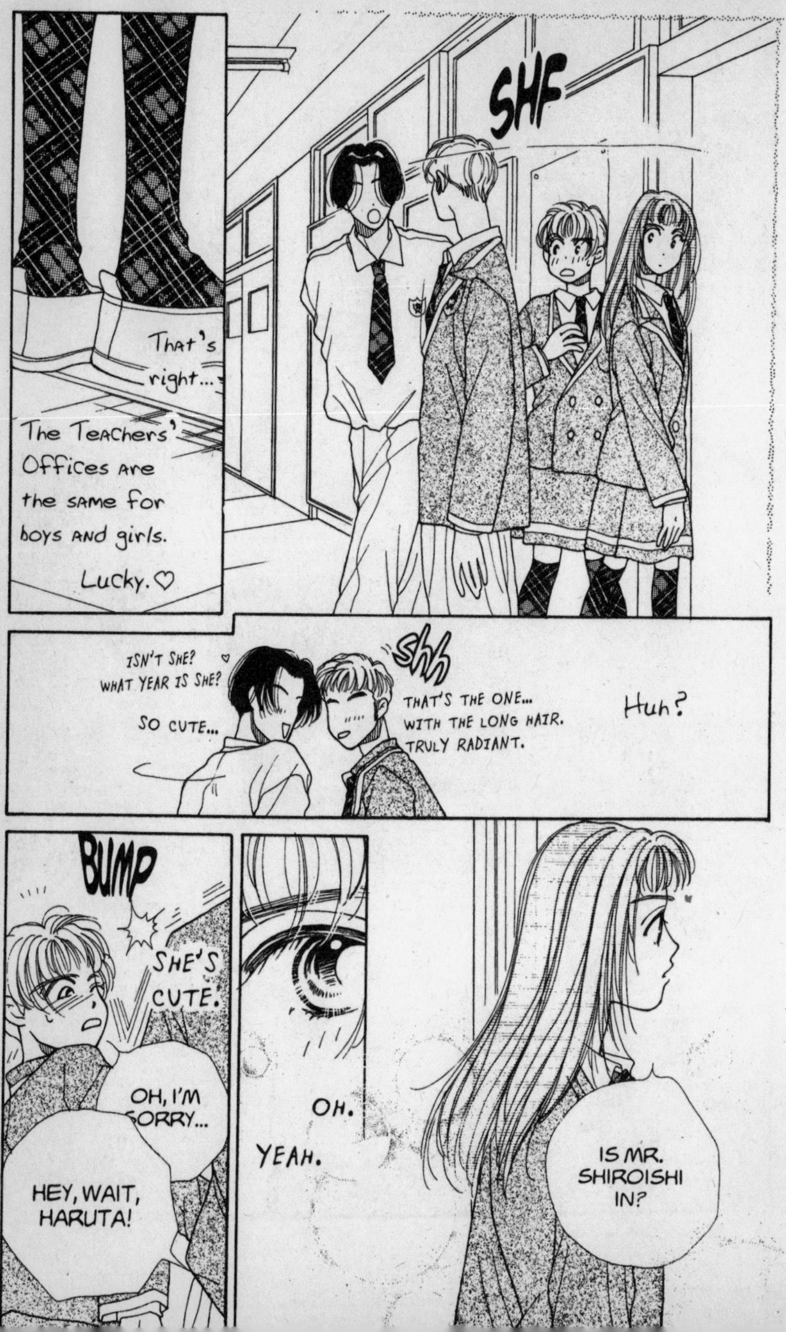
SHF
That's right...
The Teachers' Offices are the same for boys and girls.
Lucky.♡
Huh?
shh
THAT'S THE ONE... WITH THE LONG HAIR. TRULY RADIANT.
ISN'T SHE? WHAT YEAR IS SHE?
SO CUTE...
IS MR. SHIROISHI IN?
OH.
YEAH.
BUMP
SHE'S CUTE.
OH, I'M SORRY...
HEY, WAIT, HARUTA!

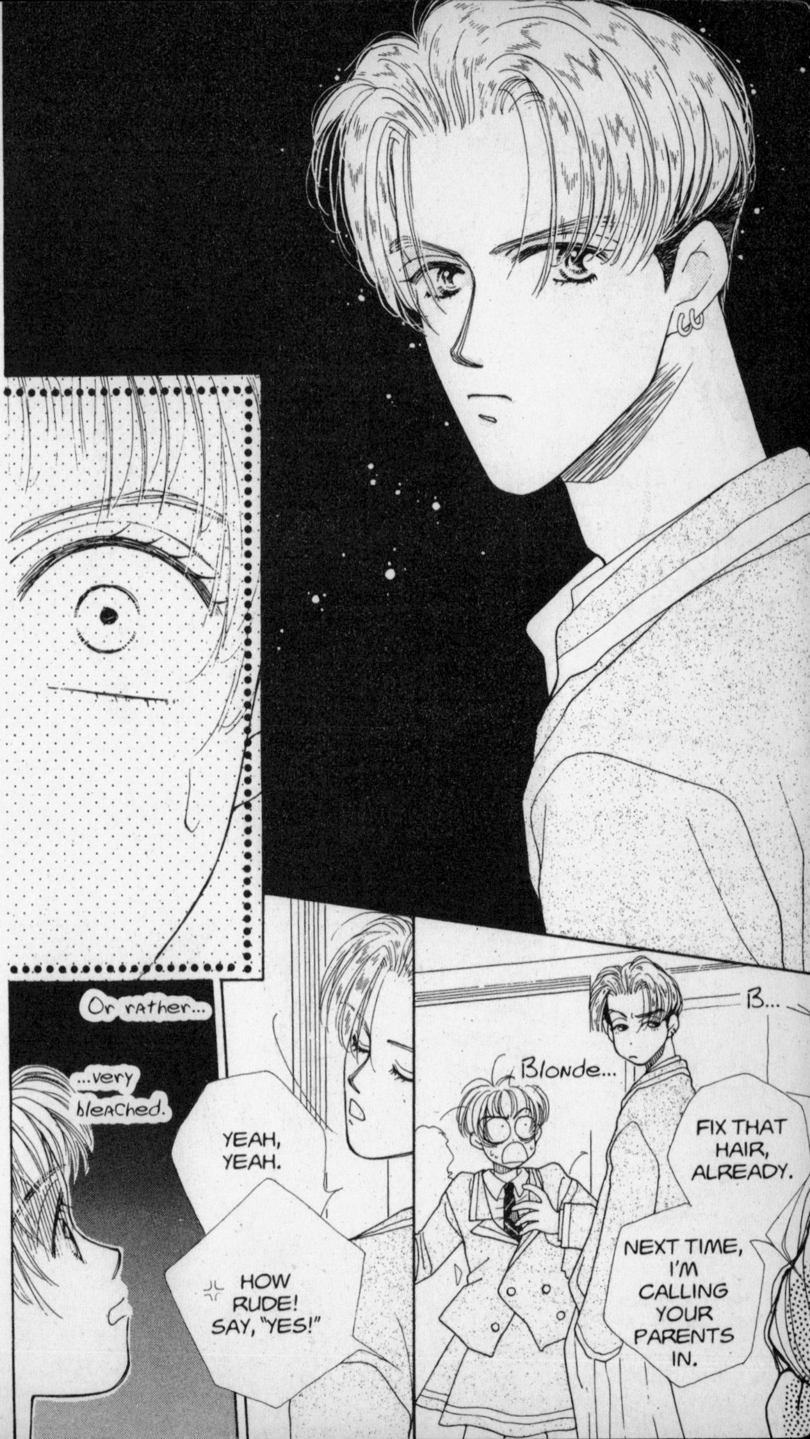
B...
Blonde...
FIX THAT HAIR, ALREADY.
NEXT TIME, I'M CALLING YOUR PARENTS IN.
YEAH, YEAH.
HOW RUDE! SAY, "YES!"
Or rather...
...very bleached.

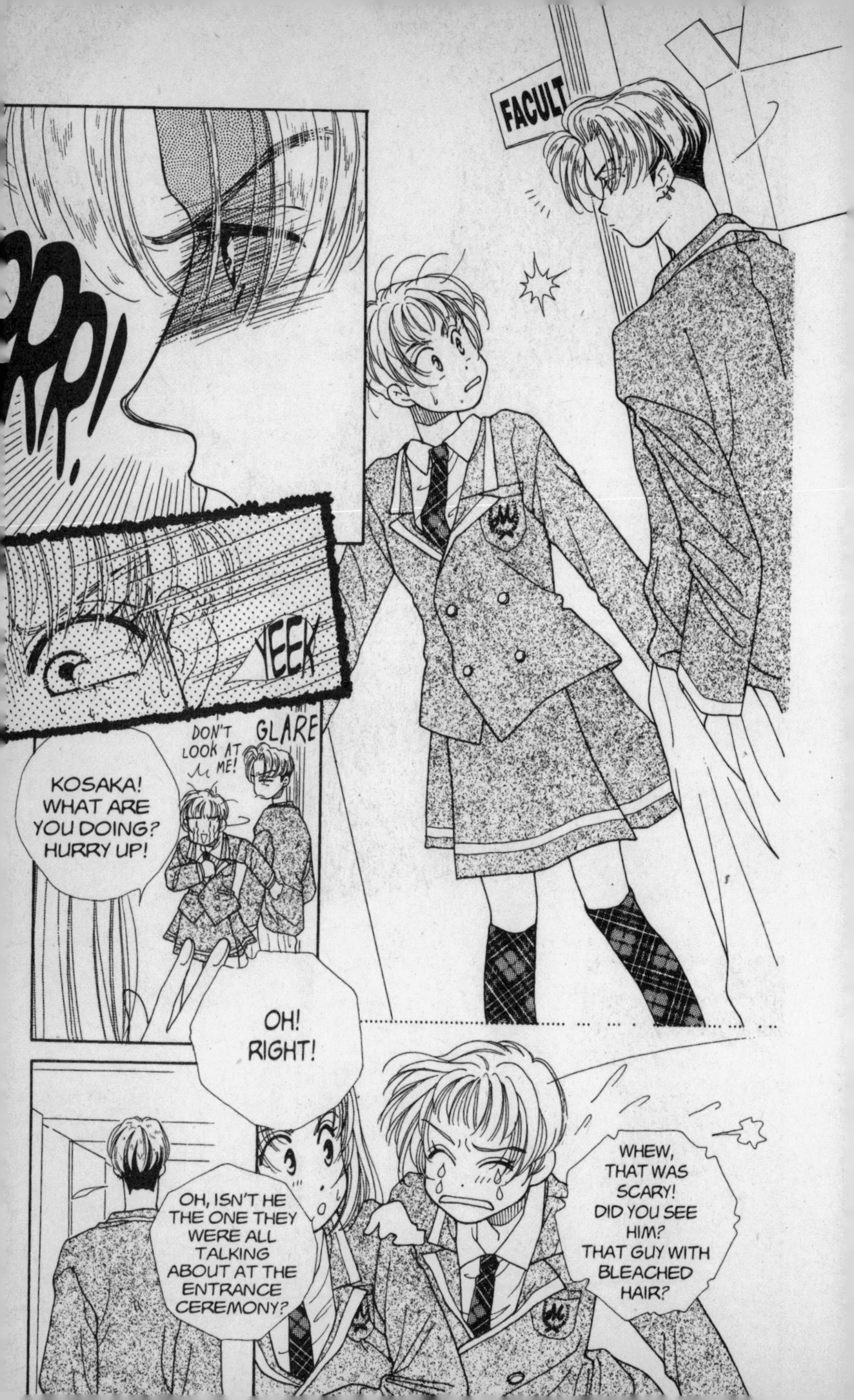

FACULT
YEEK
GLARE
DON'T LOOK AT ME!
KOSAKA! WHAT ARE YOU DOING? HURRY UP!
OH! RIGHT!
WHEW, THAT WAS SCARY! DID YOU SEE HIM? THAT GUY WITH BLEACHED HAIR?
OH, ISN'T HE THE ONE THEY WERE ALL TALKING ABOUT AT THE ENTRANCE CEREMONY?

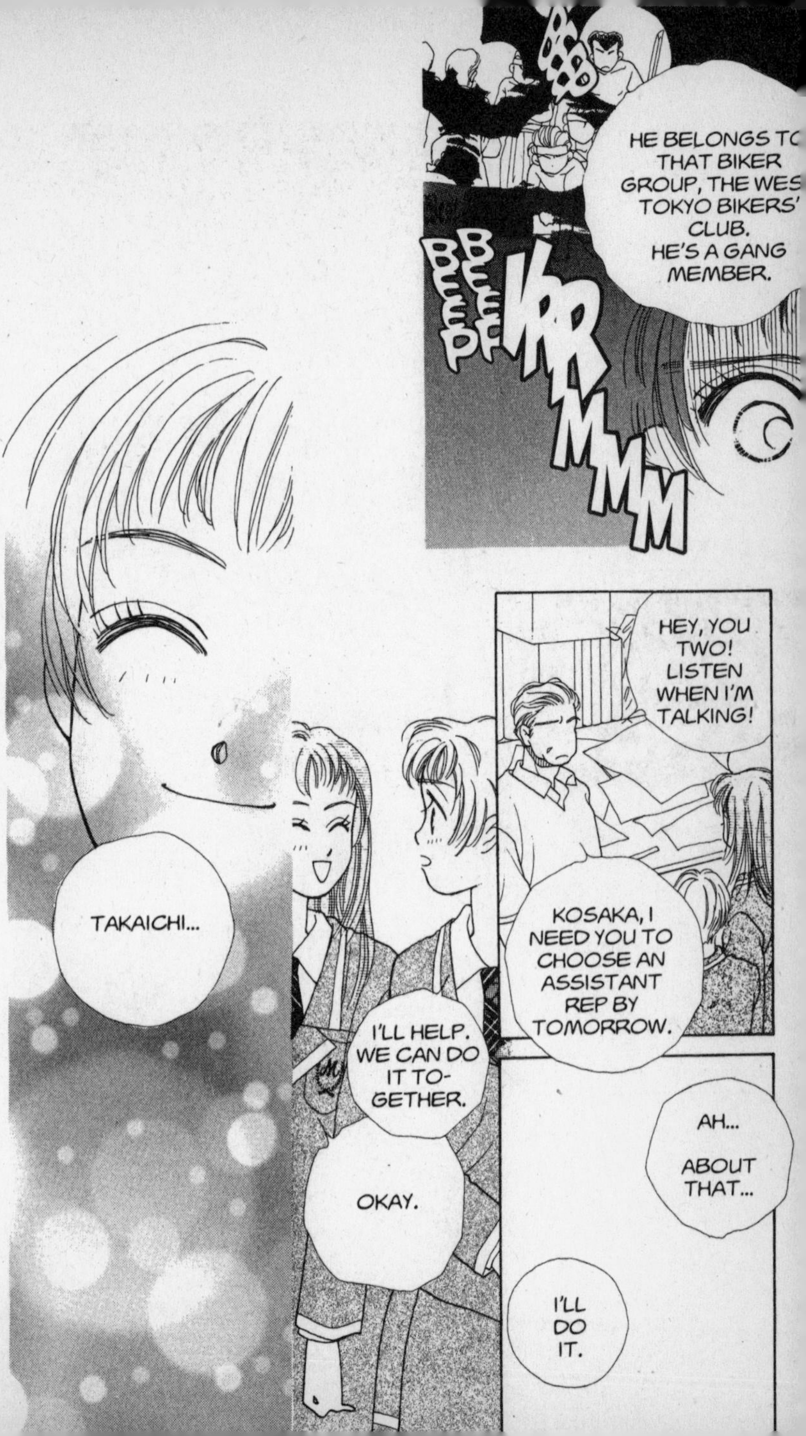
HE BELONGS TC THAT BIKER GROUP, THE WES TOKYO BIKERS' CLUB. HE'S A GANG MEMBER.
BEEEP BEEEP
VRRMMMMM
TAKAICHI...
HEY, YOU TWO! LISTEN WHEN I'M TALKING!
KOSAKA, I NEED YOU TO CHOOSE AN ASSISTANT REP BY TOMORROW.
AH... ABOUT THAT...
I'LL DO IT.
I'LL HELP. WE CAN DO IT TO-GETHER.
OKAY.

TOKYO BOYS GIRLS

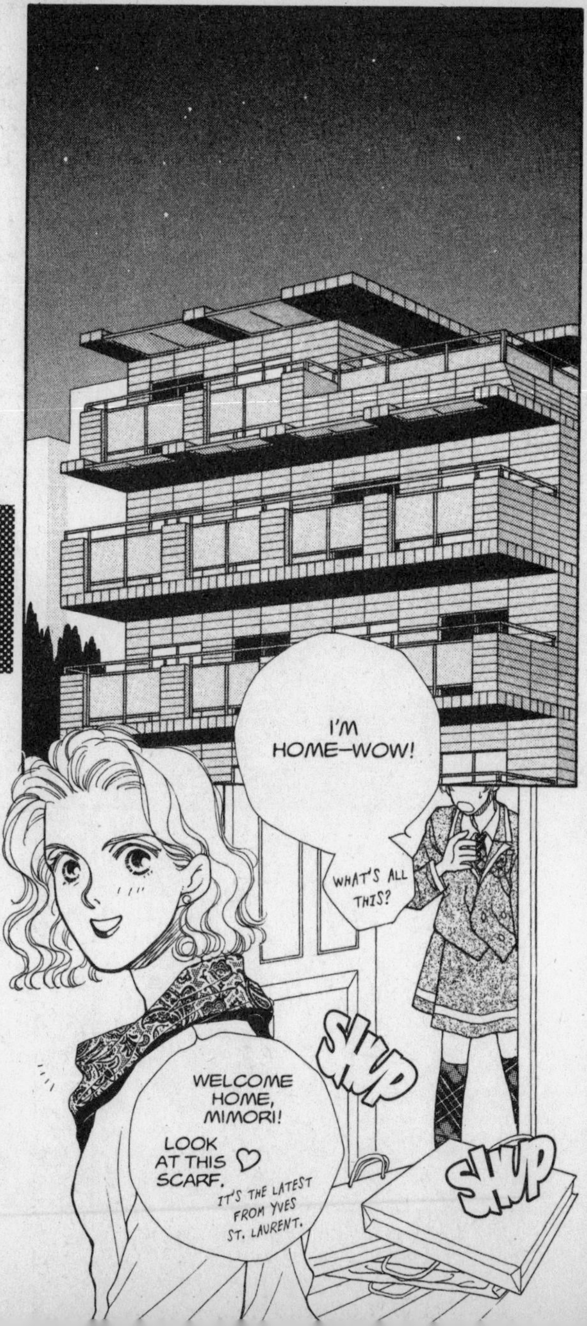
I'M HOME—WOW!
WHAT'S ALL THIS?
SHUP
SHUP
WELCOME HOME, MIMORI!
LOOK AT THIS SCARF. ♡
IT'S THE LATEST FROM YVES ST. LAURENT.

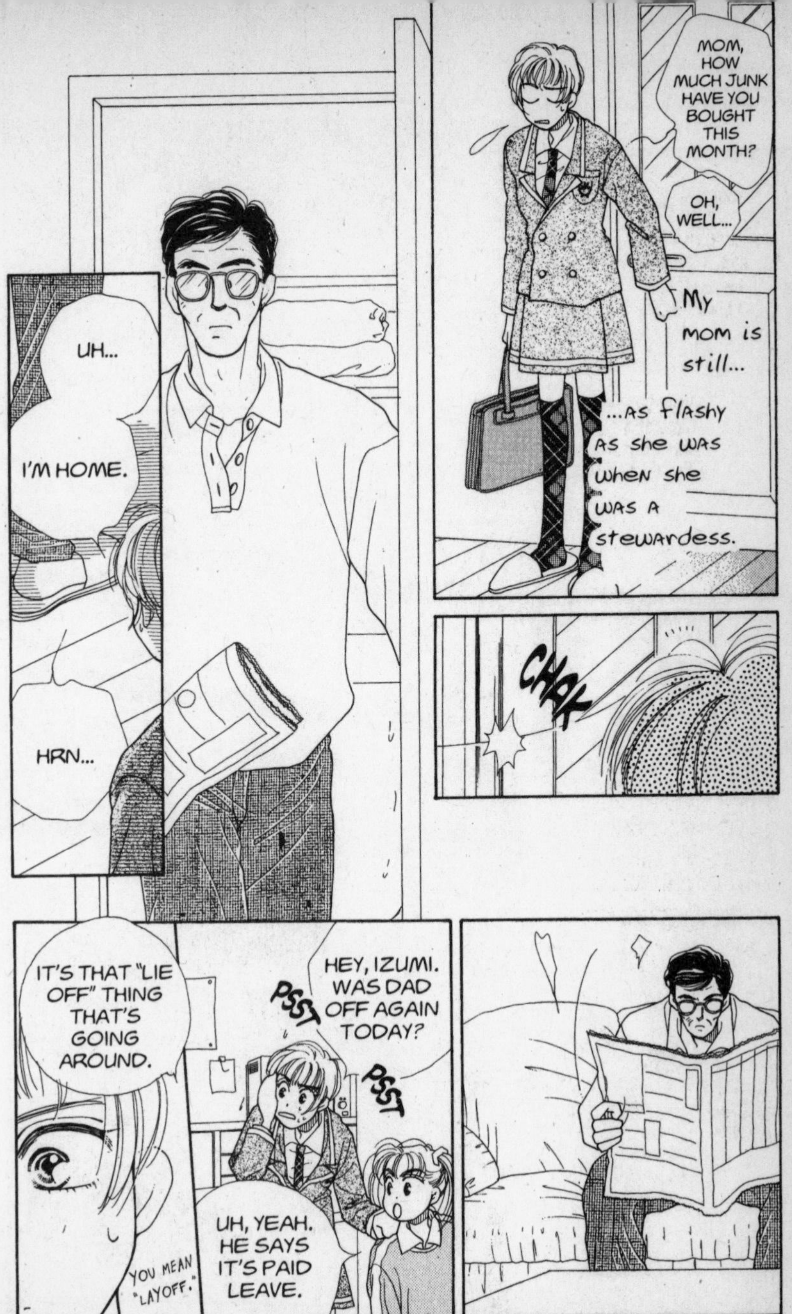
MOM, HOW MUCH JUNK HAVE YOU BOUGHT THIS MONTH?
OH, WELL...
My mom is still...
...as flashy as she was when she was a stewardess.
CHAK
UH...
I'M HOME.
HRN...
HEY, IZUMI. WAS DAD OFF AGAIN TODAY?
PSST
PSST
UH, YEAH. HE SAYS IT'S PAID LEAVE.
IT'S THAT "LIE OFF" THING THAT'S GOING AROUND.
YOU MEAN "LAYOFF."

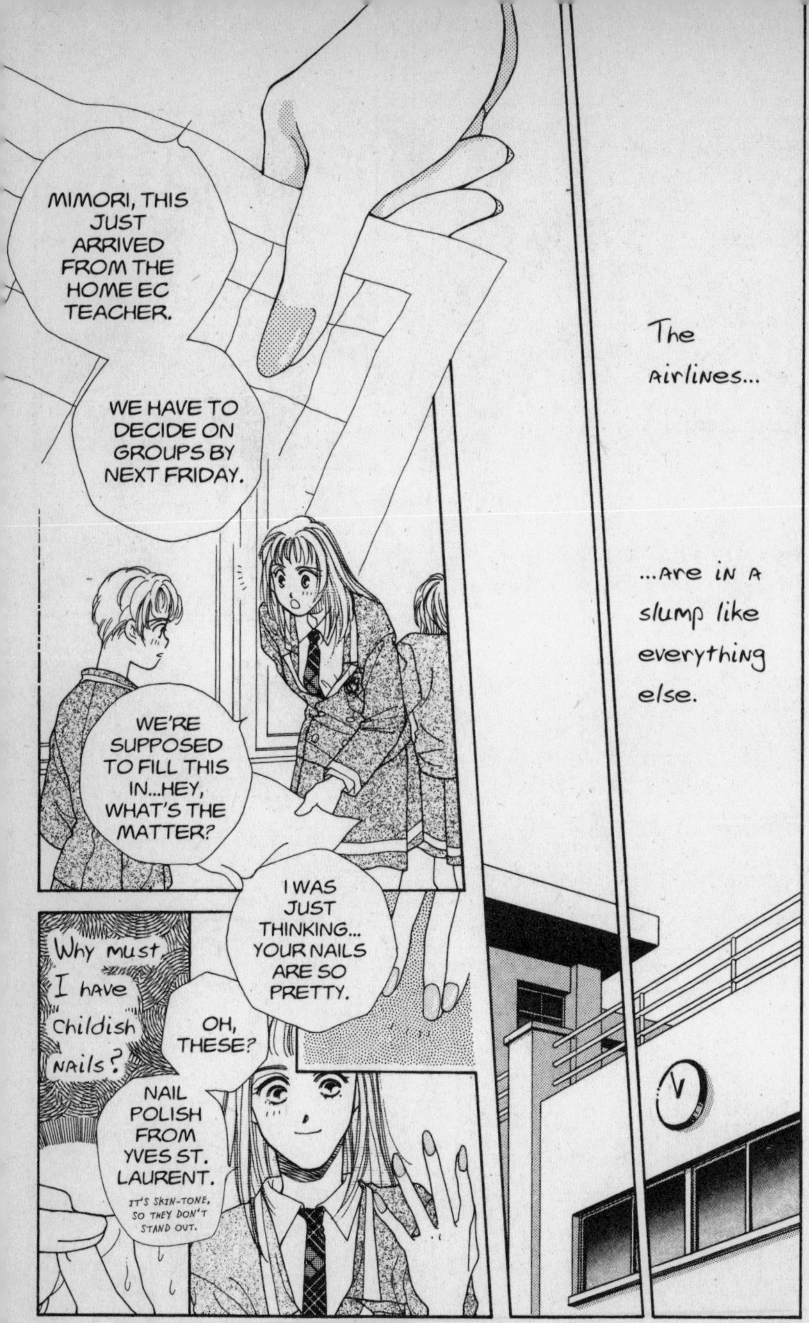
The airlines...
...are in a slump like everything else.
MIMORI, THIS JUST ARRIVED FROM THE HOME EC TEACHER.
WE HAVE TO DECIDE ON GROUPS BY NEXT FRIDAY.
WE'RE SUPPOSED TO FILL THIS IN...HEY, WHAT'S THE MATTER?
I WAS JUST THINKING... YOUR NAILS ARE SO PRETTY.
Why must I have childish nails?
OH, THESE?
NAIL POLISH FROM YVES ST. LAURENT.
IT'S SKIN-TONE, SO THEY DON'T STAND OUT.

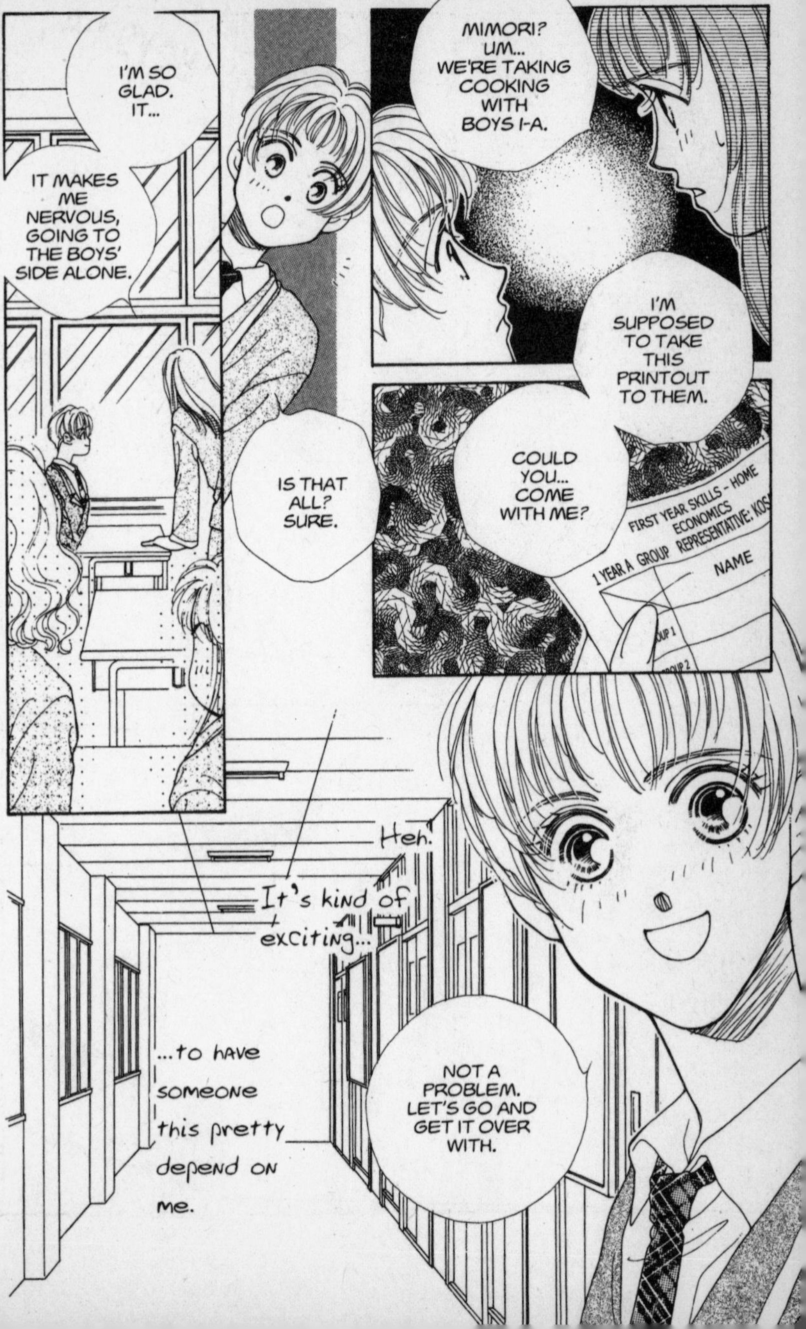
MIMORI? UM... WE'RE TAKING COOKING WITH BOYS I-A.
I'M SUPPOSED TO TAKE THIS PRINTOUT TO THEM.
COULD YOU... COME WITH ME?
FIRST YEAR SKILLS - HOME ECONOMICS
1 YEAR A GROUP REPRESENTATIVE:
NAME
IS THAT ALL? SURE.
I'M SO GLAD. IT...
IT MAKES ME NERVOUS, GOING TO THE BOYS' SIDE ALONE.
NOT A PROBLEM. LET'S GO AND GET IT OVER WITH.
Heh.
It's kind of exciting...
...to have someone this pretty depend on me.

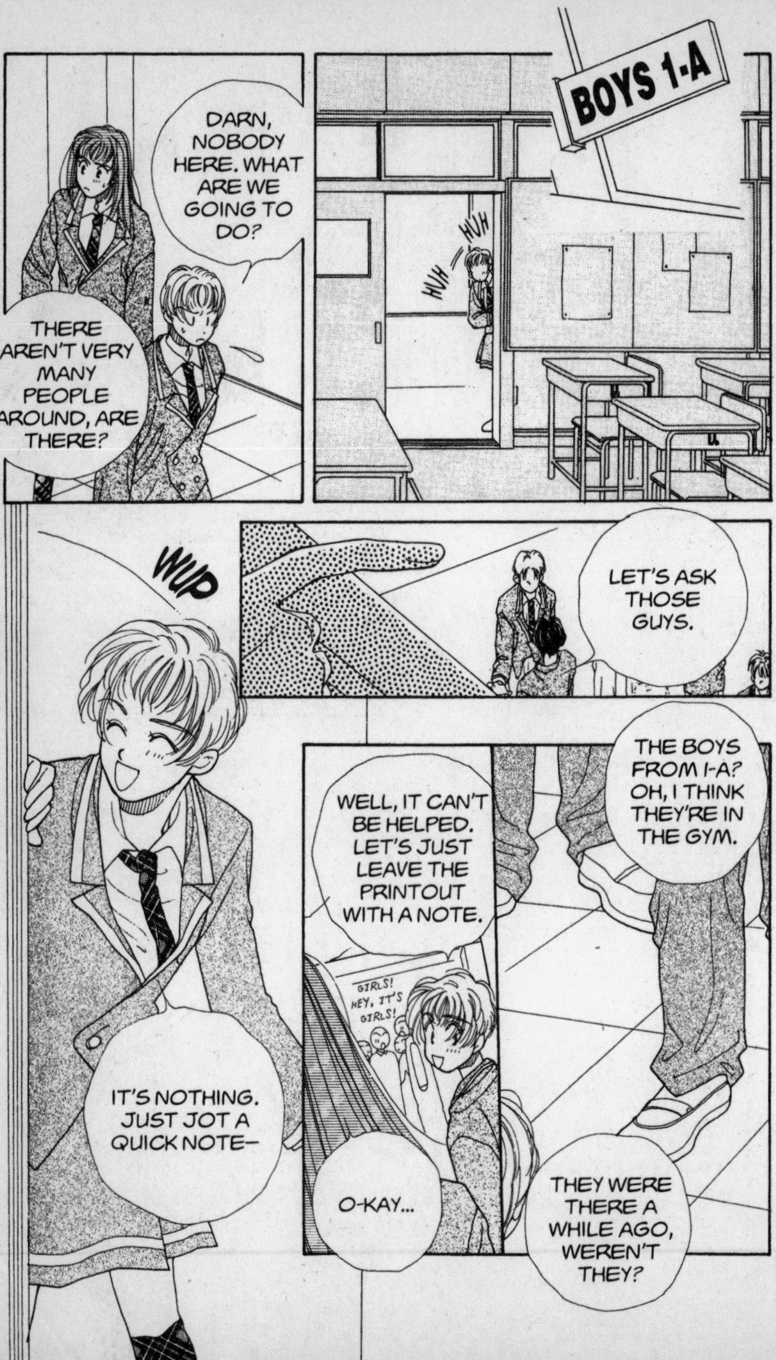
BOYS 1-A
HUH HUH
DARN, NOBODY HERE. WHAT ARE WE GOING TO DO?
THERE AREN'T VERY MANY PEOPLE AROUND, ARE THERE?
LET'S ASK THOSE GUYS.
THE BOYS FROM 1-A? OH, I THINK THEY'RE IN THE GYM.
THEY WERE THERE A WHILE AGO, WEREN'T THEY?
WELL, IT CAN'T BE HELPED. LET'S JUST LEAVE THE PRINTOUT WITH A NOTE.
GIRLS! HEY, IT'S GIRLS!
O-KAY...
WUP
IT'S NOTHING. JUST JOT A QUICK NOTE–

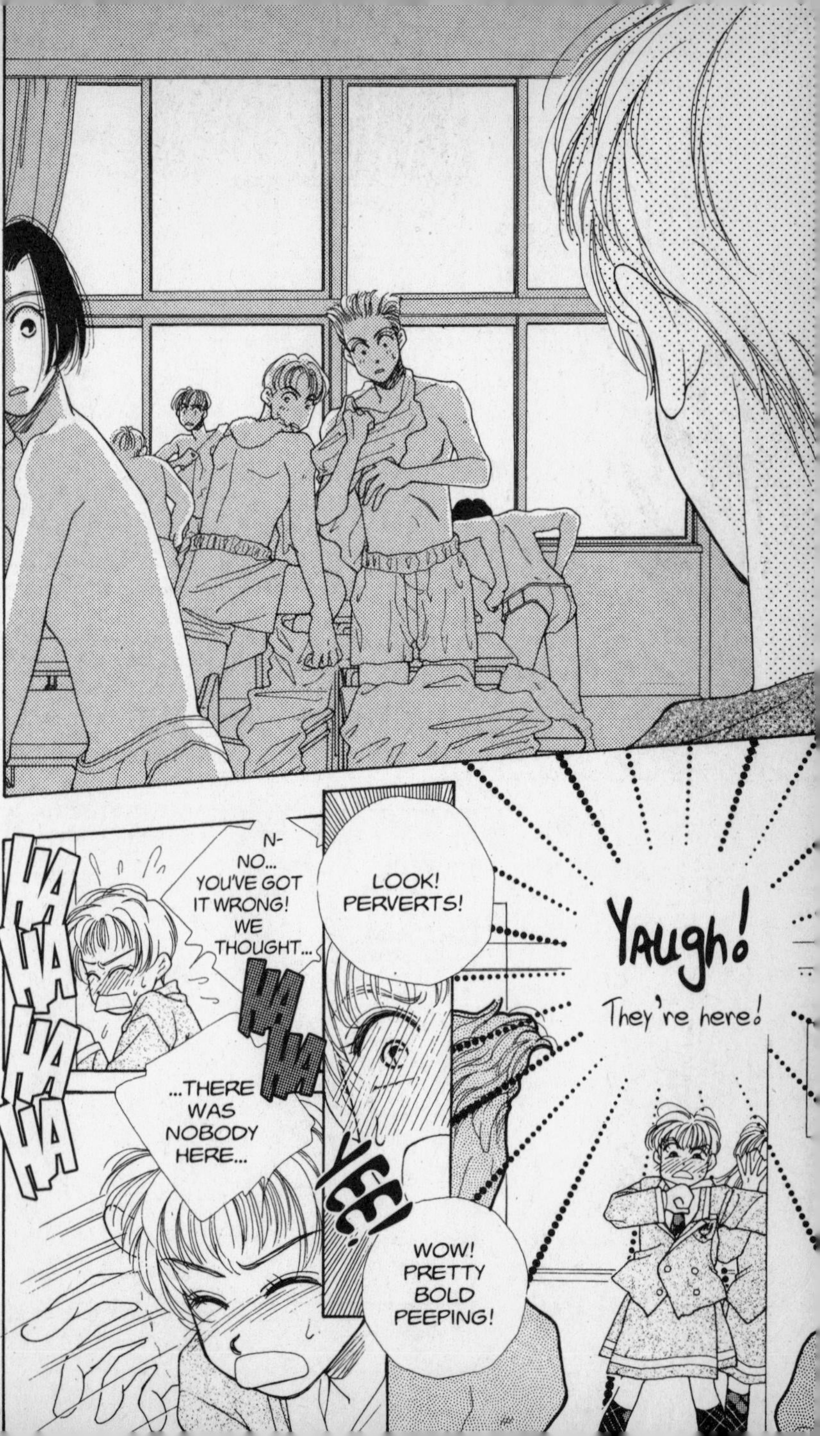
Yaugh!
They're here!
LOOK! PERVERTS!
YEE!
WOW! PRETTY BOLD PEEPING!
N- NO... YOU'VE GOT IT WRONG! WE THOUGHT...
HA HA
...THERE WAS NOBODY HERE...
HA HA HA HA HA

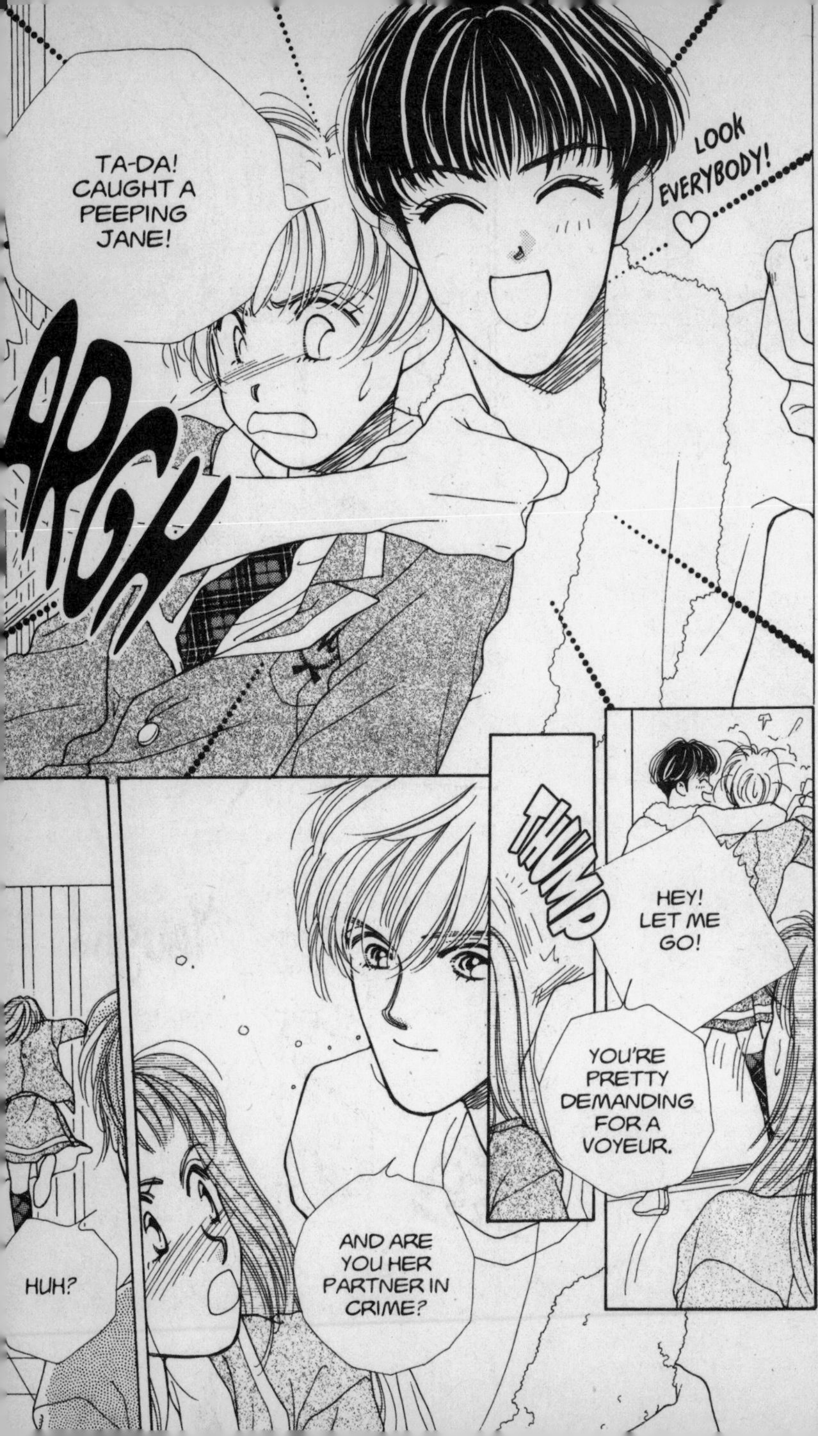
LOOK EVERYBODY! ♥
TA-DA! CAUGHT A PEEPING JANE!
ARGH
HEY! LET ME GO!
THUMP
YOU'RE PRETTY DEMANDING FOR A VOYEUR.
AND ARE YOU HER PARTNER IN CRIME?
HUH?

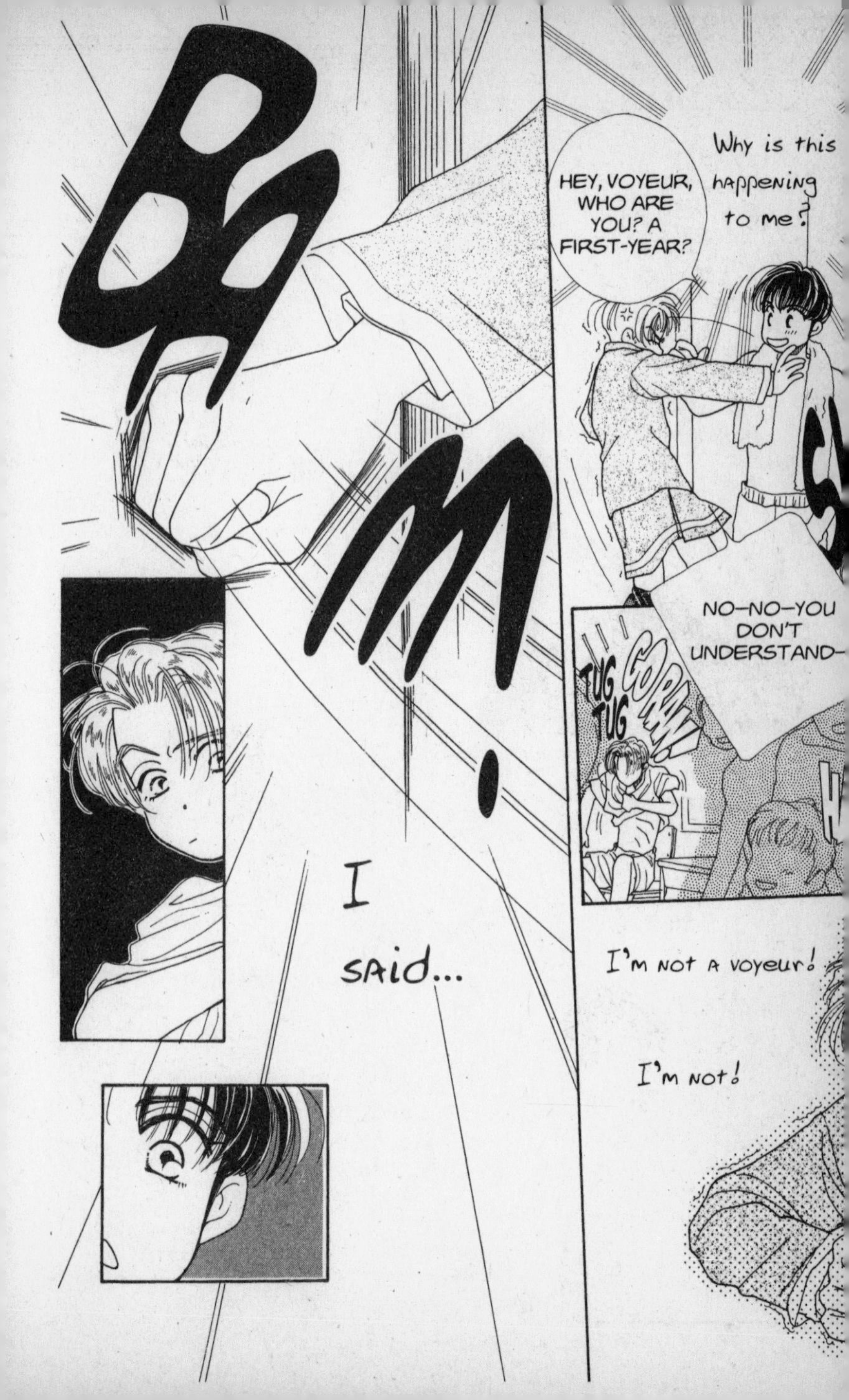

Why is this happening to me?
HEY, VOYEUR, WHO ARE YOU? A FIRST-YEAR?
NO-NO-YOU DON'T UNDERSTAND—
TUG TUG
I'm not a voyeur!
I'm not!
BAM!
I said...

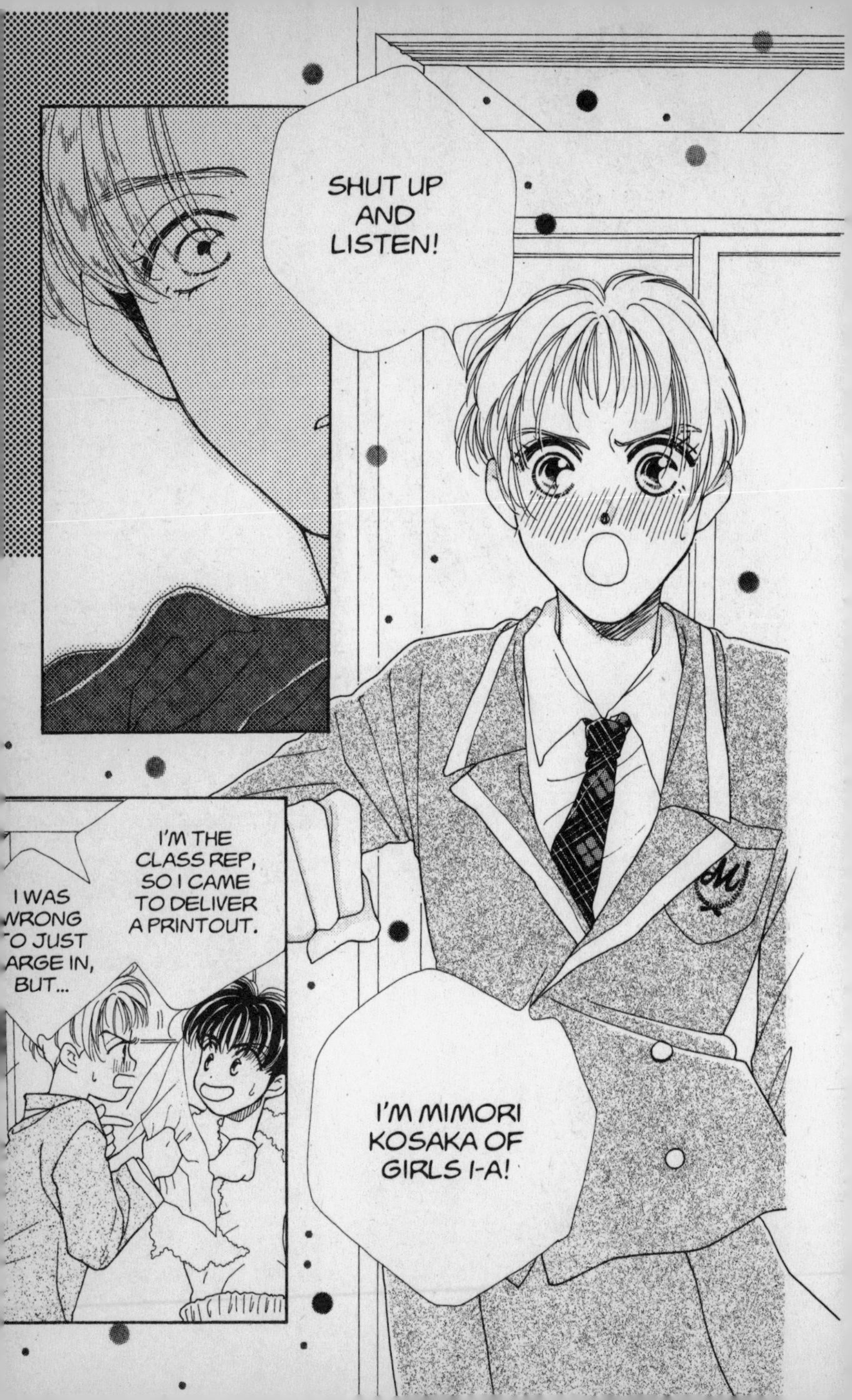
SHUT UP AND LISTEN!
I'M MIMORI KOSAKA OF GIRLS I-A!
I'M THE CLASS REP, SO I CAME TO DELIVER A PRINTOUT.
I WAS WRONG TO JUST ARGE IN, BUT...

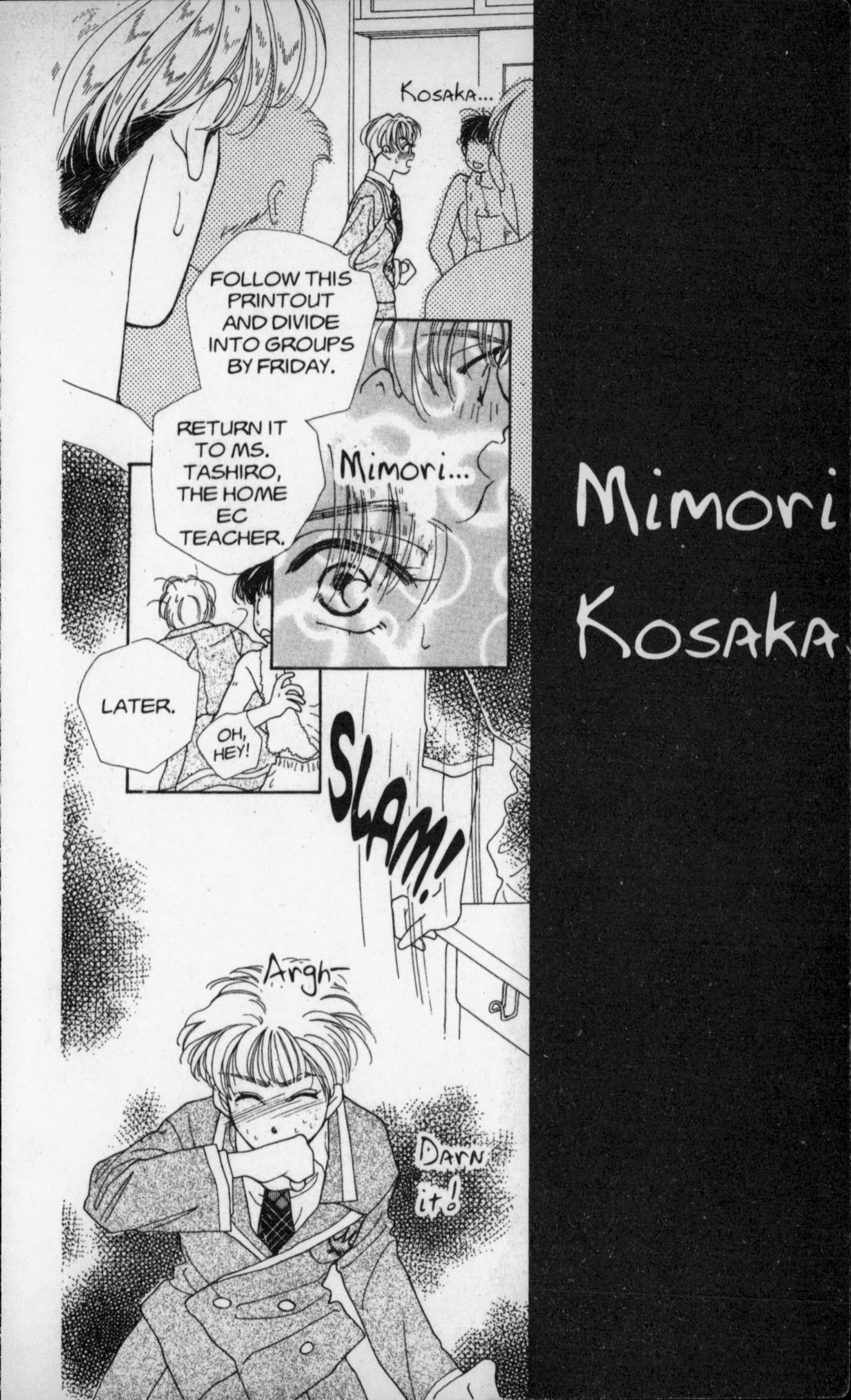
Mimori Kosaka
Kosaka...
FOLLOW THIS PRINTOUT AND DIVIDE INTO GROUPS BY FRIDAY.
RETURN IT TO MS. TASHIRO, THE HOME EC TEACHER.
Mimori...
OH, HEY!
LATER.
SLAM!
Argh
Darn it!

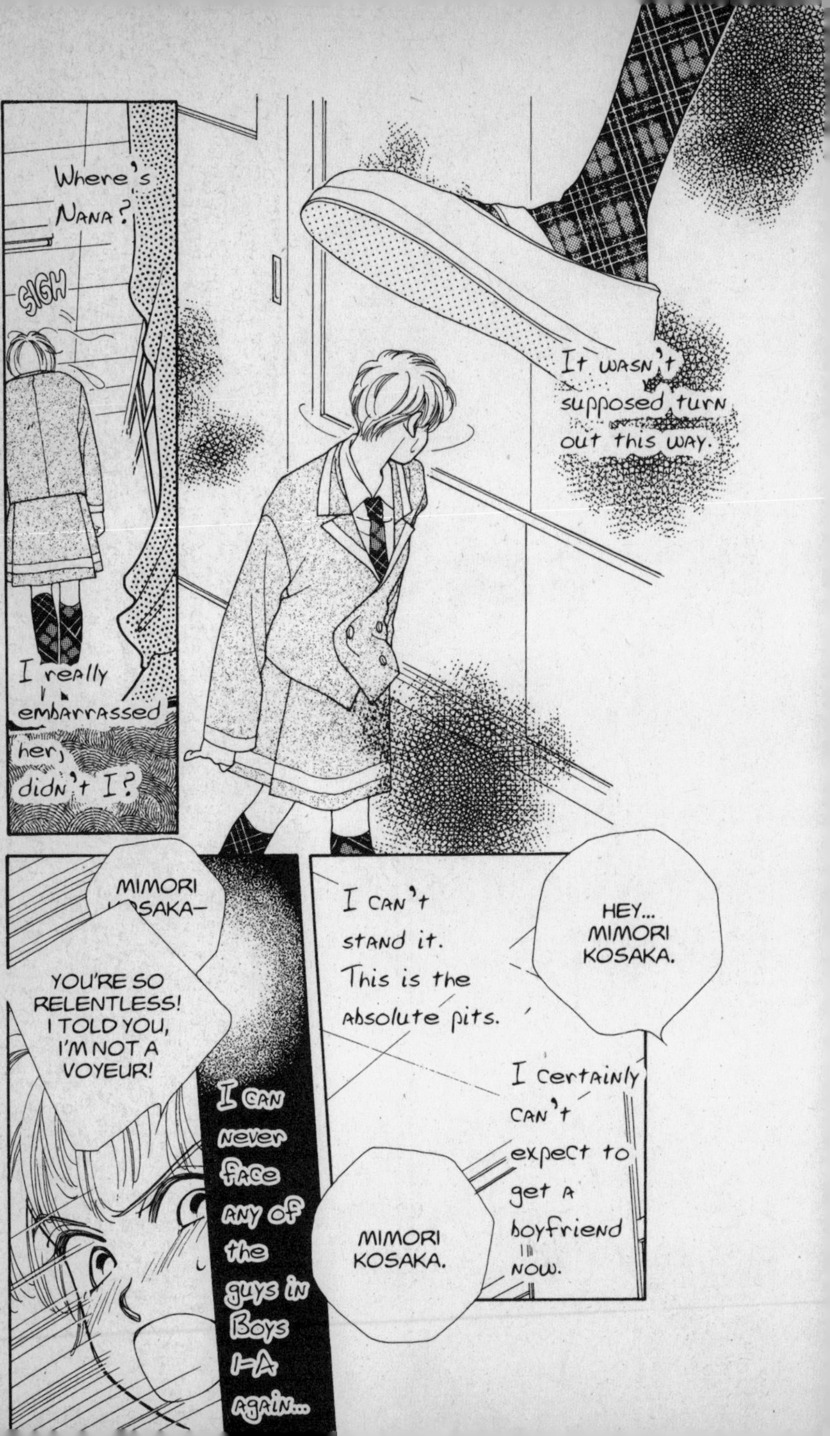
It wasn't supposed turn out this way.
Where's Nana?
SIGH
I really embarrassed her, didn't I?
HEY... MIMORI KOSAKA.
I can't stand it. This is the absolute pits.
I certainly can't expect to get a boyfriend now.
MIMORI KOSAKA.
I can never face any of the guys in Boys I-A again...
MIMORI KOSAKA—
YOU'RE SO RELENTLESS! I TOLD YOU, I'M NOT A VOYEUR!

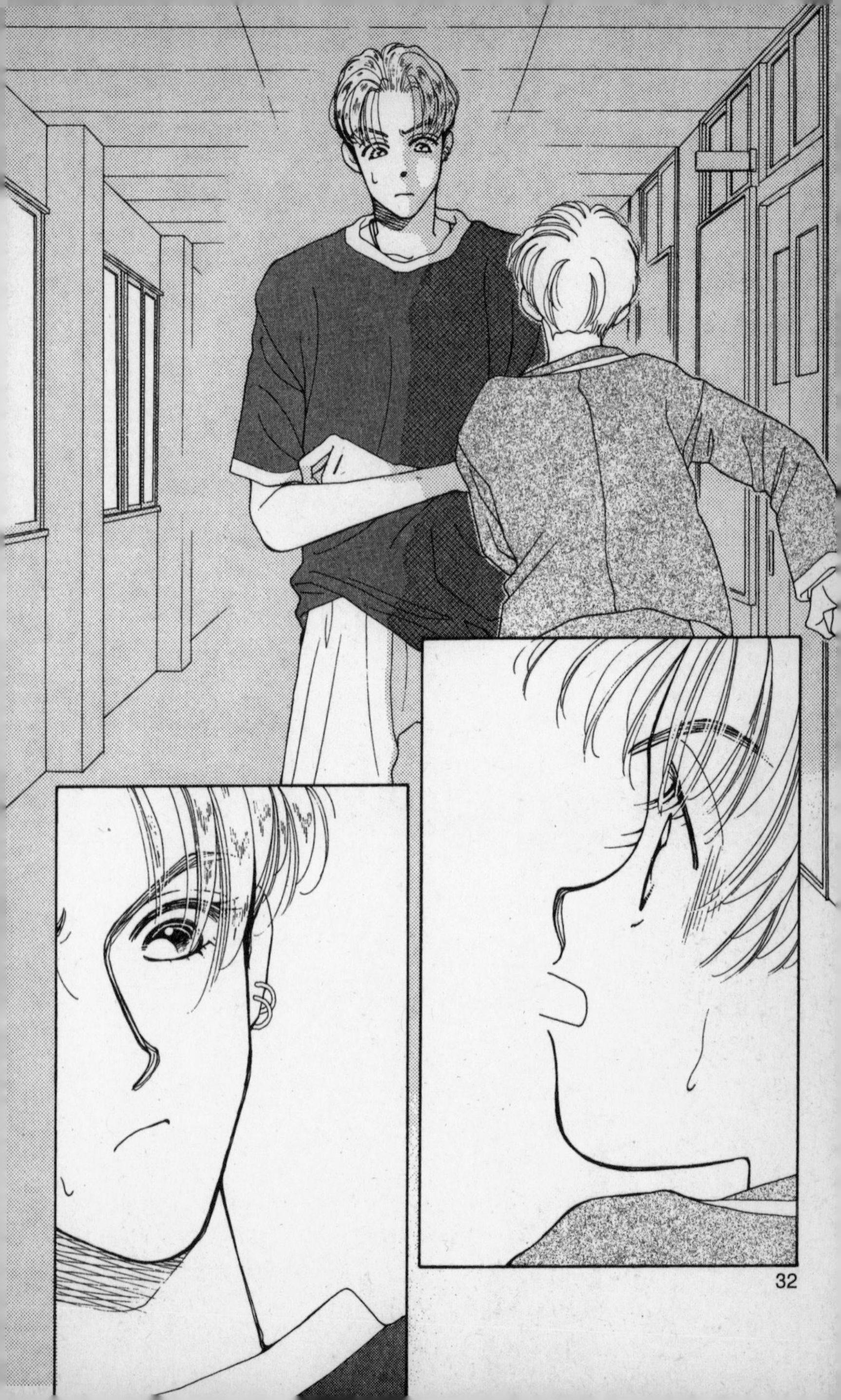

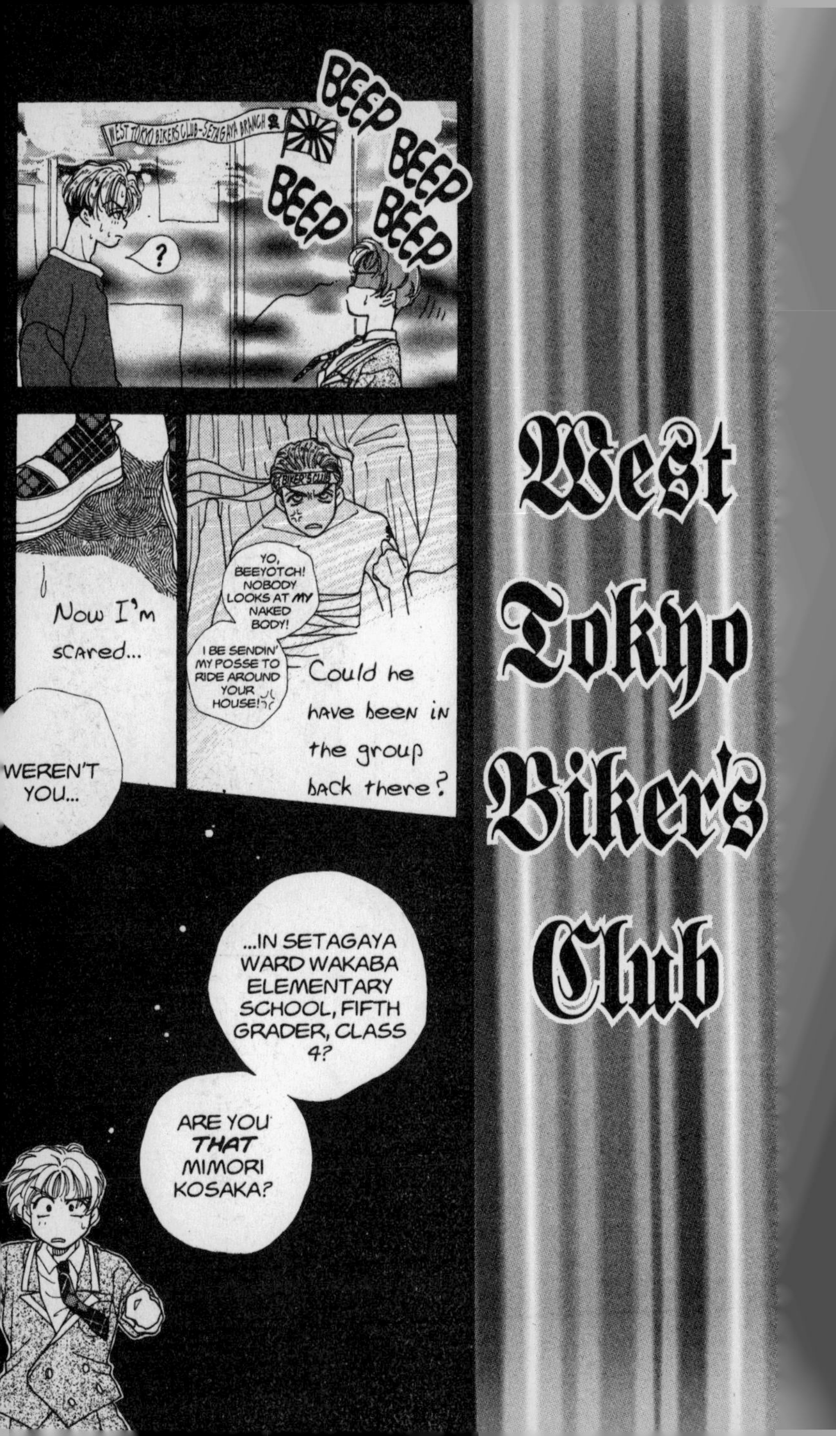
West Tokyo Biker's Club
WEST TOKYO BIKERS CLUB-SETAGAYA BRANCH
BEEP BEEP BEEP BEEP BEEP
?
BIKER'S CLUB
YO, BEEYOTCH! NOBODY LOOKS AT *MY* NAKED BODY!
I BE SENDIN' MY POSSE TO RIDE AROUND YOUR HOUSE!
Could he have been in the group back there?
Now I'm scared...
WEREN'T YOU...
...IN SETAGAYA WARD WAKABA ELEMENTARY SCHOOL, FIFTH GRADER, CLASS 4?
ARE YOU *THAT* MIMORI KOSAKA?

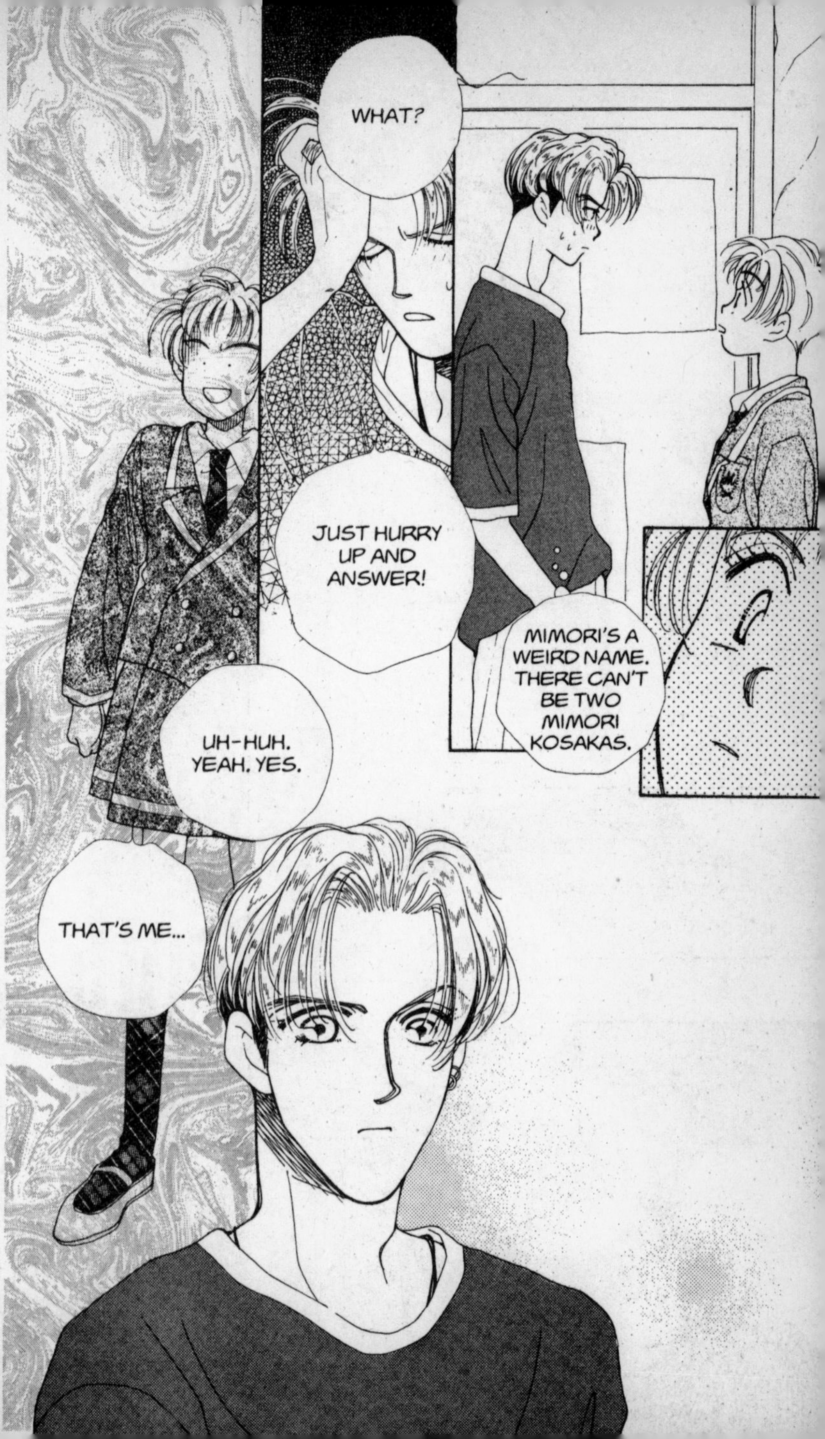
MIMORI'S A WEIRD NAME. THERE CAN'T BE TWO MIMORI KOSAKAS.
WHAT?
JUST HURRY UP AND ANSWER!
UH-HUH. YEAH. YES.
THAT'S ME...

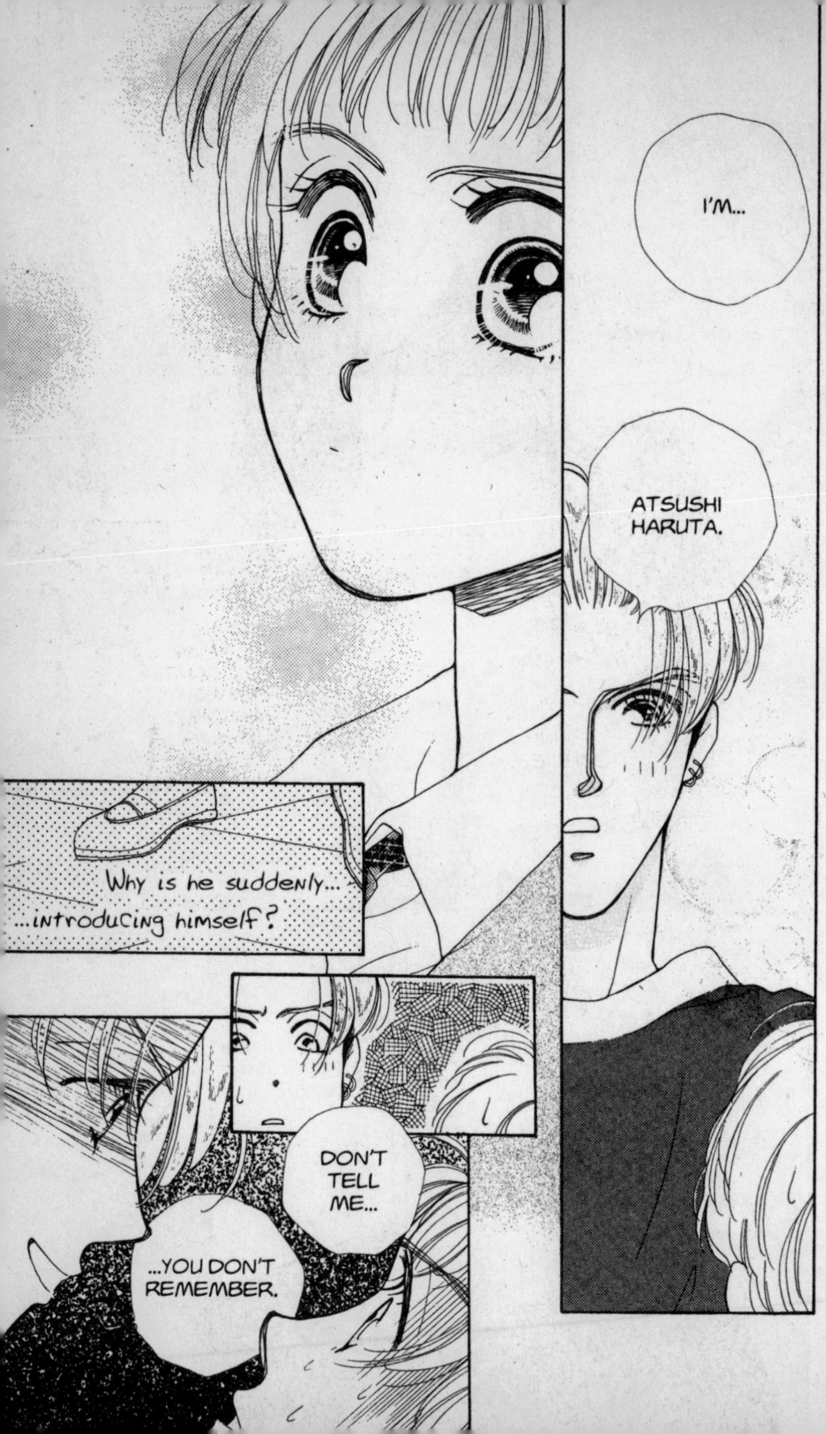
I'M...
ATSUSHI HARUTA.
Why is he suddenly...
...introducing himself?
DON'T TELL ME...
...YOU DON'T REMEMBER.

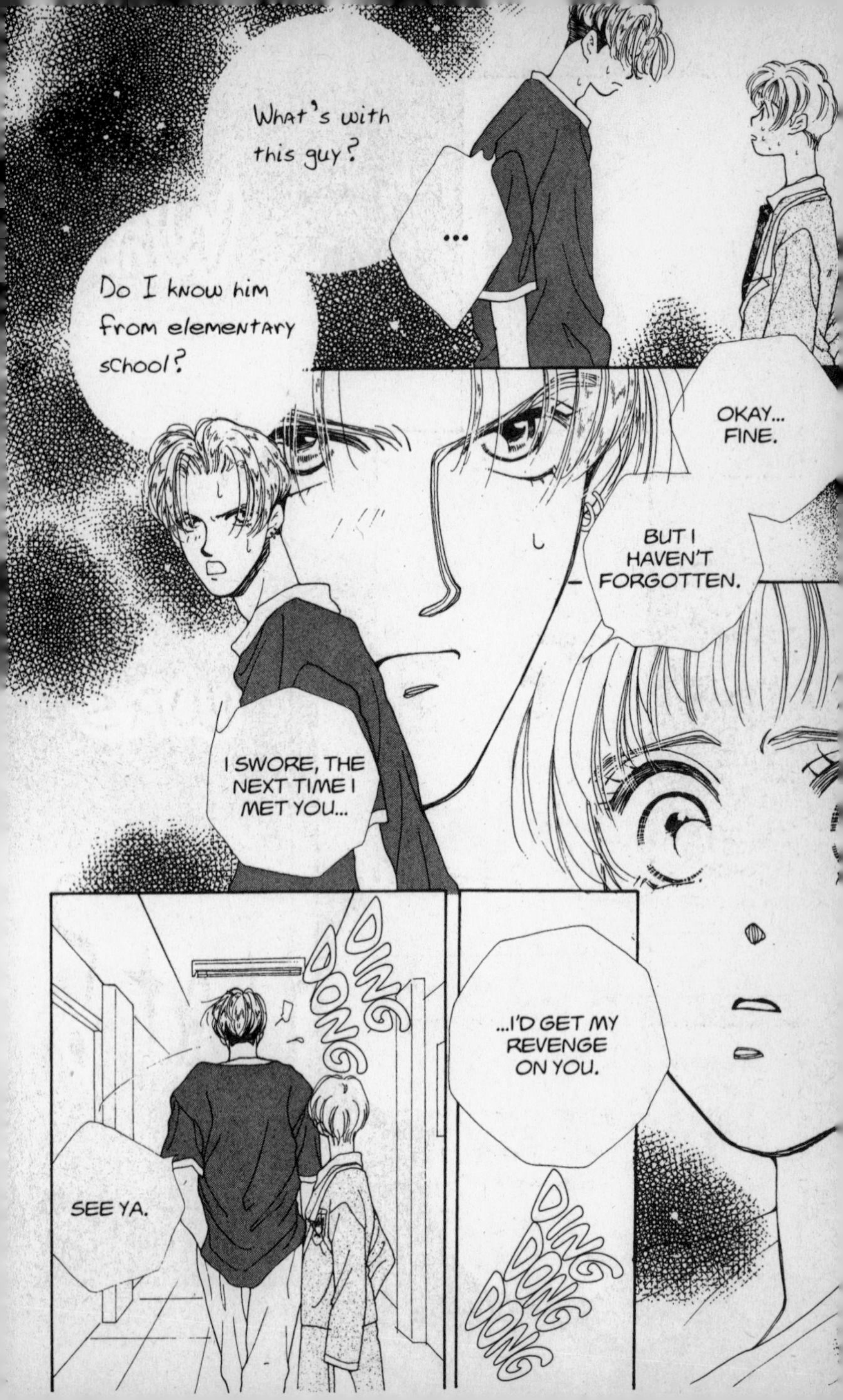
...
What's with this guy?
Do I know him from elementary school?
OKAY... FINE.
BUT I HAVEN'T FORGOTTEN.
I SWORE, THE NEXT TIME I MET YOU...
...I'D GET MY REVENGE ON YOU.
DING DONG DONG DONG
DING DONG
SEE YA.

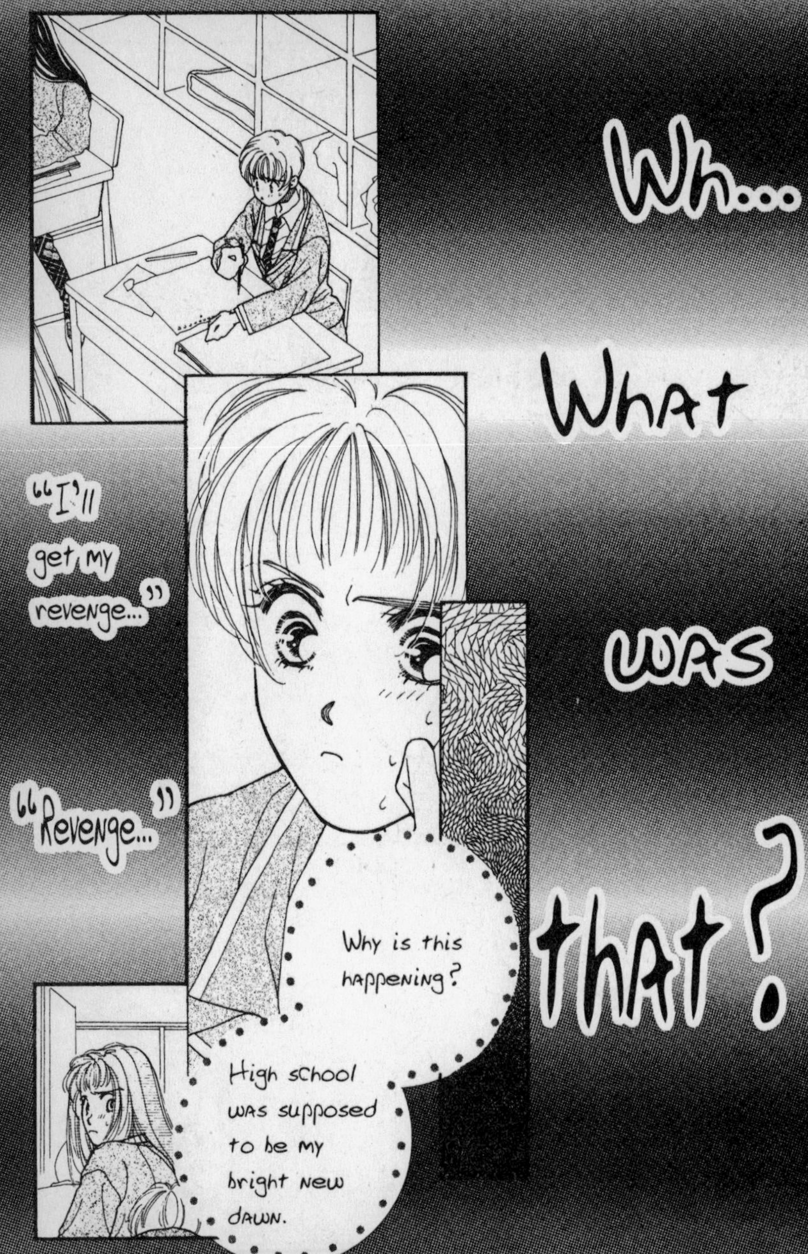
Wh... What was that?
"I'll get my revenge..."
"Revenge..."
Why is this happening?
High school was supposed to be my bright new dawn.

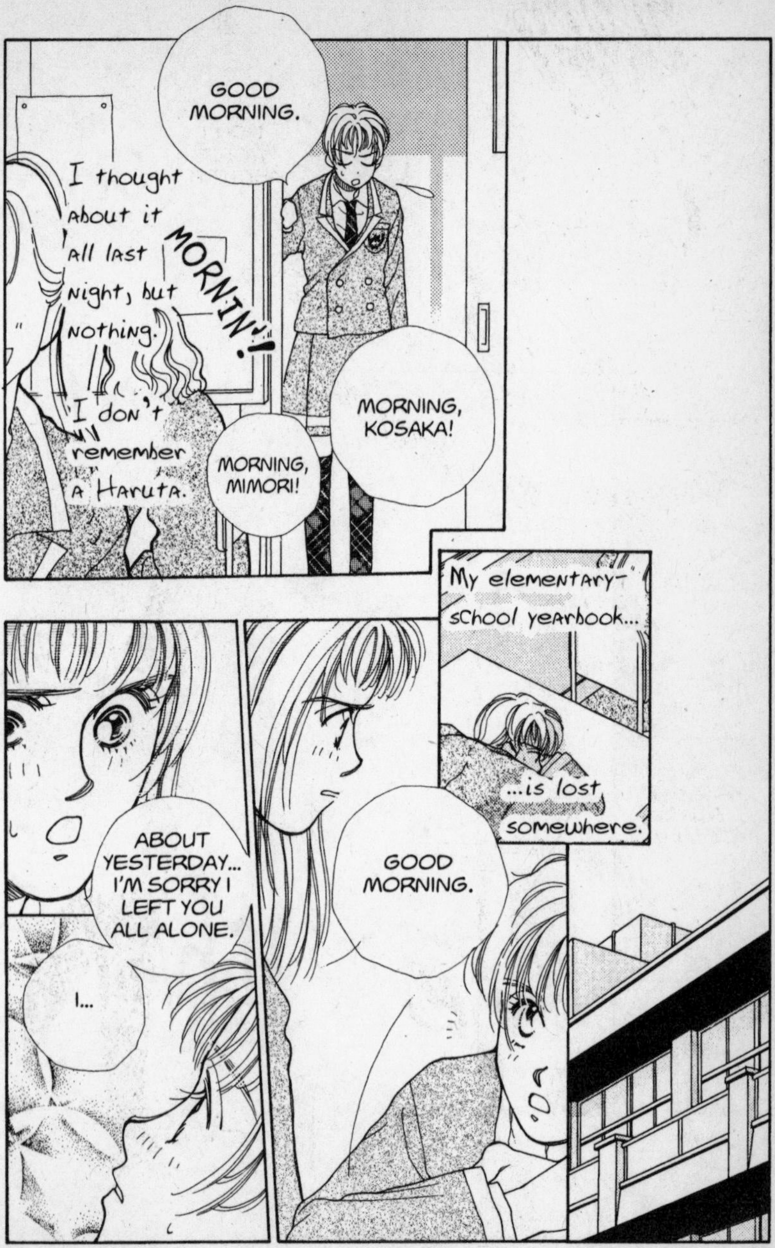
GOOD MORNING.
MORNING, KOSAKA!
MORNIN'!
I thought about it all last night, but nothing.
MORNING, MIMORI!
I don't remember a Haruta.
My elementary-school yearbook...
...is lost somewhere.
GOOD MORNING.
ABOUT YESTERDAY... I'M SORRY I LEFT YOU ALL ALONE.
I...

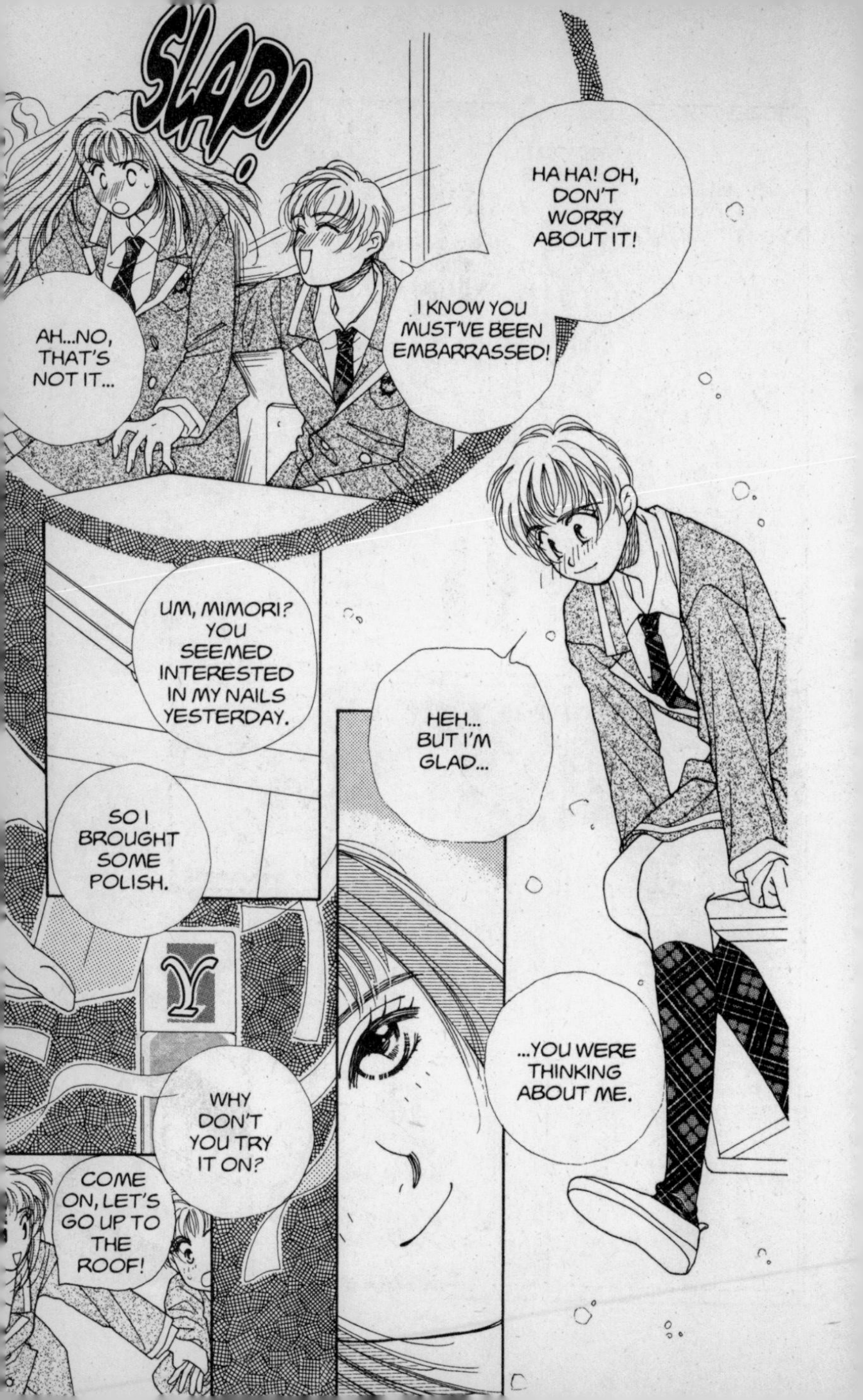
HA HA! OH, DON'T WORRY ABOUT IT!
SLAP!
I KNOW YOU MUST'VE BEEN EMBARRASSED!
AH...NO, THAT'S NOT IT...
HEH... BUT I'M GLAD...
...YOU WERE THINKING ABOUT ME.
UM, MIMORI? YOU SEEMED INTERESTED IN MY NAILS YESTERDAY.
SO I BROUGHT SOME POLISH.
WHY DON'T YOU TRY IT ON?
COME ON, LET'S GO UP TO THE ROOF!

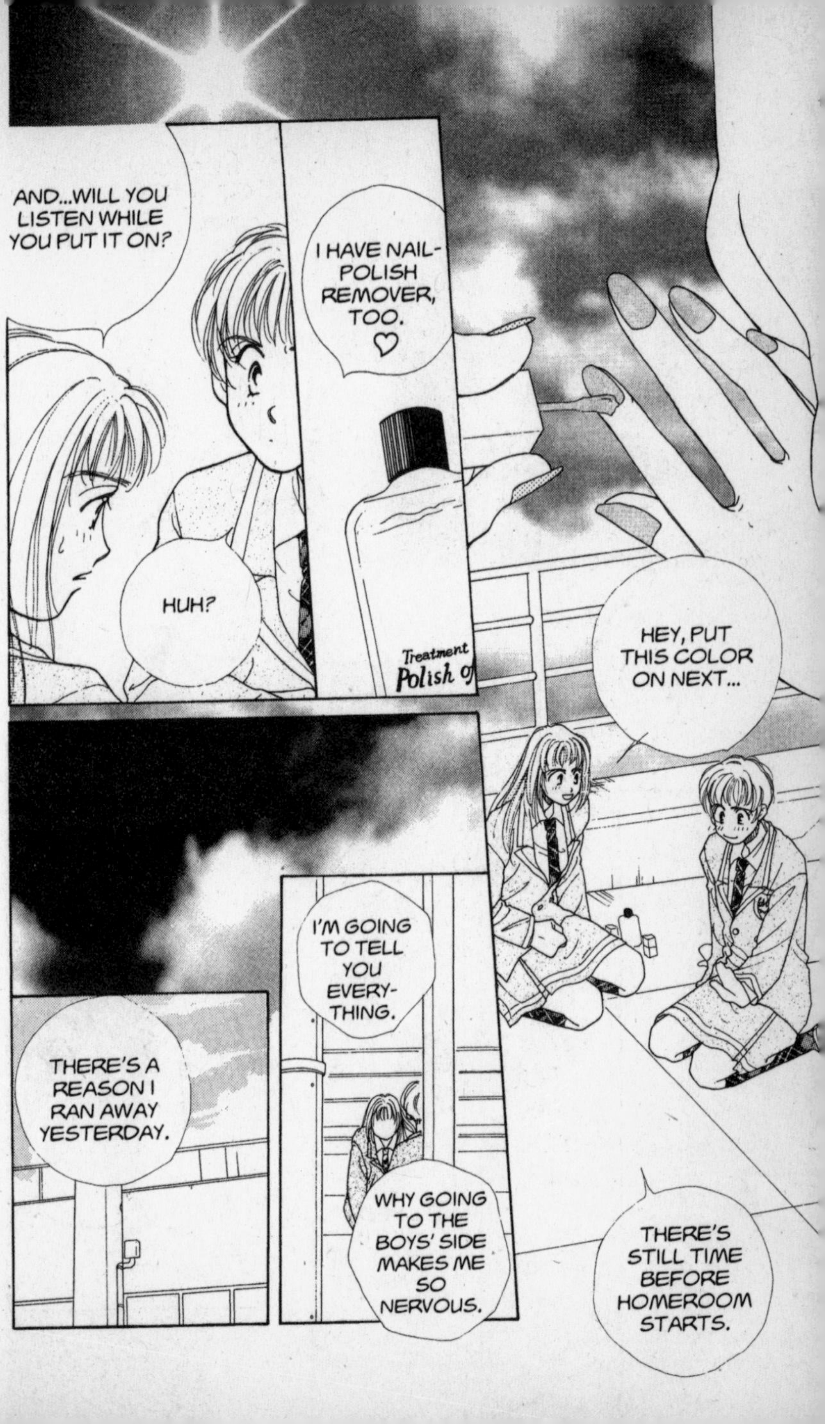
HEY, PUT THIS COLOR ON NEXT...
THERE'S STILL TIME BEFORE HOMEROOM STARTS.
I HAVE NAIL-POLISH REMOVER, TOO. ♡
Treatment Polish of
AND...WILL YOU LISTEN WHILE YOU PUT IT ON?
HUH?
I'M GOING TO TELL YOU EVERYTHING.
WHY GOING TO THE BOYS' SIDE MAKES ME SO NERVOUS.
THERE'S A REASON I RAN AWAY YESTERDAY.

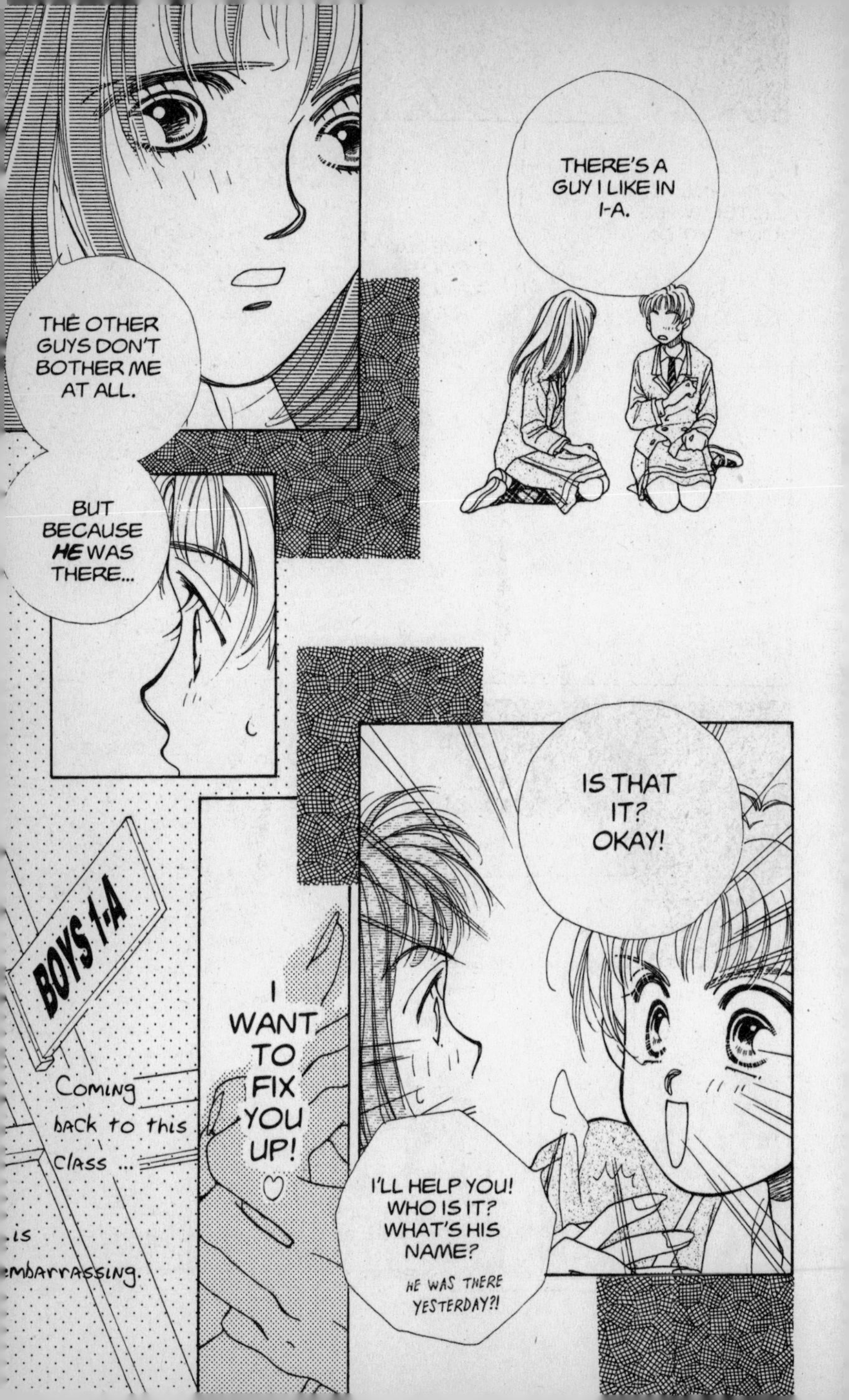
THERE'S A GUY I LIKE IN I-A.
THE OTHER GUYS DON'T BOTHER ME AT ALL.
BUT BECAUSE *HE* WAS THERE...
IS THAT IT? OKAY!
I'LL HELP YOU! WHO IS IT? WHAT'S HIS NAME?
HE WAS THERE YESTERDAY?!
I WANT TO FIX YOU UP! ♡
BOYS 1-A
Coming back to this class ...
...is embarrassing.

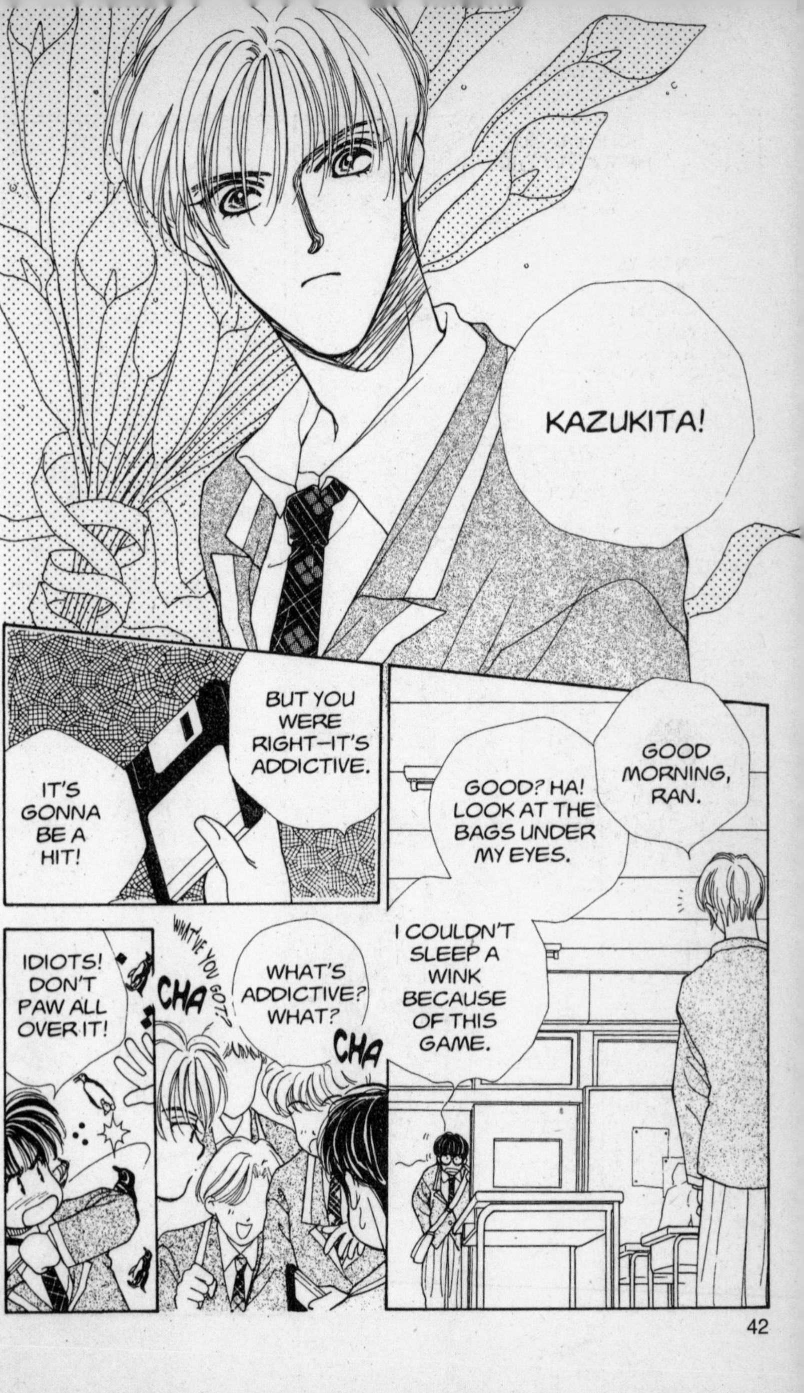
KAZUKITA!
GOOD MORNING, RAN.
GOOD? HA! LOOK AT THE BAGS UNDER MY EYES.
I COULDN'T SLEEP A WINK BECAUSE OF THIS GAME.
BUT YOU WERE RIGHT—IT'S ADDICTIVE.
IT'S GONNA BE A HIT!
CHA
WHAT'S ADDICTIVE? WHAT?
WHAT'VE YOU GOT?
CHA
IDIOTS! DON'T PAW ALL OVER IT!

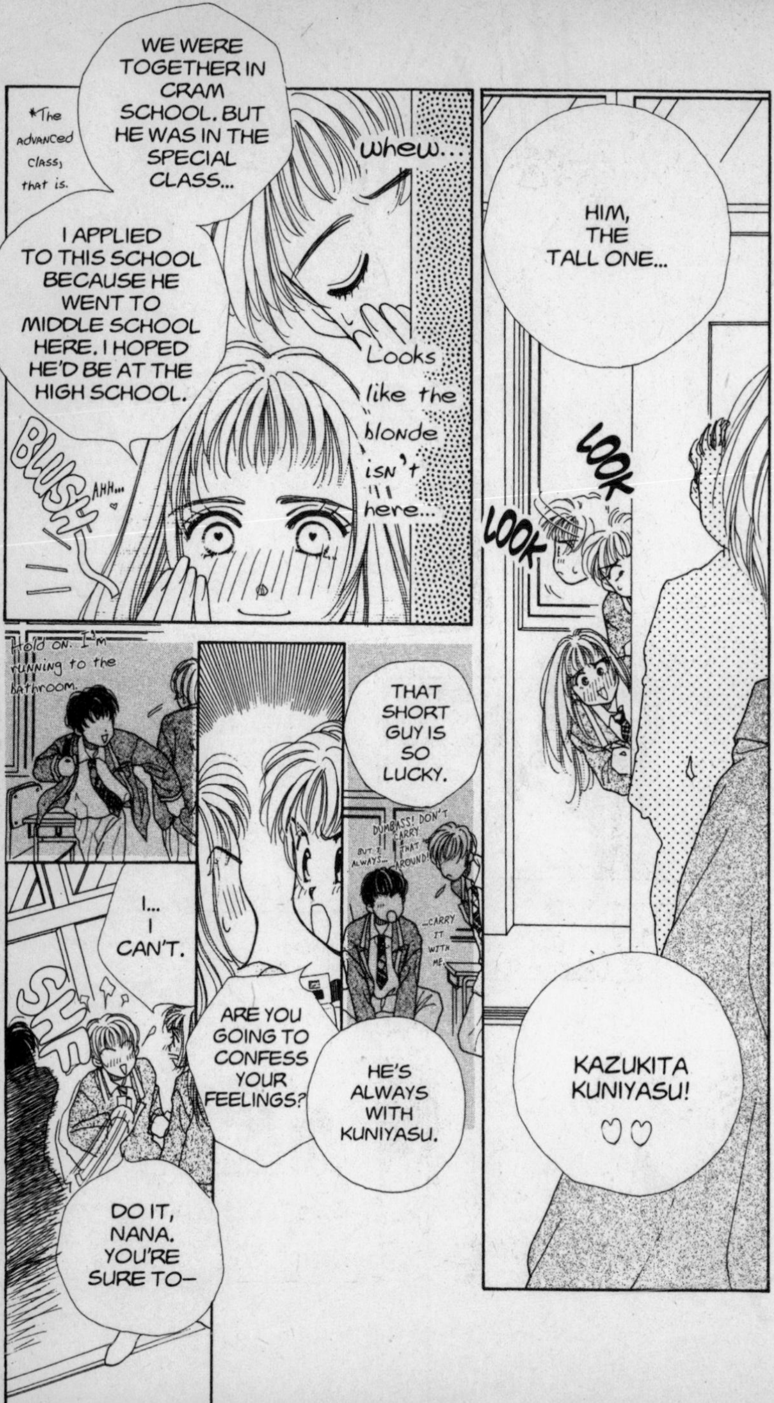
HIM, THE TALL ONE...
LOOK
LOOK
KAZUKITA KUNIYASU!
whew...
Looks like the blonde isn't here...
WE WERE TOGETHER IN CRAM SCHOOL. BUT HE WAS IN THE SPECIAL CLASS...
*The advanced class, that is.
I APPLIED TO THIS SCHOOL BECAUSE HE WENT TO MIDDLE SCHOOL HERE. I HOPED HE'D BE AT THE HIGH SCHOOL.
BLUSH
AHH...
THAT SHORT GUY IS SO LUCKY.
DUMBASS! DON'T CARRY THAT AROUND!
BUT I ALWAYS...
...CARRY IT WITH ME.
HE'S ALWAYS WITH KUNIYASU.
ARE YOU GOING TO CONFESS YOUR FEELINGS?
Hold on. I'm running to the bathroom.
I... I CAN'T.
SHF
DO IT, NANA. YOU'RE SURE TO—

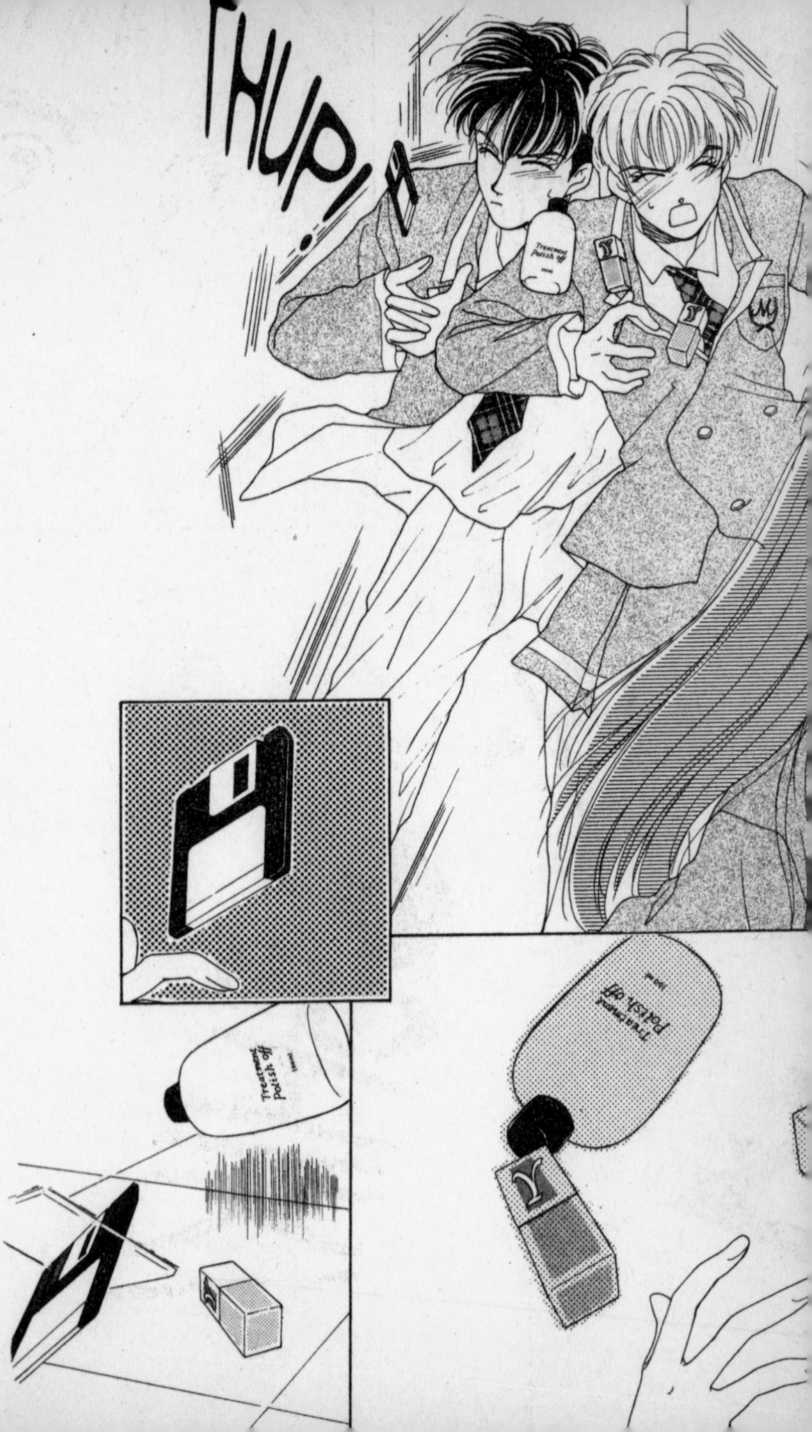
THUP!!
Treatment Polish off
Treatment Polish off
Treatment Polish off

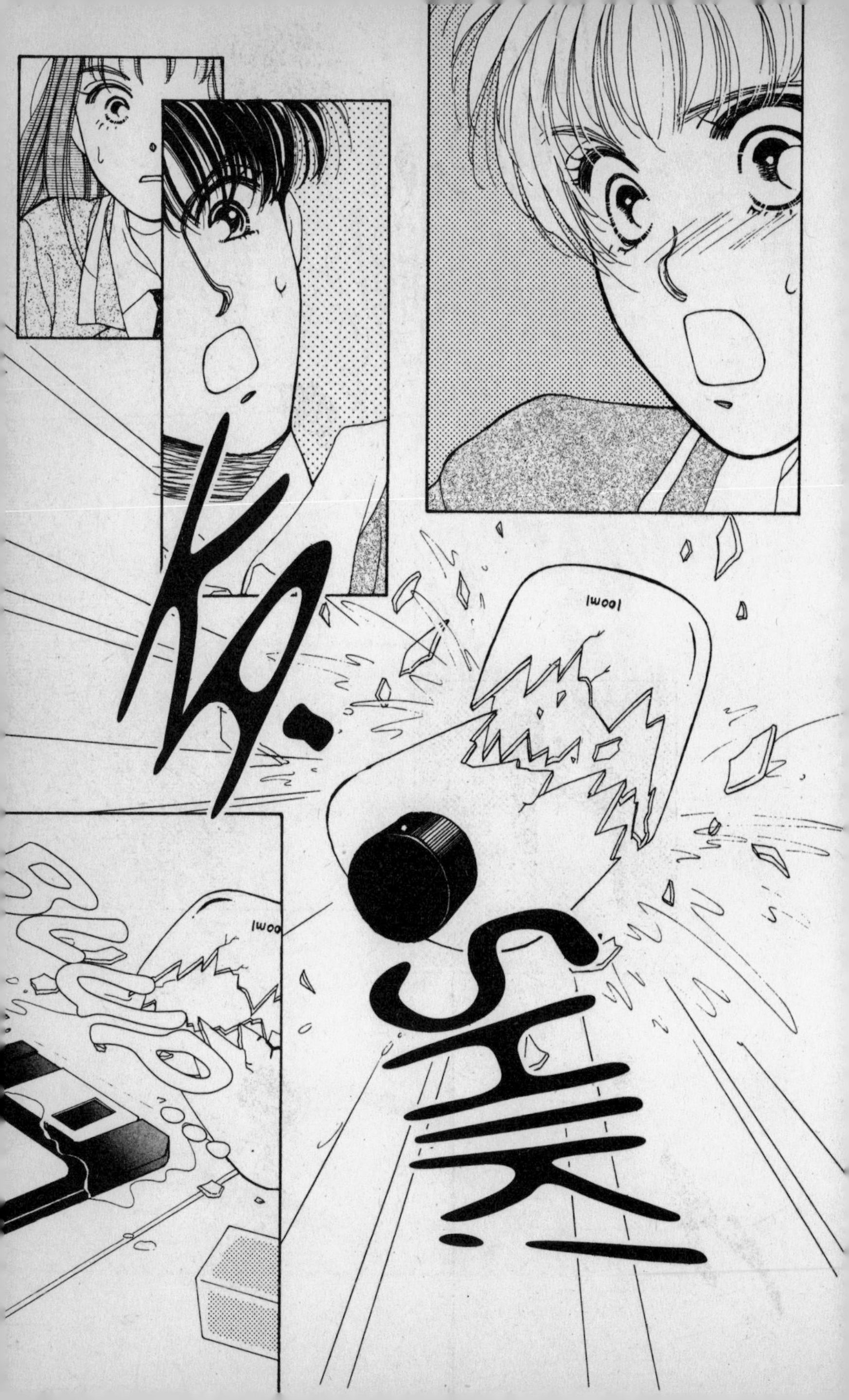
KA-
SHIK!

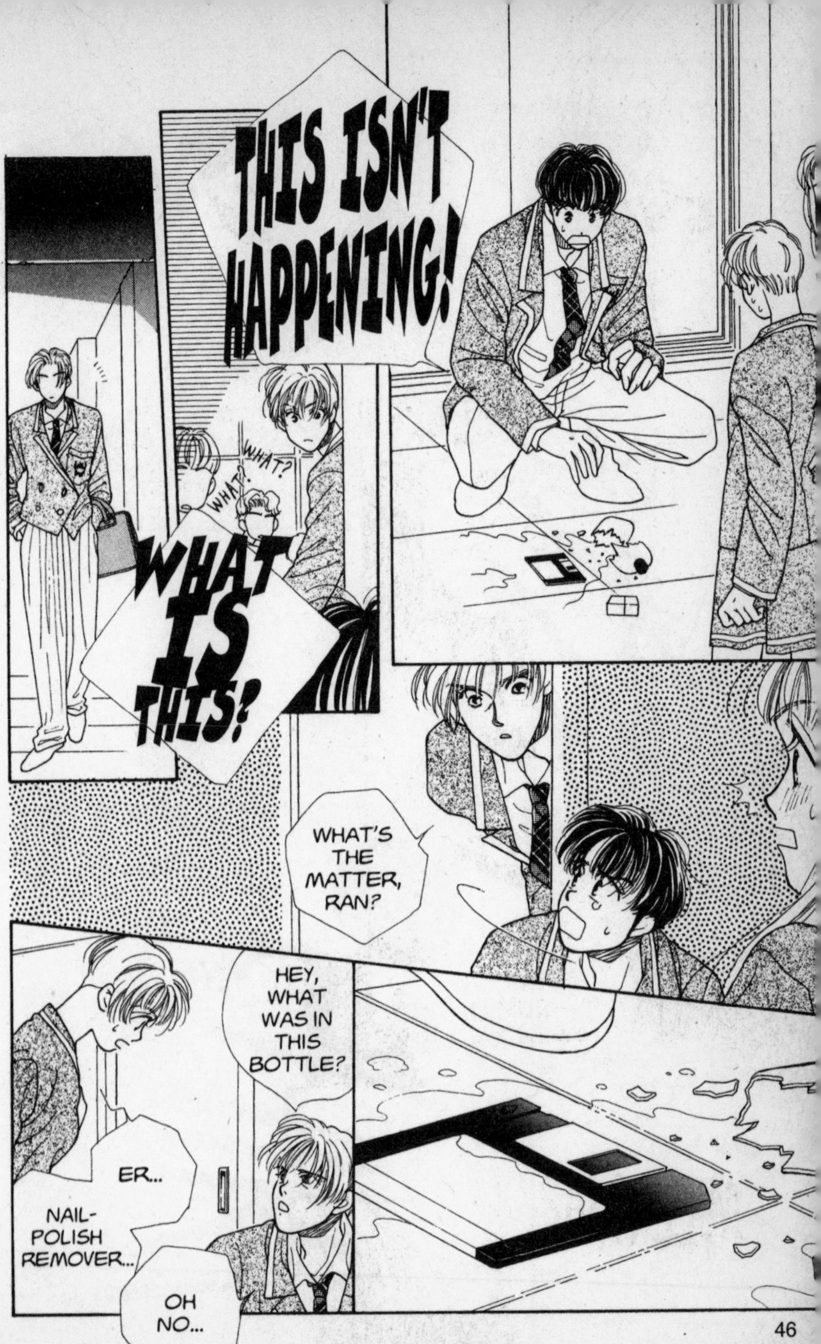
THIS ISN'T HAPPENING!
WHAT?
WHAT?
WHAT IS THIS?
WHAT'S THE MATTER, RAN?
HEY, WHAT WAS IN THIS BOTTLE?
ER...
NAIL-POLISH REMOVER...
OH NO...

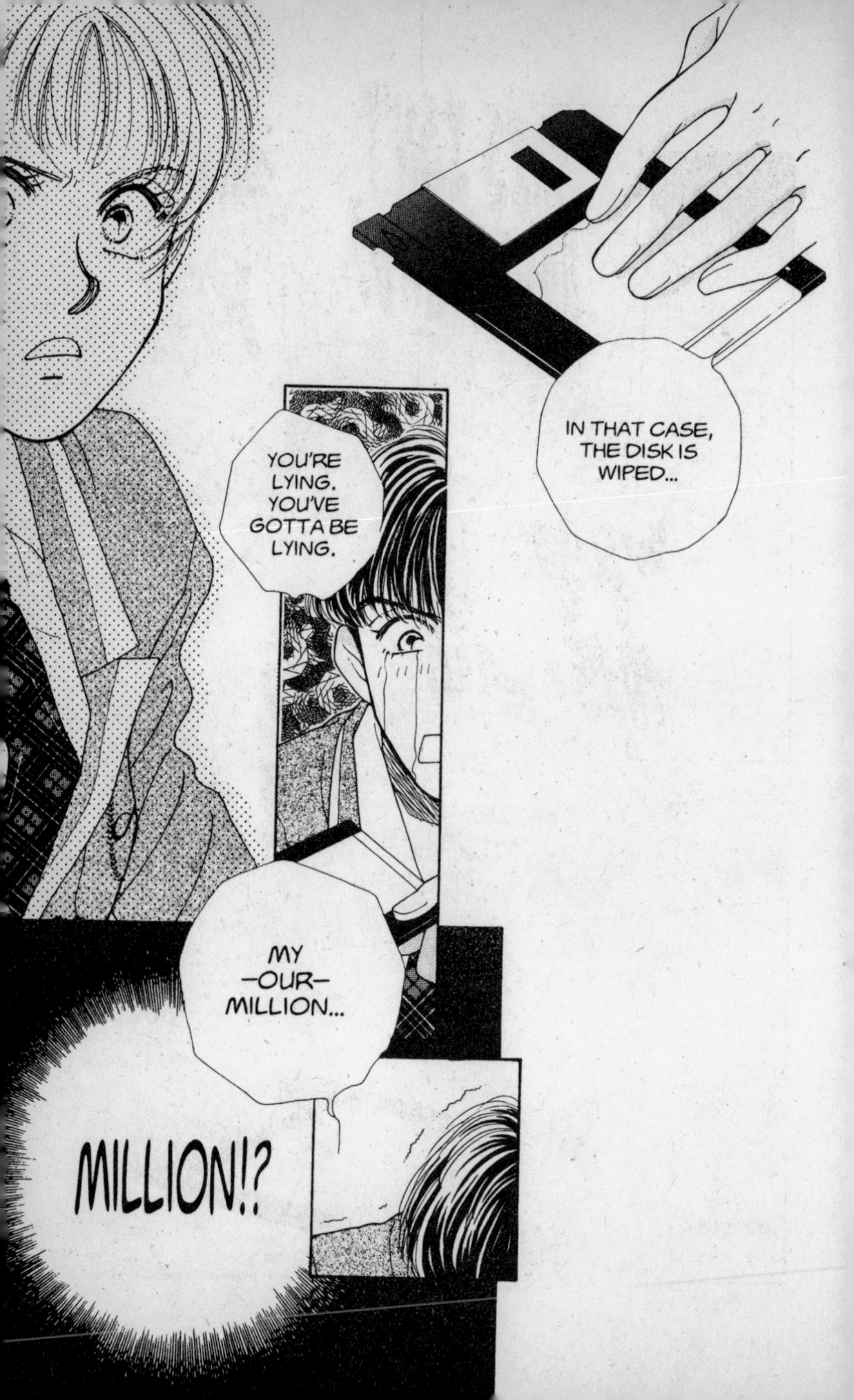
IN THAT CASE, THE DISK IS WIPED...
YOU'RE LYING. YOU'VE GOTTA BE LYING.
MY -OUR- MILLION...
MILLION!?

IT WOULD'VE BEEN BETTER IF IT HAD CRACKED...
DI—NG DO—NG
DO—NG DI—NG
LOOKS LIKE HOME-ROOM'S STARTING...
HE'S SNAPPED.
YOU GIRLS GO BACK TO CLASS.
DI—NG DO—NG
COME ON, RAN. LET'S GO.
DI—NG

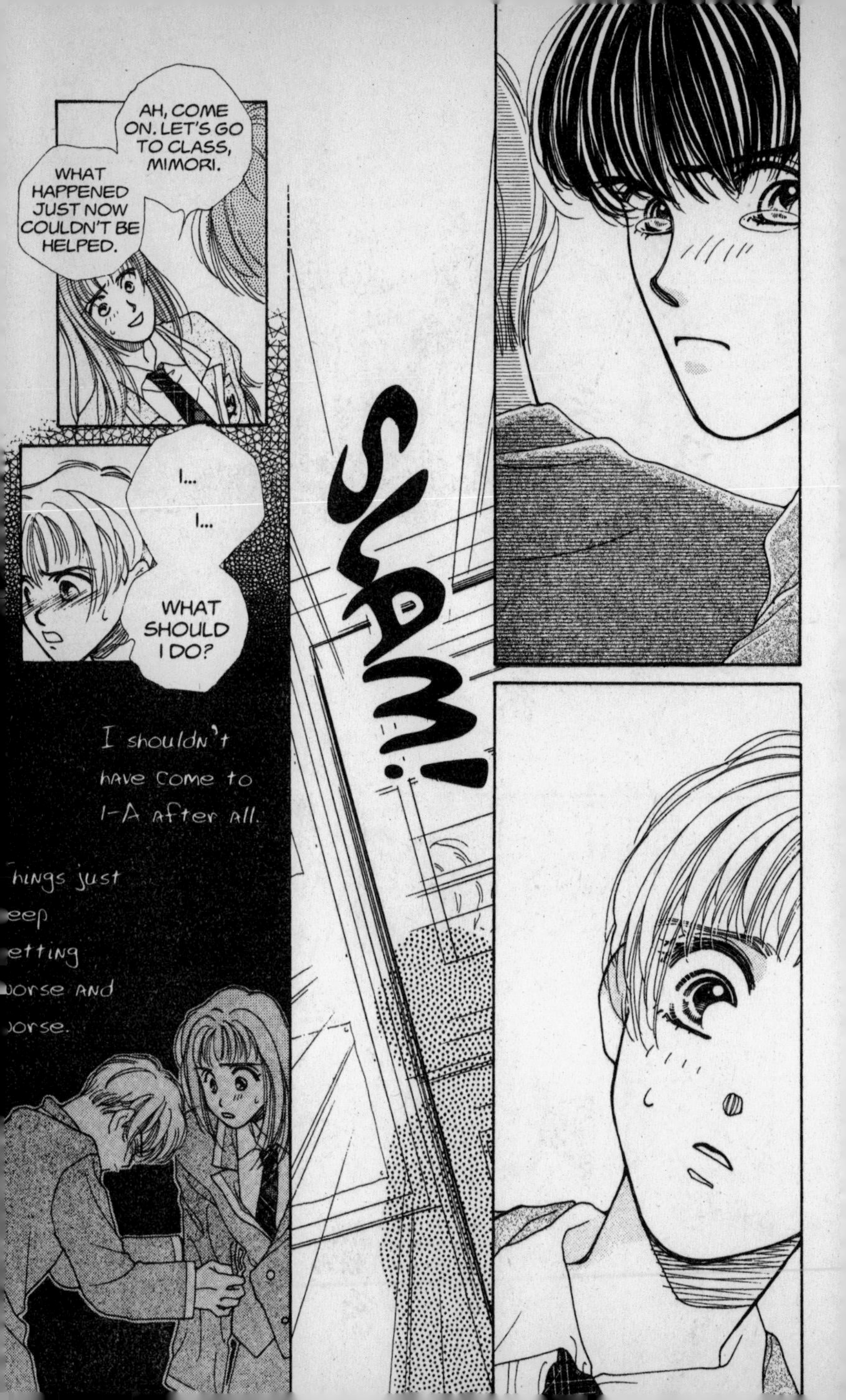
SLAM!
AH, COME ON. LET'S GO TO CLASS, MIMORI.
WHAT HAPPENED JUST NOW COULDN'T BE HELPED.
I... I...
WHAT SHOULD I DO?
I shouldn't have come to 1-A after all.
hings just eep etting orse and orse.

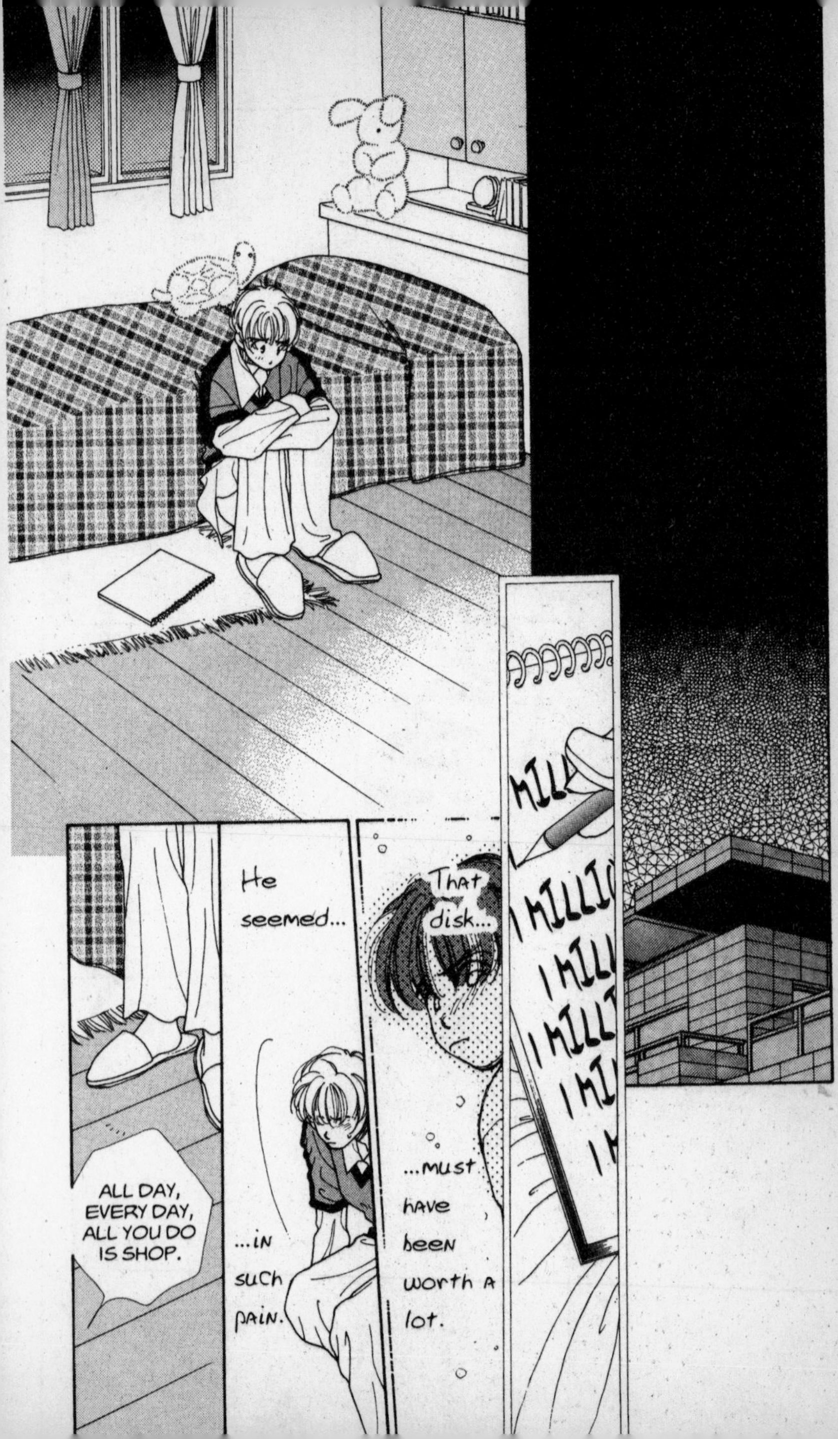
That disk...
...must have been worth a lot.
He seemed...
...in such pain.
ALL DAY, EVERY DAY, ALL YOU DO IS SHOP.

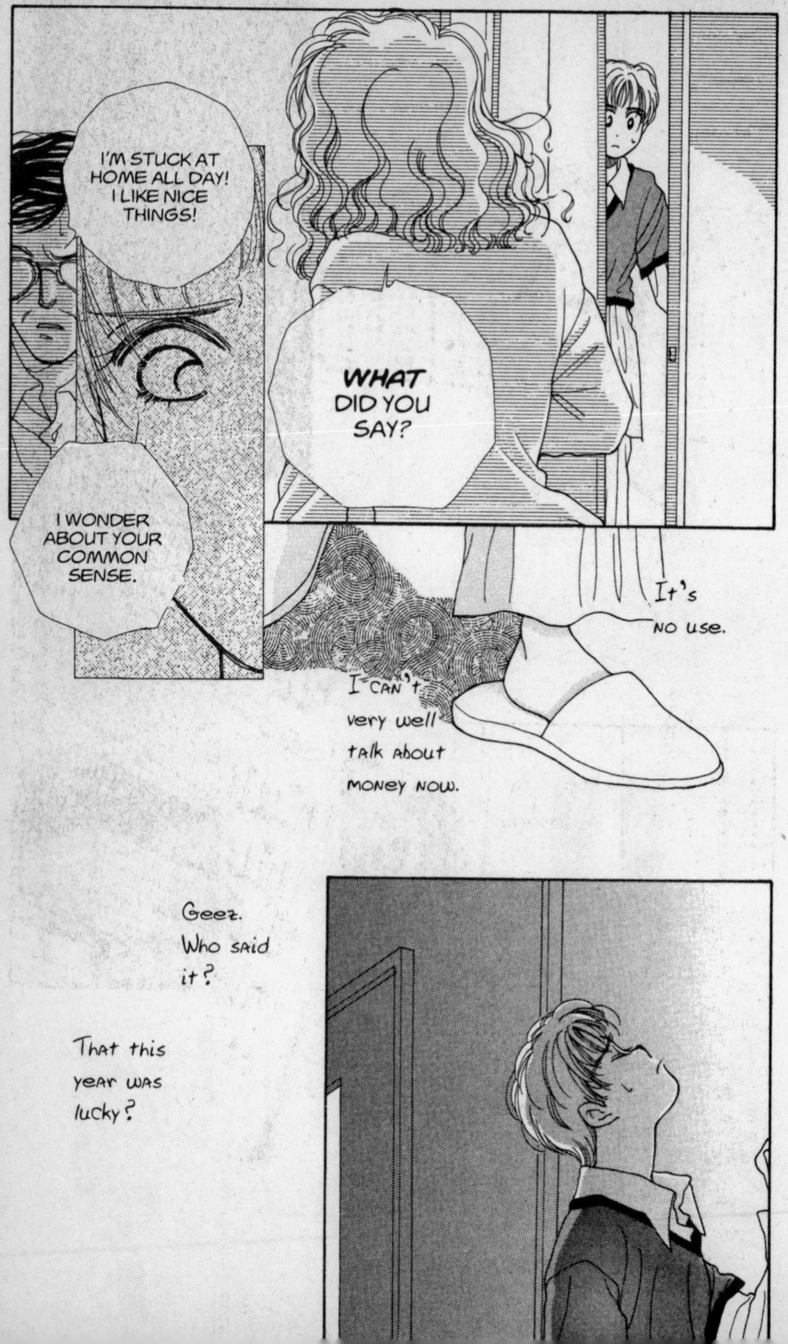
WHAT DID YOU SAY?
I'M STUCK AT HOME ALL DAY! I LIKE NICE THINGS!
I WONDER ABOUT YOUR COMMON SENSE.
It's no use.
I can't very well talk about money now.
Geez. Who said it?
That this year was lucky?

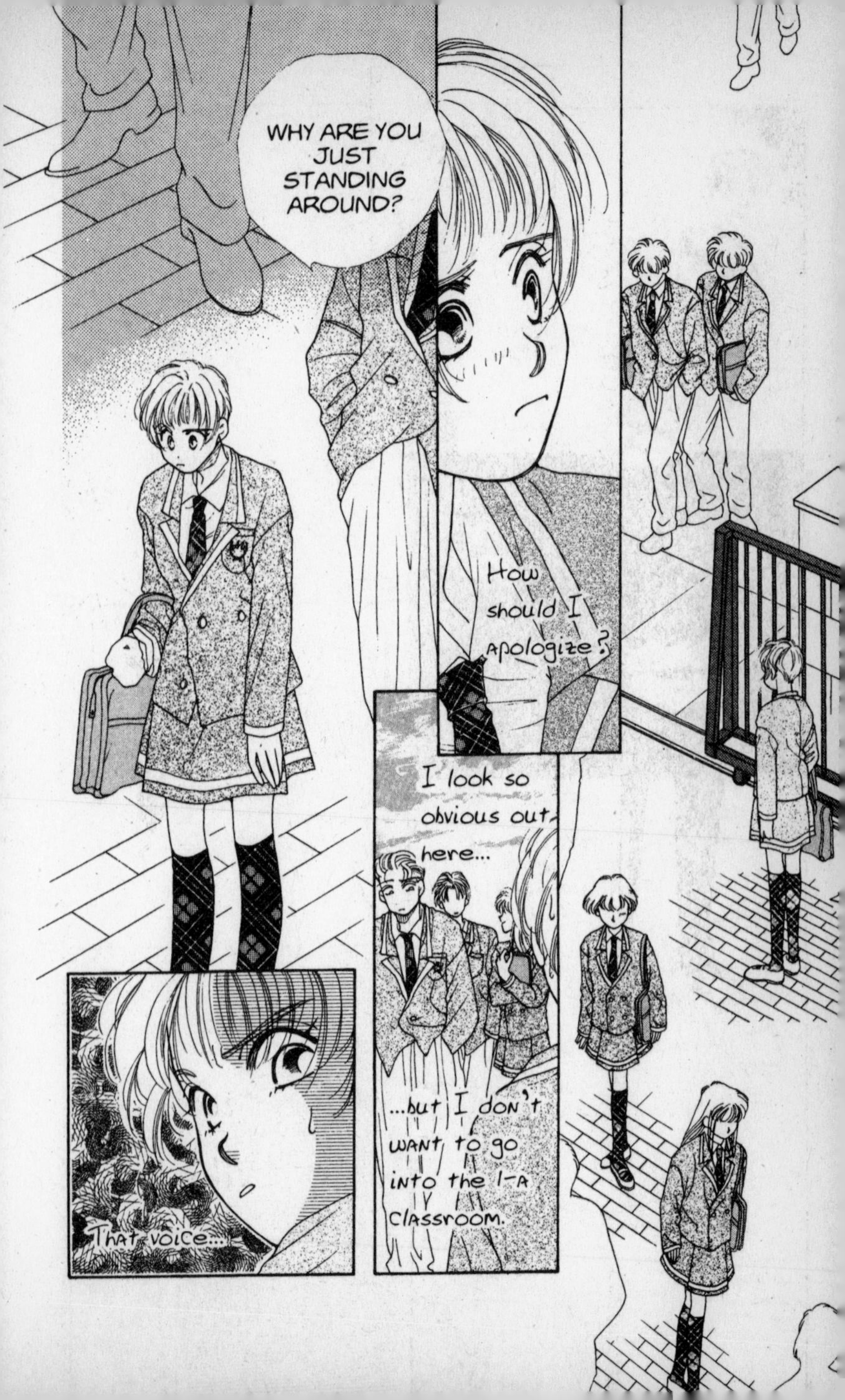
How should I apologize?
I look so obvious out here...
...but I don't want to go into the 1-A classroom.
WHY ARE YOU JUST STANDING AROUND?
That voice...

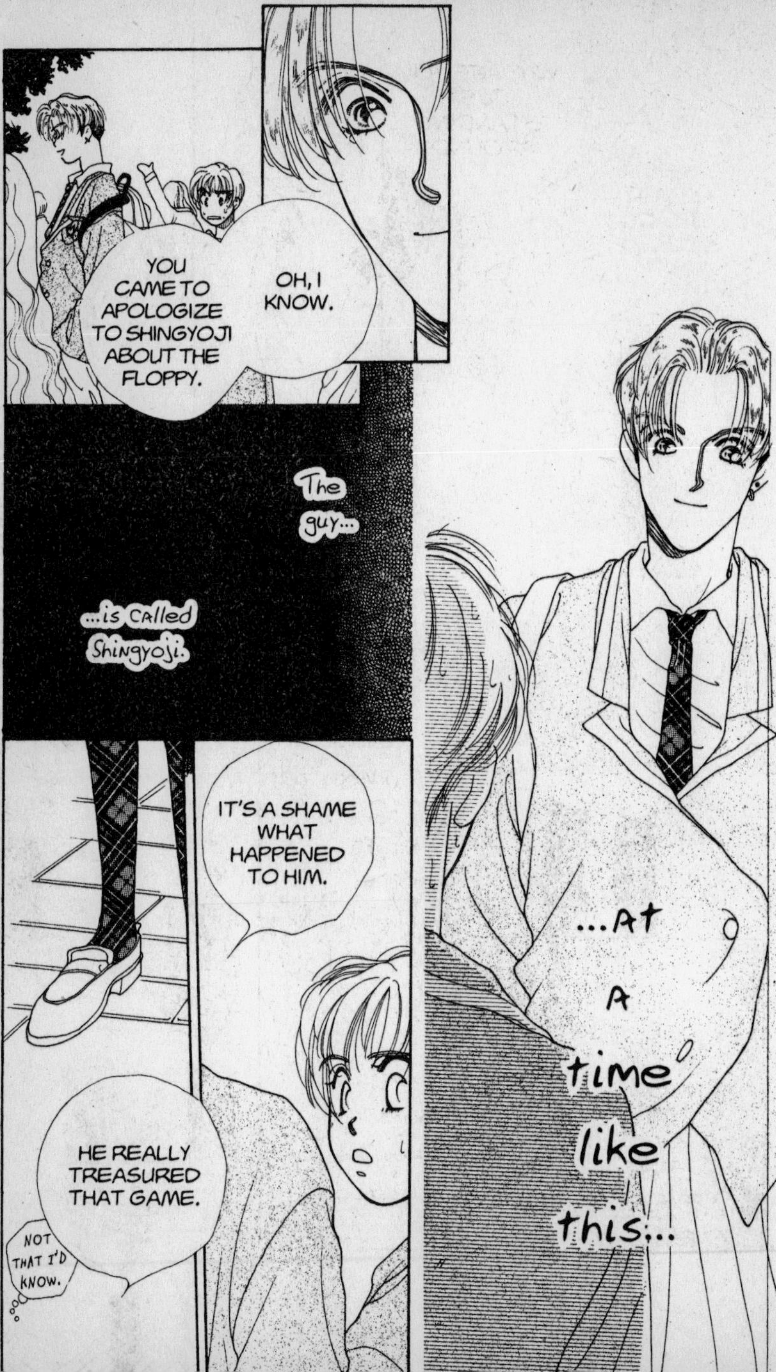
...At a time like this...
OH, I KNOW.
YOU CAME TO APOLOGIZE TO SHINGYOJI ABOUT THE FLOPPY.
The guy...
...is called Shingyoji.
IT'S A SHAME WHAT HAPPENED TO HIM.
HE REALLY TREASURED THAT GAME.
NOT THAT I'D KNOW.

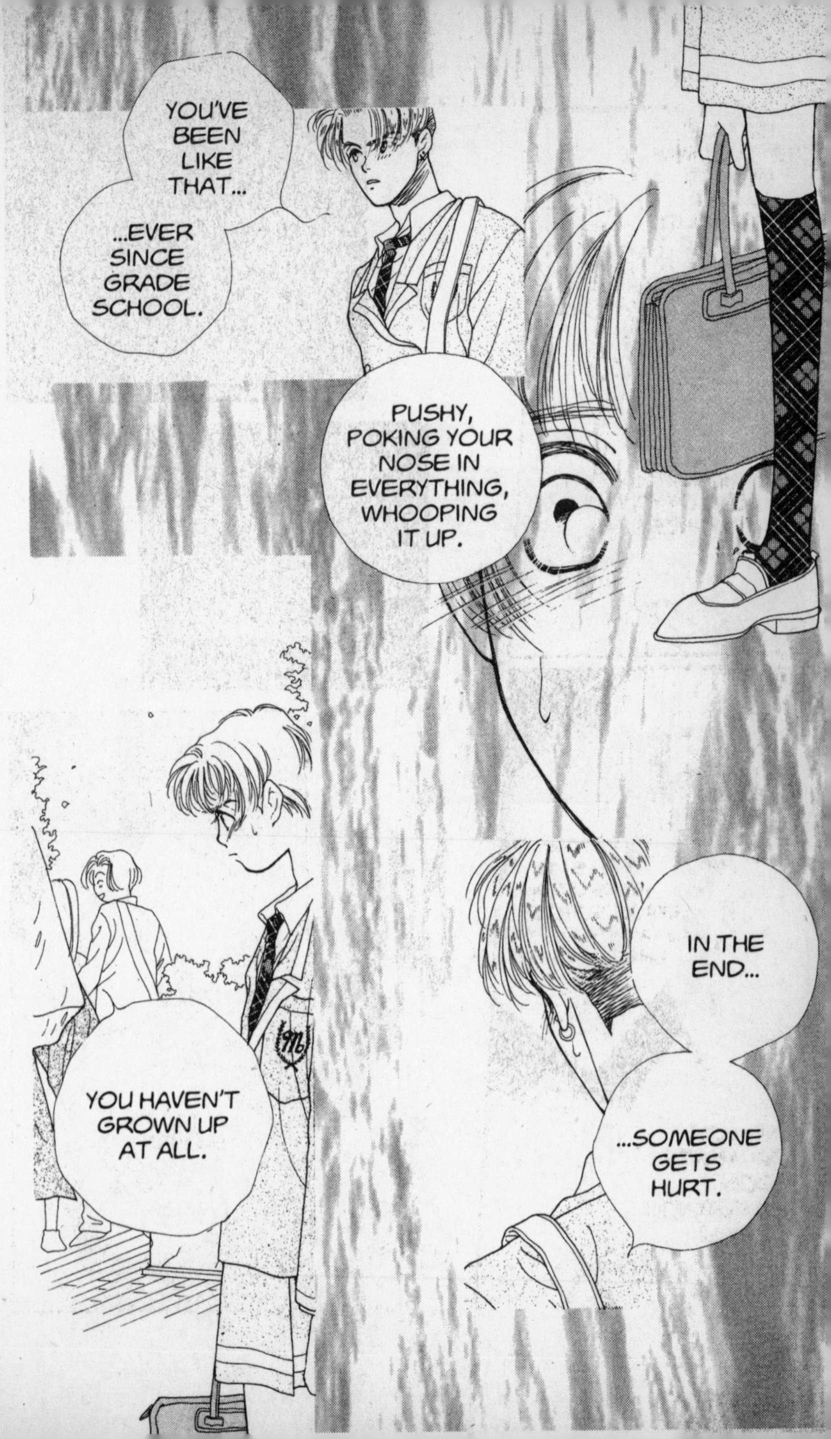
YOU'VE BEEN LIKE THAT...
...EVER SINCE GRADE SCHOOL.
PUSHY, POKING YOUR NOSE IN EVERYTHING, WHOOPING IT UP.
IN THE END...
...SOMEONE GETS HURT.
YOU HAVEN'T GROWN UP AT ALL.

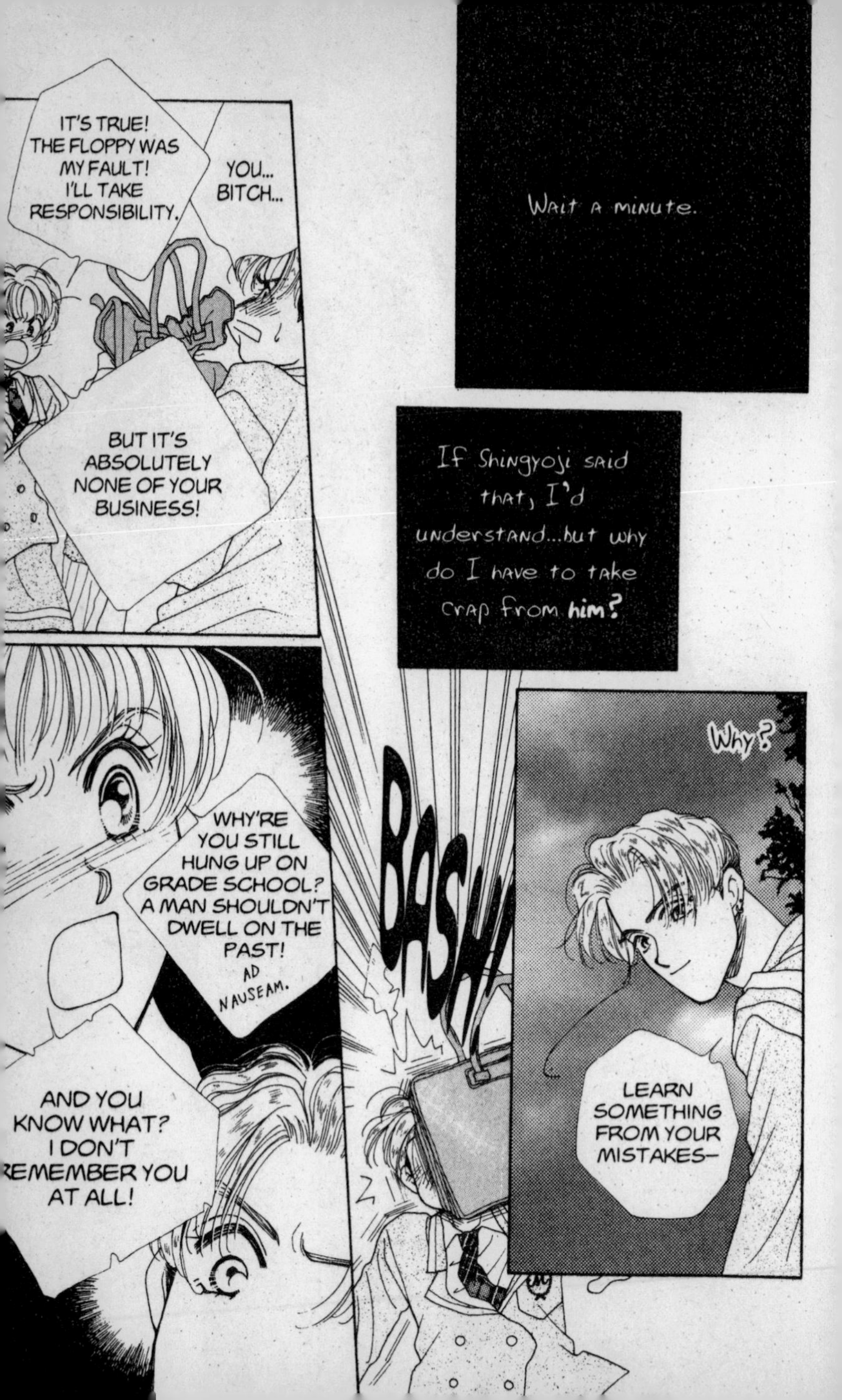

Wait a minute.
If Shingyoji said that, I'd understand...but why do I have to take crap from **him**?
Why?
LEARN SOMETHING FROM YOUR MISTAKES—
BASH
IT'S TRUE! THE FLOPPY WAS MY FAULT! I'LL TAKE RESPONSIBILITY.
YOU... BITCH...
BUT IT'S ABSOLUTELY NONE OF YOUR BUSINESS!
WHY'RE YOU STILL HUNG UP ON GRADE SCHOOL? A MAN SHOULDN'T DWELL ON THE PAST!
AD NAUSEAM.
AND YOU KNOW WHAT? I DON'T REMEMBER YOU AT ALL!

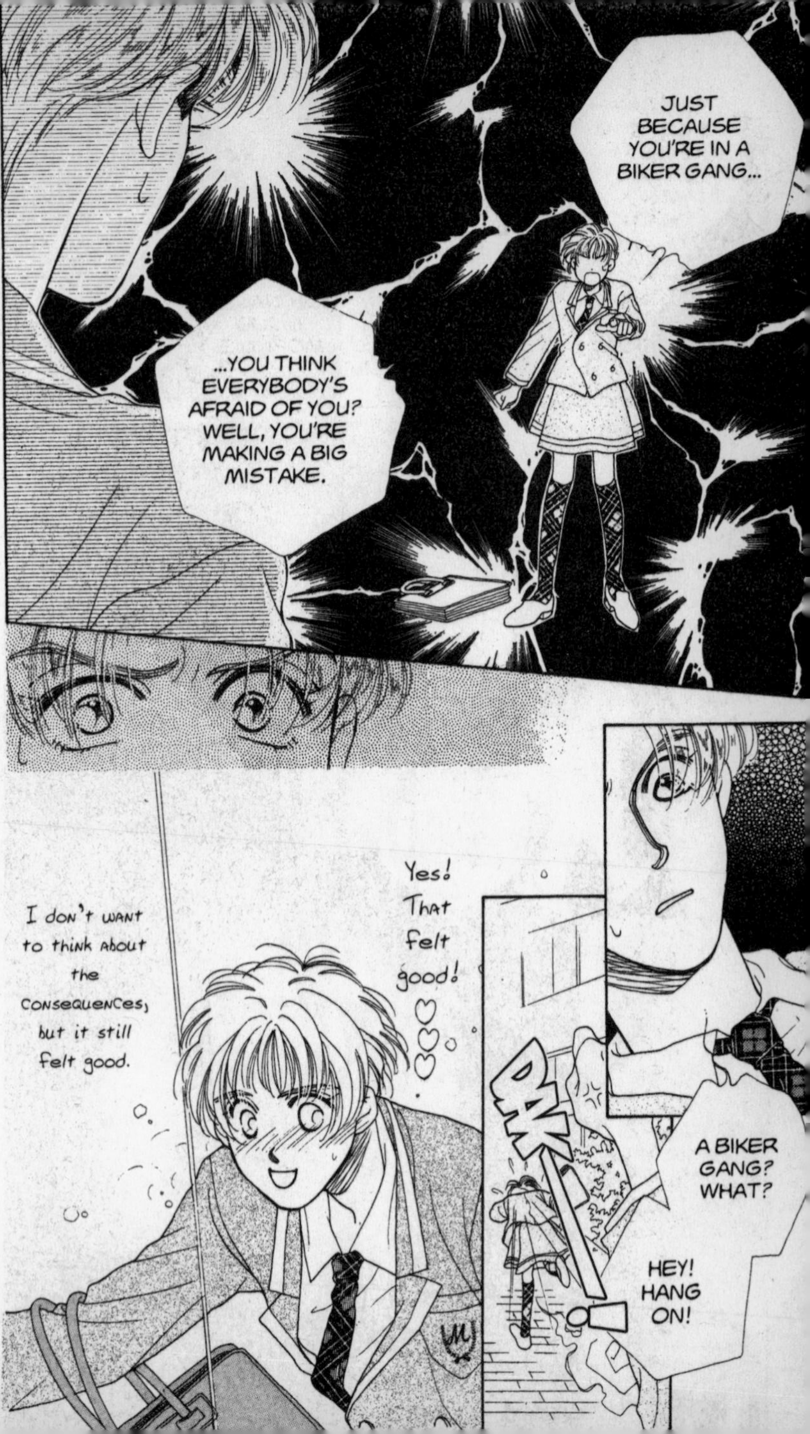
JUST BECAUSE YOU'RE IN A BIKER GANG...
...YOU THINK EVERYBODY'S AFRAID OF YOU? WELL, YOU'RE MAKING A BIG MISTAKE.
A BIKER GANG? WHAT?
DAK
HEY! HANG ON!
Yes! That felt good!
I don't want to think about the consequences, but it still felt good.

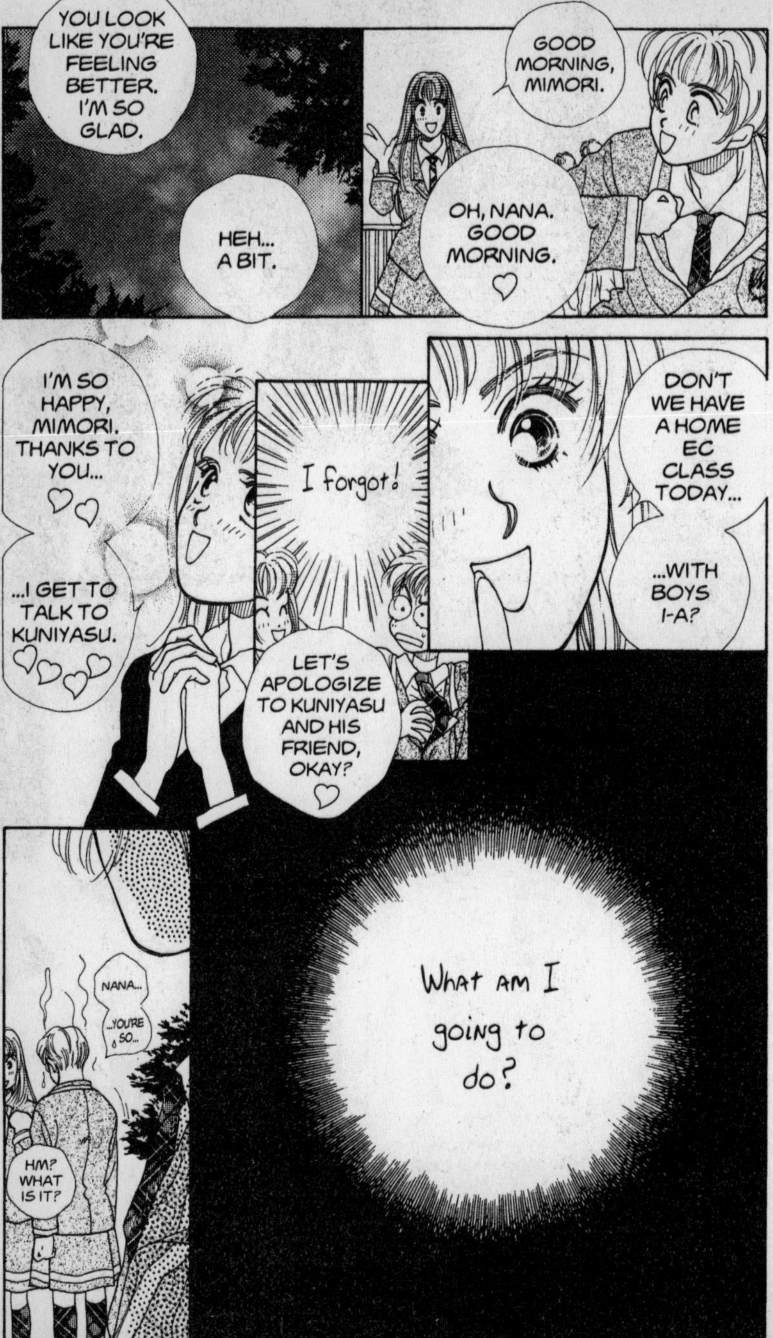
GOOD MORNING, MIMORI.
OH, NANA. GOOD MORNING. ♡
YOU LOOK LIKE YOU'RE FEELING BETTER. I'M SO GLAD.
HEH... A BIT.
DON'T WE HAVE A HOME EC CLASS TODAY...
...WITH BOYS I-A?
I forgot!
LET'S APOLOGIZE TO KUNIYASU AND HIS FRIEND, OKAY? ♡
I'M SO HAPPY, MIMORI. THANKS TO YOU... ♡♡
...I GET TO TALK TO KUNIYASU. ♡♡♡♡
What am I going to do?
NANA...
...YOU'RE SO...
HM? WHAT IS IT?

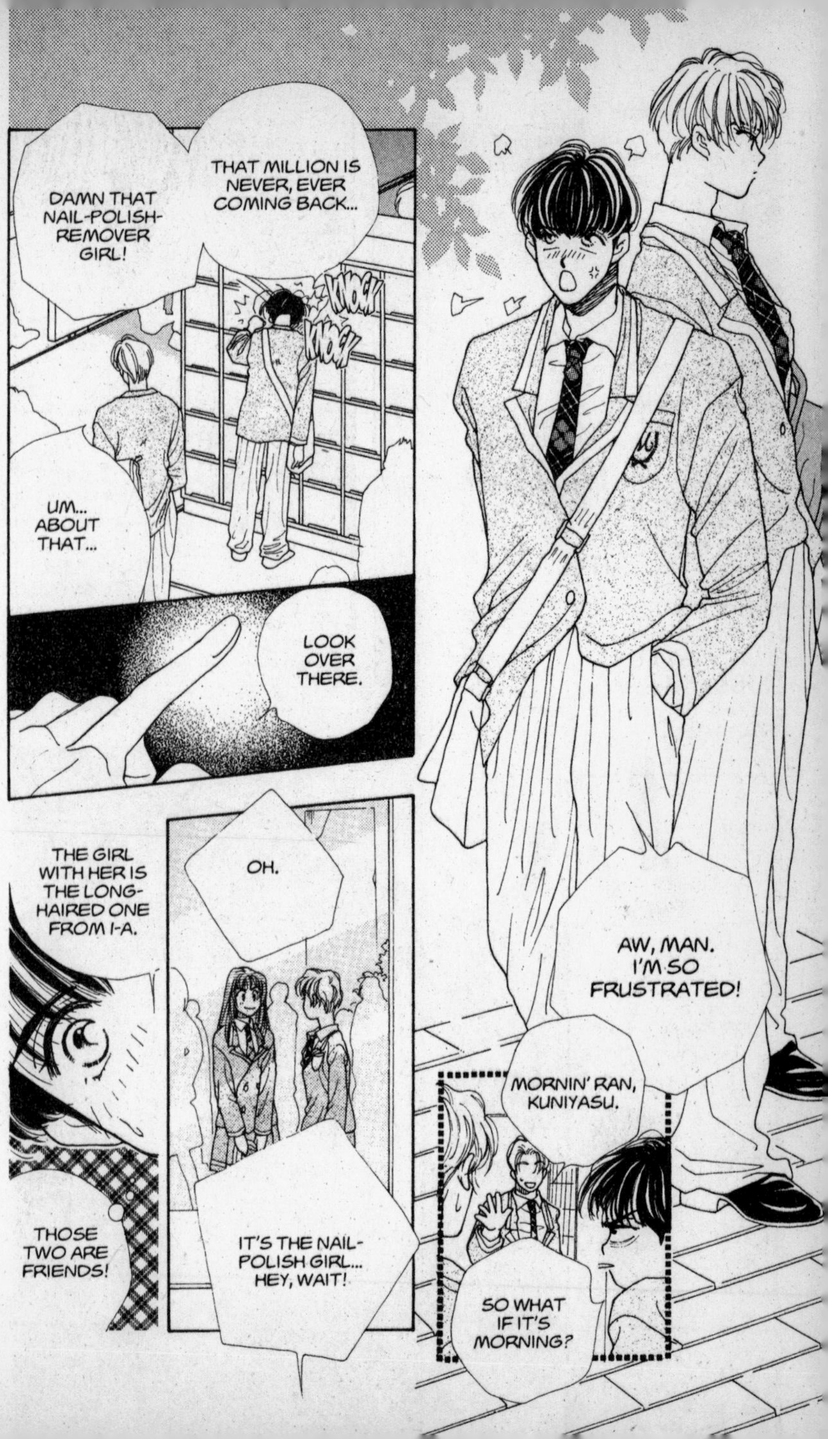
AW, MAN. I'M SO FRUSTRATED!
MORNIN' RAN, KUNIYASU.
SO WHAT IF IT'S MORNING?
THAT MILLION IS NEVER, EVER COMING BACK...
DAMN THAT NAIL-POLISH-REMOVER GIRL!
KNOCK
KNOCK
UM... ABOUT THAT...
LOOK OVER THERE.
OH.
IT'S THE NAIL-POLISH GIRL... HEY, WAIT!
THE GIRL WITH HER IS THE LONG-HAIRED ONE FROM I-A.
THOSE TWO ARE FRIENDS!

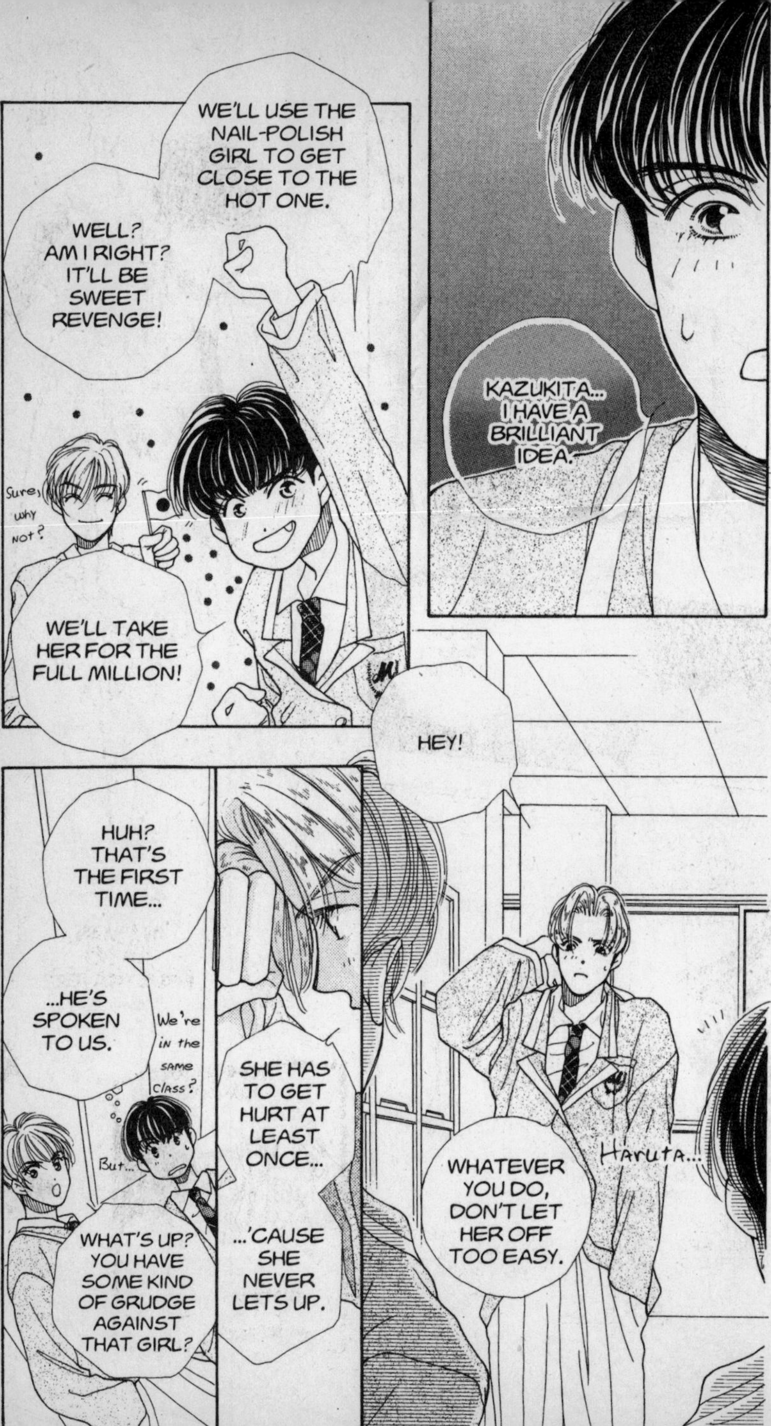
KAZUKITA... I HAVE A BRILLIANT IDEA.
WE'LL USE THE NAIL-POLISH GIRL TO GET CLOSE TO THE HOT ONE.
WELL? AM I RIGHT? IT'LL BE SWEET REVENGE!
Sure, why not?
WE'LL TAKE HER FOR THE FULL MILLION!
HEY!
WHATEVER YOU DO, DON'T LET HER OFF TOO EASY.
Haruta...
SHE HAS TO GET HURT AT LEAST ONCE...
...'CAUSE SHE NEVER LETS UP.
HUH? THAT'S THE FIRST TIME...
...HE'S SPOKEN TO US.
We're in the same class?
But...
WHAT'S UP? YOU HAVE SOME KIND OF GRUDGE AGAINST THAT GIRL?

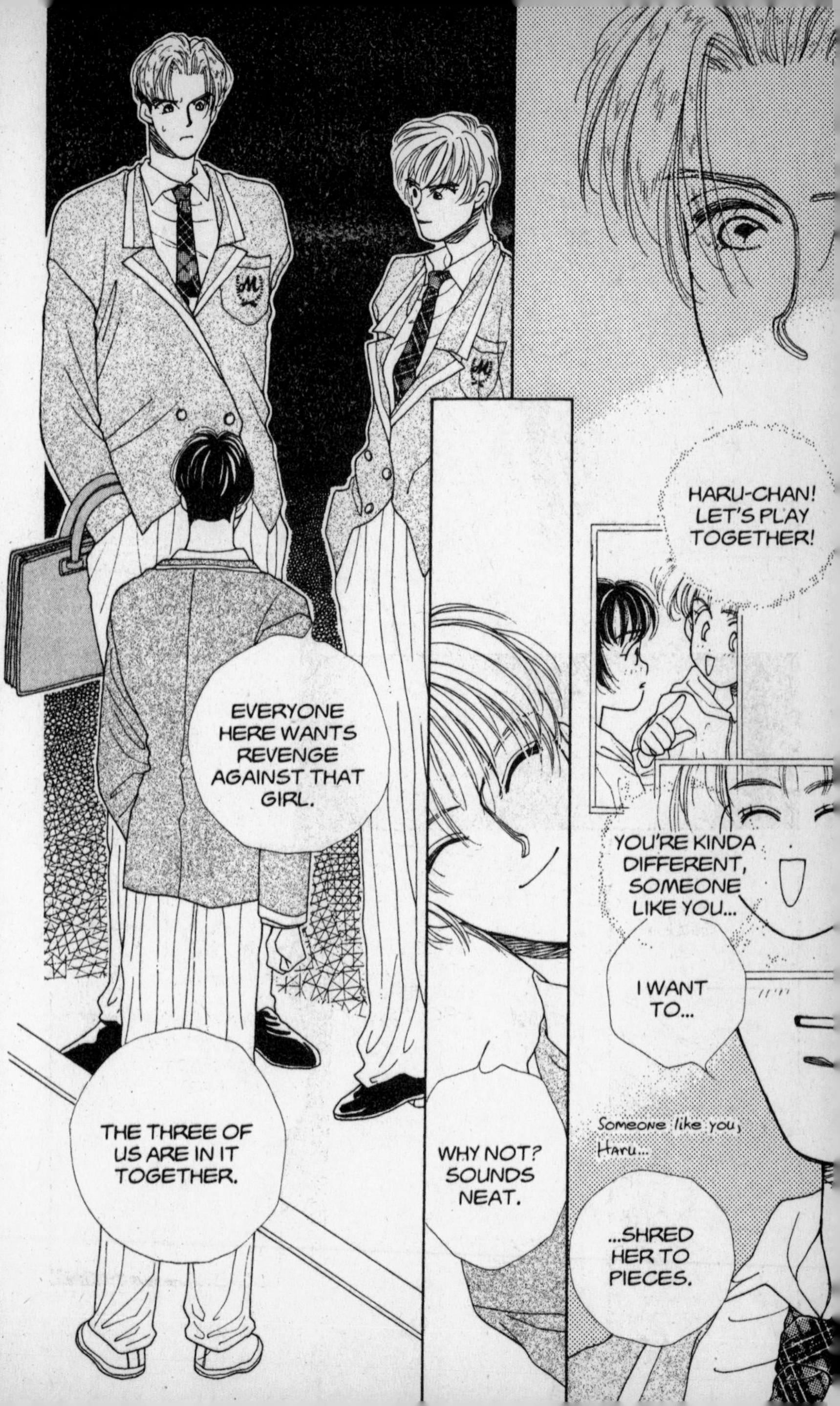

HARU-CHAN! LET'S PLAY TOGETHER!
YOU'RE KINDA DIFFERENT, SOMEONE LIKE YOU...
I WANT TO...
Someone like you, Haru...
...SHRED HER TO PIECES.
WHY NOT? SOUNDS NEAT.
EVERYONE HERE WANTS REVENGE AGAINST THAT GIRL.
THE THREE OF US ARE IN IT TOGETHER.

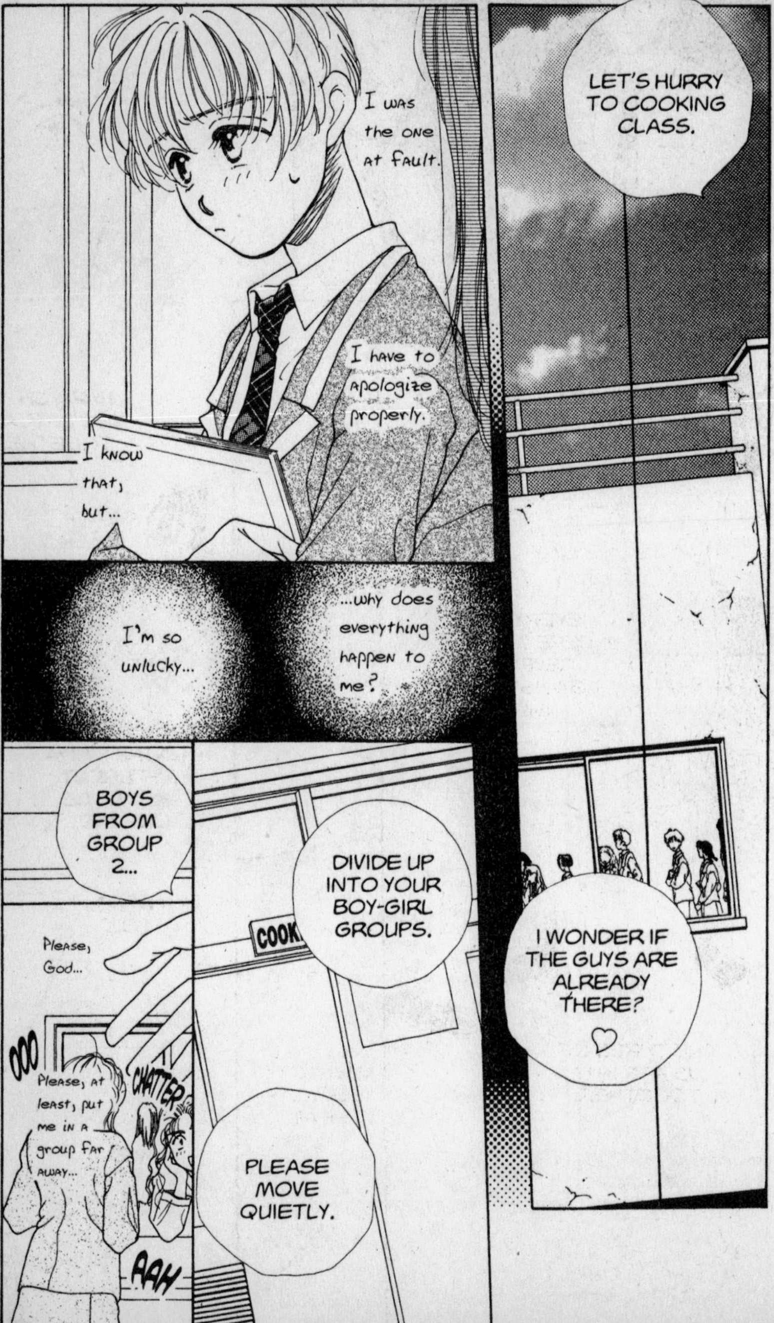
LET'S HURRY TO COOKING CLASS.
I WONDER IF THE GUYS ARE ALREADY THERE? ♡
I was the one at fault.
I have to apologize properly.
I know that, but...
...why does everything happen to me?
I'm so unlucky...
DIVIDE UP INTO YOUR BOY-GIRL GROUPS.
COOK
PLEASE MOVE QUIETLY.
BOYS FROM GROUP 2...
Please, God...
OOO
CHATTER
Please, at least, put me in a group far away...
AAH

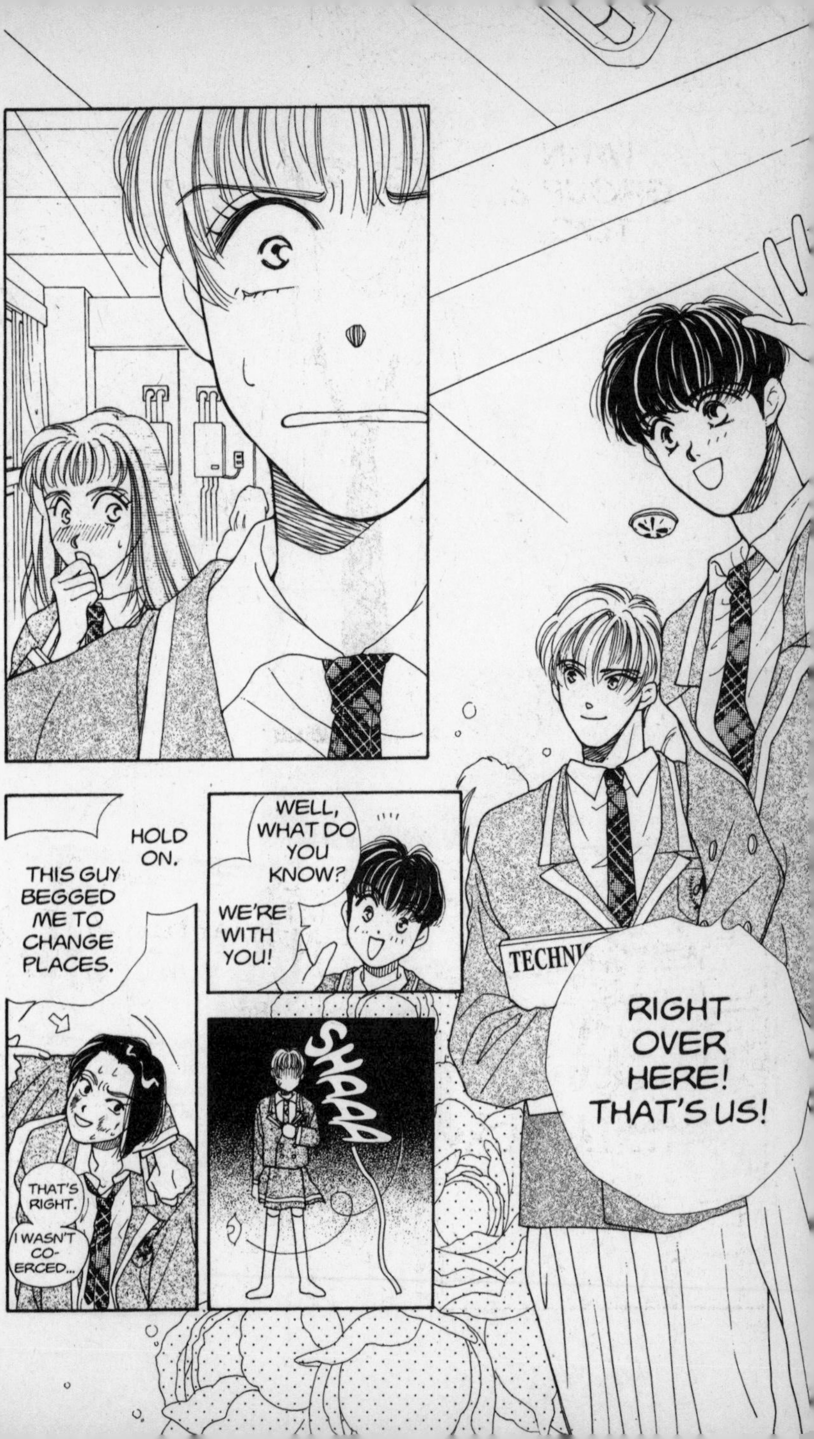
RIGHT OVER HERE! THAT'S US!
WELL, WHAT DO YOU KNOW?
WE'RE WITH YOU!
HOLD ON.
THIS GUY BEGGED ME TO CHANGE PLACES.
SHAAA
THAT'S RIGHT.
I WASN'T CO-ERCED...

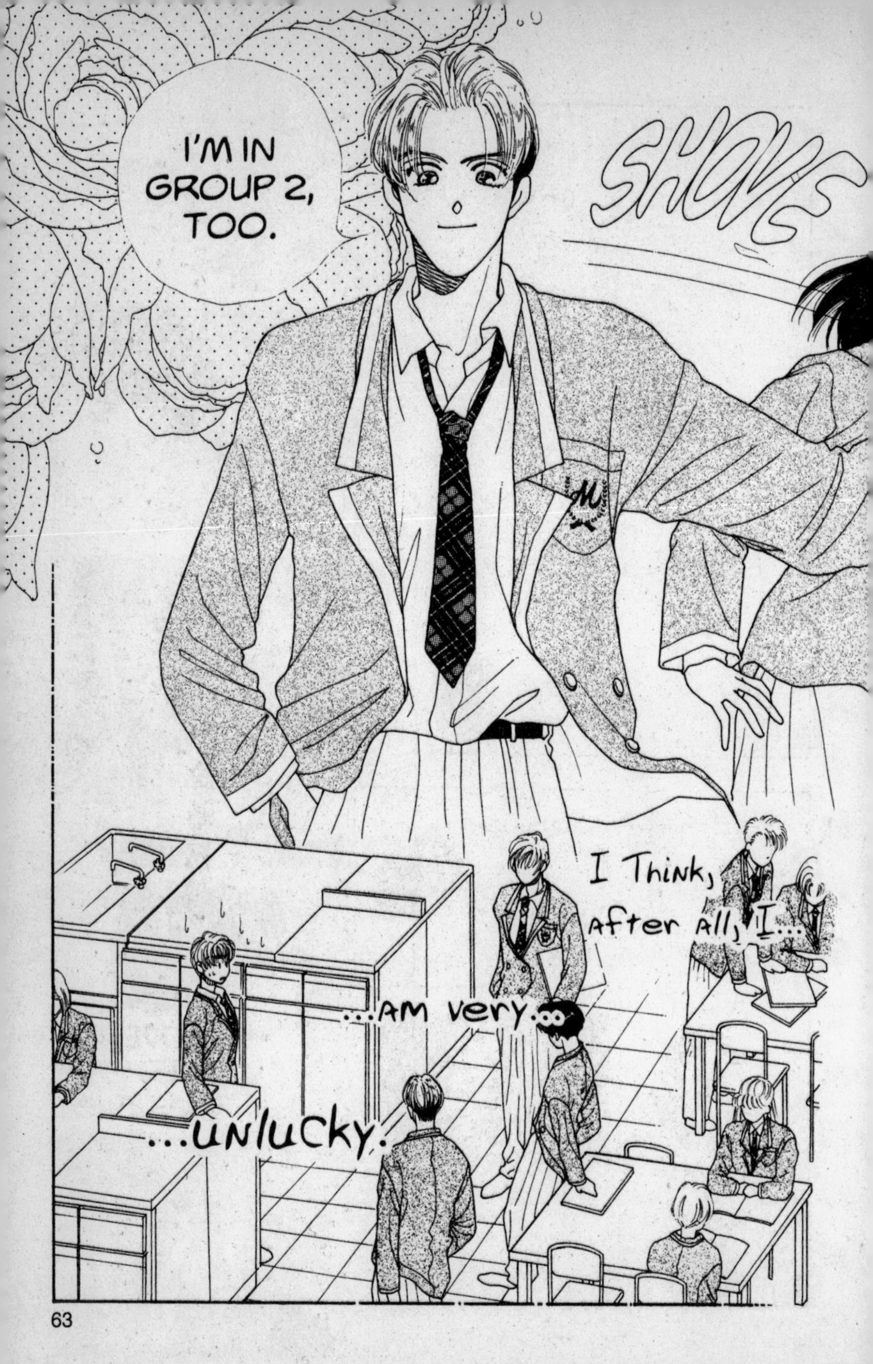
I'M IN GROUP 2, TOO.
SHOVE
I Think, after all, I...
...am very...
...unlucky.

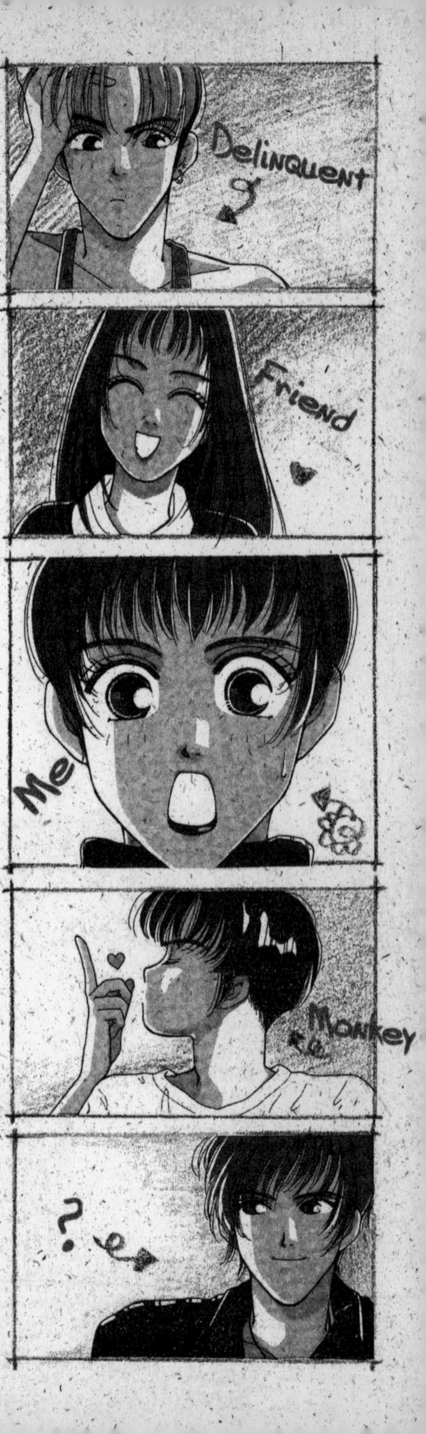
Delinquent
Friend
Me
Monkey
?

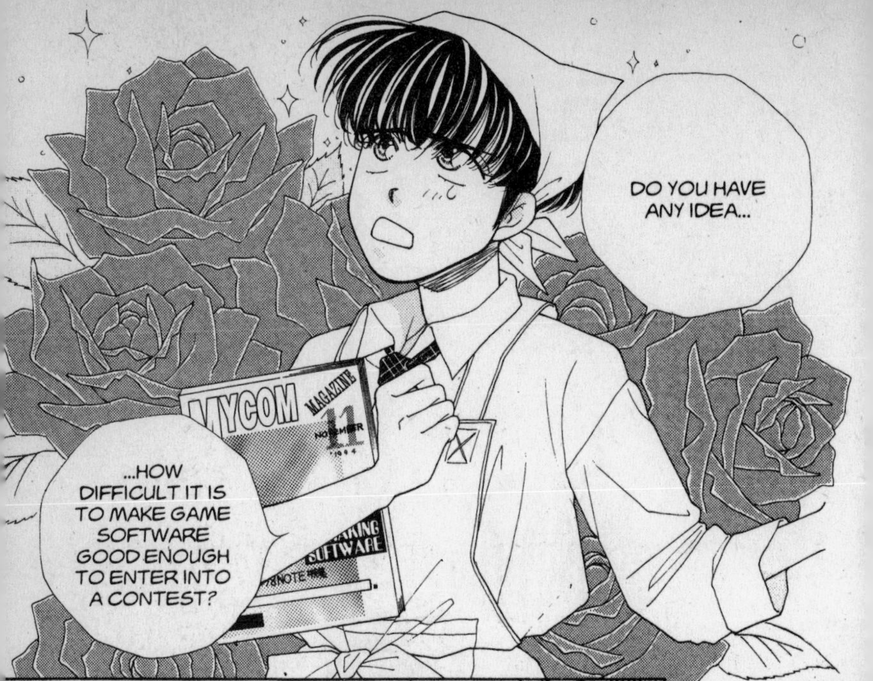
DO YOU HAVE ANY IDEA...
MYCOM
MAGAZINE
11
SOFTWARE
...HOW DIFFICULT IT IS TO MAKE GAME SOFTWARE GOOD ENOUGH TO ENTER INTO A CONTEST?

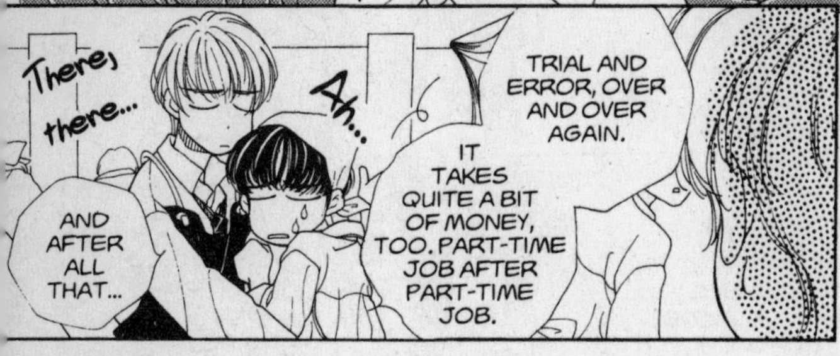
TRIAL AND ERROR, OVER AND OVER AGAIN.
IT TAKES QUITE A BIT OF MONEY, TOO. PART-TIME JOB AFTER PART-TIME JOB.
Ah...
There, there...
AND AFTER ALL THAT...

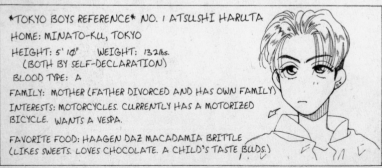

TOKYO BOYS REFERENCE NO. 1 ATSUSHI HARUTA

HOME: MINATO-KU, TOKYO

HEIGHT: 5' 10" WEIGHT: 132 lbs.
(BOTH BY SELF-DECLARATION)

BLOOD TYPE: A

FAMILY: MOTHER (FATHER DIVORCED AND HAS OWN FAMILY)

INTERESTS: MOTORCYCLES. CURRENTLY HAS A MOTORIZED BICYCLE. WANTS A VESPA.

FAVORITE FOOD: HAAGEN DAZ MACADAMIA BRITTLE (LIKES SWEETS. LOVES CHOCOLATE. A CHILD'S TASTE BUDS.)

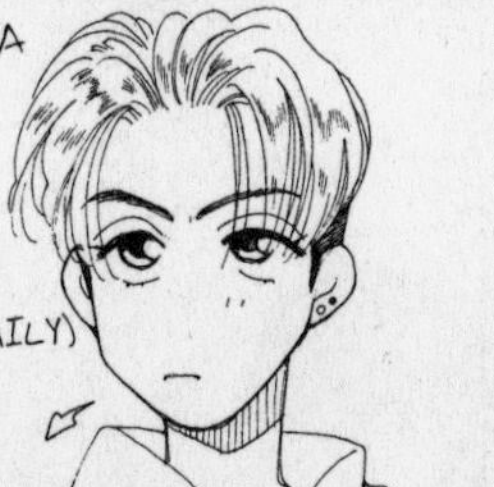

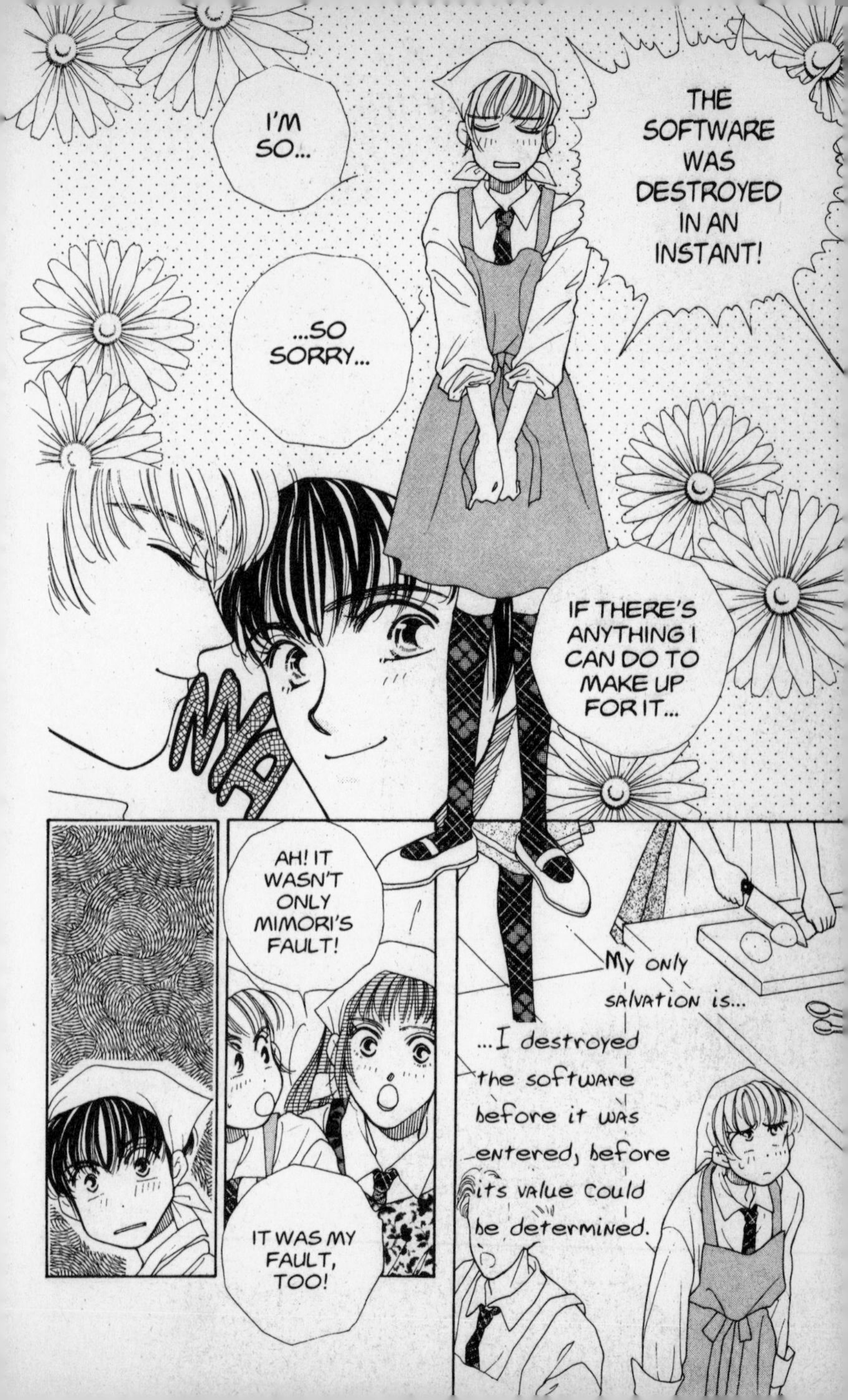
THE SOFTWARE WAS DESTROYED IN AN INSTANT!
I'M SO...
...SO SORRY...
IF THERE'S ANYTHING I CAN DO TO MAKE UP FOR IT...
My only salvation is...
...I destroyed the software before it was entered, before its value could be determined.
AH! IT WASN'T ONLY MIMORI'S FAULT!
IT WAS MY FAULT, TOO!

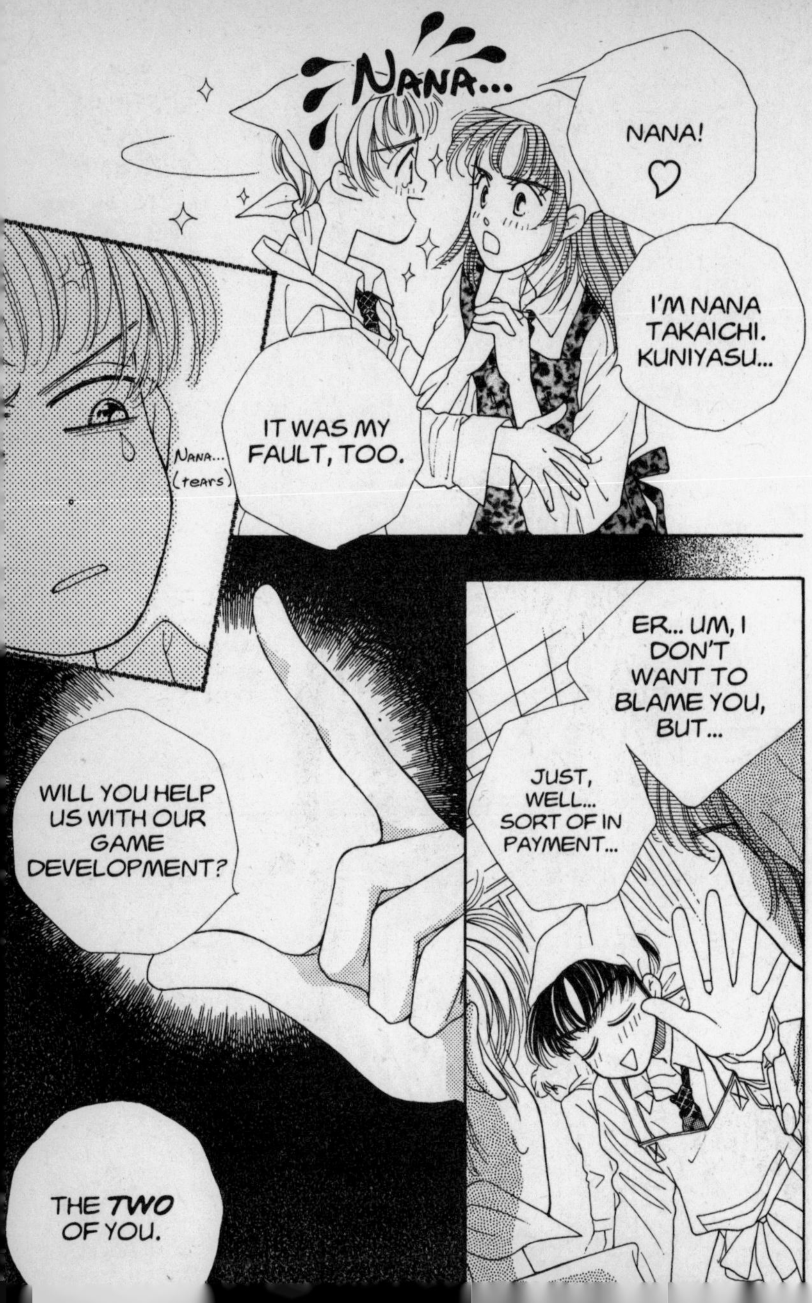
NANA!
♡
NANA...
I'M NANA TAKAICHI. KUNIYASU...
IT WAS MY FAULT, TOO.
NANA...
(tears)
ER... UM, I DON'T WANT TO BLAME YOU, BUT...
JUST, WELL... SORT OF IN PAYMENT...
WILL YOU HELP US WITH OUR GAME DEVELOPMENT?
THE *TWO* OF YOU.

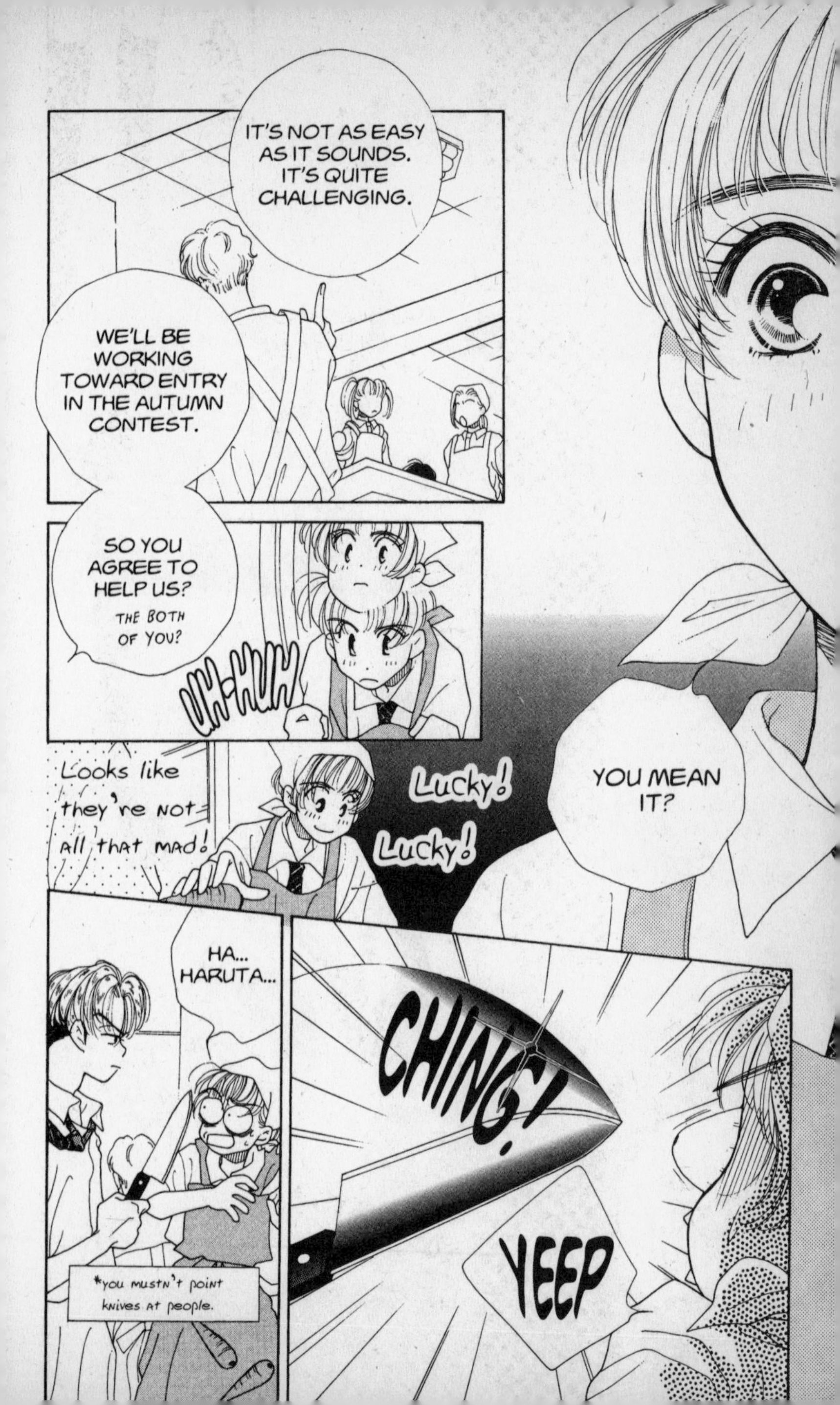
YOU MEAN IT?
IT'S NOT AS EASY AS IT SOUNDS. IT'S QUITE CHALLENGING.
WE'LL BE WORKING TOWARD ENTRY IN THE AUTUMN CONTEST.
SO YOU AGREE TO HELP US?
THE BOTH OF YOU?
UH-HUH
Looks like they're not all that mad!
Lucky!
Lucky!
CHING!
YEEP
HA... HARUTA...
*you mustn't point knives at people.

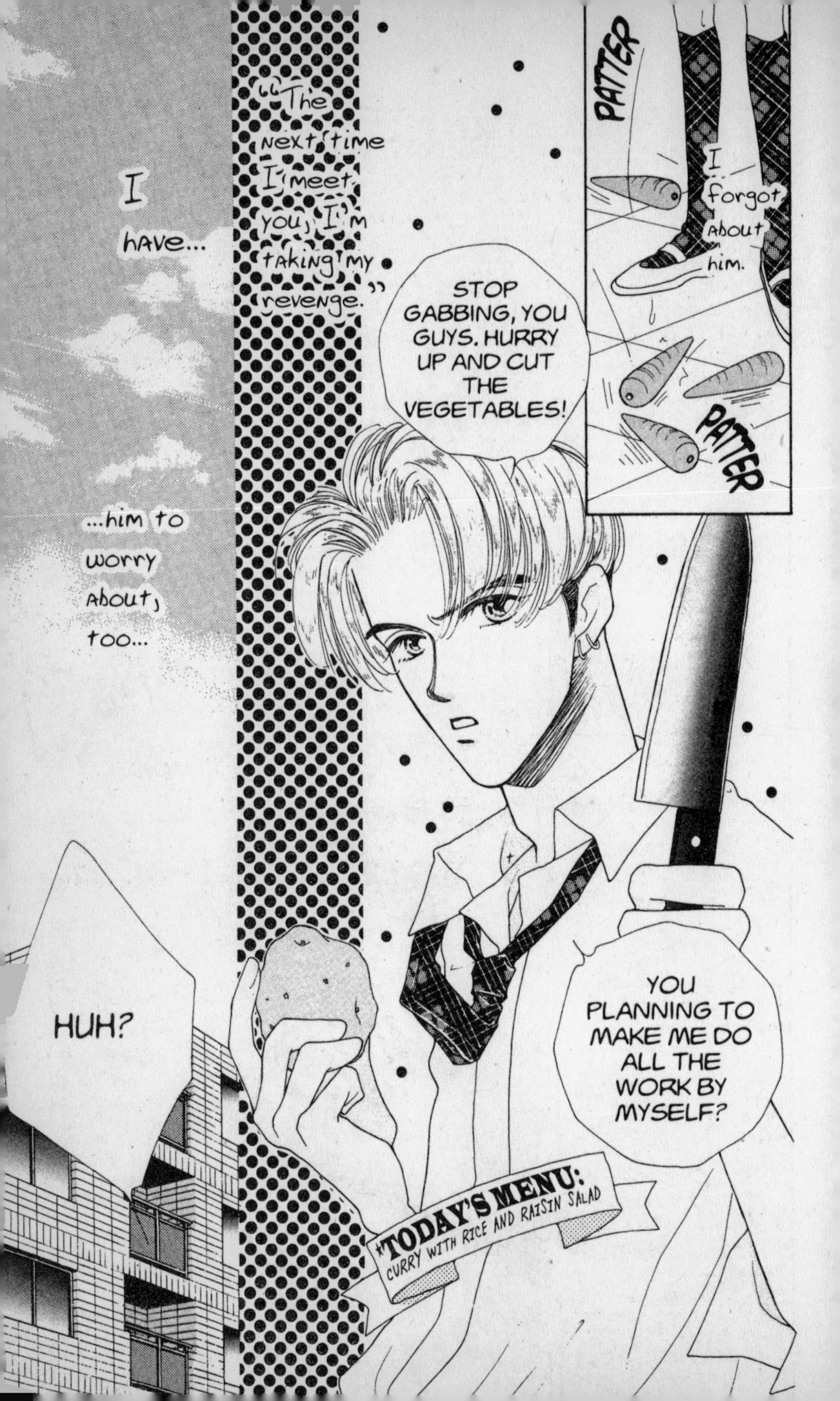
PATTER
I forgot about him.
PATTER
STOP GABBING, YOU GUYS. HURRY UP AND CUT THE VEGETABLES!
YOU PLANNING TO MAKE ME DO ALL THE WORK BY MYSELF?
*TODAY'S MENU: CURRY WITH RICE AND RAISIN SALAD
"The next time I meet you, I'm taking my revenge."
I have...
...him to worry about, too...
HUH?

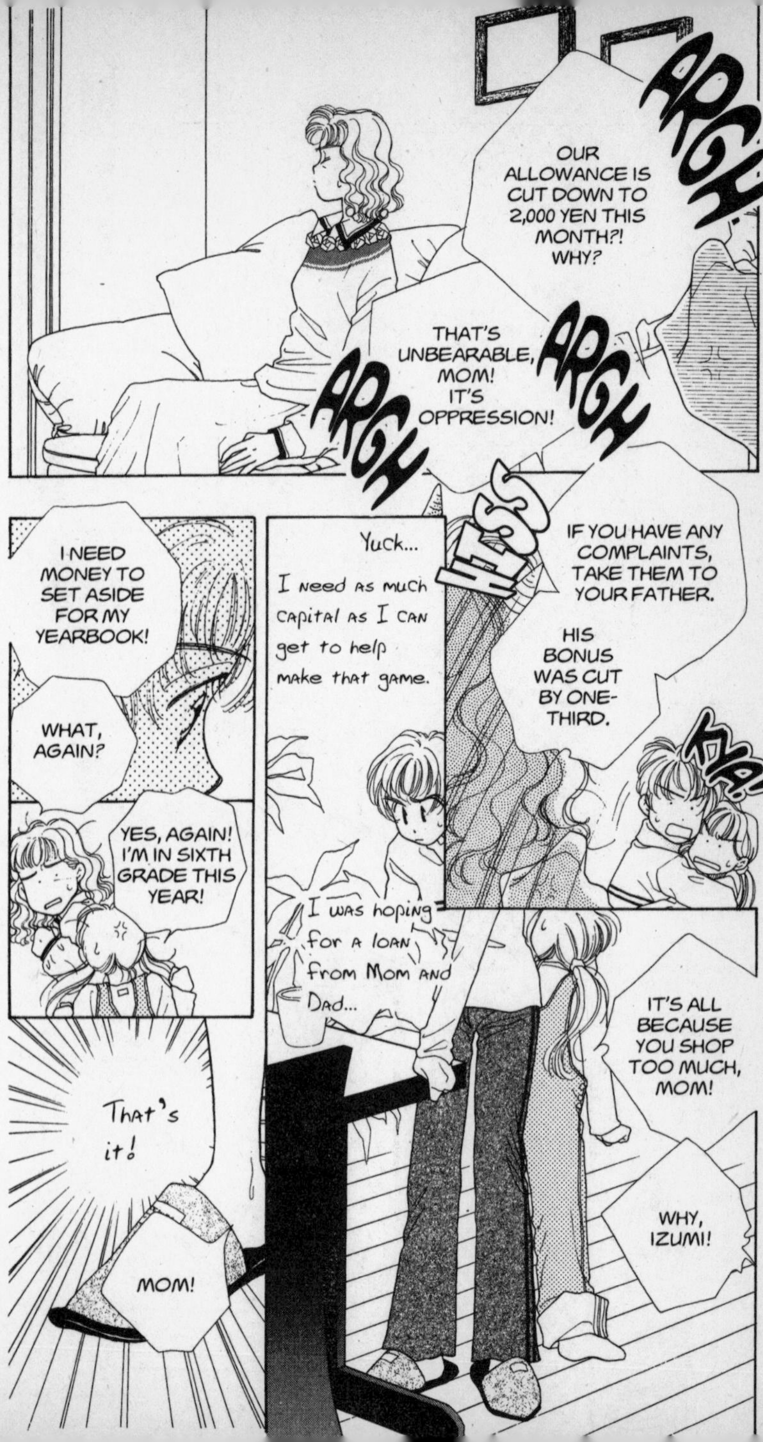
ARGH
OUR ALLOWANCE IS CUT DOWN TO 2,000 YEN THIS MONTH?! WHY?
ARGH
THAT'S UNBEARABLE, MOM! IT'S OPPRESSION!
ARGH
IF YOU HAVE ANY COMPLAINTS, TAKE THEM TO YOUR FATHER.
HIS BONUS WAS CUT BY ONE-THIRD.
KYA!
Yuck...
I need as much capital as I can get to help make that game.
I NEED MONEY TO SET ASIDE FOR MY YEARBOOK!
WHAT, AGAIN?
YES, AGAIN! I'M IN SIXTH GRADE THIS YEAR!
IT'S ALL BECAUSE YOU SHOP TOO MUCH, MOM!
WHY, IZUMI!
I was hoping for a loan from Mom and Dad...
That's it!
MOM!

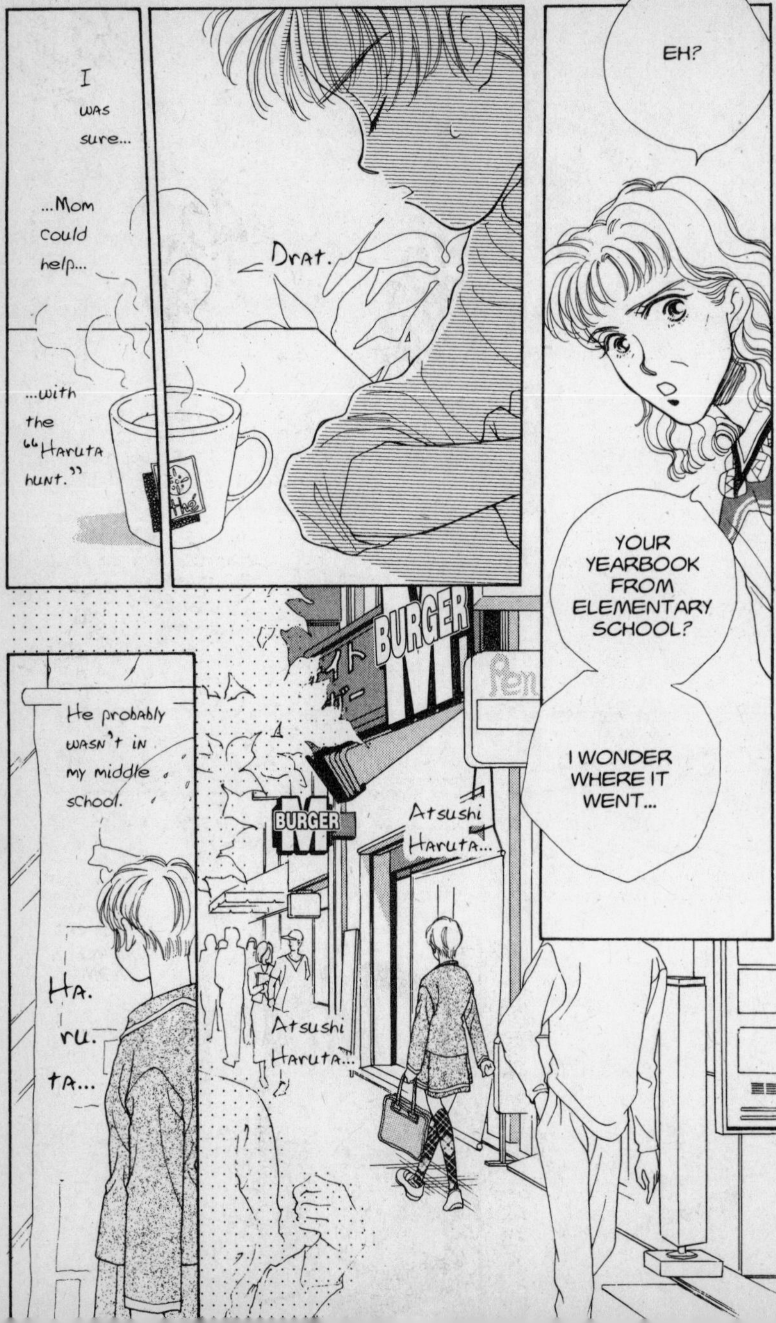
EH?
YOUR YEARBOOK FROM ELEMENTARY SCHOOL?
I WONDER WHERE IT WENT...
Drat.
I was sure...
...Mom could help...
...with the "Haruta hunt."
BURGER
BURGER
Atsushi Haruta...
Atsushi Haruta...
He probably wasn't in my middle school.
Ha. ru. ta...

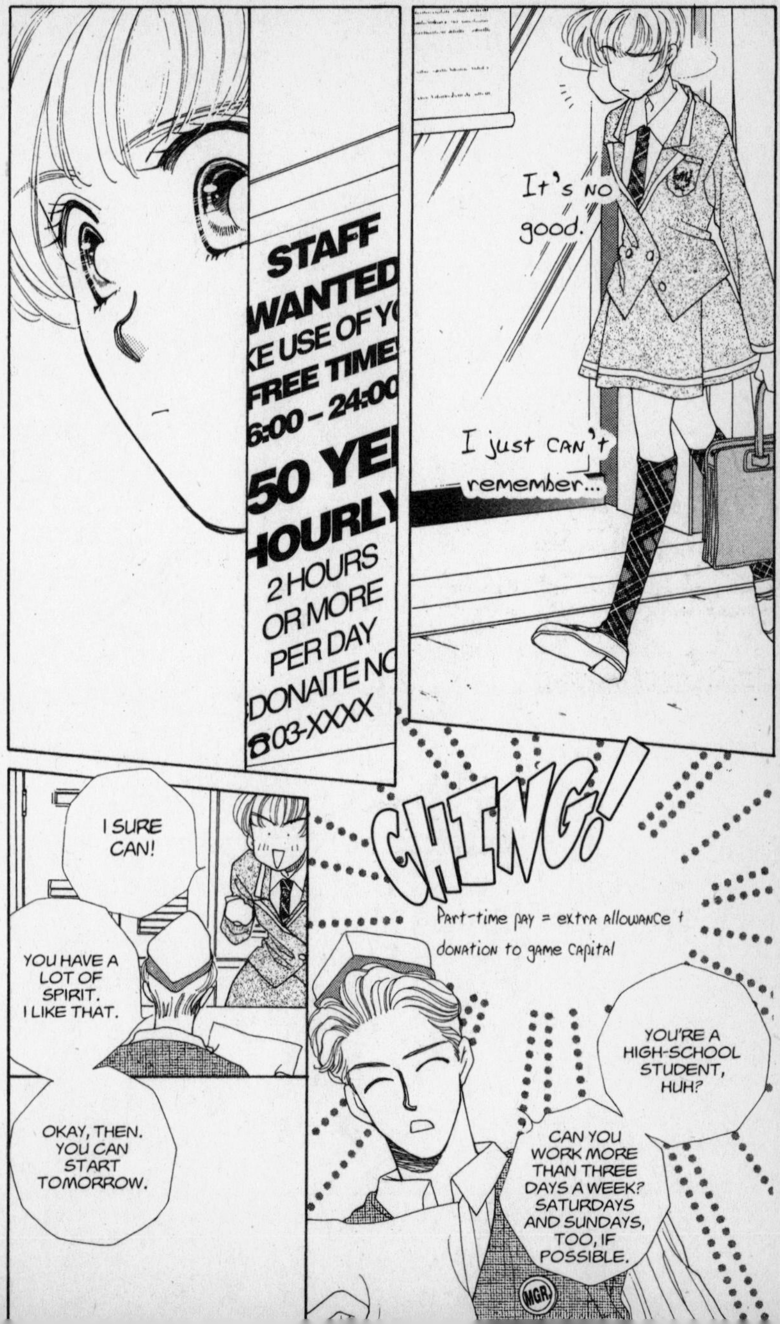

It's no good.
I just can't remember...
STAFF
WANTED
KE USE OF YO
FREE TIME
6:00 – 24:00
50 YE
HOURLY
2 HOURS
OR MORE
PER DAY
DONAITE NO
☎03-XXXX
CHING!
Part-time pay = extra allowance + donation to game capital
YOU'RE A HIGH-SCHOOL STUDENT, HUH?
CAN YOU WORK MORE THAN THREE DAYS A WEEK? SATURDAYS AND SUNDAYS, TOO, IF POSSIBLE.
MGR.
I SURE CAN!
YOU HAVE A LOT OF SPIRIT. I LIKE THAT.
OKAY, THEN. YOU CAN START TOMORROW.

TOKYO BOYS GIRLS

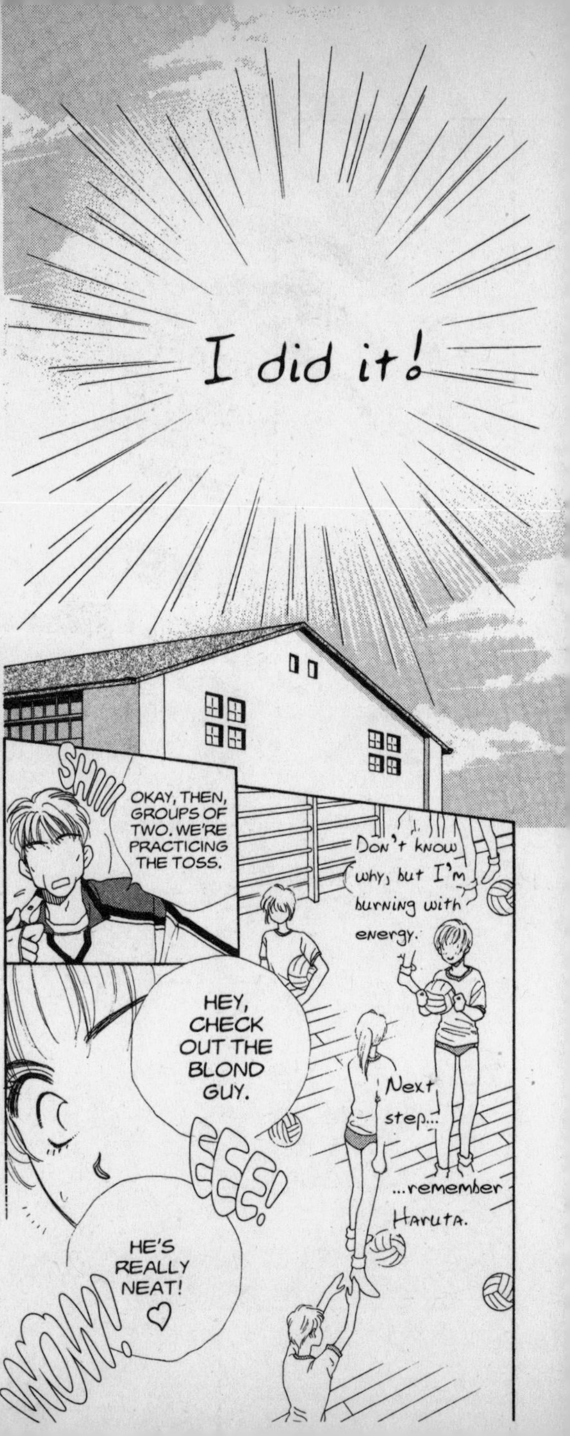
I did it!
Don't know why, but I'm burning with energy.
Next step...
...remember Haruta.
OKAY, THEN, GROUPS OF TWO. WE'RE PRACTICING THE TOSS.
HEY, CHECK OUT THE BLOND GUY.
HE'S REALLY NEAT! ♡
WOW!

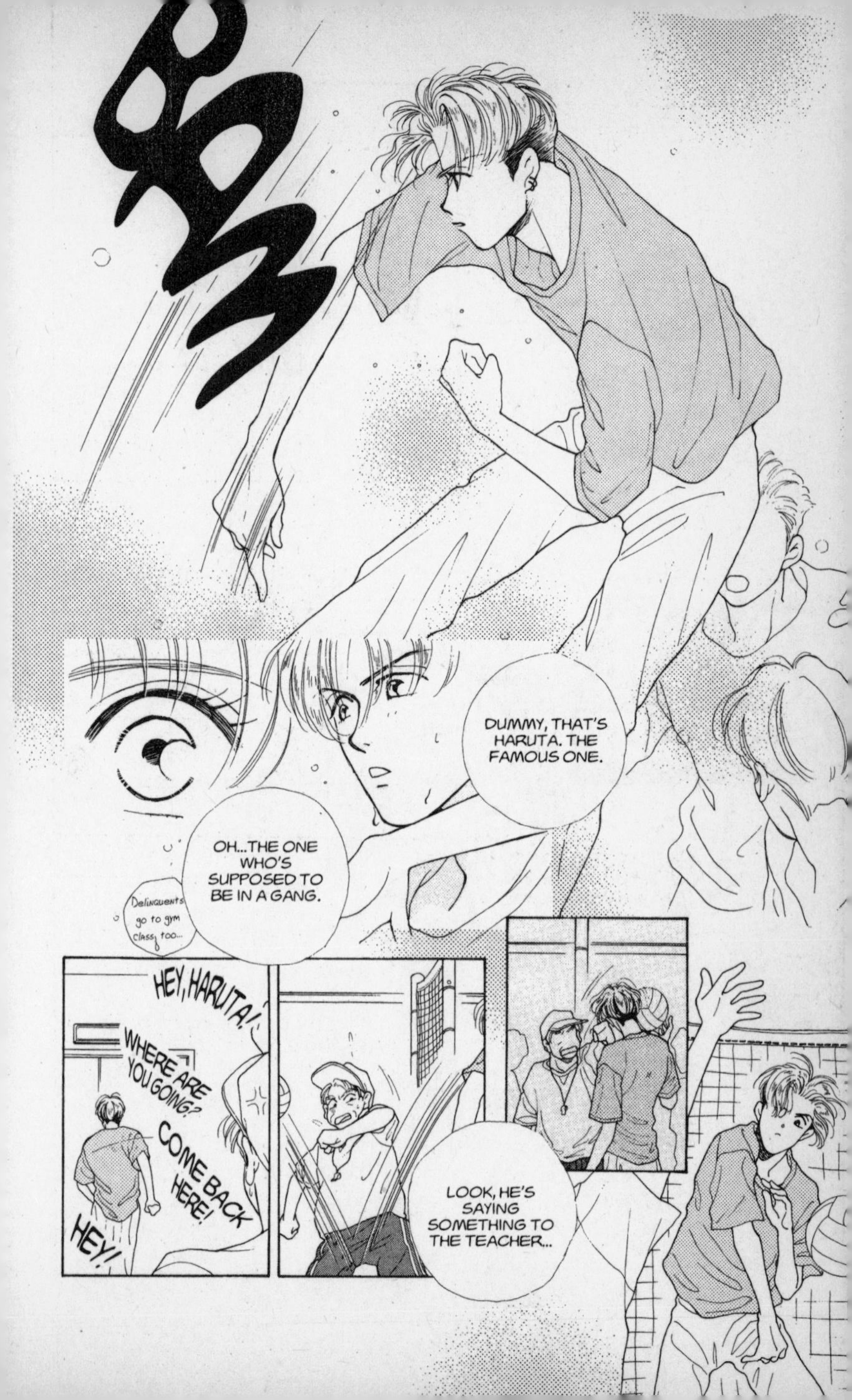
BAM
DUMMY, THAT'S HARUTA. THE FAMOUS ONE.
OH...THE ONE WHO'S SUPPOSED TO BE IN A GANG.
Delinquents go to gym class too...
LOOK, HE'S SAYING SOMETHING TO THE TEACHER...
HEY, HARUTA!
WHERE ARE YOU GOING?
COME BACK HERE!
HEY!

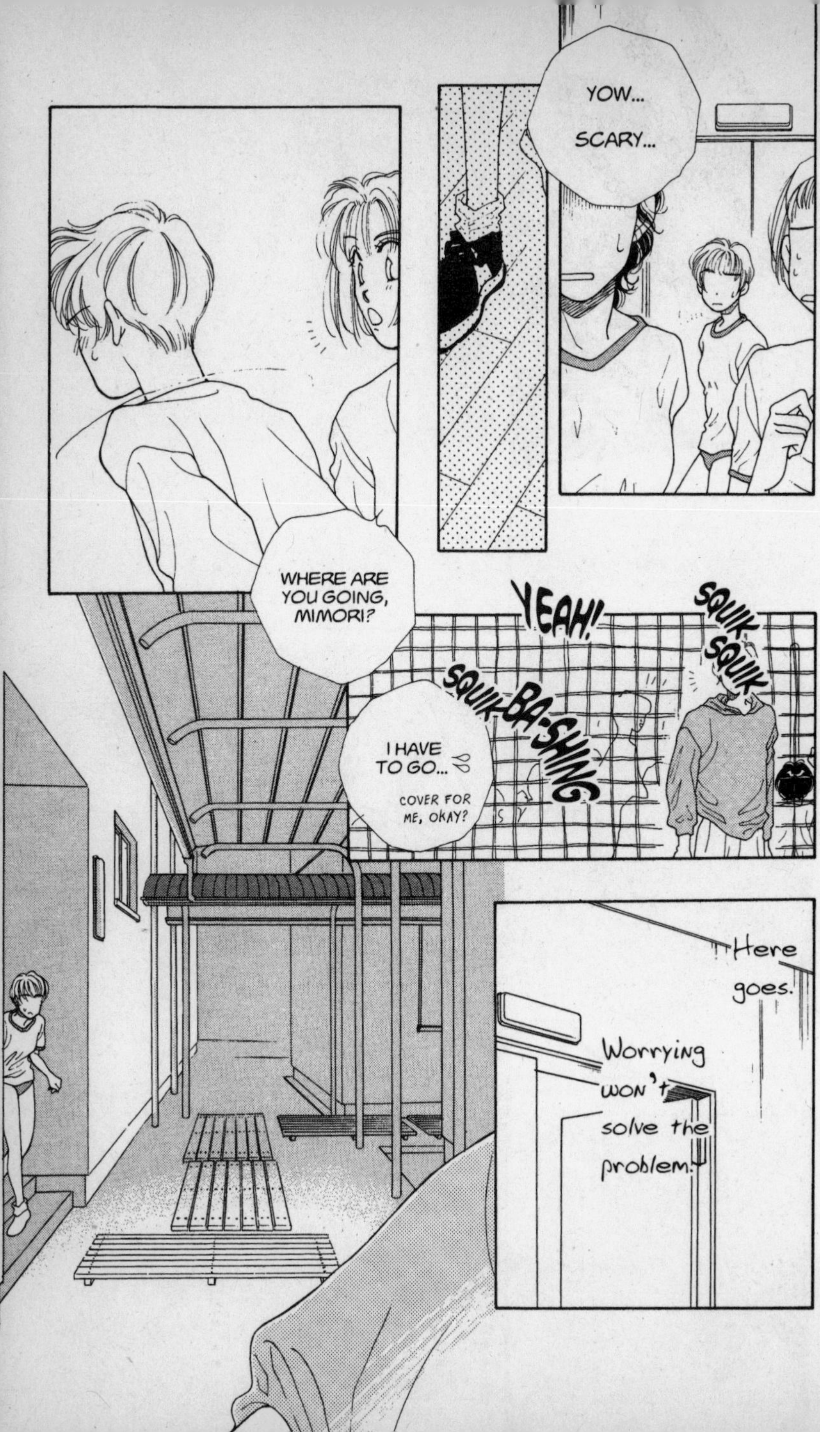
YOW... SCARY...
WHERE ARE YOU GOING, MIMORI?
SQUIK SQUIK
YEAH!
SQUIK-BA-SHING
I HAVE TO GO...
COVER FOR ME, OKAY?
Here goes.
Worrying won't solve the problem.

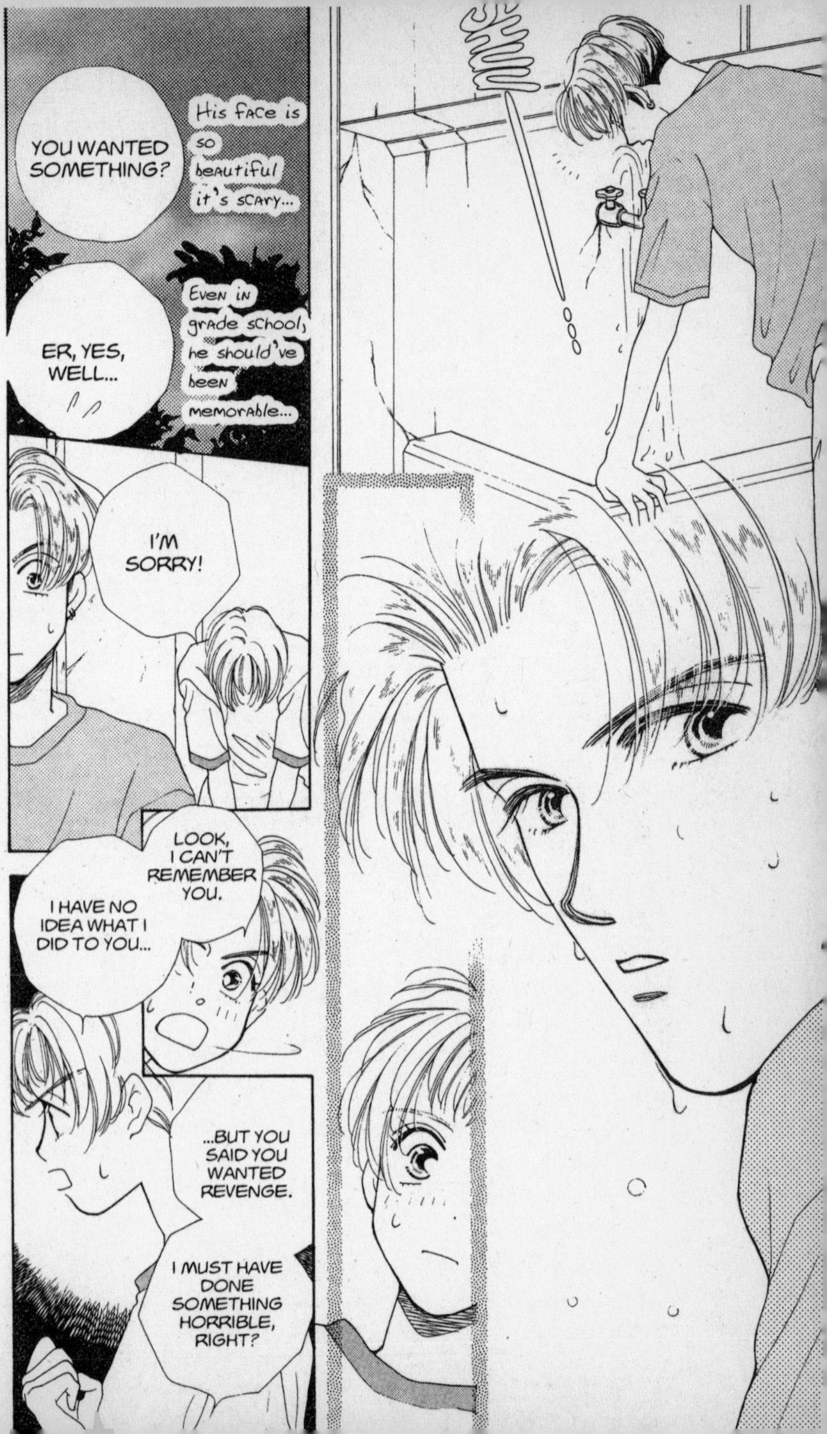
His face is so beautiful it's scary...
YOU WANTED SOMETHING?
Even in grade school, he should've been memorable...
ER, YES, WELL...
I'M SORRY!
LOOK, I CAN'T REMEMBER YOU.
I HAVE NO IDEA WHAT I DID TO YOU...
...BUT YOU SAID YOU WANTED REVENGE.
I MUST HAVE DONE SOMETHING HORRIBLE, RIGHT?

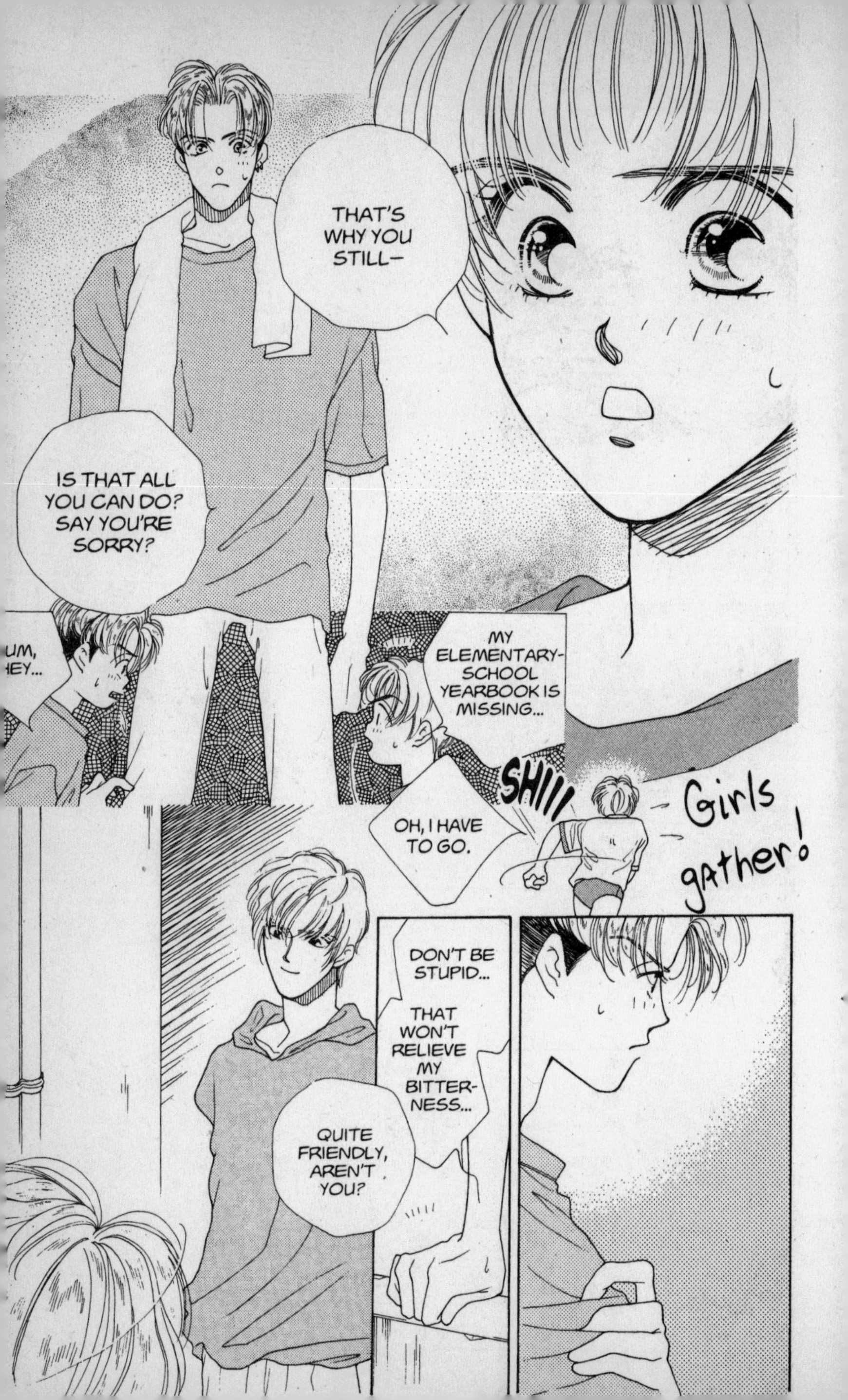
THAT'S WHY YOU STILL—
IS THAT ALL YOU CAN DO? SAY YOU'RE SORRY?
MY ELEMENTARY-SCHOOL YEARBOOK IS MISSING...
UM, HEY...
SHIII
Girls gather!
OH, I HAVE TO GO.
DON'T BE STUPID...
THAT WON'T RELIEVE MY BITTERNESS...
QUITE FRIENDLY, AREN'T YOU?

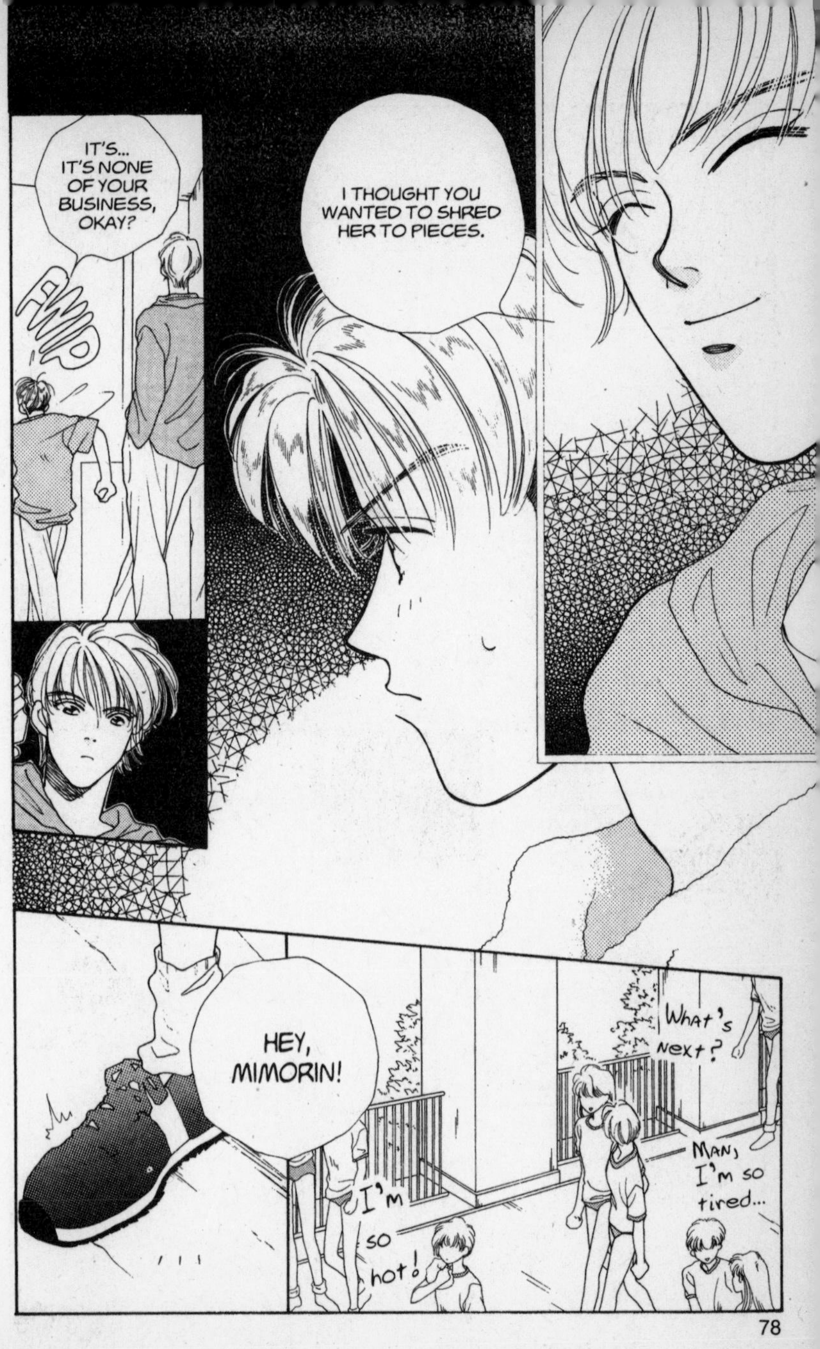
I THOUGHT YOU WANTED TO SHRED HER TO PIECES.
IT'S... IT'S NONE OF YOUR BUSINESS, OKAY?
FWIP
What's next?
Man, I'm so tired...
I'm so hot!
HEY, MIMORIN!

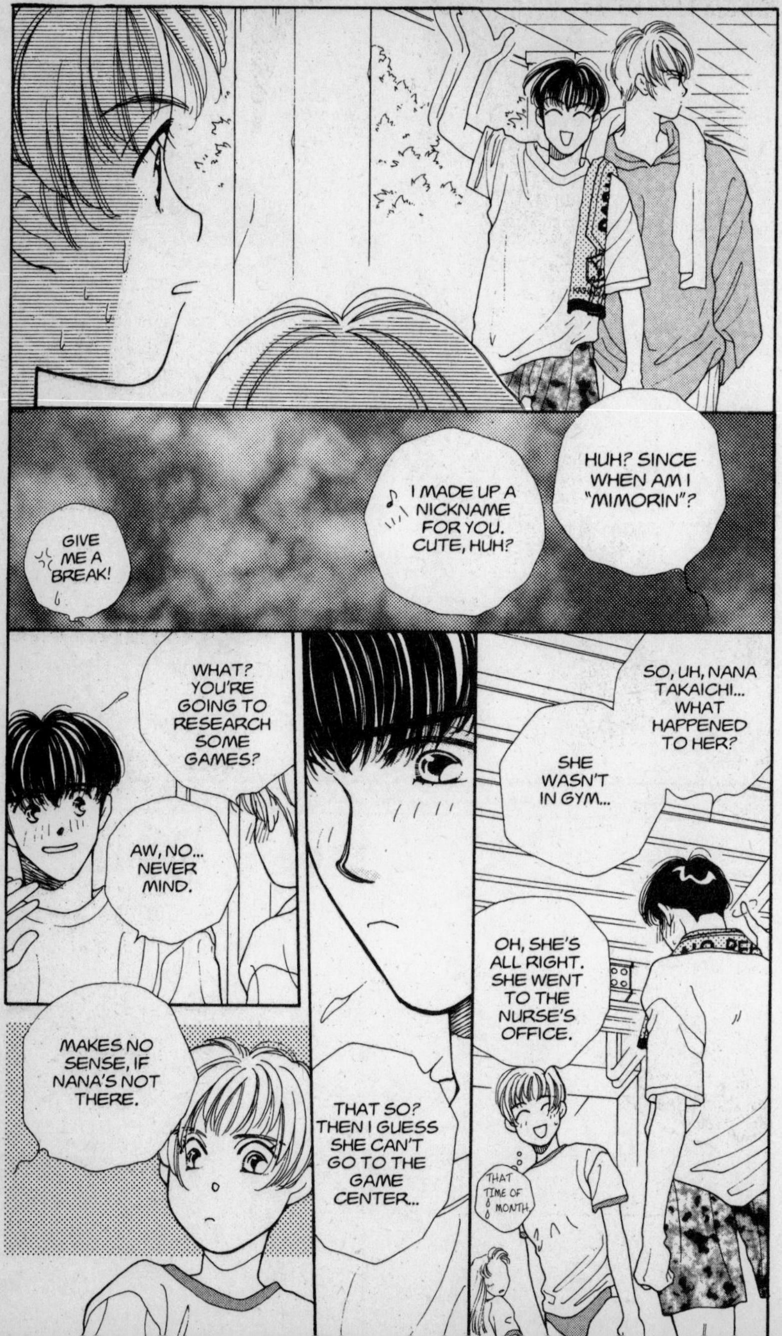
HUH? SINCE WHEN AM I "MIMORIN"?
I MADE UP A NICKNAME FOR YOU. CUTE, HUH?
GIVE ME A BREAK!
SO, UH, NANA TAKAICHI... WHAT HAPPENED TO HER?
SHE WASN'T IN GYM...
OH, SHE'S ALL RIGHT. SHE WENT TO THE NURSE'S OFFICE.
THAT TIME OF MONTH
THAT SO? THEN I GUESS SHE CAN'T GO TO THE GAME CENTER...
WHAT? YOU'RE GOING TO RESEARCH SOME GAMES?
AW, NO... NEVER MIND.
MAKES NO SENSE, IF NANA'S NOT THERE.

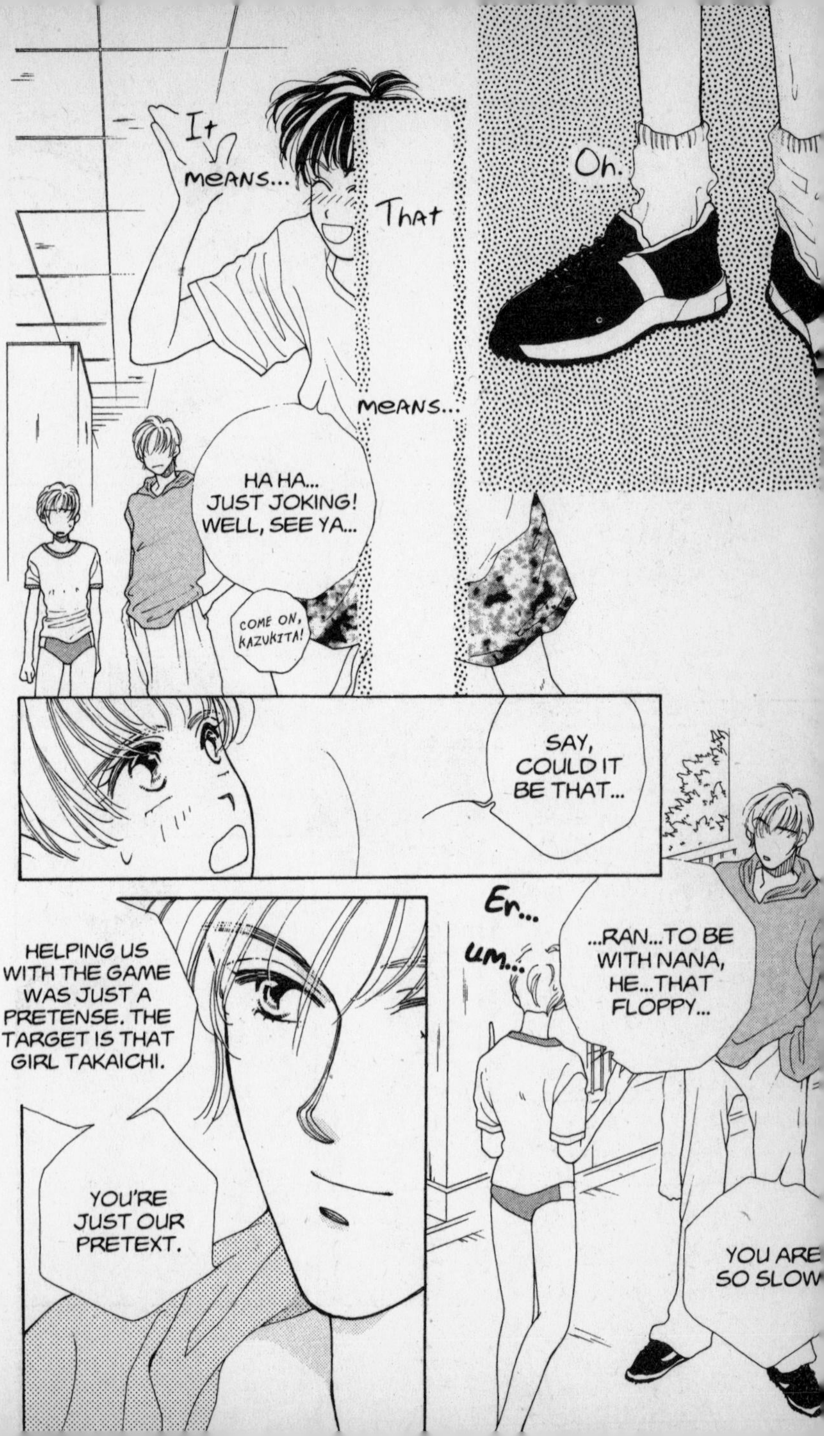
Oh.
That means...
It means...
HA HA... JUST JOKING! WELL, SEE YA...
COME ON, KAZUKITA!
SAY, COULD IT BE THAT...
...RAN...TO BE WITH NANA, HE...THAT FLOPPY...
Er... um...
YOU ARE SO SLOW
HELPING US WITH THE GAME WAS JUST A PRETENSE. THE TARGET IS THAT GIRL TAKAICHI.
YOU'RE JUST OUR PRETEXT.

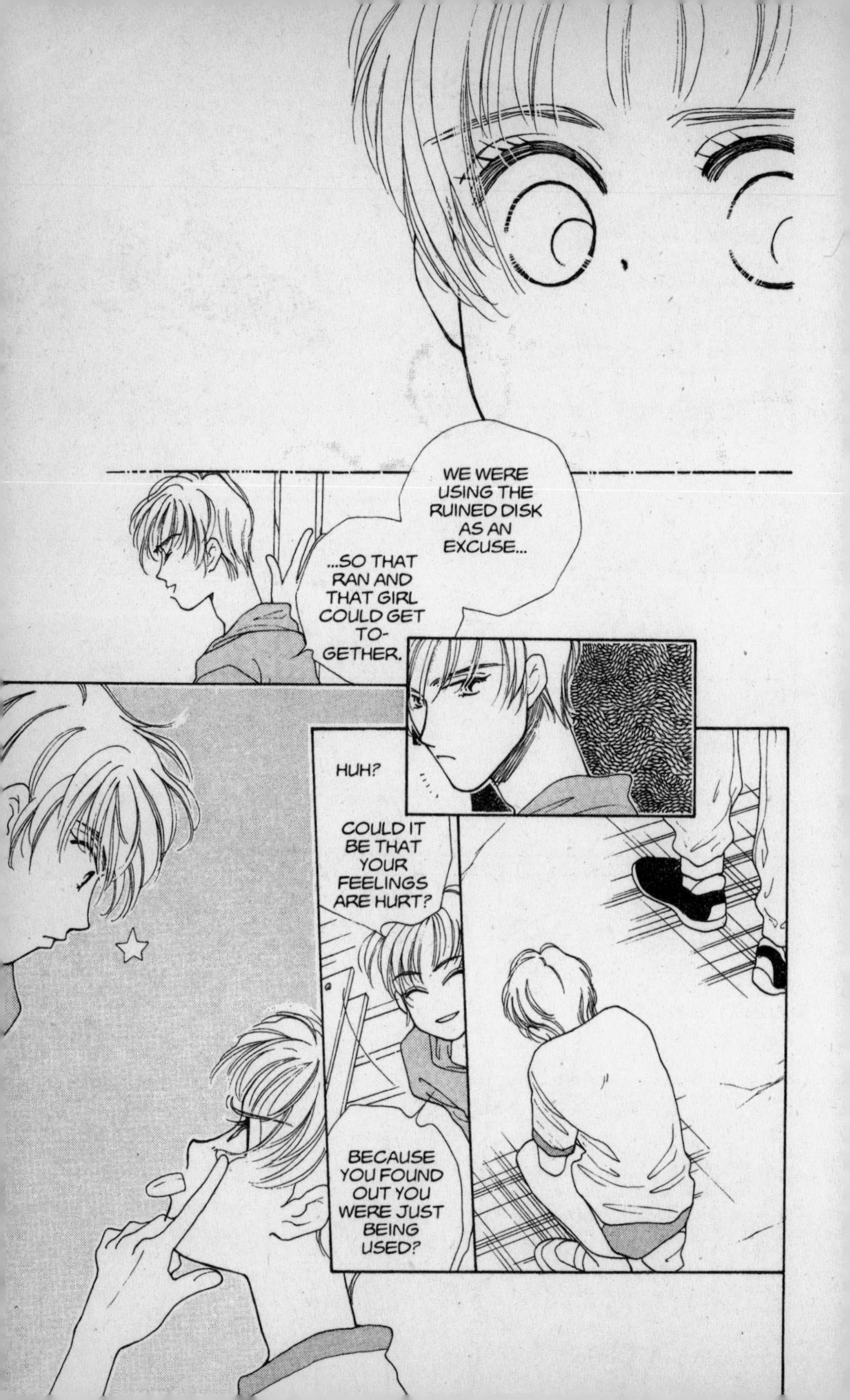
WE WERE USING THE RUINED DISK AS AN EXCUSE...
...SO THAT RAN AND THAT GIRL COULD GET TO-GETHER.
HUH?
COULD IT BE THAT YOUR FEELINGS ARE HURT?
BECAUSE YOU FOUND OUT YOU WERE JUST BEING USED?

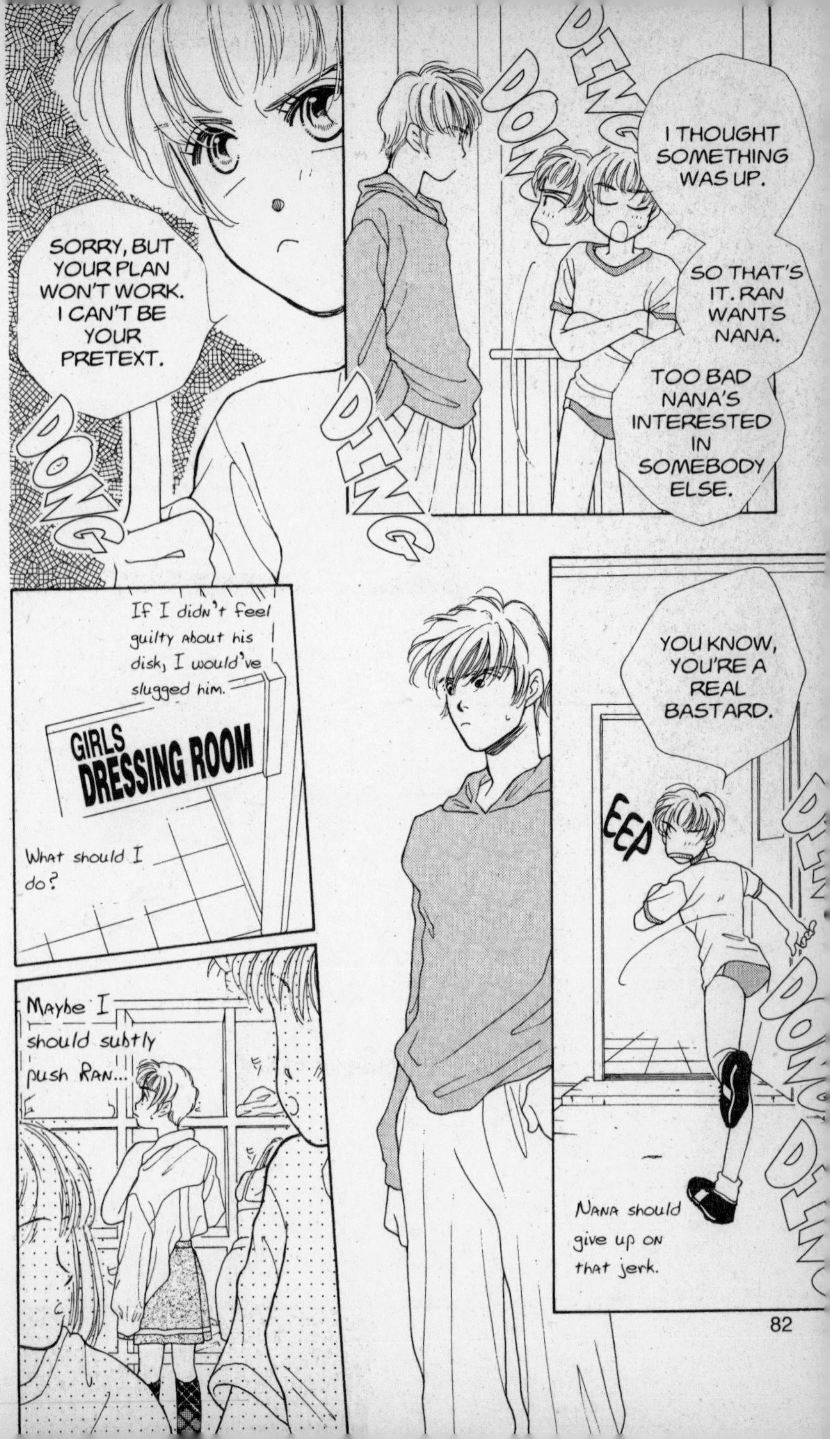
DING
DONG
I THOUGHT SOMETHING WAS UP.
SO THAT'S IT. RAN WANTS NANA.
TOO BAD NANA'S INTERESTED IN SOMEBODY ELSE.
DING
SORRY, BUT YOUR PLAN WON'T WORK. I CAN'T BE YOUR PRETEXT.
DONG
YOU KNOW, YOU'RE A REAL BASTARD.
EEP
DING
DONG
DING
Nana should give up on that jerk.
If I didn't feel guilty about his disk, I would've slugged him.
GIRLS DRESSING ROOM
What should I do?
Maybe I should subtly push Ran...

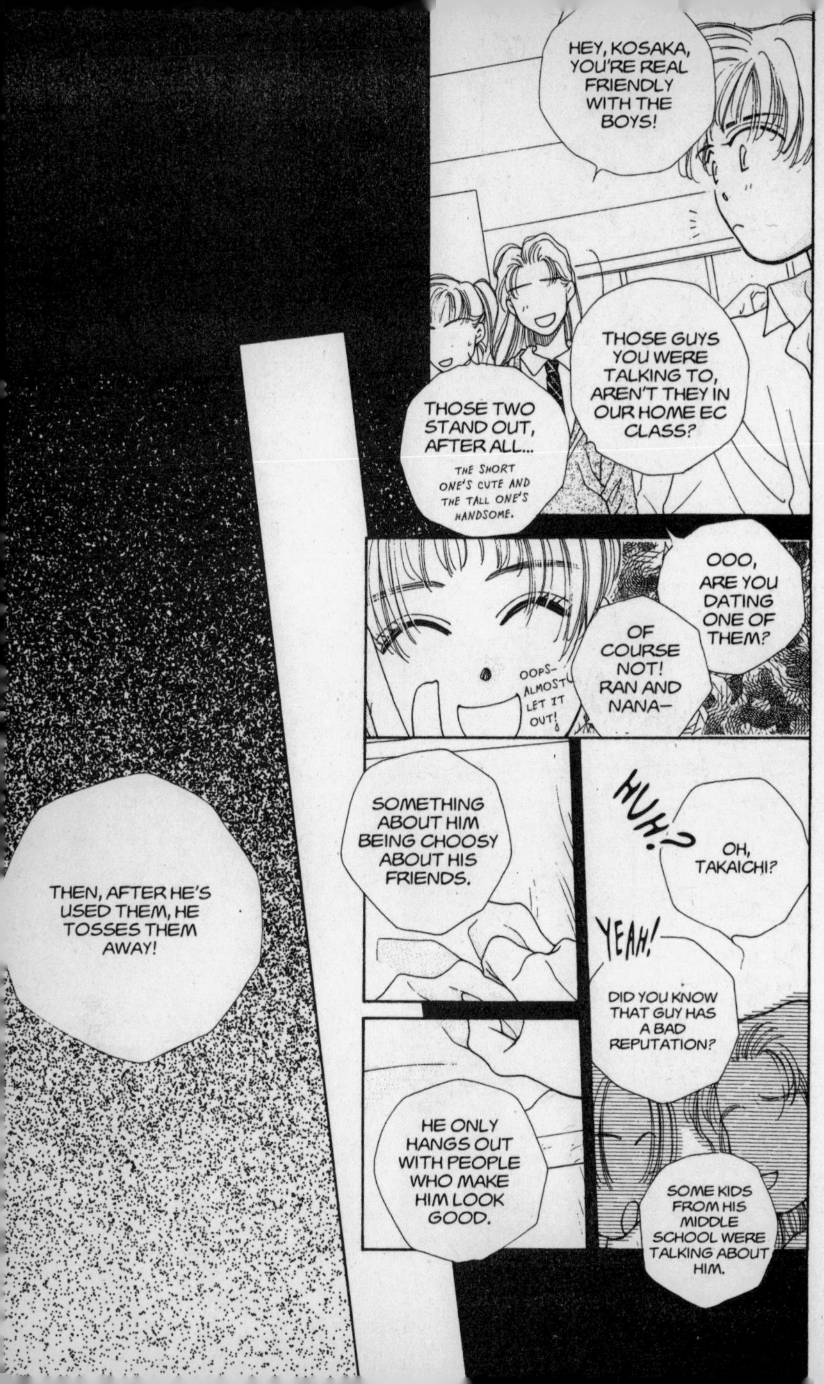
HEY, KOSAKA, YOU'RE REAL FRIENDLY WITH THE BOYS!
THOSE GUYS YOU WERE TALKING TO, AREN'T THEY IN OUR HOME EC CLASS?
THOSE TWO STAND OUT, AFTER ALL...
THE SHORT ONE'S CUTE AND THE TALL ONE'S HANDSOME.
OOO, ARE YOU DATING ONE OF THEM?
OF COURSE NOT! RAN AND NANA-
OOPS- ALMOST LET IT OUT!
HUH?
OH, TAKAICHI?
YEAH!
DID YOU KNOW THAT GUY HAS A BAD REPUTATION?
SOME KIDS FROM HIS MIDDLE SCHOOL WERE TALKING ABOUT HIM.
SOMETHING ABOUT HIM BEING CHOOSY ABOUT HIS FRIENDS.
HE ONLY HANGS OUT WITH PEOPLE WHO MAKE HIM LOOK GOOD.
THEN, AFTER HE'S USED THEM, HE TOSSES THEM AWAY!

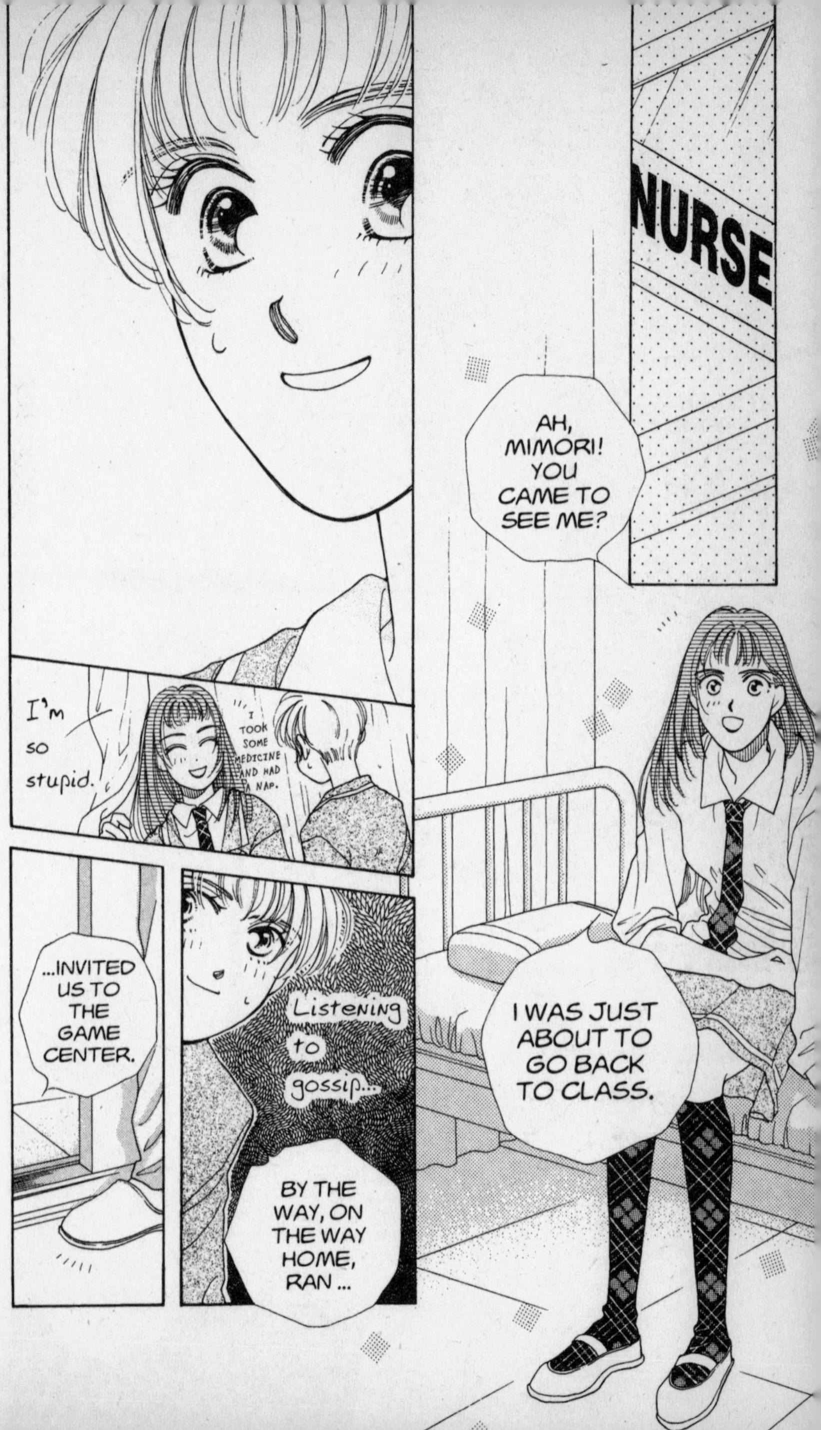
NURSE
AH, MIMORI! YOU CAME TO SEE ME?
I WAS JUST ABOUT TO GO BACK TO CLASS.
I TOOK SOME MEDICINE AND HAD A NAP.
I'm so stupid.
Listening to gossip...
BY THE WAY, ON THE WAY HOME, RAN ...
...INVITED US TO THE GAME CENTER.

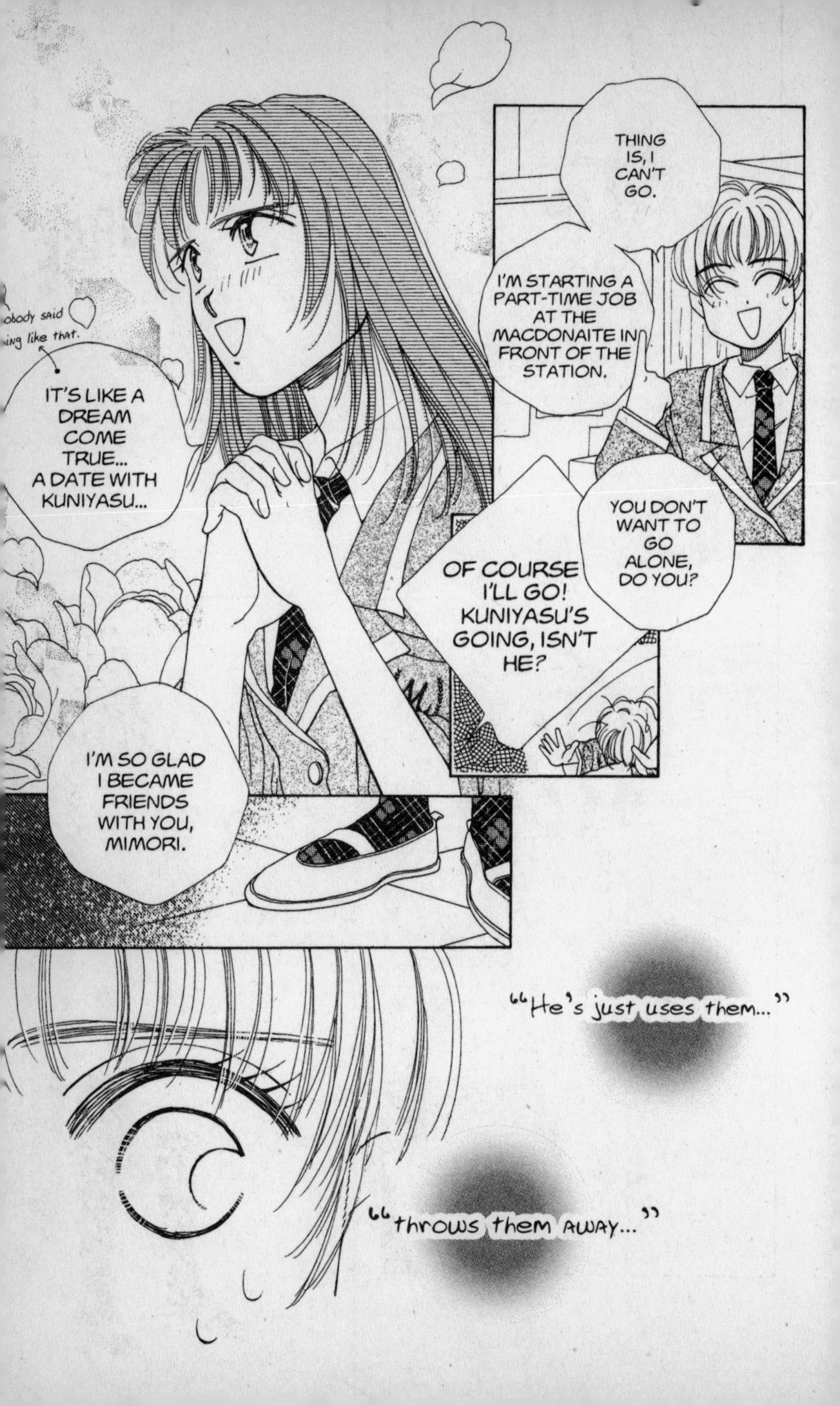
THING IS, I CAN'T GO.
I'M STARTING A PART-TIME JOB AT THE MACDONAITE IN FRONT OF THE STATION.
YOU DON'T WANT TO GO ALONE, DO YOU?
OF COURSE I'LL GO! KUNIYASU'S GOING, ISN'T HE?
IT'S LIKE A DREAM COME TRUE... A DATE WITH KUNIYASU...
obody said
ing like that.
I'M SO GLAD I BECAME FRIENDS WITH YOU, MIMORI.
"He's just uses them..."
"throws them away..."

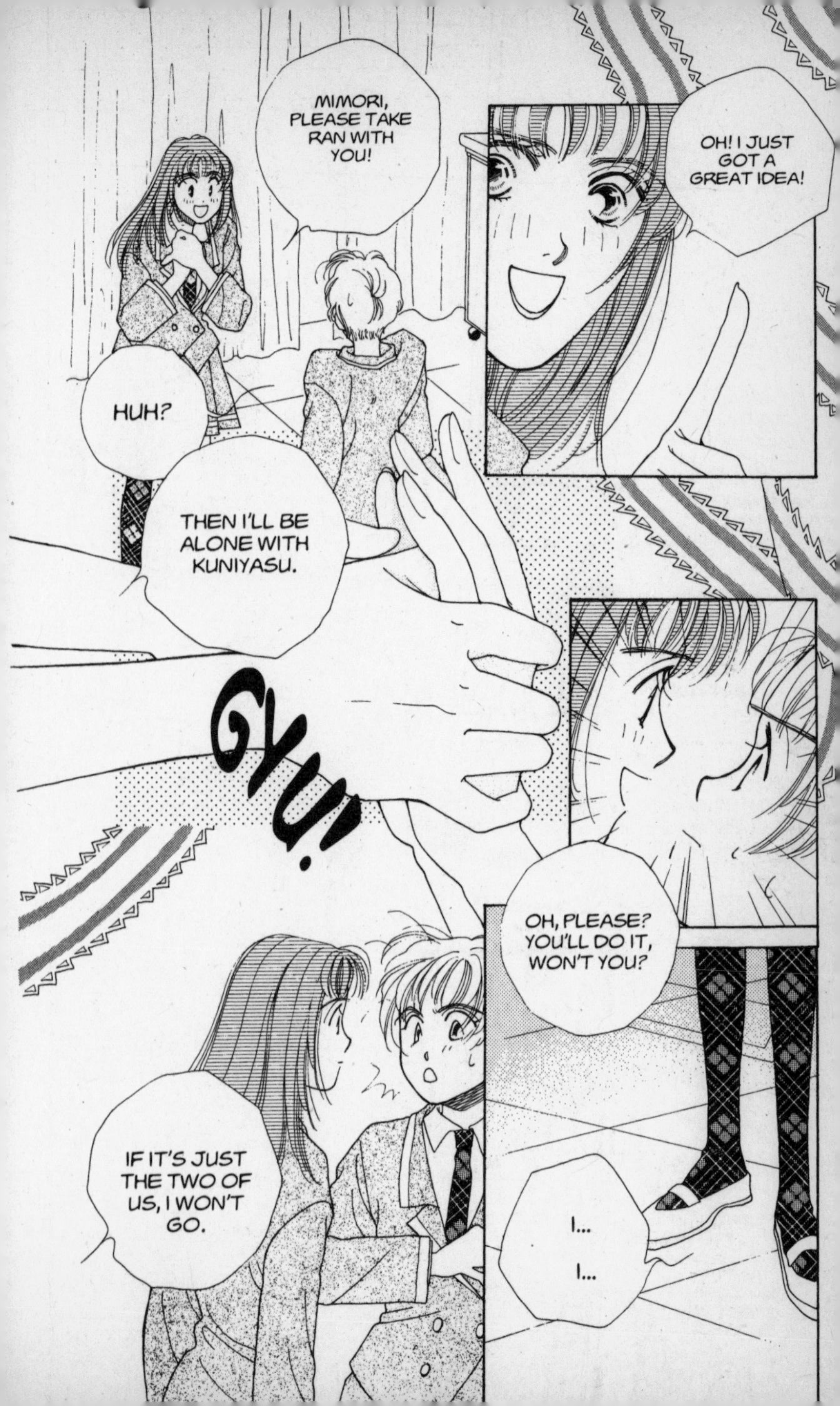
OH! I JUST GOT A GREAT IDEA!
MIMORI, PLEASE TAKE RAN WITH YOU!
HUH?
THEN I'LL BE ALONE WITH KUNIYASU.
GYU!
OH, PLEASE? YOU'LL DO IT, WON'T YOU?
I... I...
IF IT'S JUST THE TWO OF US, I WON'T GO.

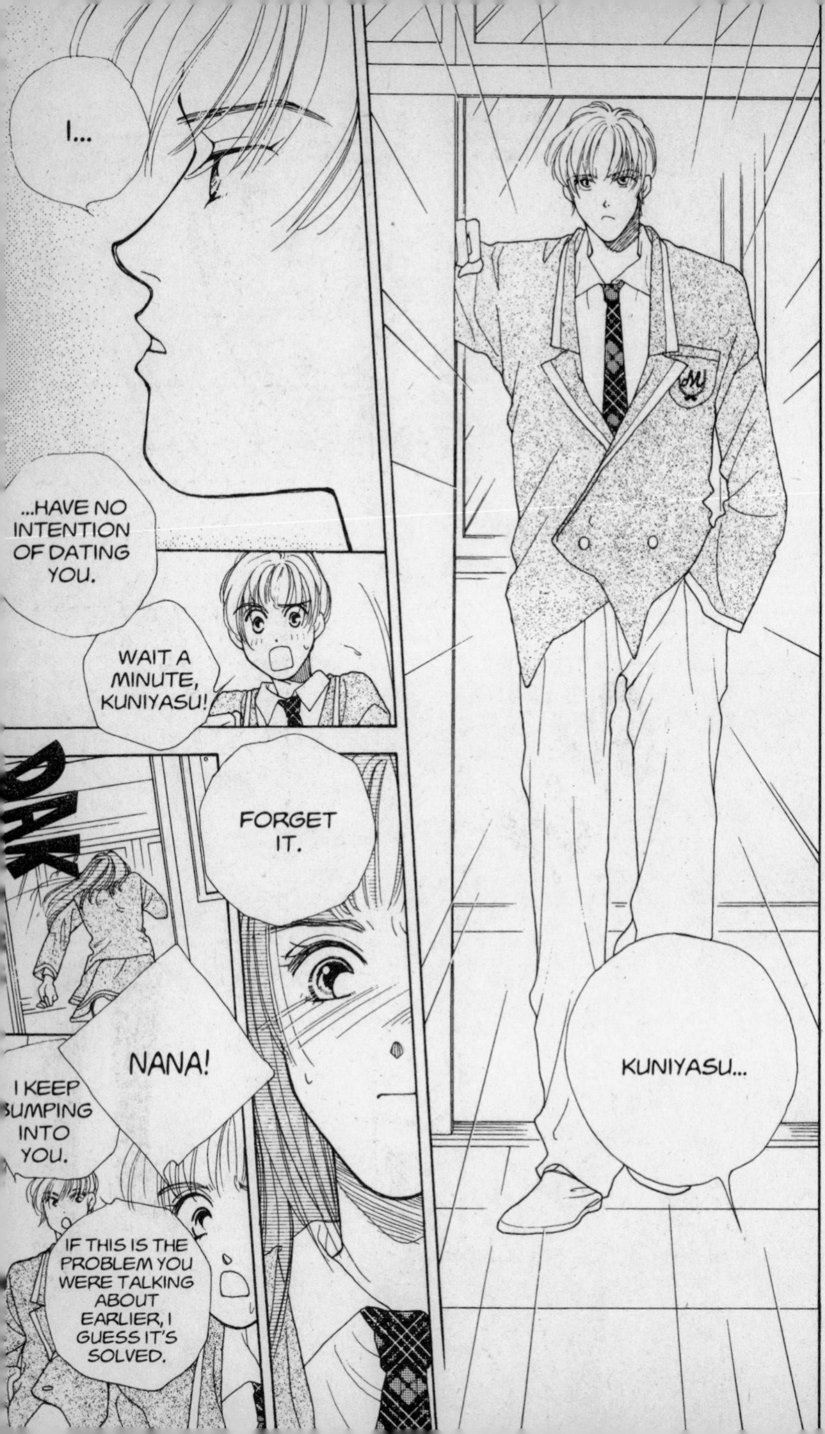
KUNIYASU...
I...
...HAVE NO INTENTION OF DATING YOU.
WAIT A MINUTE, KUNIYASU!
FORGET IT.
DAK
NANA!
I KEEP BUMPING INTO YOU.
IF THIS IS THE PROBLEM YOU WERE TALKING ABOUT EARLIER, I GUESS IT'S SOLVED.

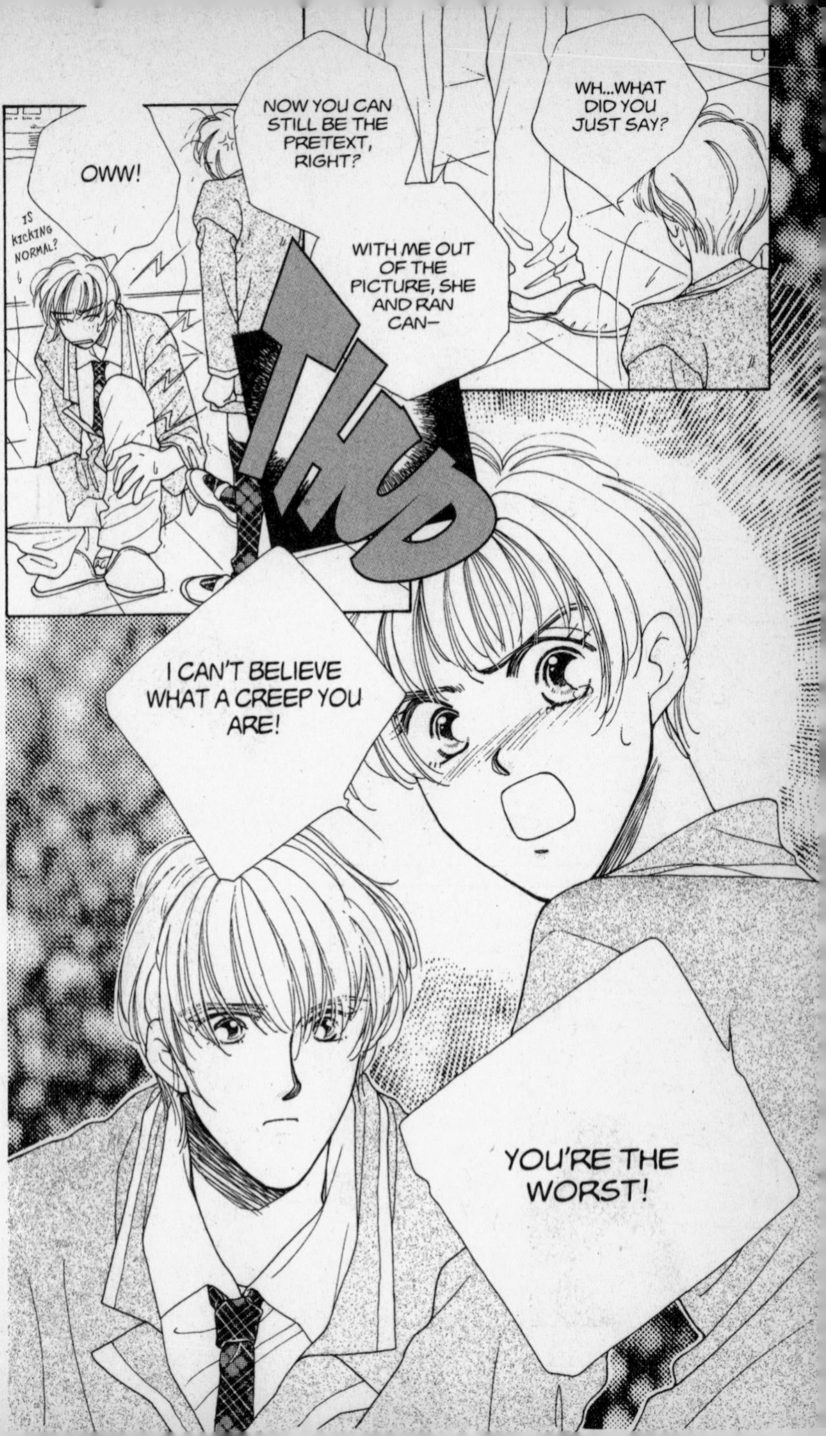
WH...WHAT DID YOU JUST SAY?
NOW YOU CAN STILL BE THE PRETEXT, RIGHT?
WITH ME OUT OF THE PICTURE, SHE AND RAN CAN—
THUD
OWW!
IS KICKING NORMAL?
I CAN'T BELIEVE WHAT A CREEP YOU ARE!
YOU'RE THE WORST!

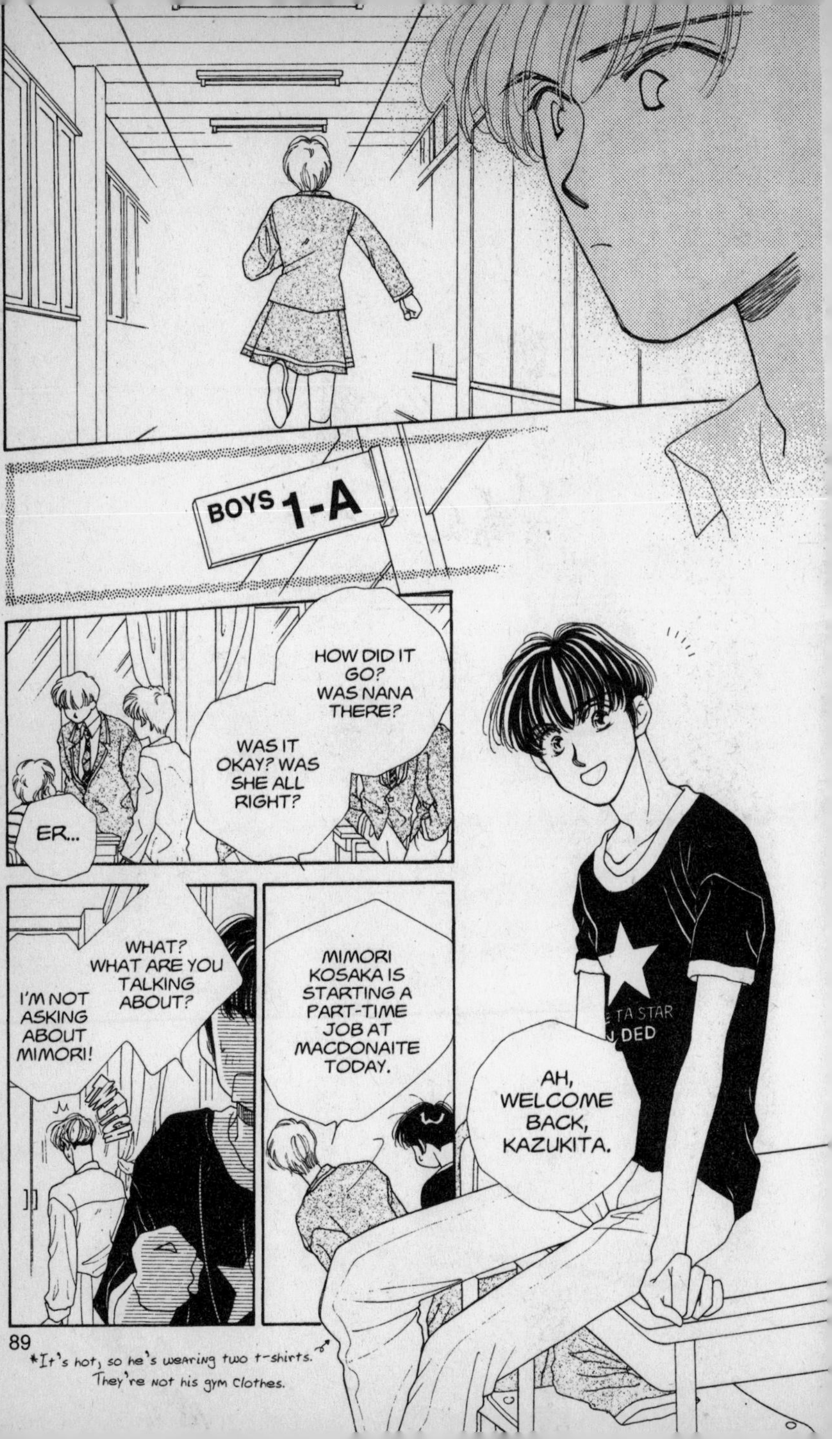
BOYS 1-A
AH, WELCOME BACK, KAZUKITA.
HOW DID IT GO? WAS NANA THERE?
WAS IT OKAY? WAS SHE ALL RIGHT?
ER...
MIMORI KOSAKA IS STARTING A PART-TIME JOB AT MACDONAITE TODAY.
WHAT? WHAT ARE YOU TALKING ABOUT?
I'M NOT ASKING ABOUT MIMORI!

*It's hot, so he's wearing two t-shirts. They're not his gym clothes.

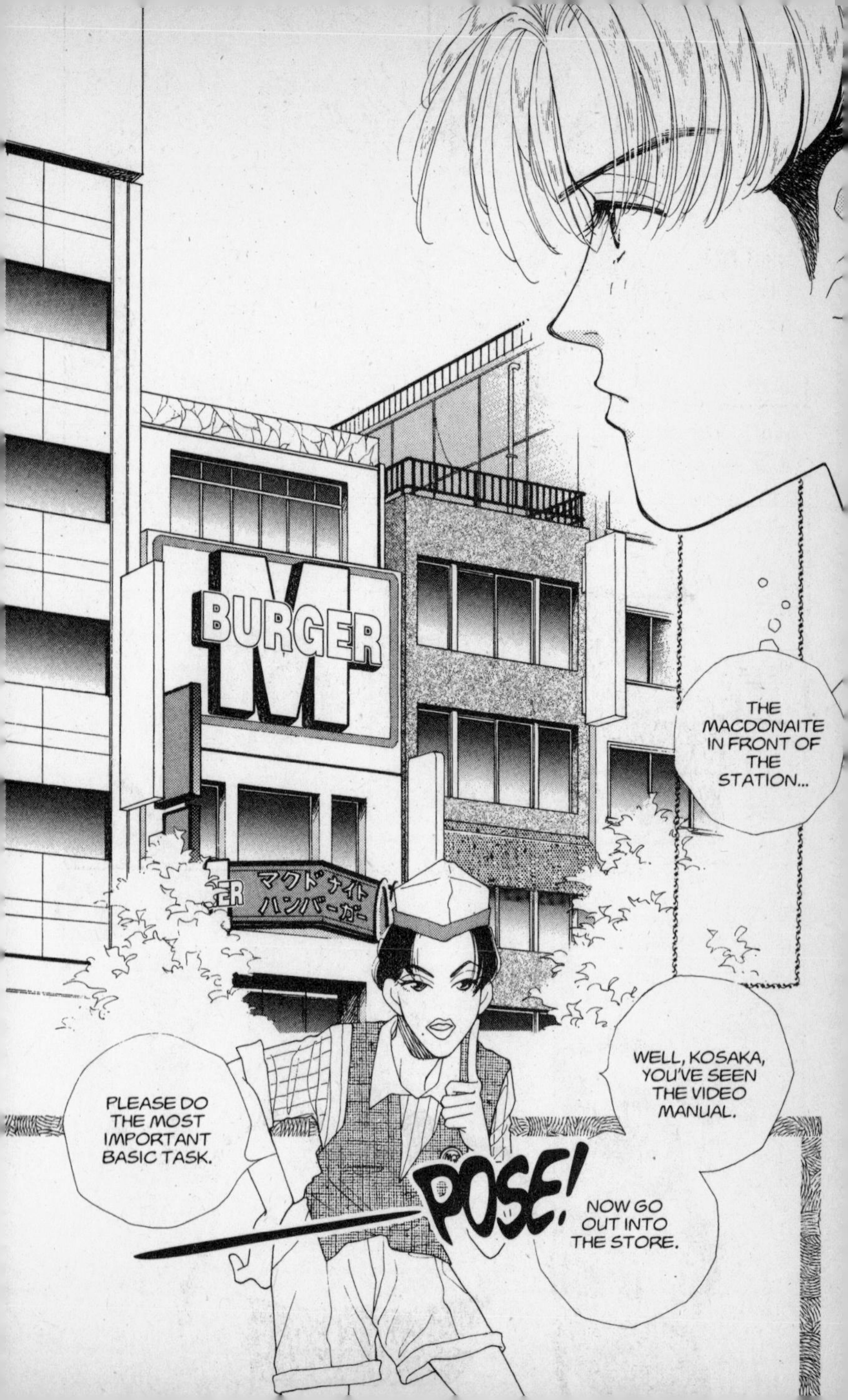
THE MACDONAITE IN FRONT OF THE STATION...
BURGER
マクドナイト
ハンバーガー
WELL, KOSAKA, YOU'VE SEEN THE VIDEO MANUAL.
NOW GO OUT INTO THE STORE.
POSE!
PLEASE DO THE MOST IMPORTANT BASIC TASK.

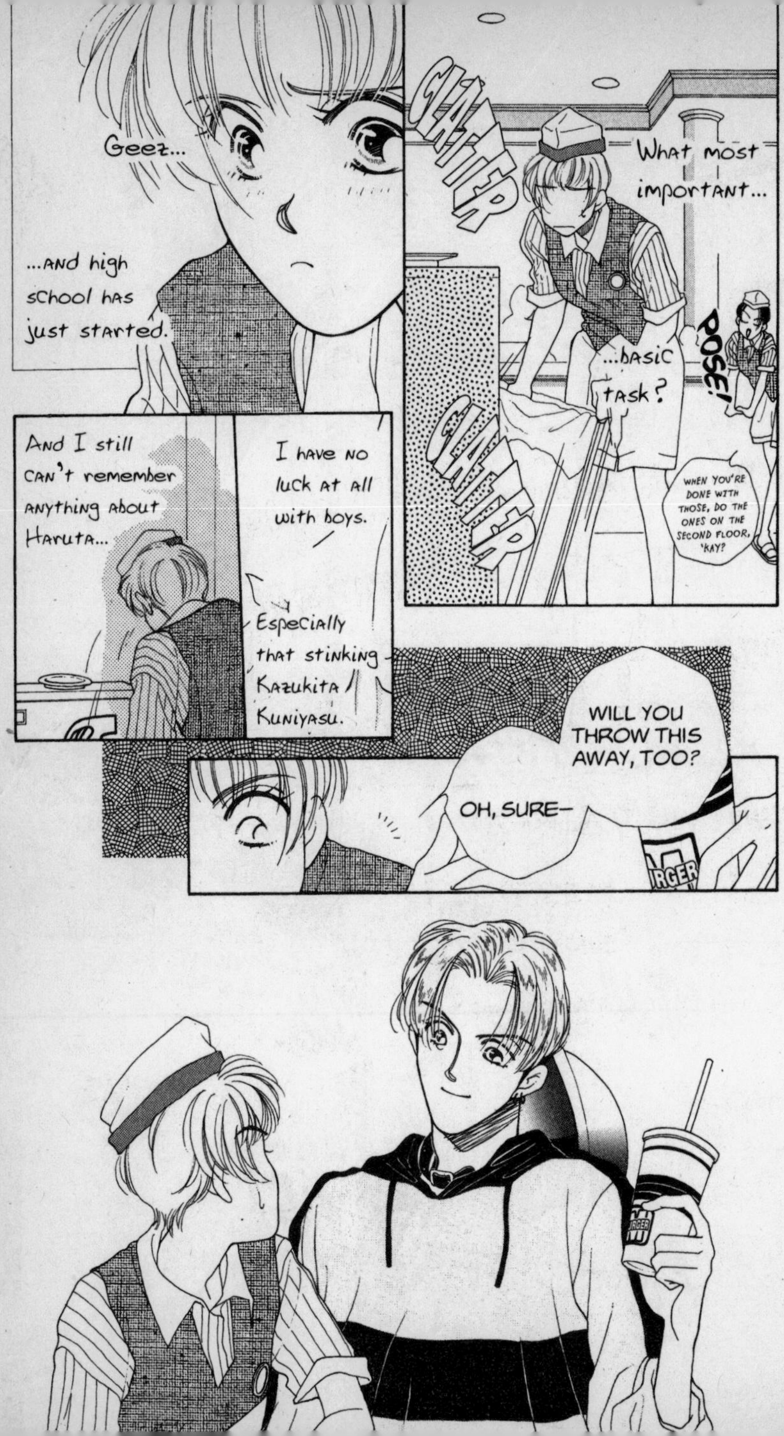
CLATTER
What most important...
POSE!
...basic task?
CLATTER
WHEN YOU'RE DONE WITH THOSE, DO THE ONES ON THE SECOND FLOOR, 'KAY?
Geez...
...and high school has just started.
I have no luck at all with boys.
Especially that stinking Kazukita Kuniyasu.
And I still can't remember anything about Haruta...
WILL YOU THROW THIS AWAY, TOO?
OH, SURE—
RGER
RGER

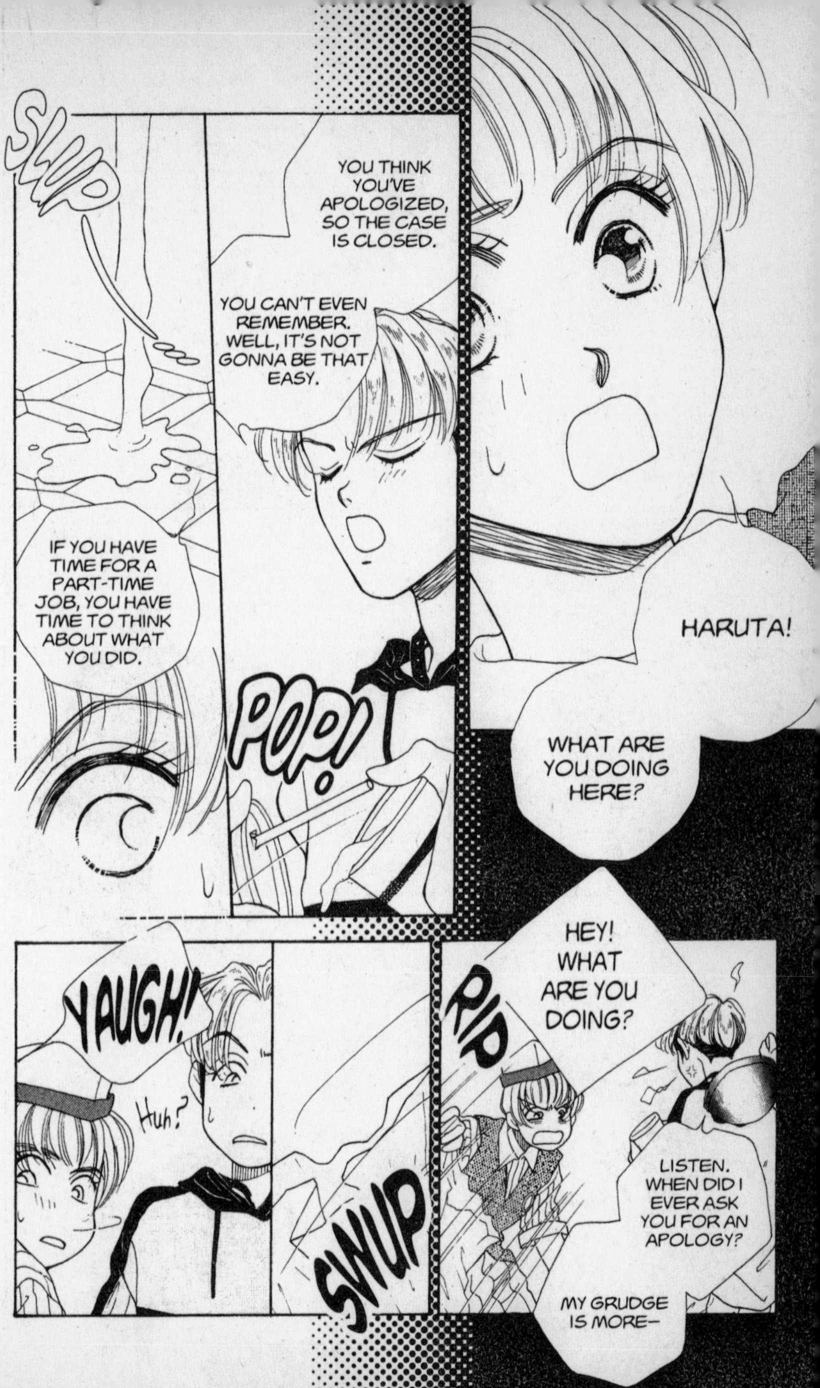
HARUTA!
WHAT ARE YOU DOING HERE?
YOU THINK YOU'VE APOLOGIZED, SO THE CASE IS CLOSED.
YOU CAN'T EVEN REMEMBER. WELL, IT'S NOT GONNA BE THAT EASY.
POP!
SWIP
IF YOU HAVE TIME FOR A PART-TIME JOB, YOU HAVE TIME TO THINK ABOUT WHAT YOU DID.
HEY! WHAT ARE YOU DOING?
RIP
LISTEN. WHEN DID I EVER ASK YOU FOR AN APOLOGY?
MY GRUDGE IS MORE—
SWUP
YAUGH!
Huh?

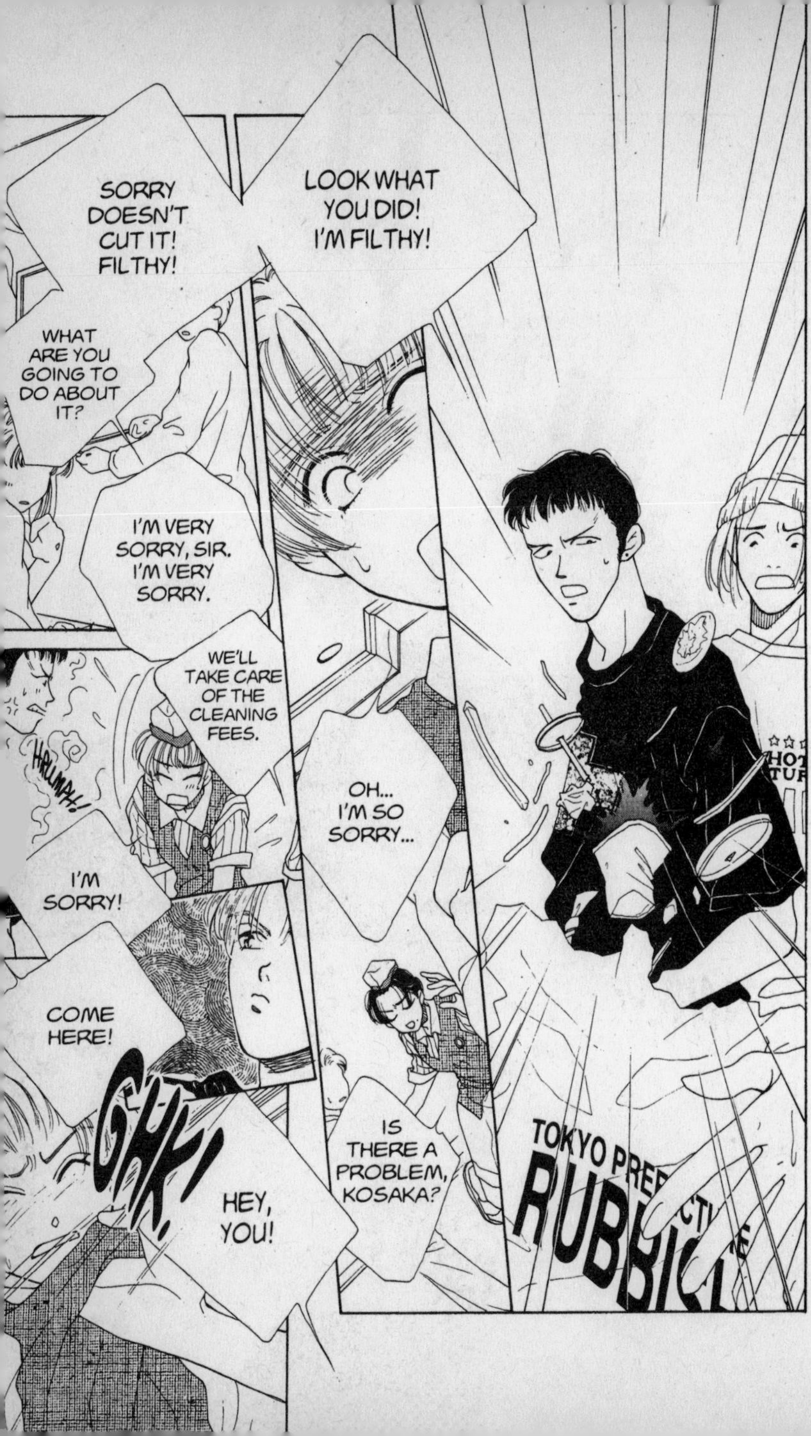
LOOK WHAT YOU DID! I'M FILTHY!
OH... I'M SO SORRY...
IS THERE A PROBLEM, KOSAKA?
SORRY DOESN'T CUT IT! FILTHY!
WHAT ARE YOU GOING TO DO ABOUT IT?
I'M VERY SORRY, SIR. I'M VERY SORRY.
WE'LL TAKE CARE OF THE CLEANING FEES.
HRUMPH!
I'M SORRY!
COME HERE!
GHK!
HEY, YOU!

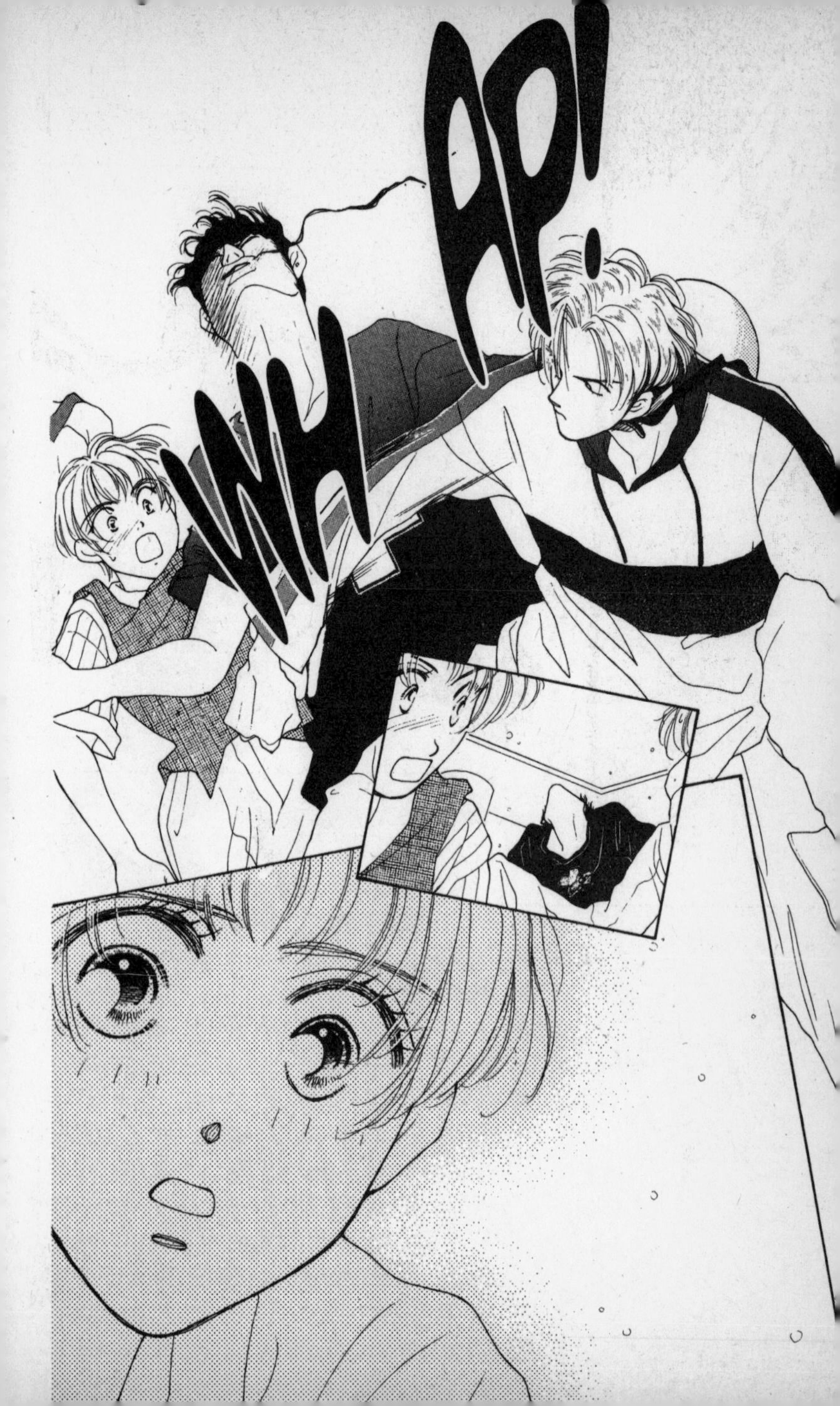
WHAP!

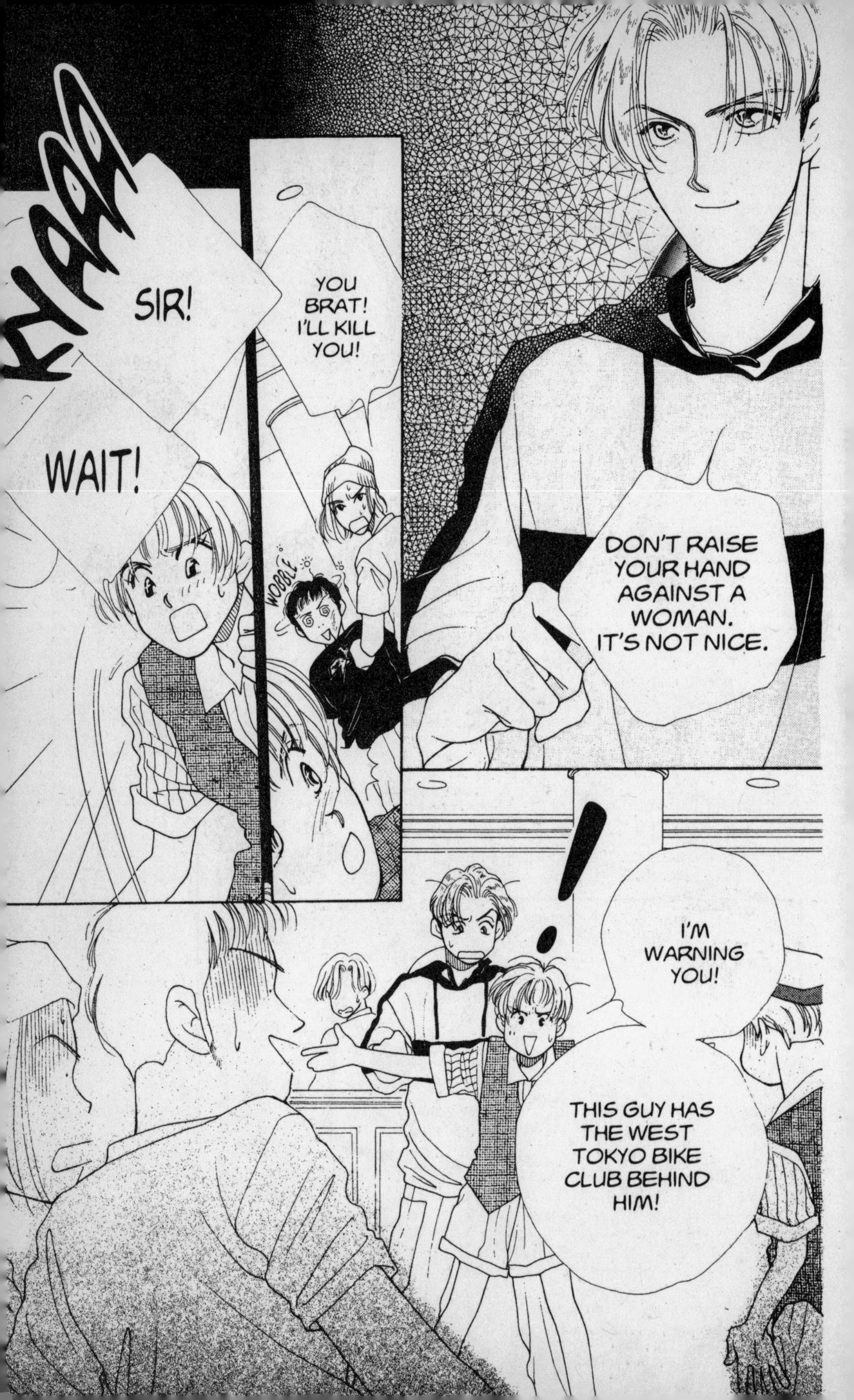
DON'T RAISE YOUR HAND AGAINST A WOMAN. IT'S NOT NICE.
YOU BRAT! I'LL KILL YOU!
WOBBLE
KYAAA
SIR!
WAIT!
!
I'M WARNING YOU!
THIS GUY HAS THE WEST TOKYO BIKE CLUB BEHIND HIM!

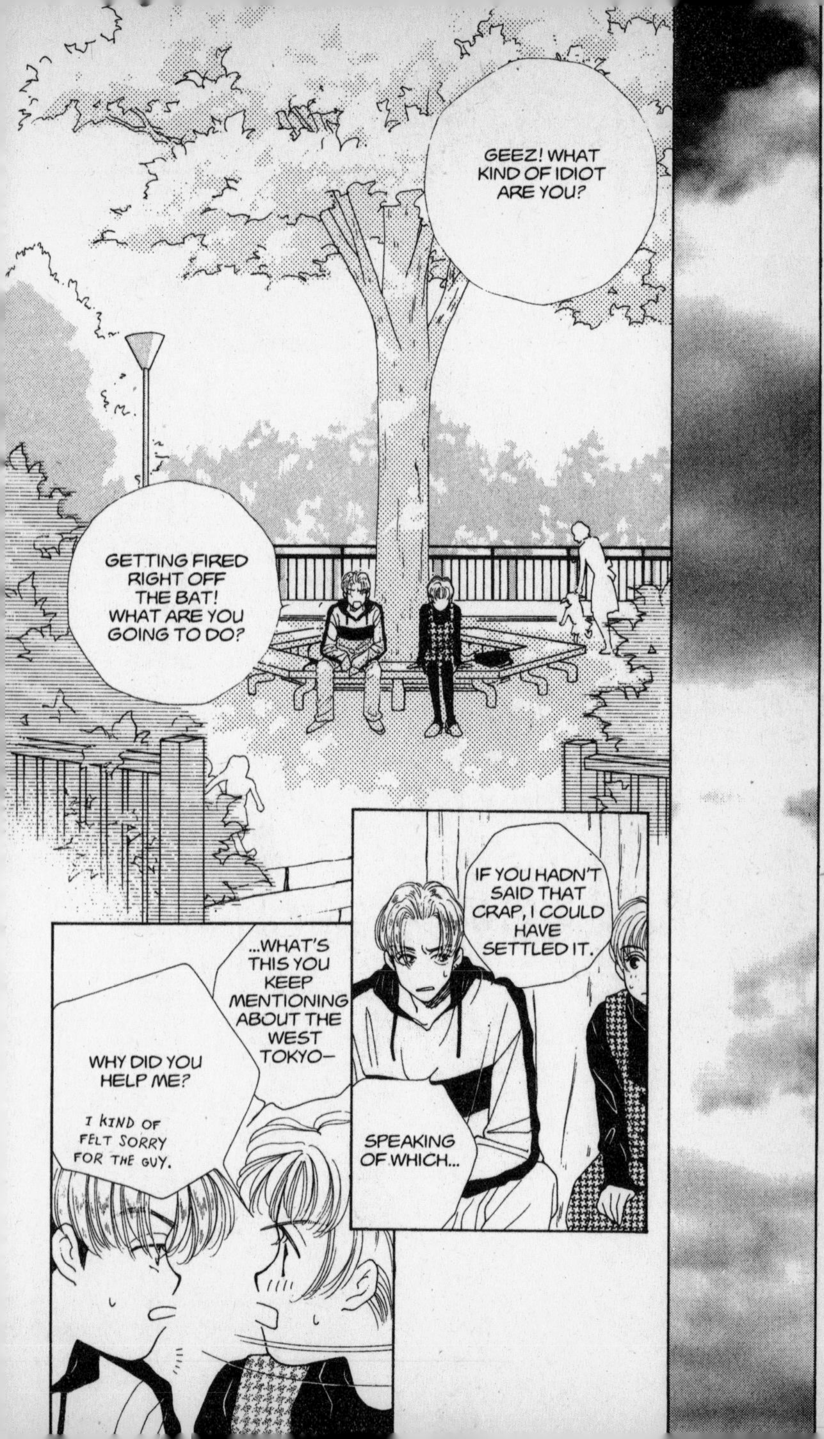
GEEZ! WHAT KIND OF IDIOT ARE YOU?
GETTING FIRED RIGHT OFF THE BAT! WHAT ARE YOU GOING TO DO?
IF YOU HADN'T SAID THAT CRAP, I COULD HAVE SETTLED IT.
SPEAKING OF WHICH...
...WHAT'S THIS YOU KEEP MENTIONING ABOUT THE WEST TOKYO—
WHY DID YOU HELP ME?
I KIND OF FELT SORRY FOR THE GUY.

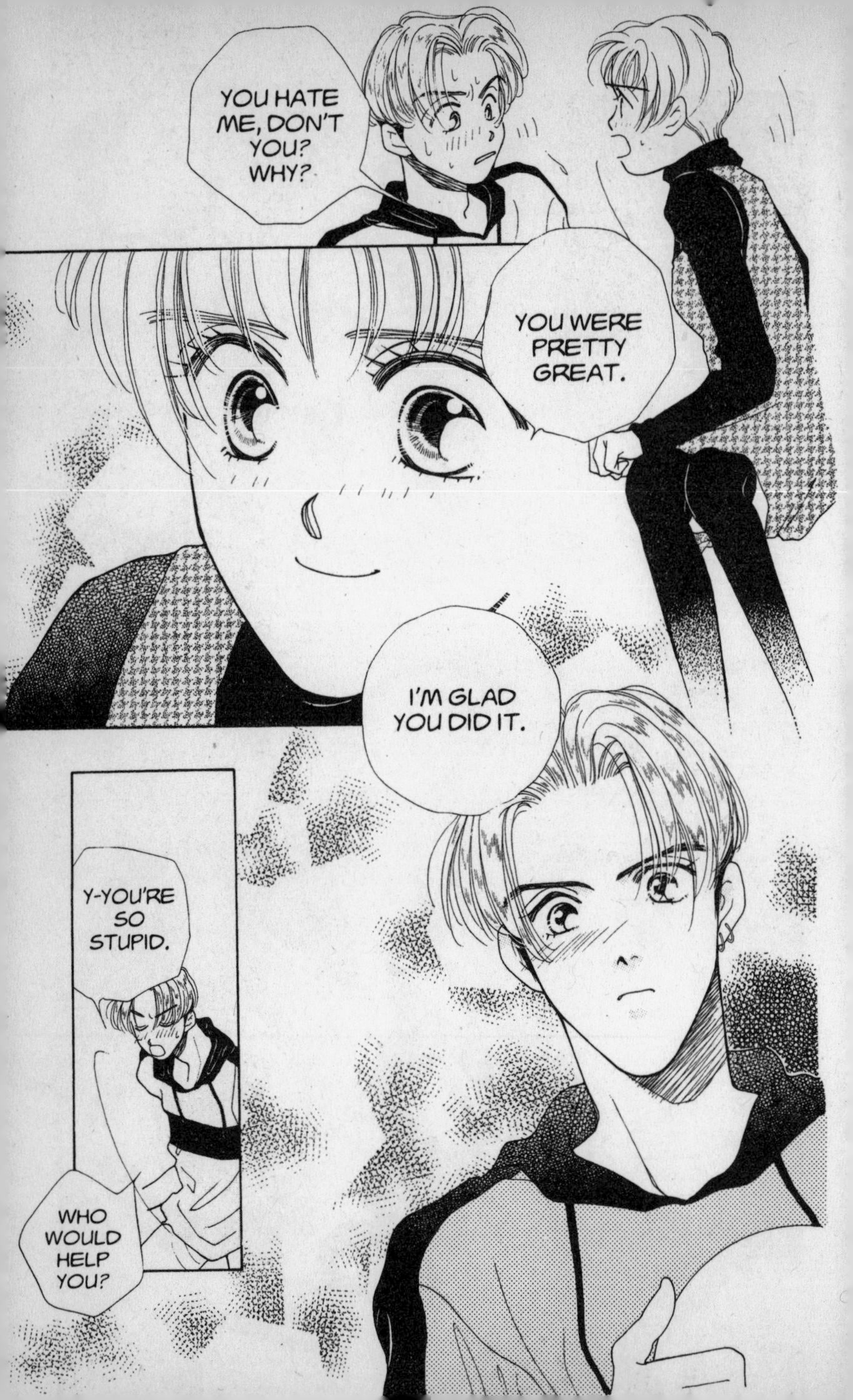
YOU HATE ME, DON'T YOU? WHY?
YOU WERE PRETTY GREAT.
I'M GLAD YOU DID IT.
Y-YOU'RE SO STUPID.
WHO WOULD HELP YOU?

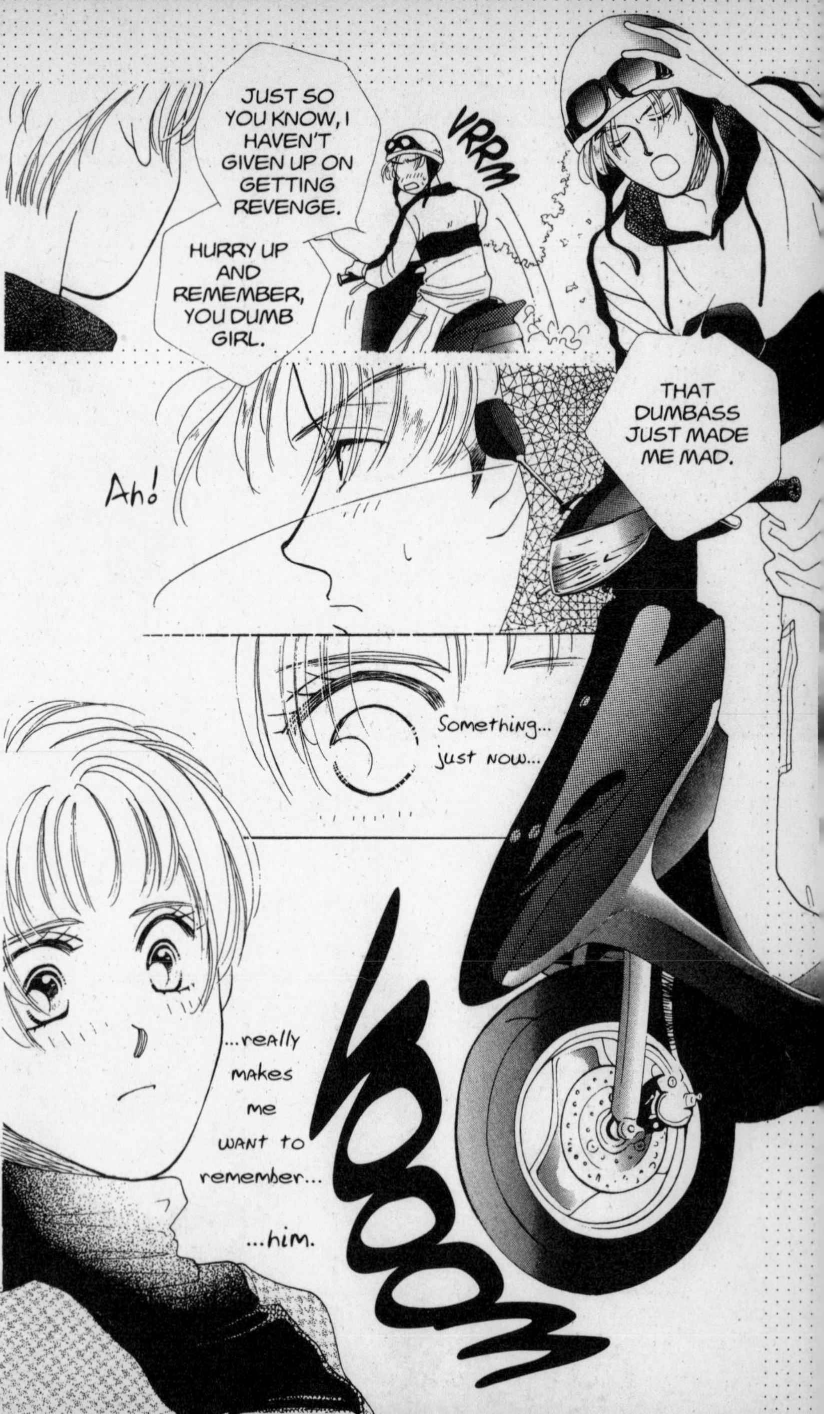
THAT DUMBASS JUST MADE ME MAD.
JUST SO YOU KNOW, I HAVEN'T GIVEN UP ON GETTING REVENGE.
HURRY UP AND REMEMBER, YOU DUMB GIRL.
VRRM
Ah!
Something... just now...
...really makes me want to remember...
...him.

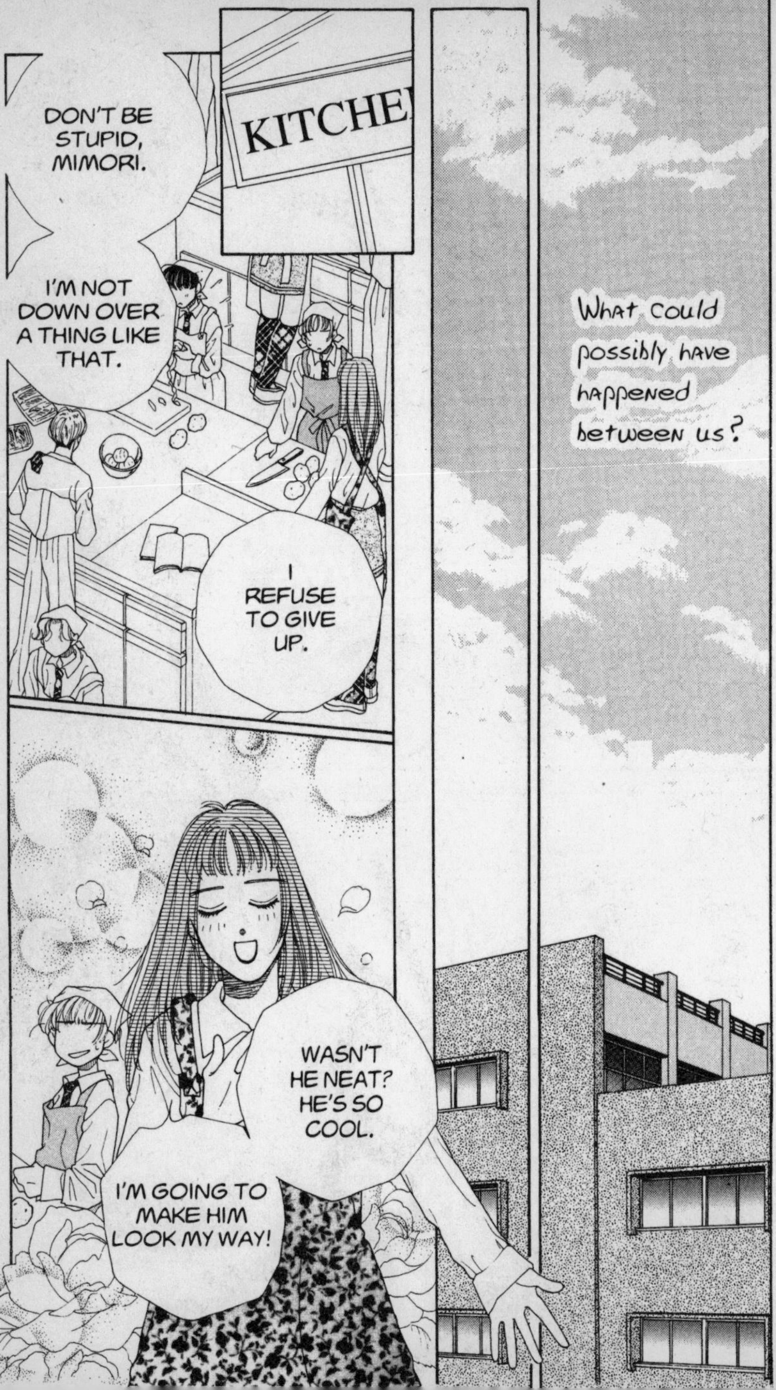
What could possibly have happened between us?
KITCHE
DON'T BE STUPID, MIMORI.
I'M NOT DOWN OVER A THING LIKE THAT.
I REFUSE TO GIVE UP.
WASN'T HE NEAT? HE'S SO COOL.
I'M GOING TO MAKE HIM LOOK MY WAY!

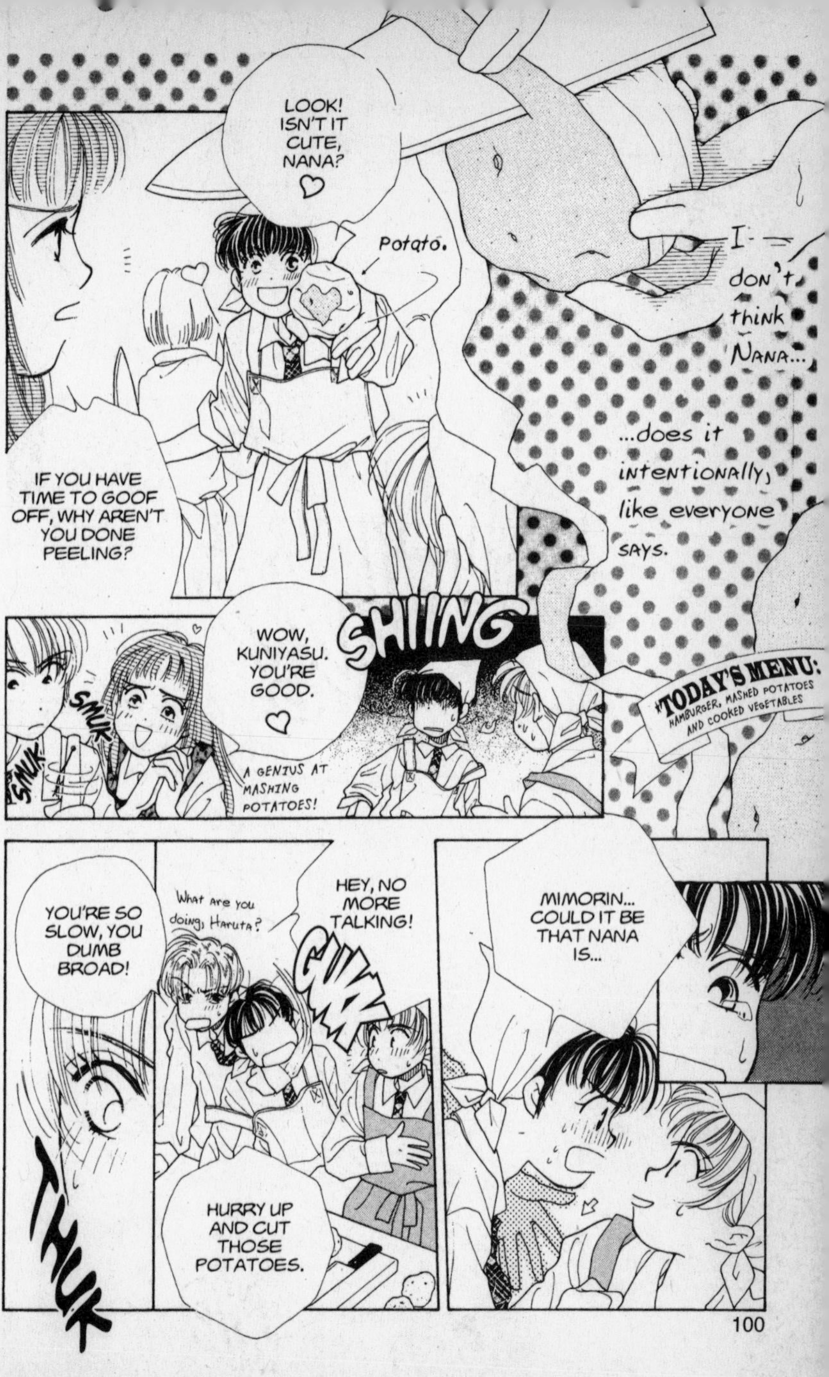
I— don't think Nana...
...does it intentionally, like everyone says.
TODAY'S MENU: HAMBURGER, MASHED POTATOES AND COOKED VEGETABLES
LOOK! ISN'T IT CUTE, NANA? ♡
Potato.
IF YOU HAVE TIME TO GOOF OFF, WHY AREN'T YOU DONE PEELING?
SHIING
WOW, KUNIYASU. YOU'RE GOOD. ♡
A GENIUS AT MASHING POTATOES!
SMUK SMUK
MIMORIN... COULD IT BE THAT NANA IS...
HEY, NO MORE TALKING!
What are you doing, Haruta?
GUK
HURRY UP AND CUT THOSE POTATOES.
YOU'RE SO SLOW, YOU DUMB BROAD!
THUK

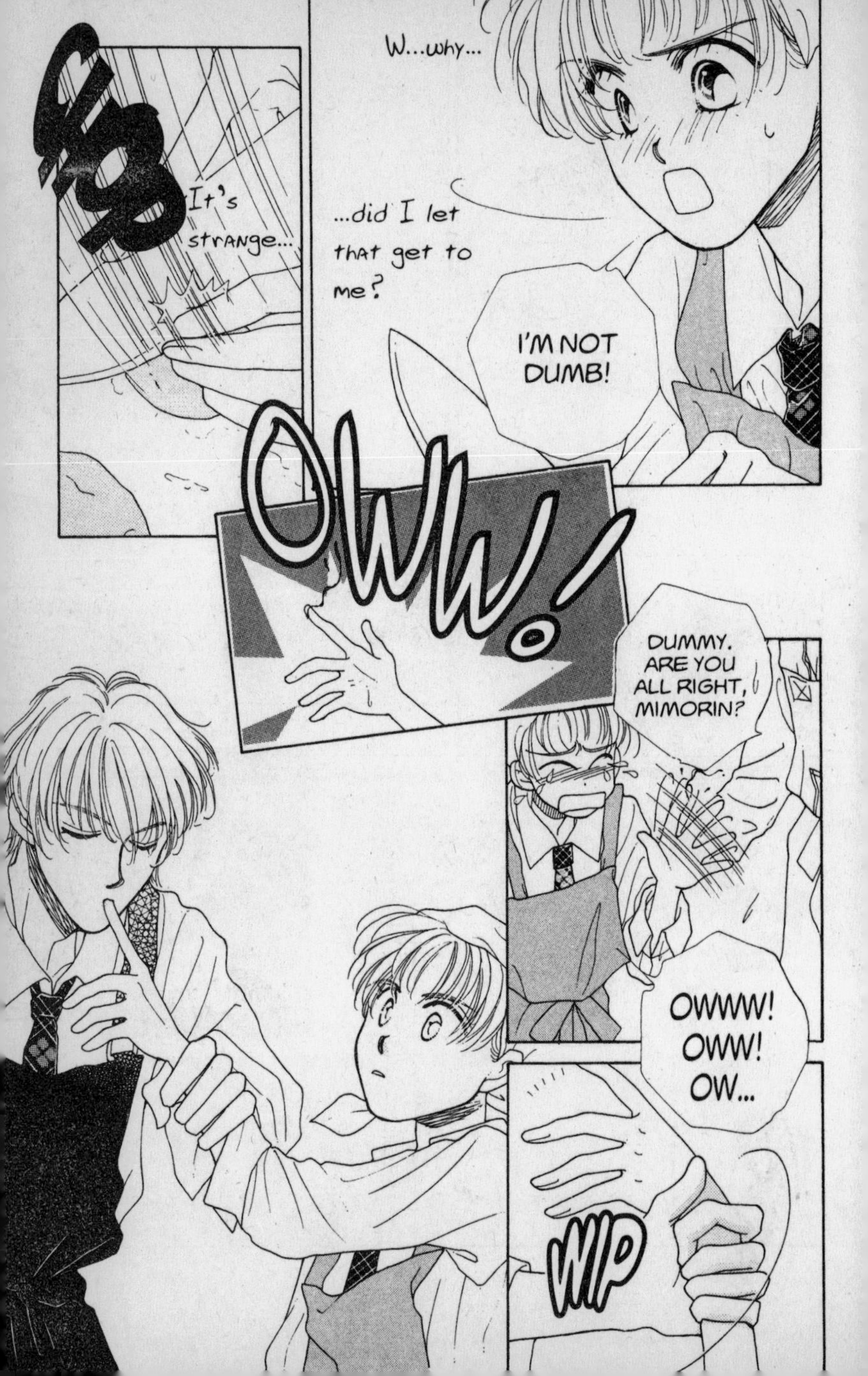
W...why...
...did I let that get to me?
I'M NOT DUMB!
CLIP
It's strange...
OWW!
DUMMY. ARE YOU ALL RIGHT, MIMORIN?
OWWW! OWW! OW...
WIP

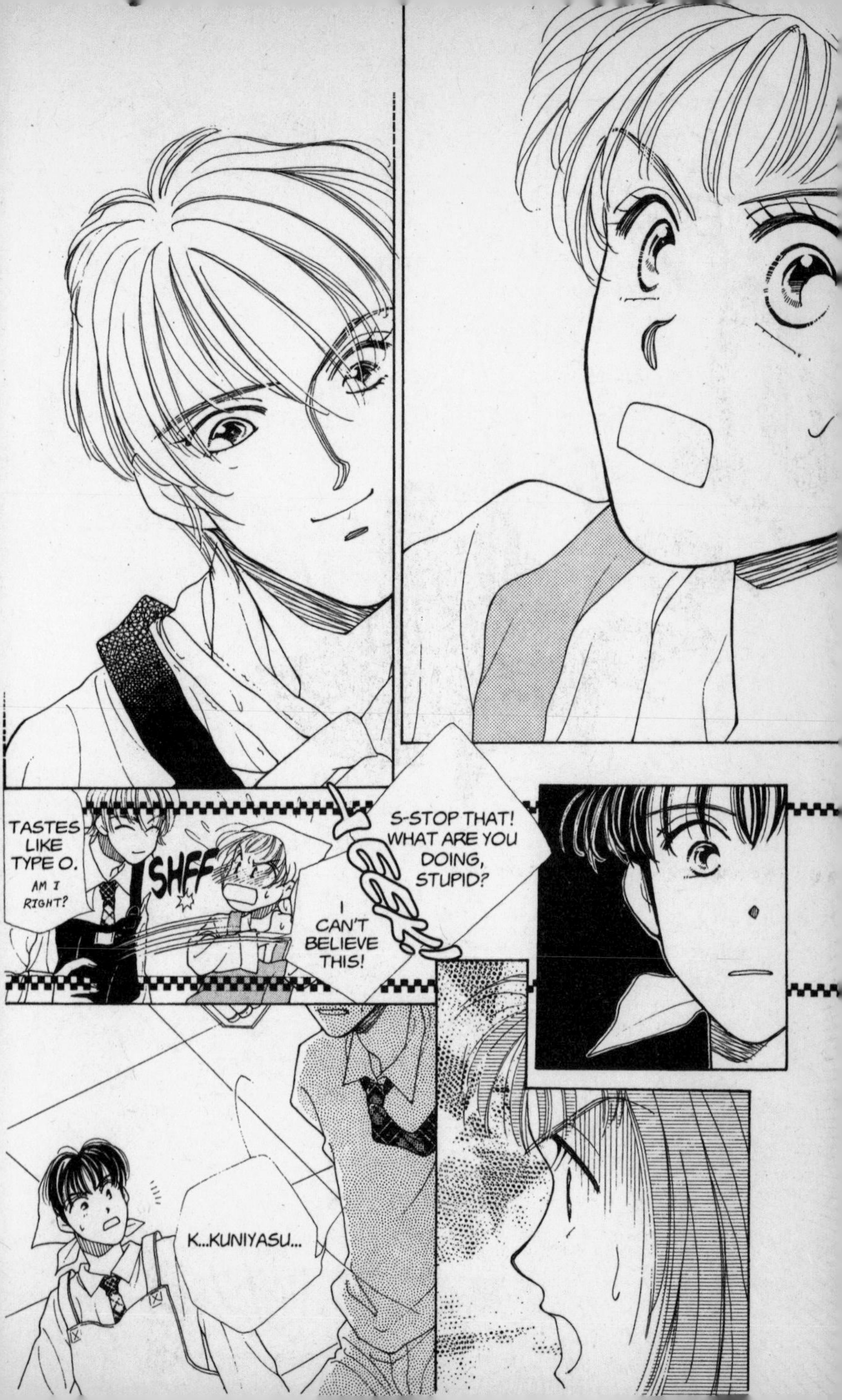
TASTES LIKE TYPE O.
AM I RIGHT?
SHFF
S-STOP THAT! WHAT ARE YOU DOING, STUPID?
I CAN'T BELIEVE THIS!
K...KUNIYASU...

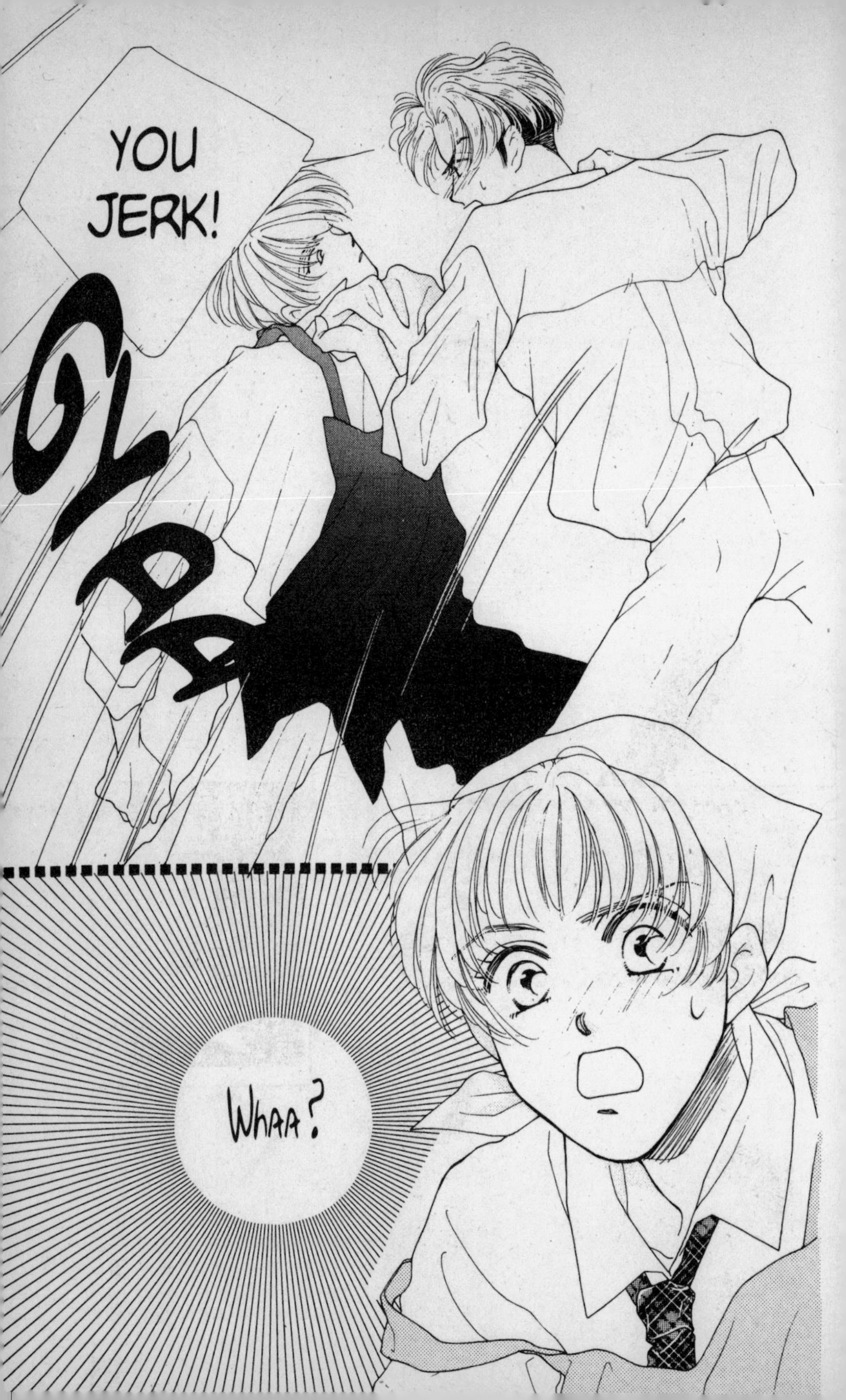
YOU JERK!
WHAA?

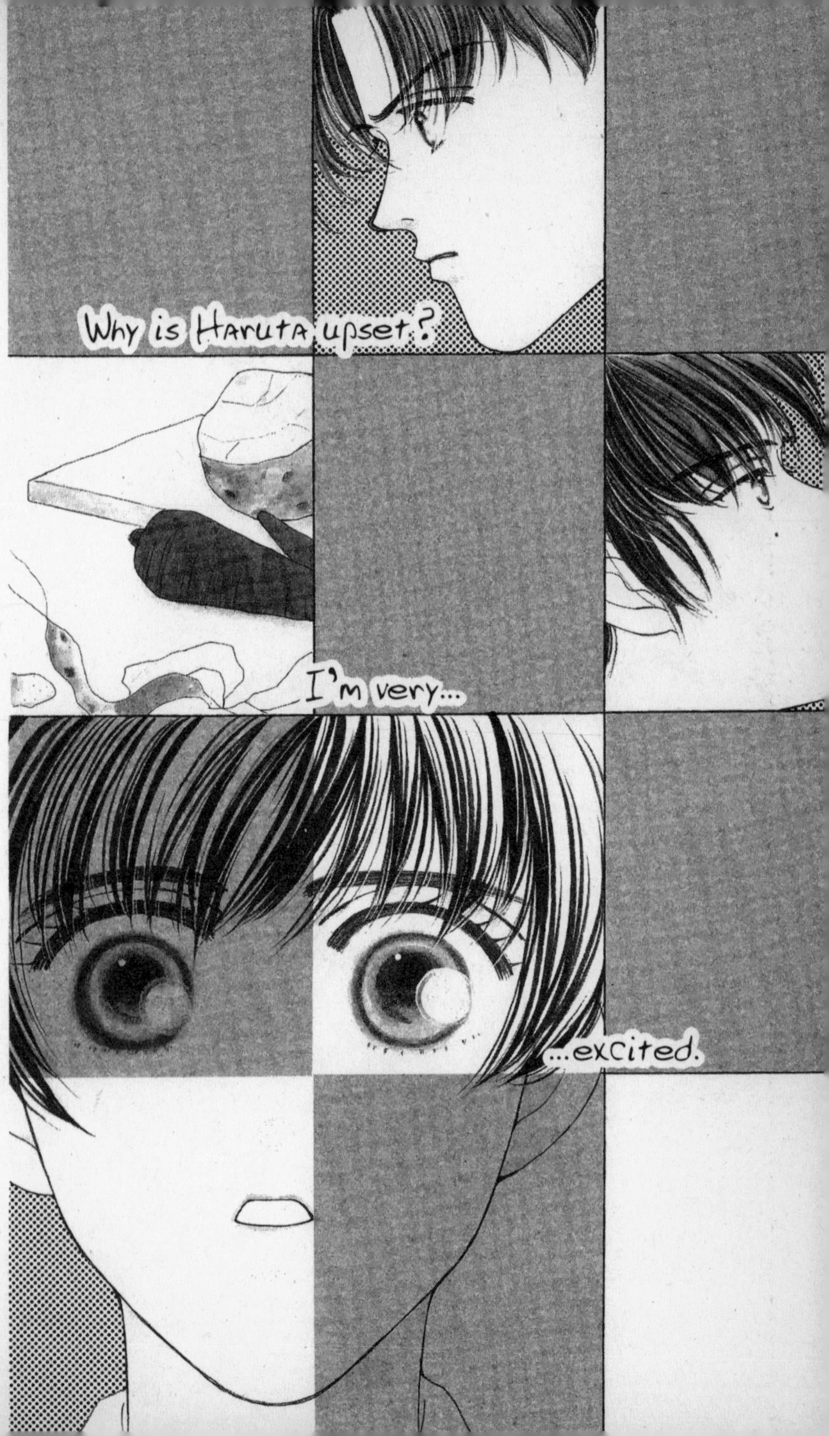
Why is Haruta upset?
I'm very...
...excited.

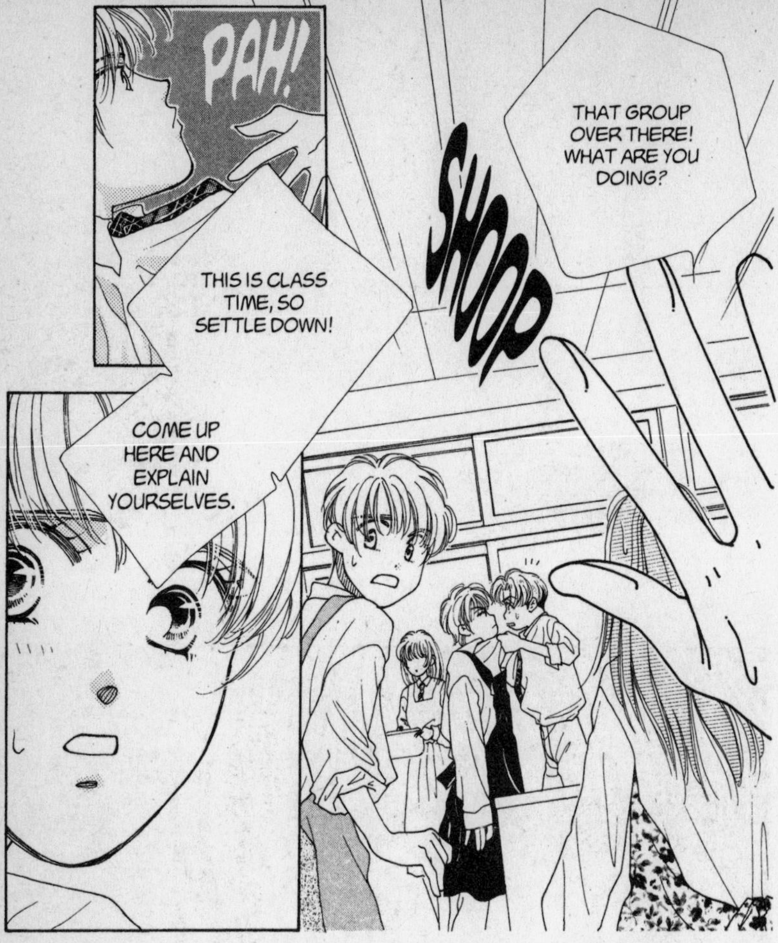
THAT GROUP OVER THERE! WHAT ARE YOU DOING?
SHOOP
PAH!
THIS IS CLASS TIME, SO SETTLE DOWN!
COME UP HERE AND EXPLAIN YOURSELVES.

TOKYO GIRLS PROFILE NO. 1 MIMORI KOSAKA

HOME: MEGURO WARD, TOKYO
HEIGHT : 5' 2" WEIGHT: ABOUT 97lbs
BLOOD TYPE: A
FAMILY: MOTHER, FATHER AND ONE YOUNGER SISTER
HOBBIES: NOTHING IN PARTICULAR. PLAYING GAMES LIKE BASKETBALL (PLAYED IT IN MIDDLE SCHOOL).
HISTORY OF BOYFRIENDS: NONE IN 15 YEARS (HAS ONLY ASSOCIATED WITH BOYS IN CLUB ACTIVITIES).

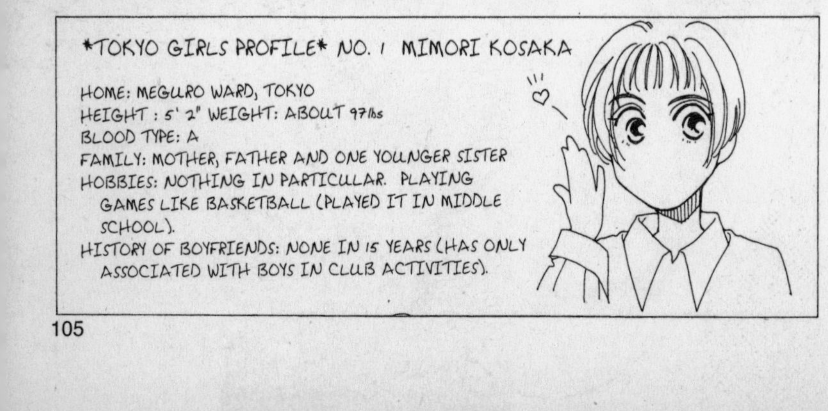

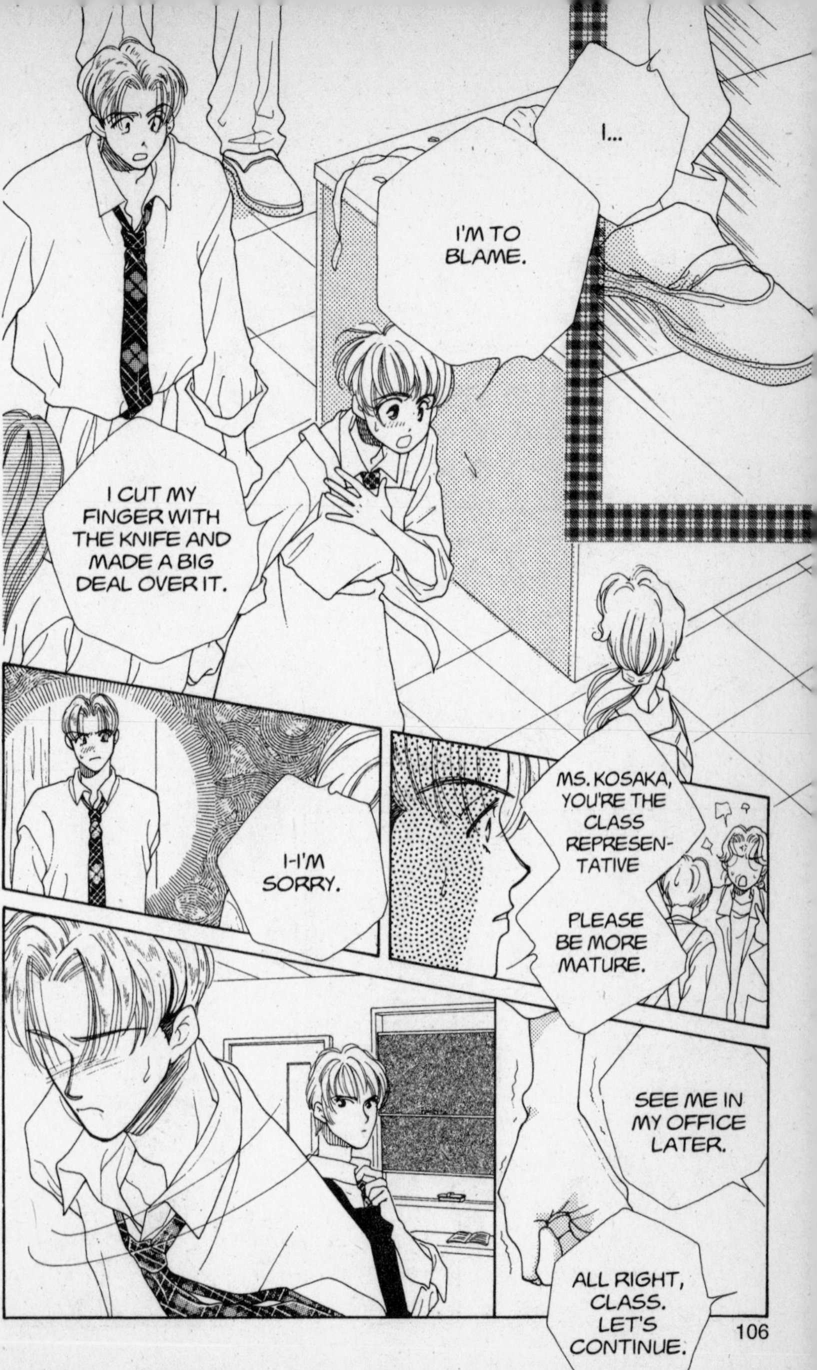
I...
I'M TO BLAME.
I CUT MY FINGER WITH THE KNIFE AND MADE A BIG DEAL OVER IT.
MS. KOSAKA, YOU'RE THE CLASS REPRESEN-TATIVE
PLEASE BE MORE MATURE.
I-I'M SORRY.
SEE ME IN MY OFFICE LATER.
ALL RIGHT, CLASS. LET'S CONTINUE.

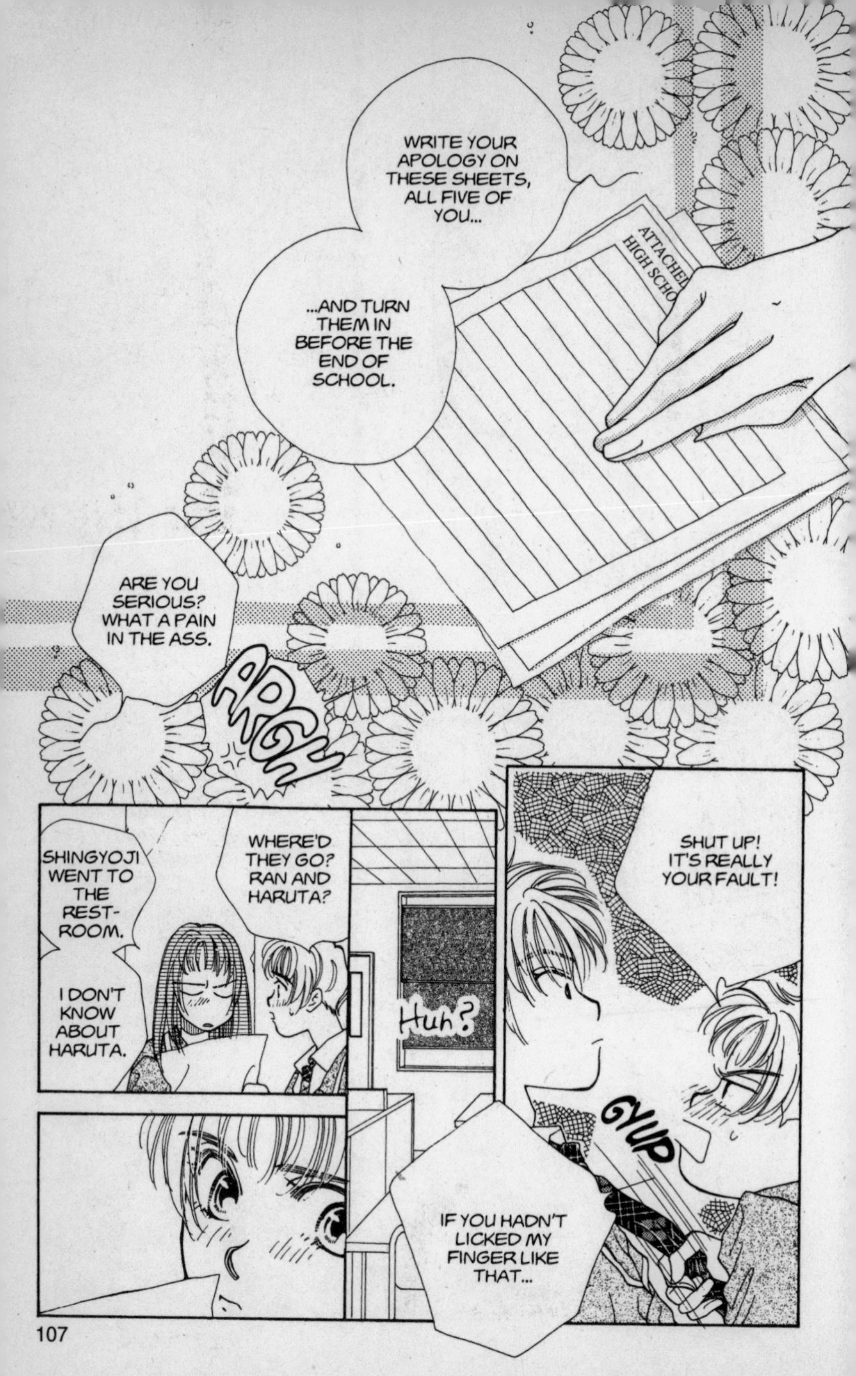
WRITE YOUR APOLOGY ON THESE SHEETS, ALL FIVE OF YOU...
...AND TURN THEM IN BEFORE THE END OF SCHOOL.
ARE YOU SERIOUS? WHAT A PAIN IN THE ASS.
ARGH
SHUT UP! IT'S REALLY YOUR FAULT!
GYUP
IF YOU HADN'T LICKED MY FINGER LIKE THAT...
WHERE'D THEY GO? RAN AND HARUTA?
SHINGYOJI WENT TO THE REST-ROOM.
I DON'T KNOW ABOUT HARUTA.
Huh?

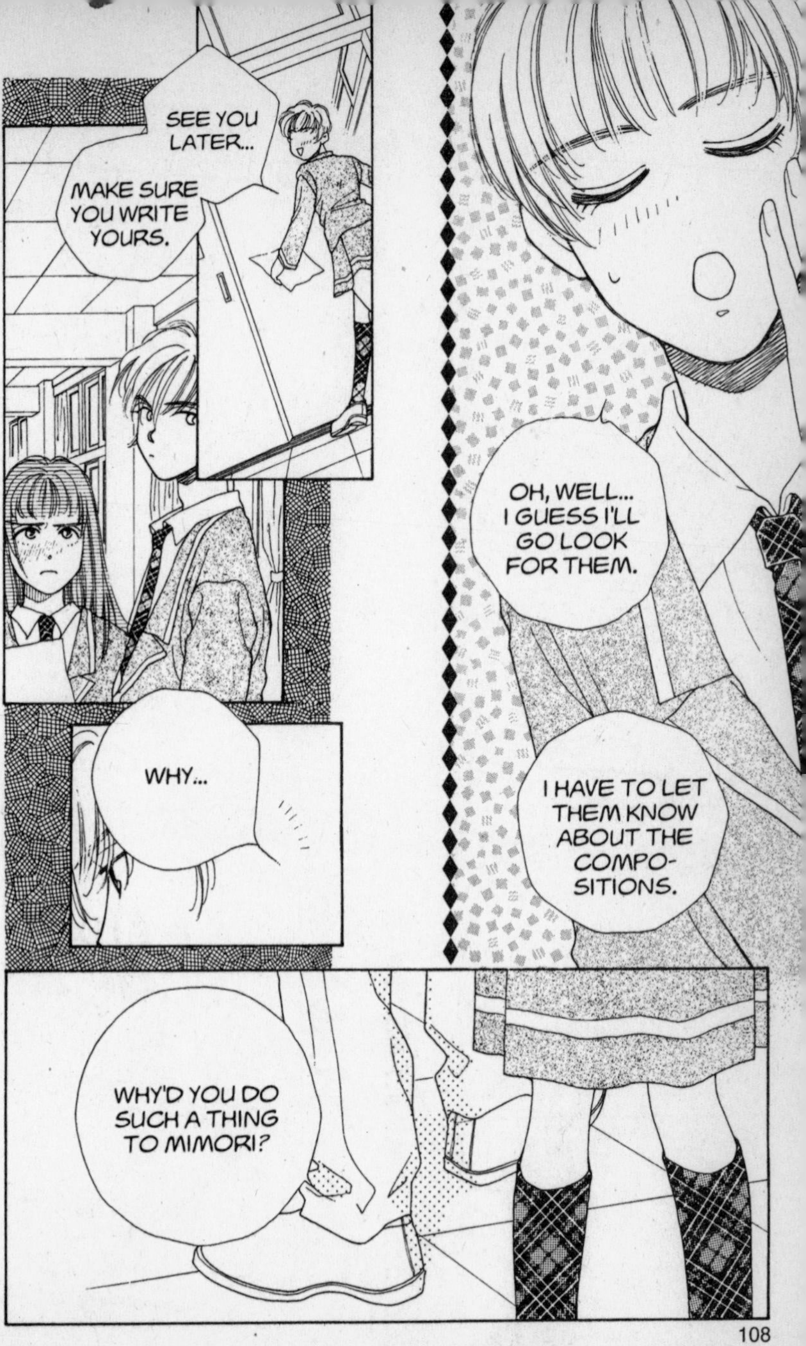
OH, WELL... I GUESS I'LL GO LOOK FOR THEM.
I HAVE TO LET THEM KNOW ABOUT THE COMPO-SITIONS.
SEE YOU LATER...
MAKE SURE YOU WRITE YOURS.
WHY...
WHY'D YOU DO SUCH A THING TO MIMORI?

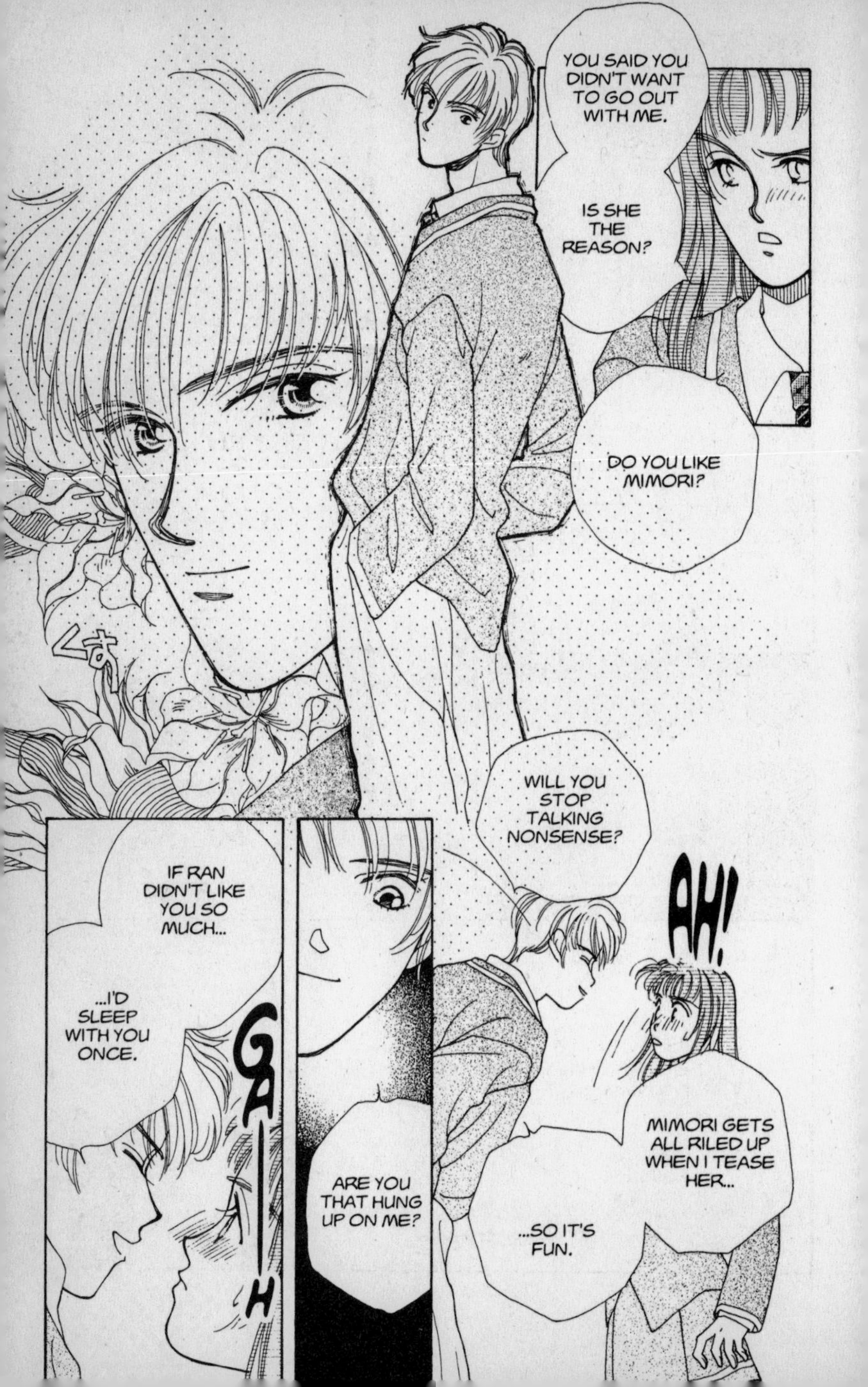
YOU SAID YOU DIDN'T WANT TO GO OUT WITH ME.
IS SHE THE REASON?
DO YOU LIKE MIMORI?
くす
WILL YOU STOP TALKING NONSENSE?
AH!
MIMORI GETS ALL RILED UP WHEN I TEASE HER...
...SO IT'S FUN.
ARE YOU THAT HUNG UP ON ME?
IF RAN DIDN'T LIKE YOU SO MUCH...
...I'D SLEEP WITH YOU ONCE.
GA—H

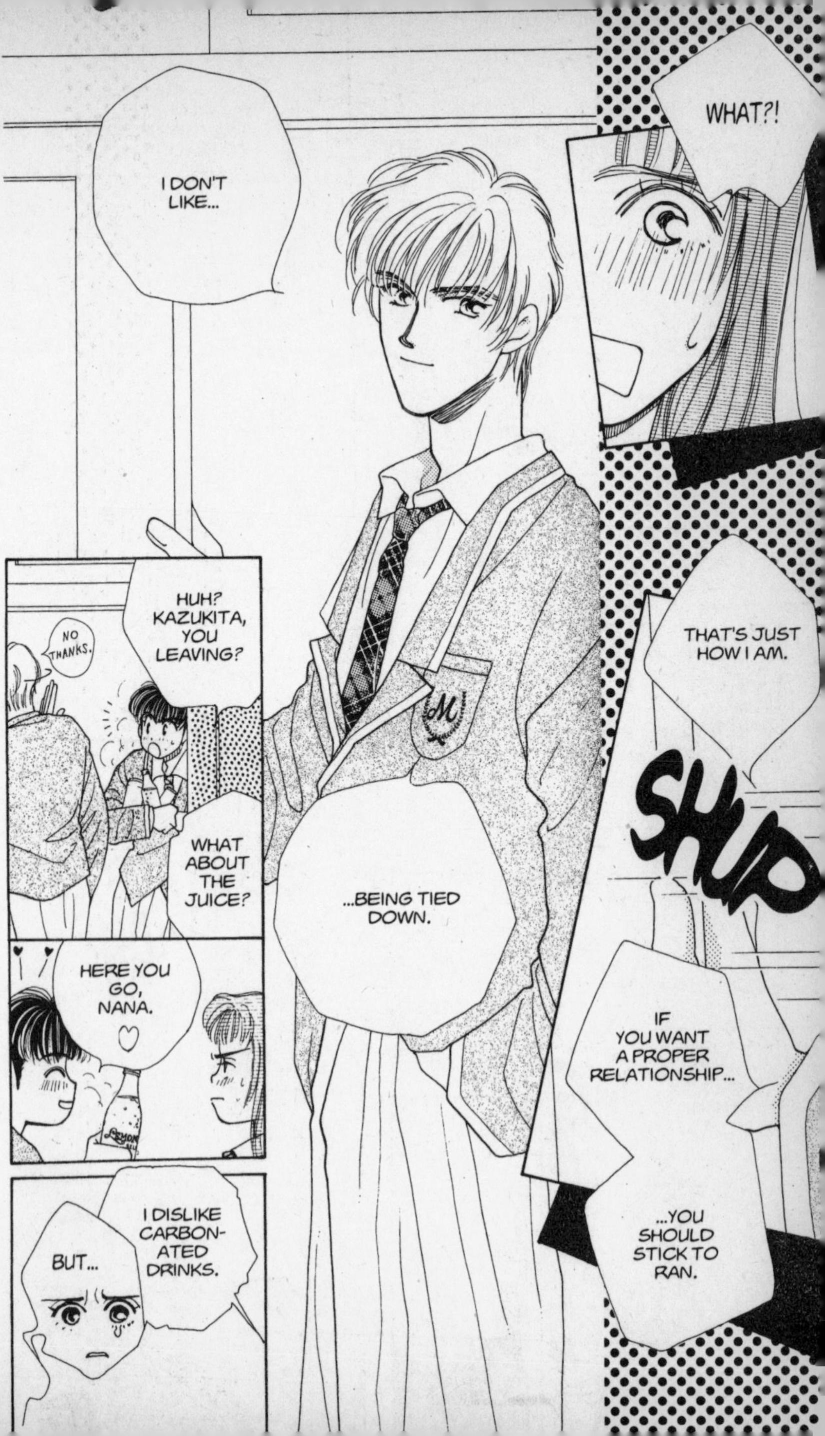
WHAT?!
THAT'S JUST HOW I AM.
SHUP
IF YOU WANT A PROPER RELATIONSHIP...
...YOU SHOULD STICK TO RAN.
I DON'T LIKE...
...BEING TIED DOWN.
HUH? KAZUKITA, YOU LEAVING?
NO THANKS.
WHAT ABOUT THE JUICE?
HERE YOU GO, NANA.
I DISLIKE CARBON-ATED DRINKS.
BUT...

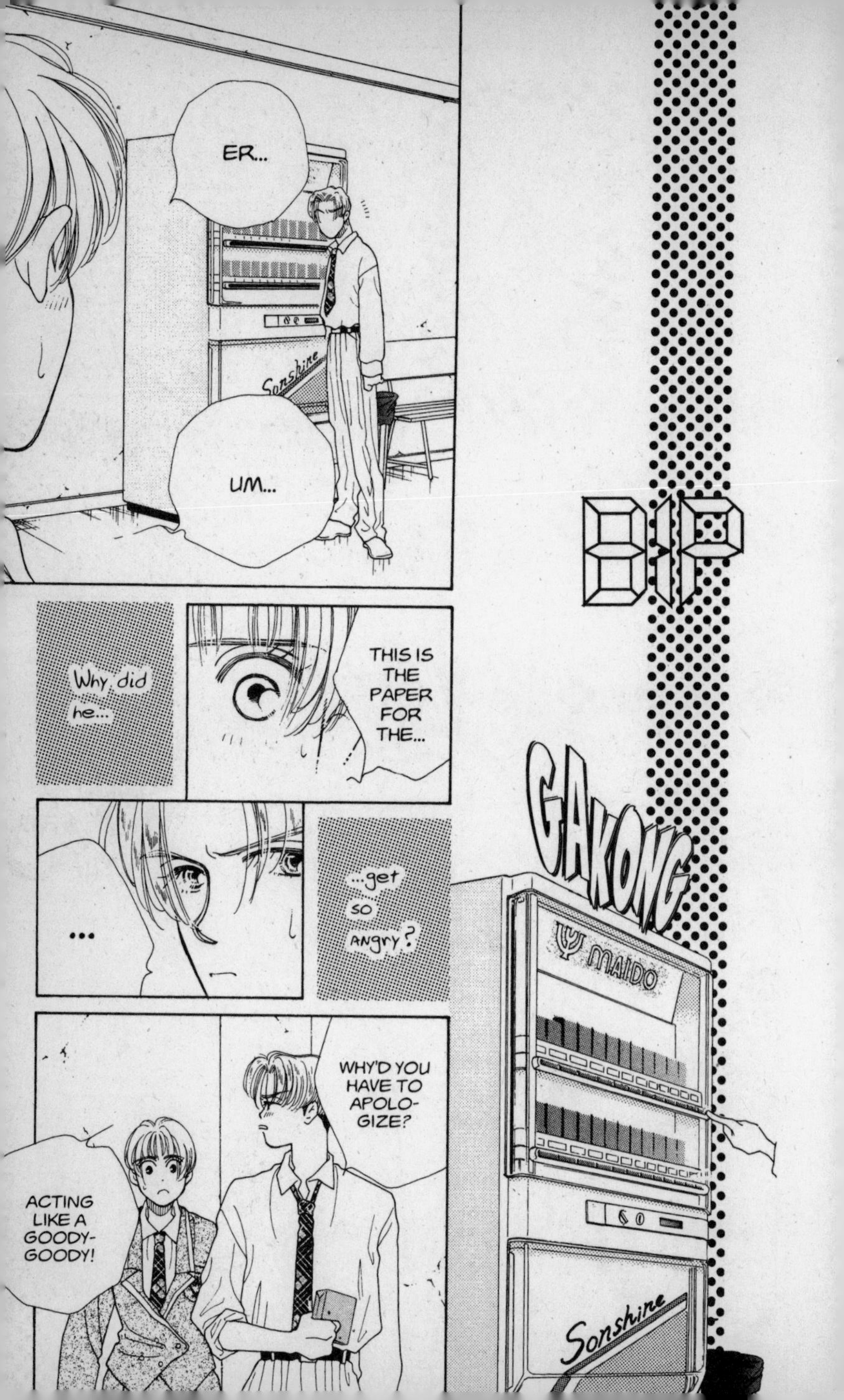
BIP
GAKONG
MAIDO
Sonshine
ER...
Sonshine
UM...
THIS IS THE PAPER FOR THE...
Why did he...
...get so angry?
...
WHY'D YOU HAVE TO APOLO-GIZE?
ACTING LIKE A GOODY-GOODY!

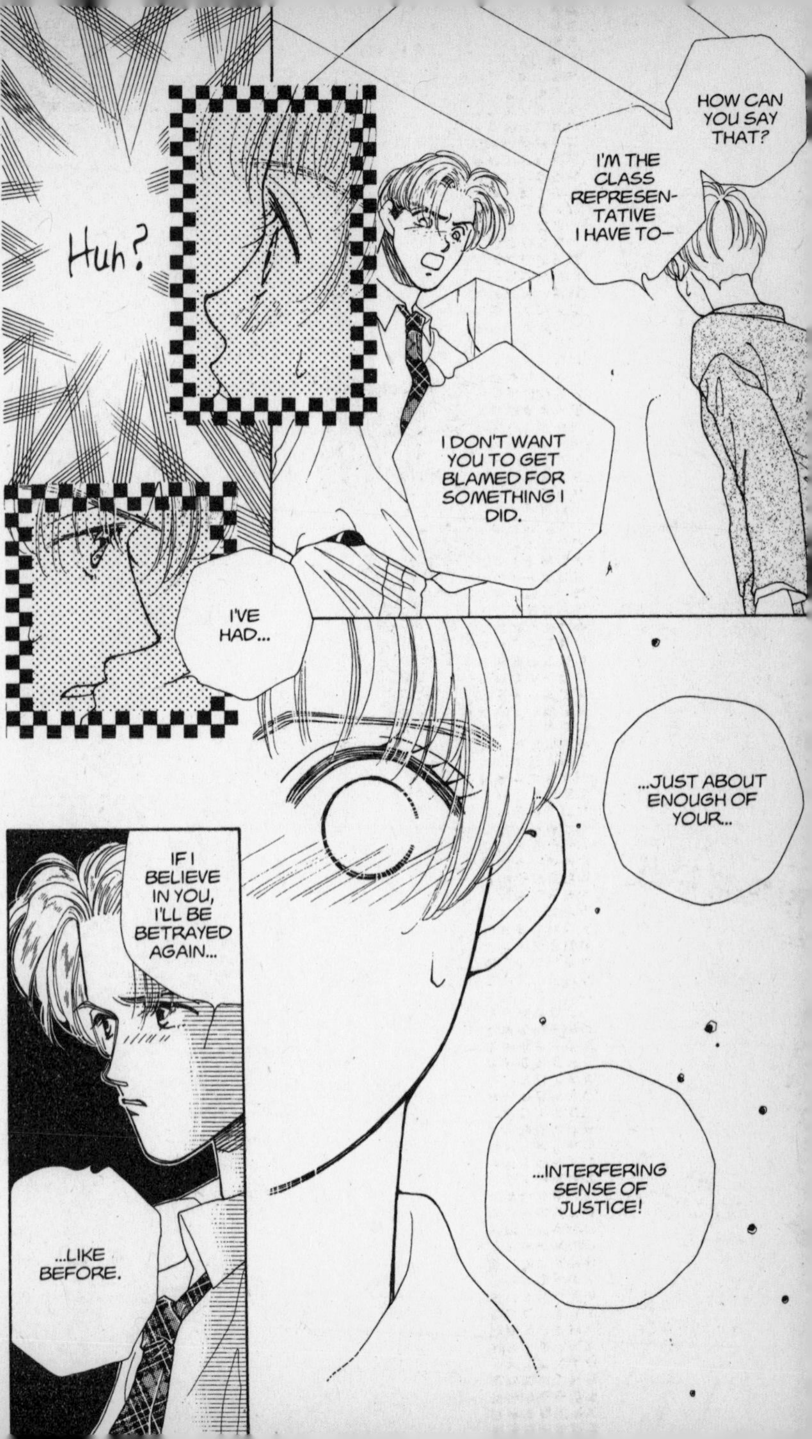
HOW CAN YOU SAY THAT?
I'M THE CLASS REPRESEN-TATIVE I HAVE TO—
I DON'T WANT YOU TO GET BLAMED FOR SOMETHING I DID.
Huh?
I'VE HAD...
...JUST ABOUT ENOUGH OF YOUR...
...INTERFERING SENSE OF JUSTICE!
IF I BELIEVE IN YOU, I'LL BE BETRAYED AGAIN...
...LIKE BEFORE.

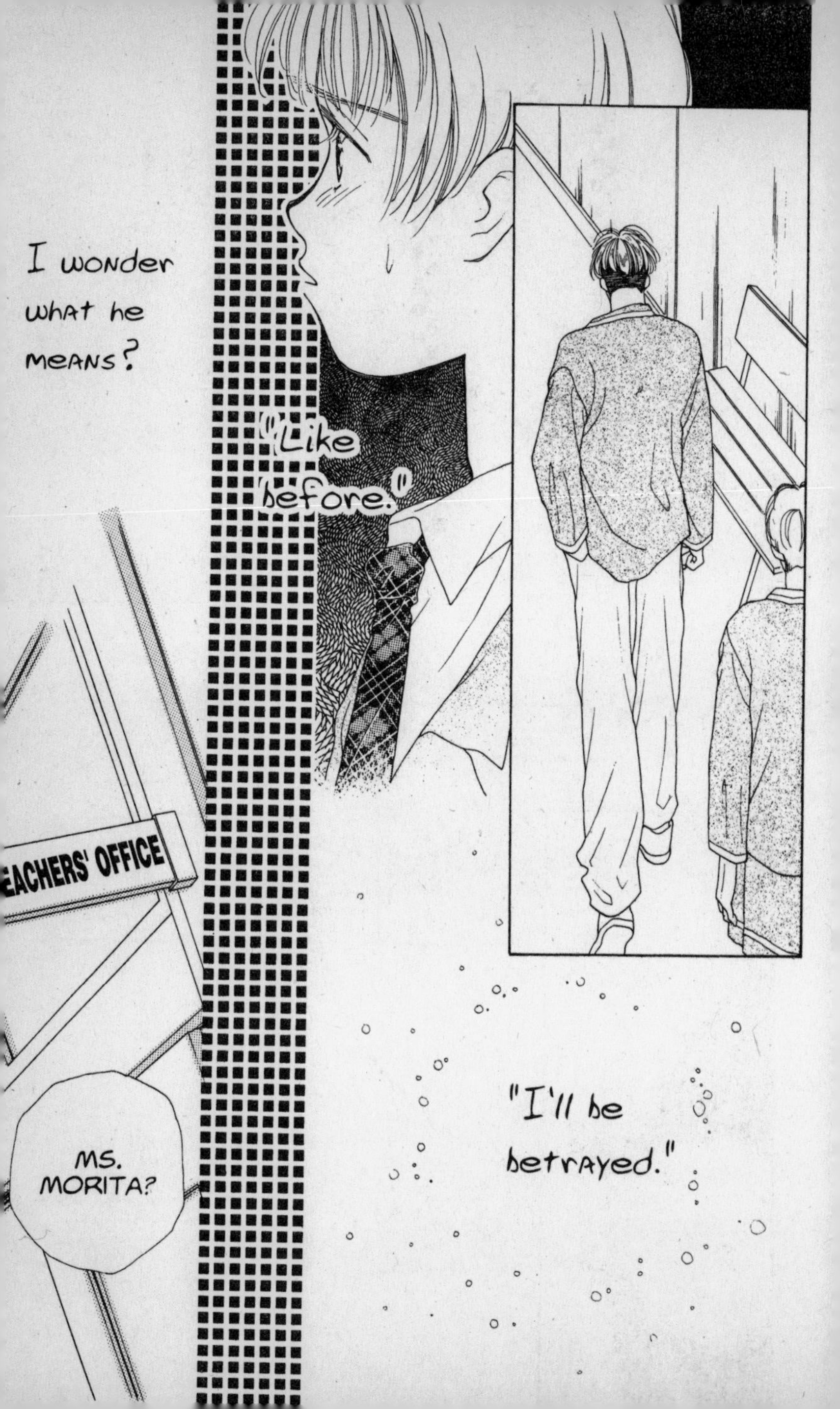
"Like before."
"I'll be betrayed."
I wonder what he means?
EACHERS' OFFICE
MS. MORITA?

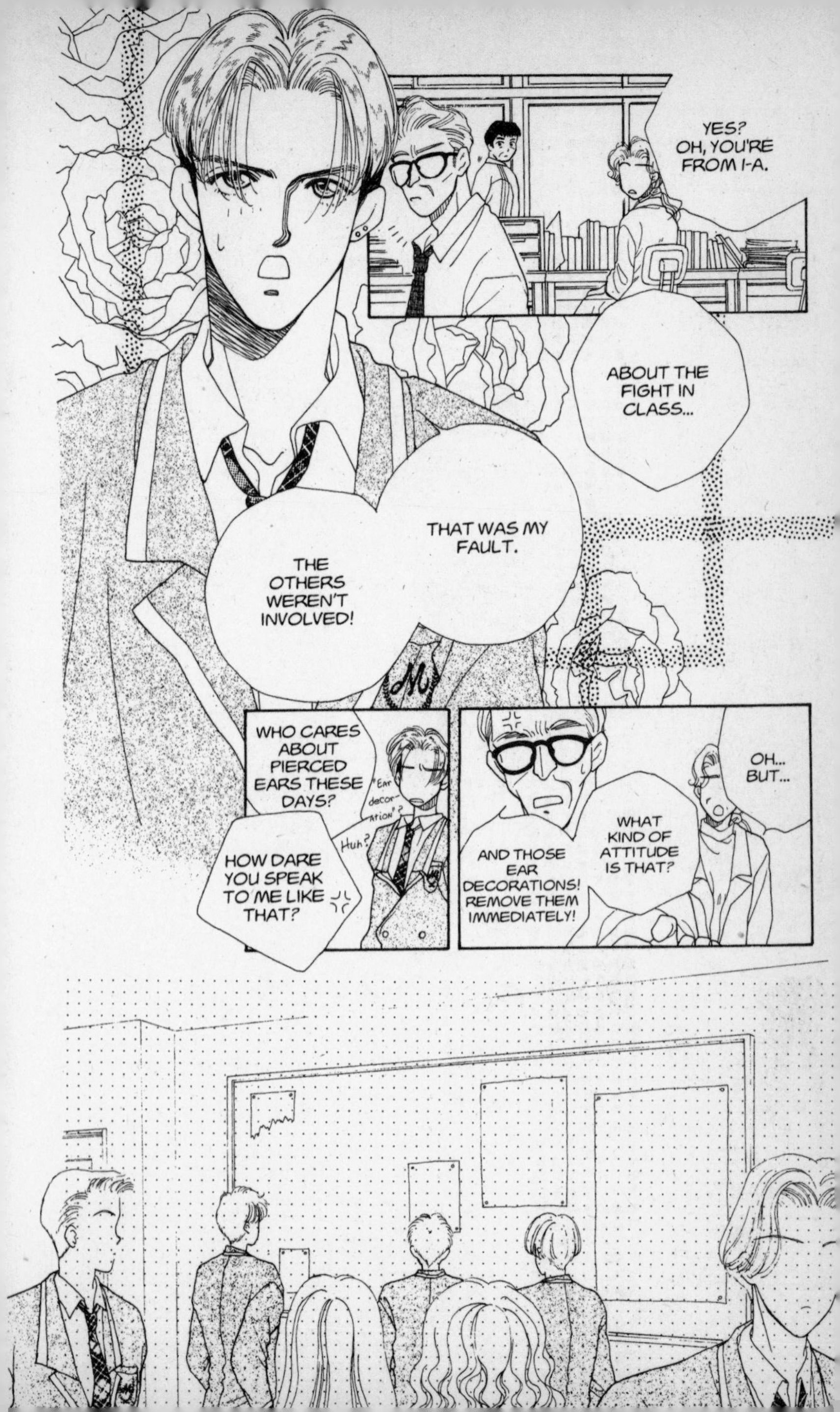
YES? OH, YOU'RE FROM I-A.
ABOUT THE FIGHT IN CLASS...
THAT WAS MY FAULT.
THE OTHERS WEREN'T INVOLVED!
OH... BUT...
WHAT KIND OF ATTITUDE IS THAT?
AND THOSE EAR DECORATIONS! REMOVE THEM IMMEDIATELY!
WHO CARES ABOUT PIERCED EARS THESE DAYS?
"Ear decoration"?
Huh?
HOW DARE YOU SPEAK TO ME LIKE THAT?

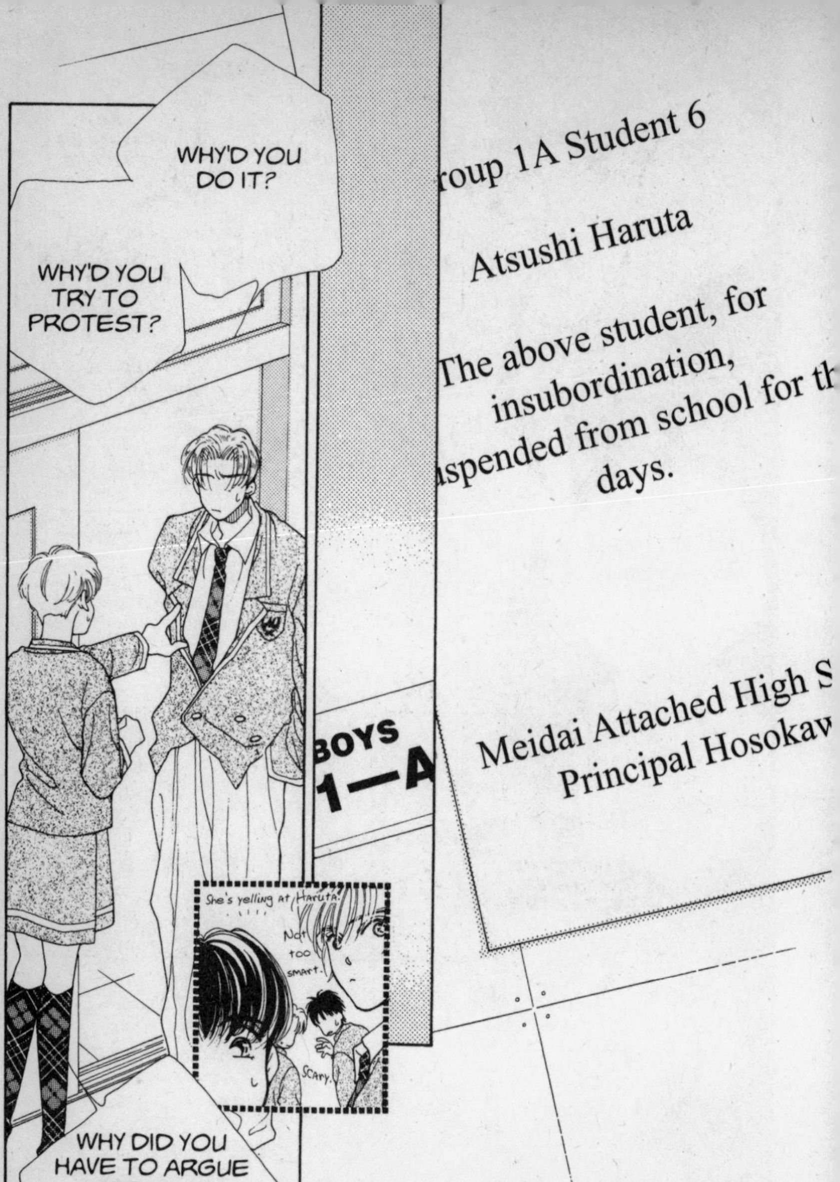
roup 1A Student 6
Atsushi Haruta
The above student, for insubordination, spended from school for th days.
Meidai Attached High S
Principal Hosokaw
BOYS 1—A
WHY'D YOU DO IT?
WHY'D YOU TRY TO PROTEST?
She's yelling at Haruta.
Not too smart.
Scary.
WHY DID YOU HAVE TO ARGUE WITH THE TEACHER IN CHARGE OF OUR GRADE LEVEL?

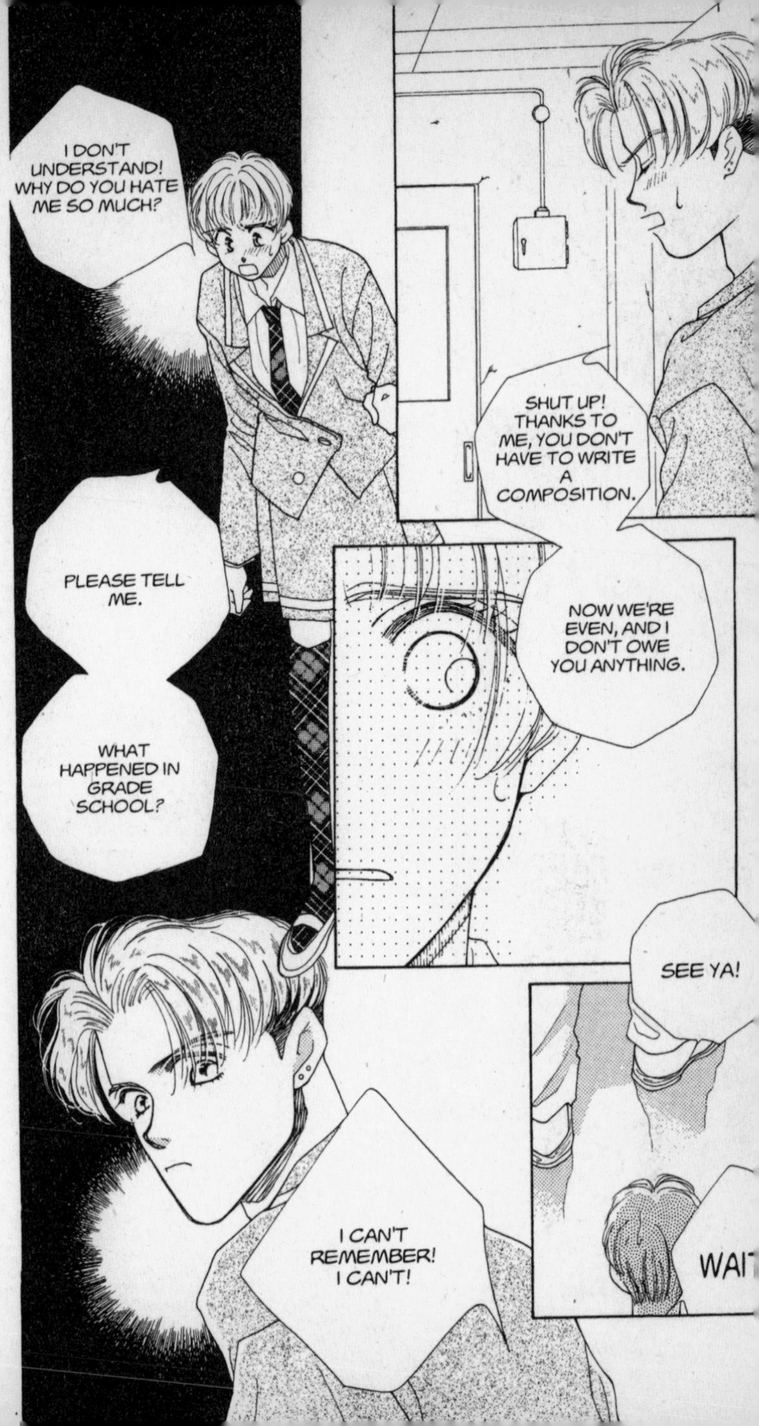
SHUT UP! THANKS TO ME, YOU DON'T HAVE TO WRITE A COMPOSITION.
NOW WE'RE EVEN, AND I DON'T OWE YOU ANYTHING.
SEE YA!
WAIT
I DON'T UNDERSTAND! WHY DO YOU HATE ME SO MUCH?
PLEASE TELL ME.
WHAT HAPPENED IN GRADE SCHOOL?
I CAN'T REMEMBER! I CAN'T!

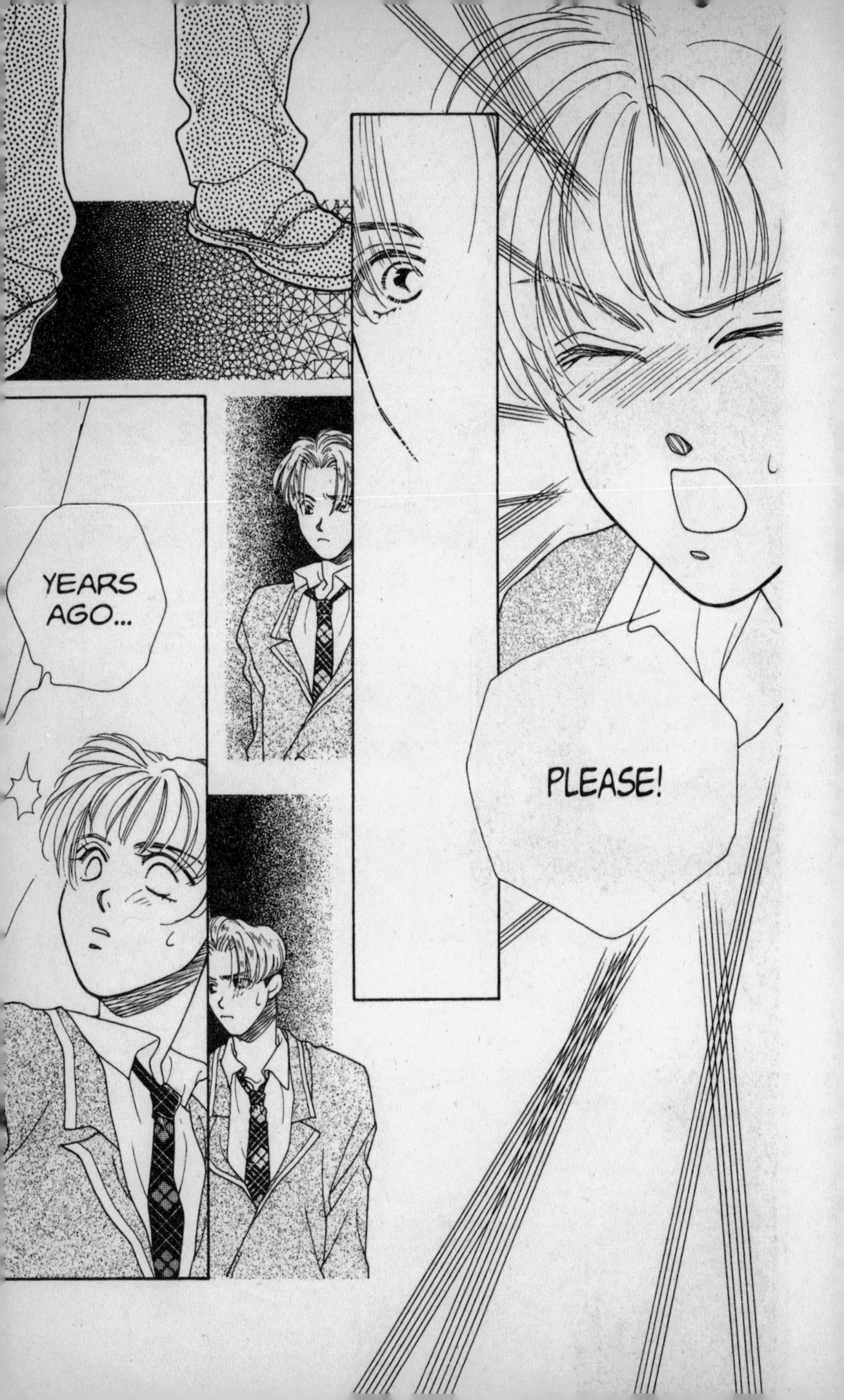
PLEASE!
YEARS AGO...

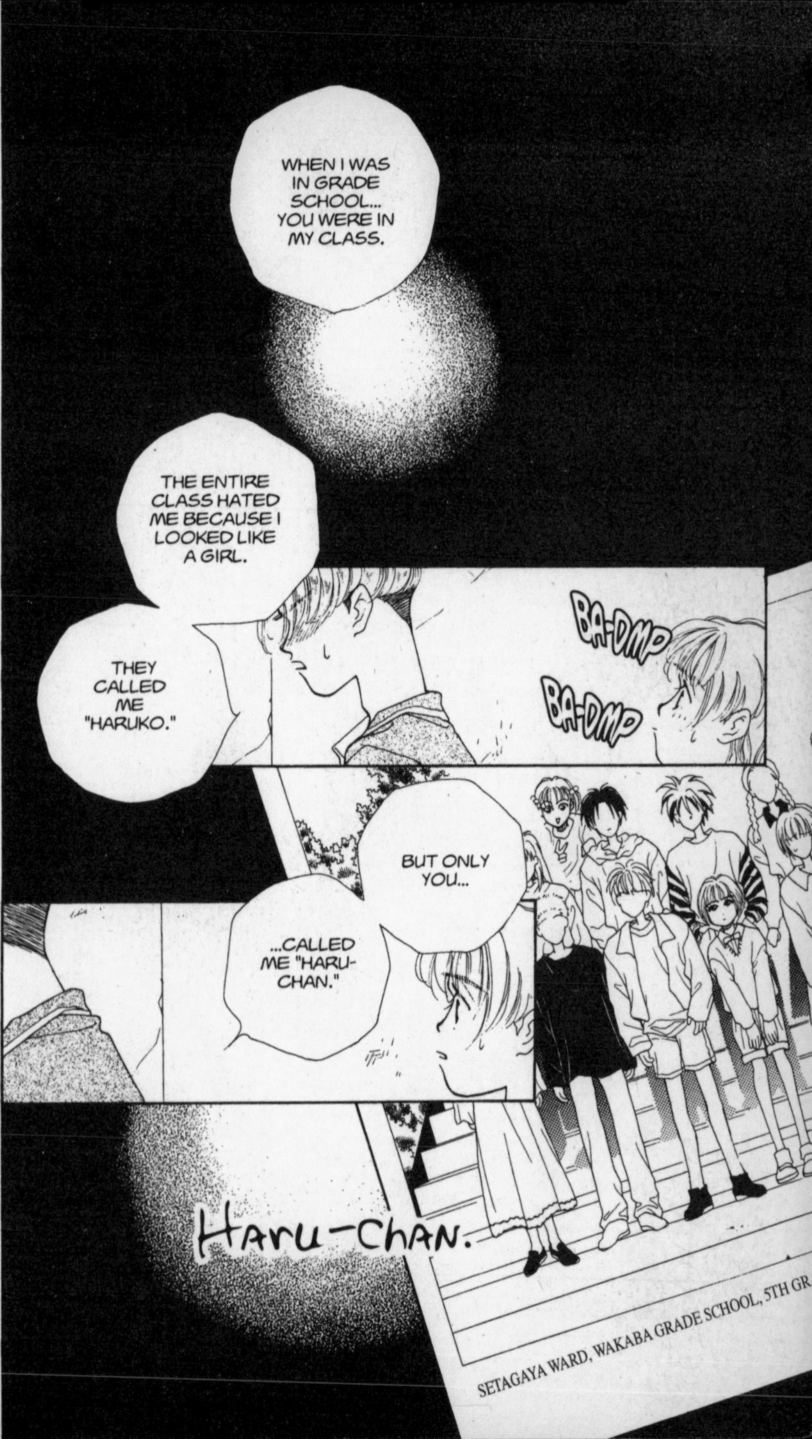
WHEN I WAS IN GRADE SCHOOL... YOU WERE IN MY CLASS.
THE ENTIRE CLASS HATED ME BECAUSE I LOOKED LIKE A GIRL.
BA-DMP
BA-DMP
THEY CALLED ME "HARUKO."
BUT ONLY YOU...
...CALLED ME "HARU-CHAN."
Haru-chan.
SETAGAYA WARD, WAKABA GRADE SCHOOL, 5TH GR

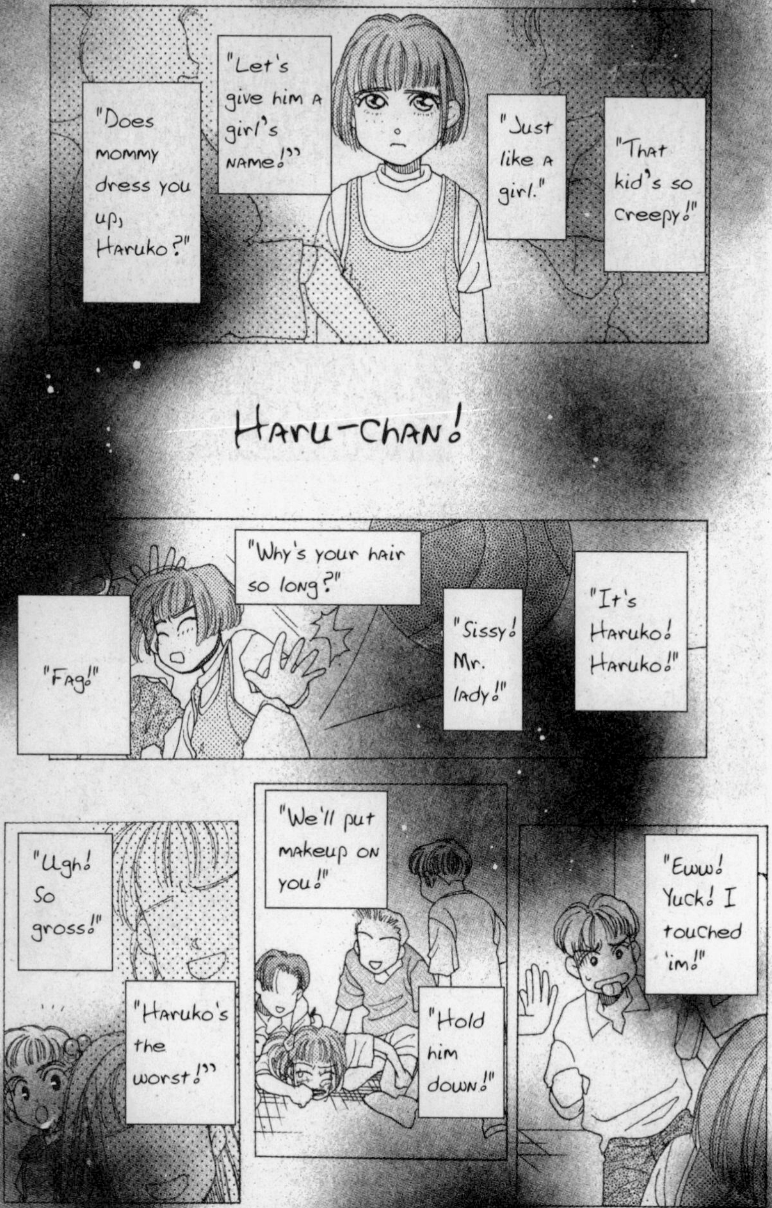
"That kid's so creepy!"
"Just like a girl."
"Let's give him a girl's name!"
"Does mommy dress you up, Haruko?"
Haru-chan!
"It's Haruko! Haruko!"
"Sissy! Mr. lady!"
"Why's your hair so long?"
"Fag!"
"Eww! Yuck! I touched 'im!"
"We'll put makeup on you!"
"Hold him down!"
"Ugh! So gross!"
"Haruko's the worst!"
...

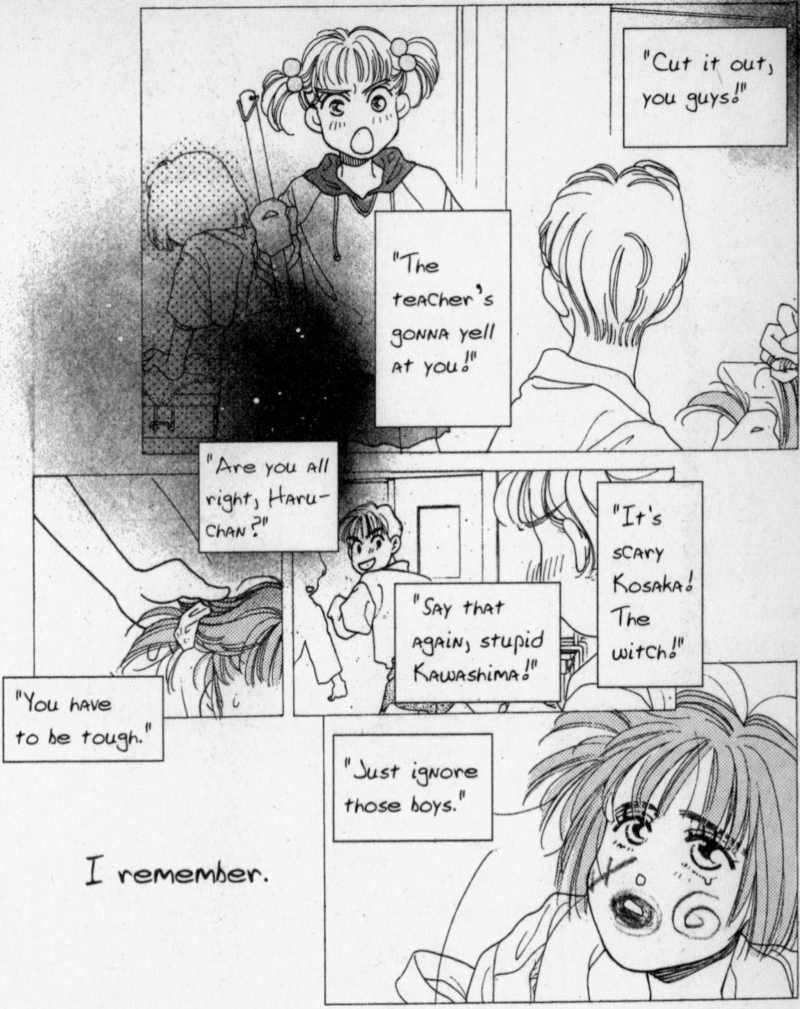
"Cut it out, you guys!"
"The teacher's gonna yell at you!"
"It's scary Kosaka! The witch!"
"Say that again, stupid Kawashima!"
"Are you all right, Haru-chan?"
"You have to be tough."
"Just ignore those boys."
I remember.

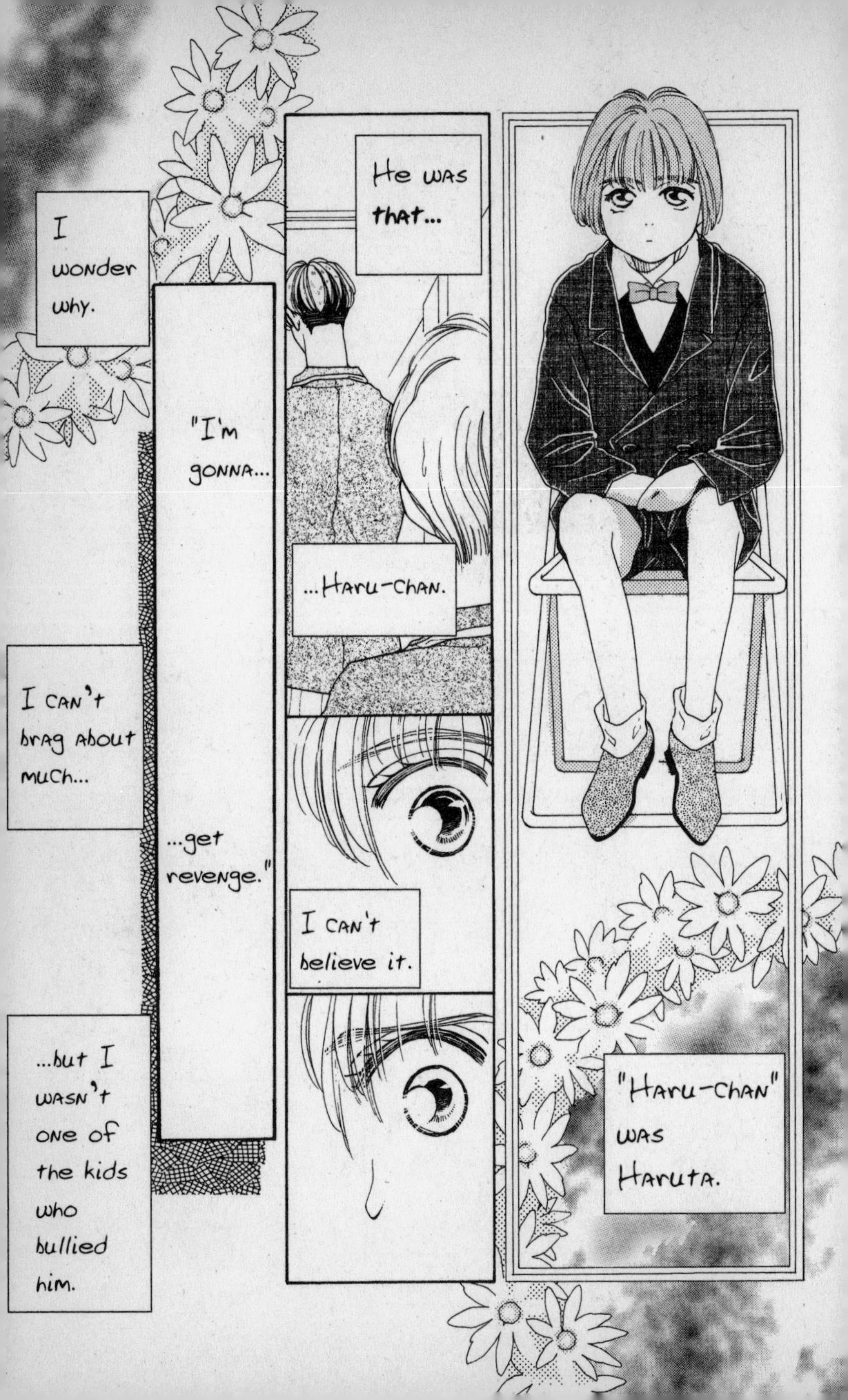
"Haru-chan" was Haruta.
He was that...
...Haru-chan.
I can't believe it.
"I'm gonna...
...get revenge."
I wonder why.
I can't brag about much...
...but I wasn't one of the kids who bullied him.

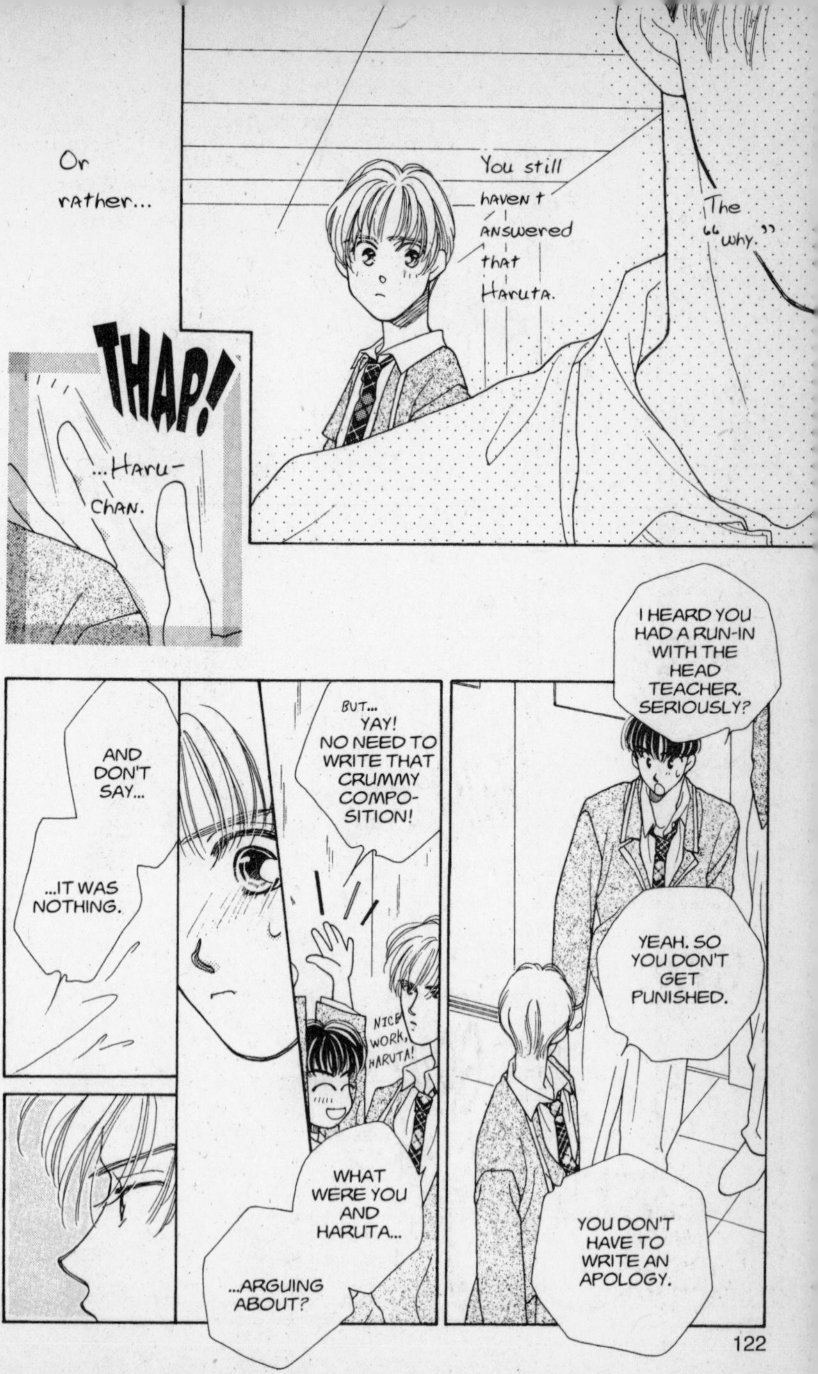

You still haven't answered that Haruta.
The "why."
Or rather...
THAP!
...Haru-chan.
I HEARD YOU HAD A RUN-IN WITH THE HEAD TEACHER. SERIOUSLY?
YEAH. SO YOU DON'T GET PUNISHED.
YOU DON'T HAVE TO WRITE AN APOLOGY.
BUT... YAY! NO NEED TO WRITE THAT CRUMMY COMPOSITION!
NICE WORK, HARUTA!
WHAT WERE YOU AND HARUTA...
...ARGUING ABOUT?
AND DON'T SAY...
...IT WAS NOTHING.

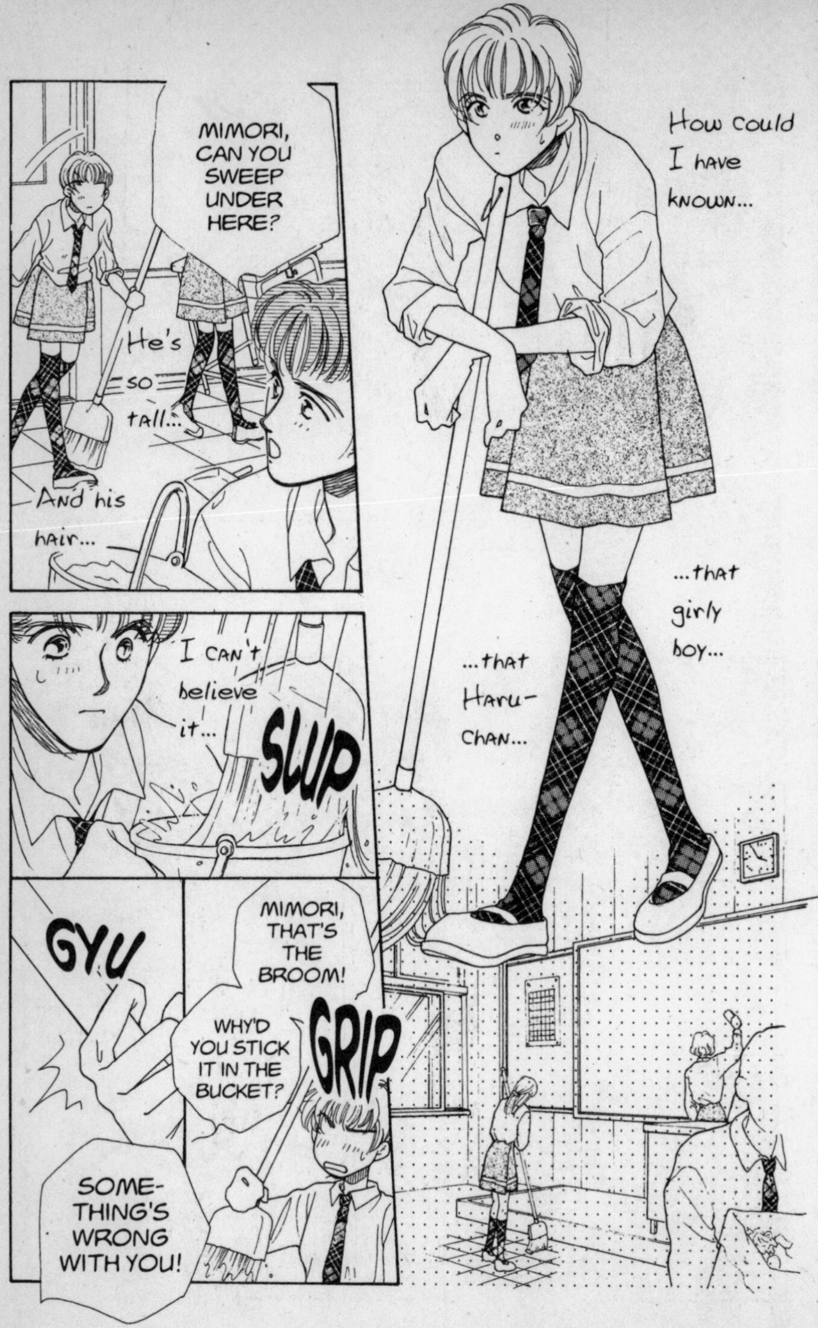
How could I have known...
...that girly boy...
...that Haru-chan...
MIMORI, CAN YOU SWEEP UNDER HERE?
He's so tall...
And his hair...
I can't believe it...
SLUP
MIMORI, THAT'S THE BROOM!
WHY'D YOU STICK IT IN THE BUCKET?
GRIP
GYU
SOME-THING'S WRONG WITH YOU!

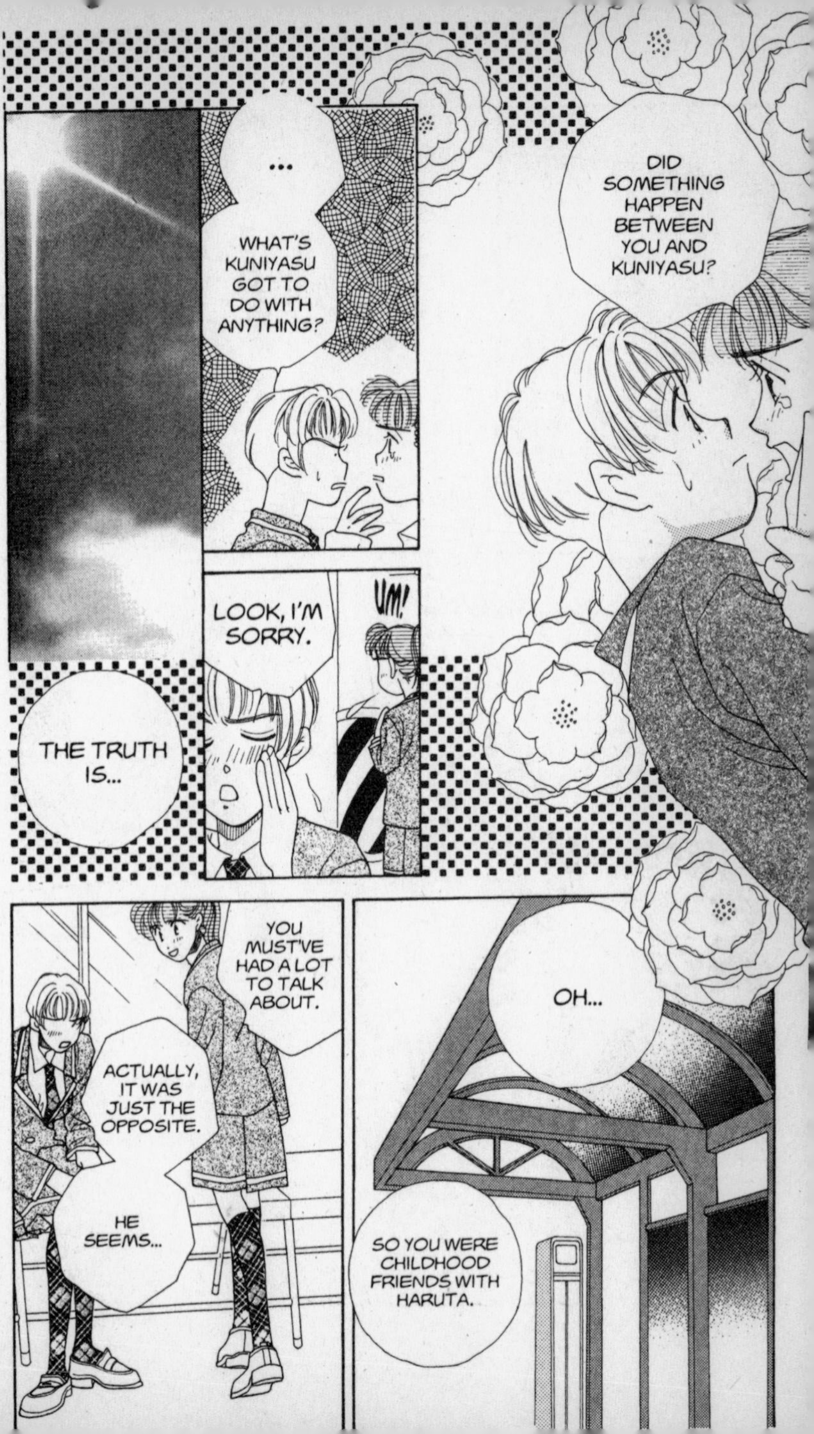
DID SOMETHING HAPPEN BETWEEN YOU AND KUNIYASU?
...
WHAT'S KUNIYASU GOT TO DO WITH ANYTHING?
UM!
LOOK, I'M SORRY.
THE TRUTH IS...
OH...
SO YOU WERE CHILDHOOD FRIENDS WITH HARUTA.
YOU MUST'VE HAD A LOT TO TALK ABOUT.
ACTUALLY, IT WAS JUST THE OPPOSITE.
HE SEEMS...

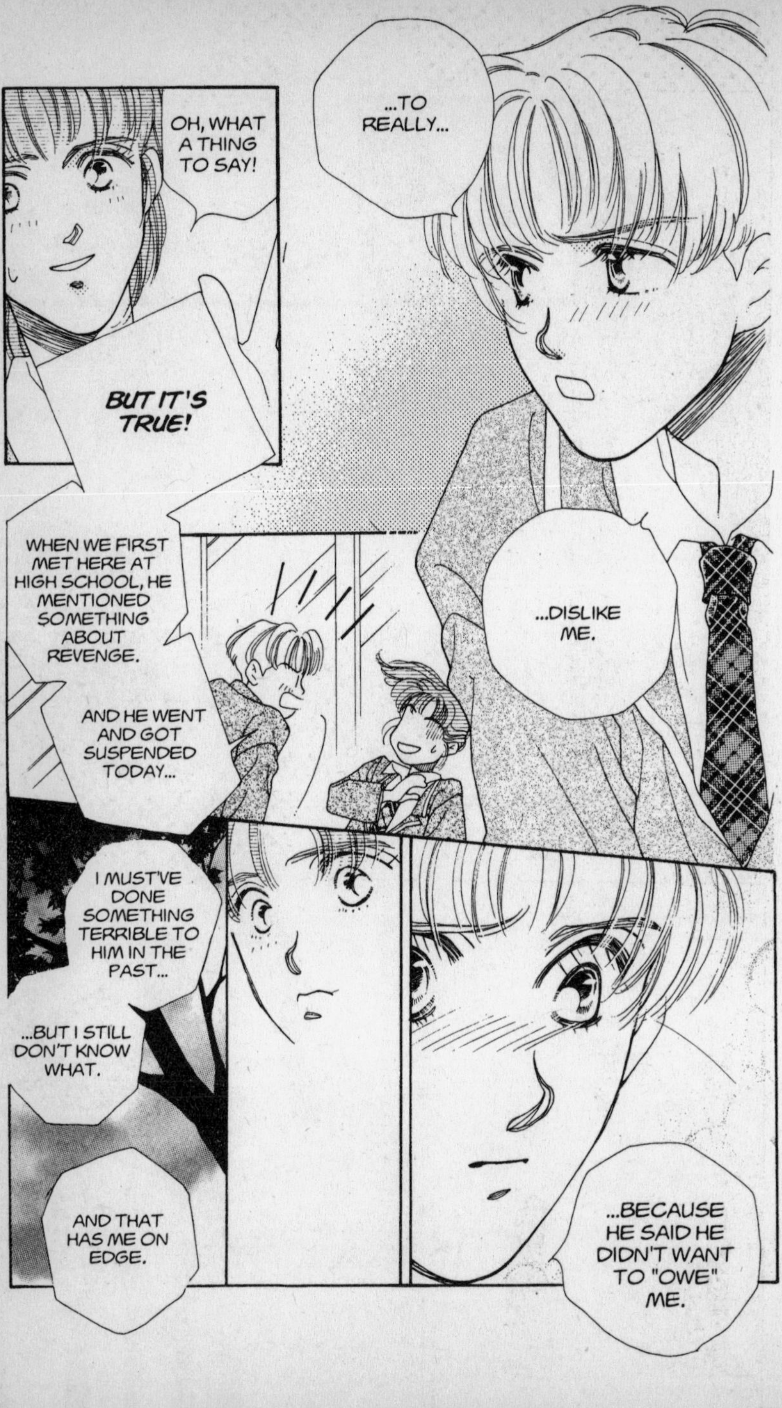
...TO REALLY...
...DISLIKE ME.
OH, WHAT A THING TO SAY!
BUT IT'S TRUE!
WHEN WE FIRST MET HERE AT HIGH SCHOOL, HE MENTIONED SOMETHING ABOUT REVENGE.
AND HE WENT AND GOT SUSPENDED TODAY...
...BECAUSE HE SAID HE DIDN'T WANT TO "OWE" ME.
I MUST'VE DONE SOMETHING TERRIBLE TO HIM IN THE PAST...
...BUT I STILL DON'T KNOW WHAT.
AND THAT HAS ME ON EDGE.

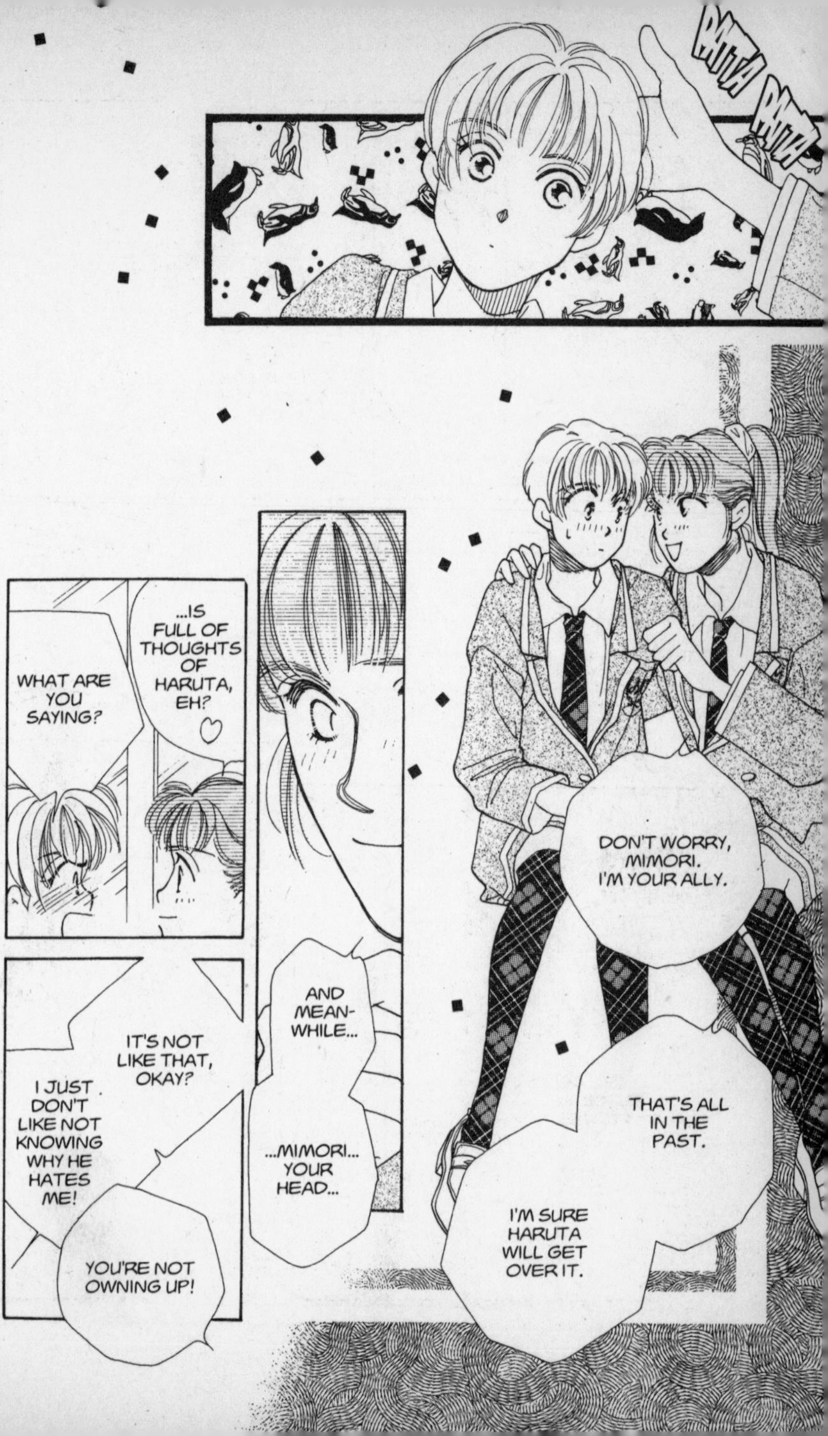
PATA PATA
DON'T WORRY, MIMORI. I'M YOUR ALLY.
THAT'S ALL IN THE PAST.
I'M SURE HARUTA WILL GET OVER IT.
AND MEAN-WHILE...
...MIMORI... YOUR HEAD...
...IS FULL OF THOUGHTS OF HARUTA, EH? ♡
WHAT ARE YOU SAYING?
IT'S NOT LIKE THAT, OKAY?
I JUST DON'T LIKE NOT KNOWING WHY HE HATES ME!
YOU'RE NOT OWNING UP!

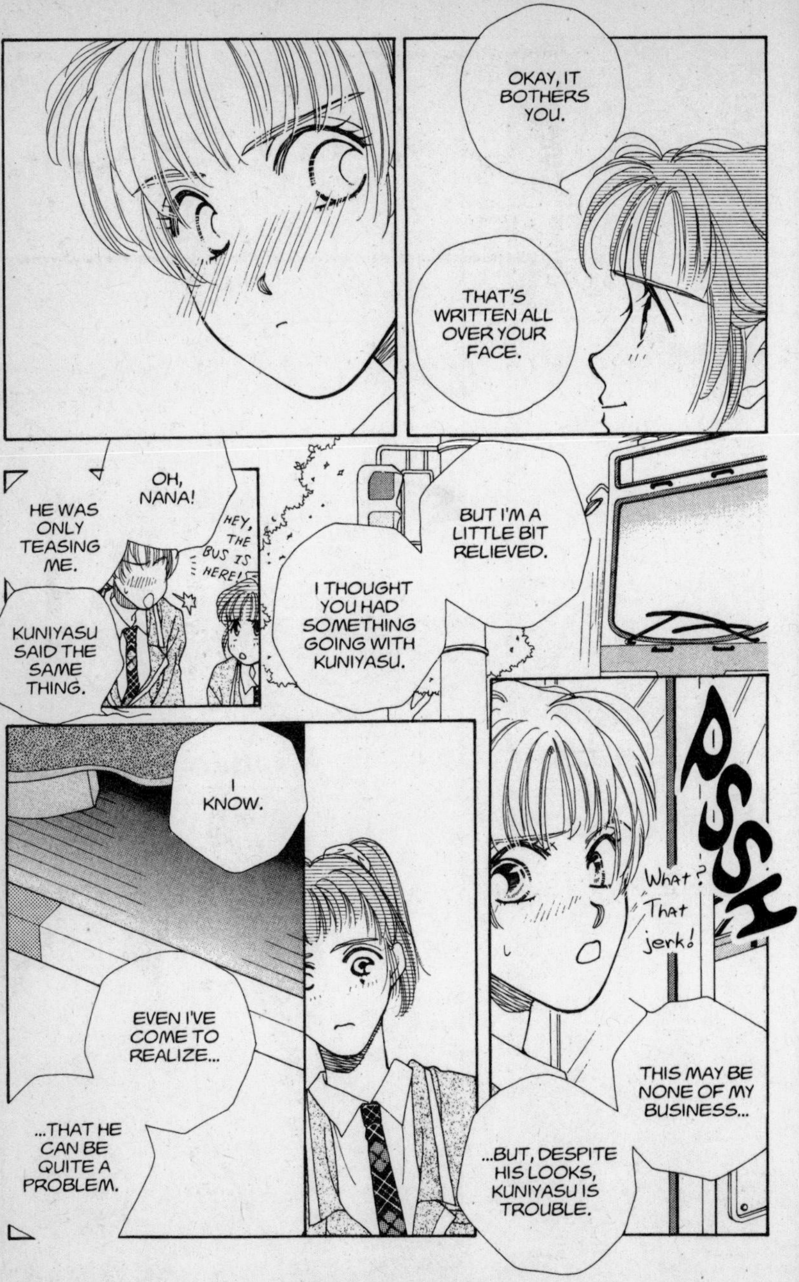
OKAY, IT BOTHERS YOU.
THAT'S WRITTEN ALL OVER YOUR FACE.
BUT I'M A LITTLE BIT RELIEVED.
I THOUGHT YOU HAD SOMETHING GOING WITH KUNIYASU.
OH, NANA!
HEY, THE BUS IS HERE!
HE WAS ONLY TEASING ME.
KUNIYASU SAID THE SAME THING.
PSSH!
What? That jerk!
THIS MAY BE NONE OF MY BUSINESS...
...BUT, DESPITE HIS LOOKS, KUNIYASU IS TROUBLE.
I KNOW.
EVEN I'VE COME TO REALIZE...
...THAT HE CAN BE QUITE A PROBLEM.

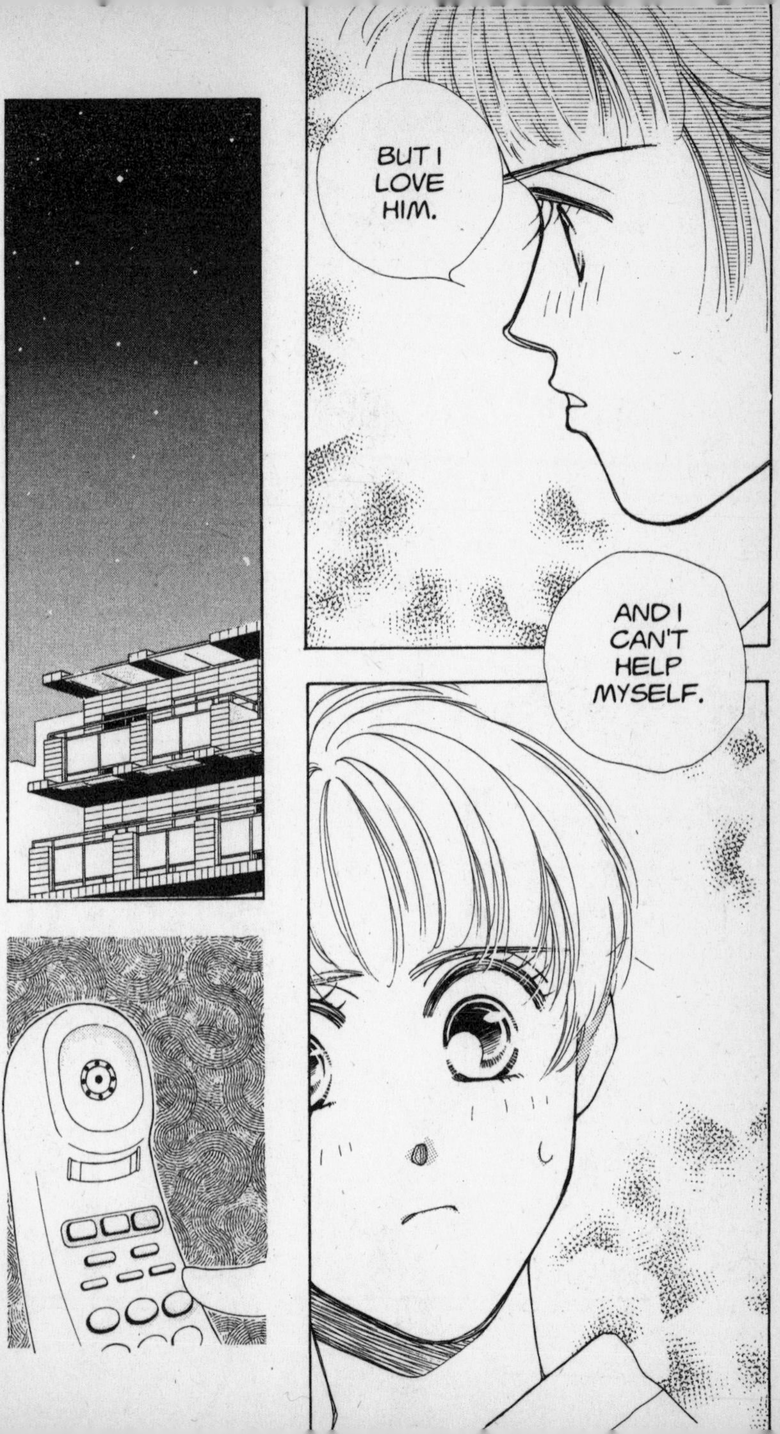
BUT I LOVE HIM.
AND I CAN'T HELP MYSELF.

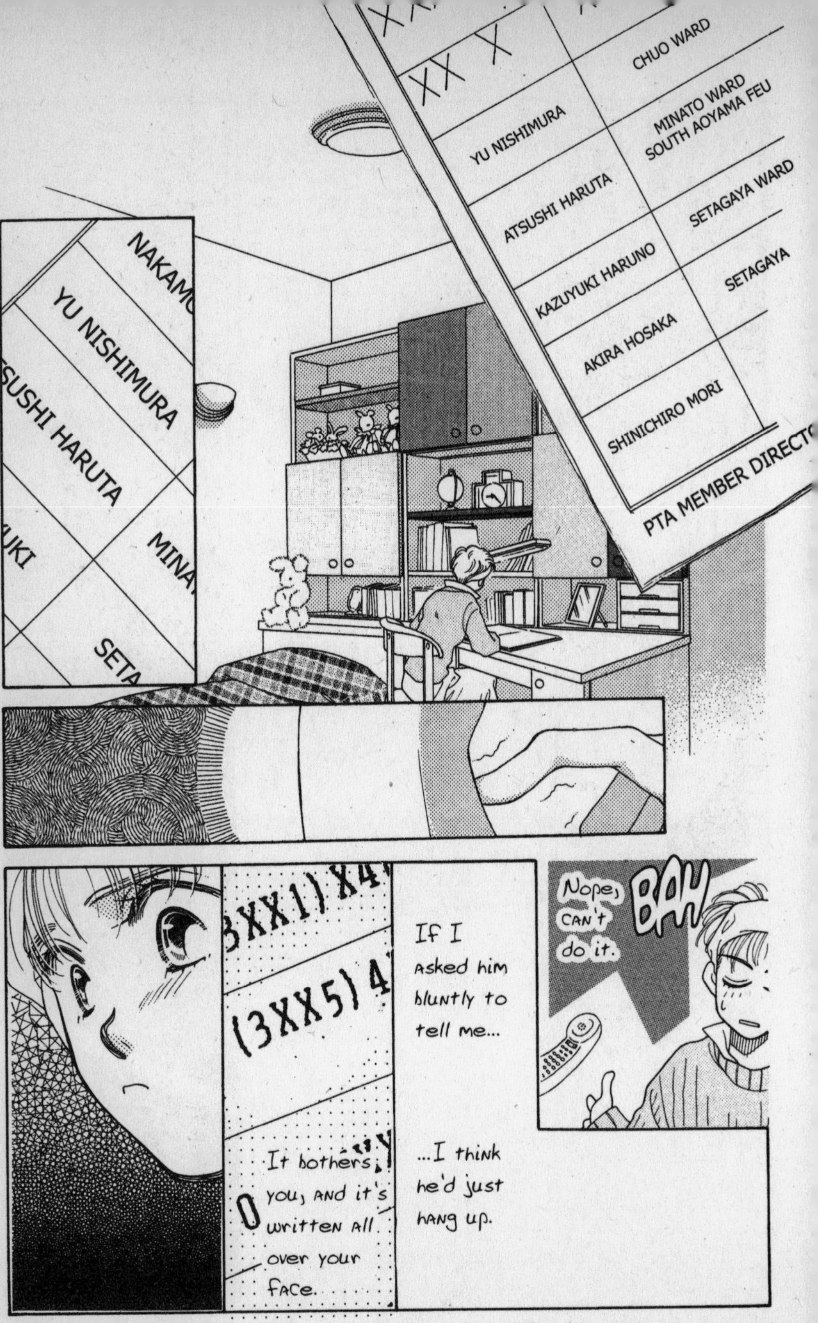
CHUO WARD
YU NISHIMURA
MINATO WARD SOUTH AOYAMA FEU
ATSUSHI HARUTA
SETAGAYA WARD
KAZUYUKI HARUNO
SETAGAYA
AKIRA HOSAKA
SHINICHIRO MORI
PTA MEMBER
YU NISHIMURA
Nope, can't do it.
BAH
If I asked him bluntly to tell me...
...I think he'd just hang up.
It bothers you, and it's written all over your face.

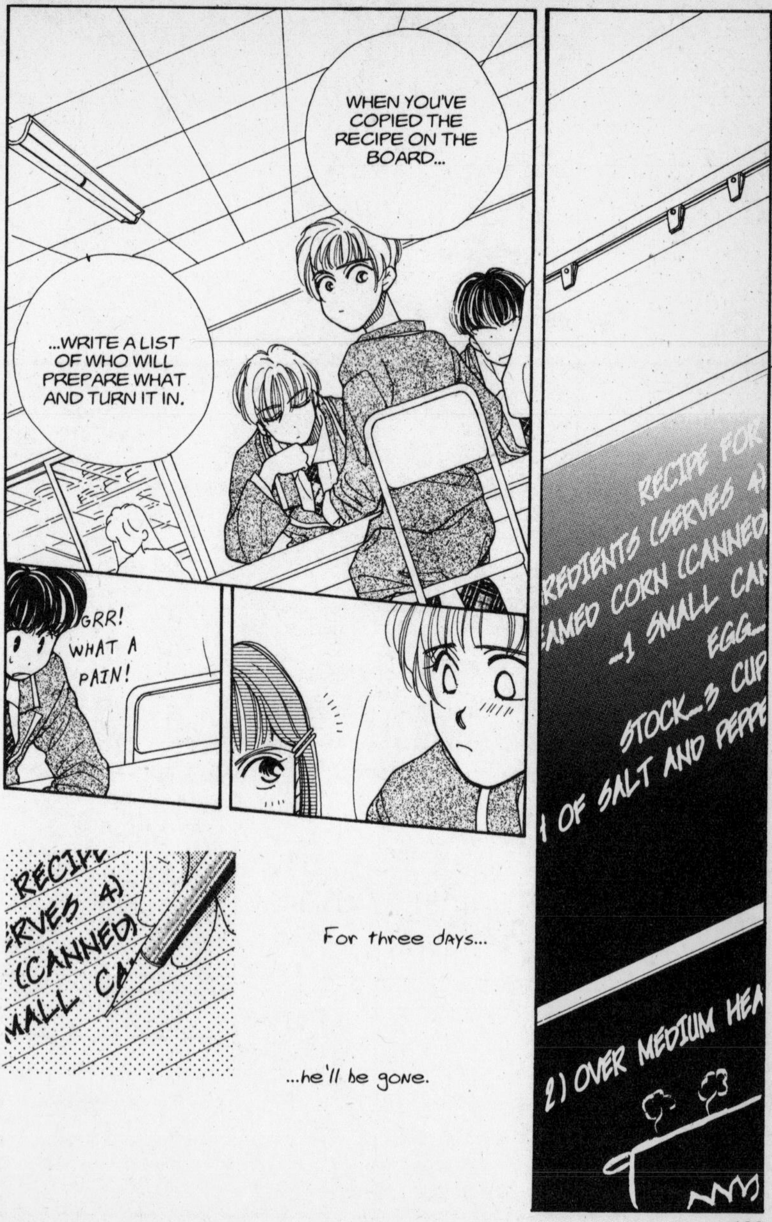
RECIPE FOR
REDIENTS (SERVES 4)
EAMED CORN (CANNED)
—1 SMALL CA
EGG...
STOCK...3 CUP
OF SALT AND PEPPE
2) OVER MEDIUM HEA
WHEN YOU'VE COPIED THE RECIPE ON THE BOARD...
...WRITE A LIST OF WHO WILL PREPARE WHAT AND TURN IT IN.
GRR! WHAT A PAIN!
For three days...
...he'll be gone.
RECI
ERVES 4)
(CANNED)
MALL CA

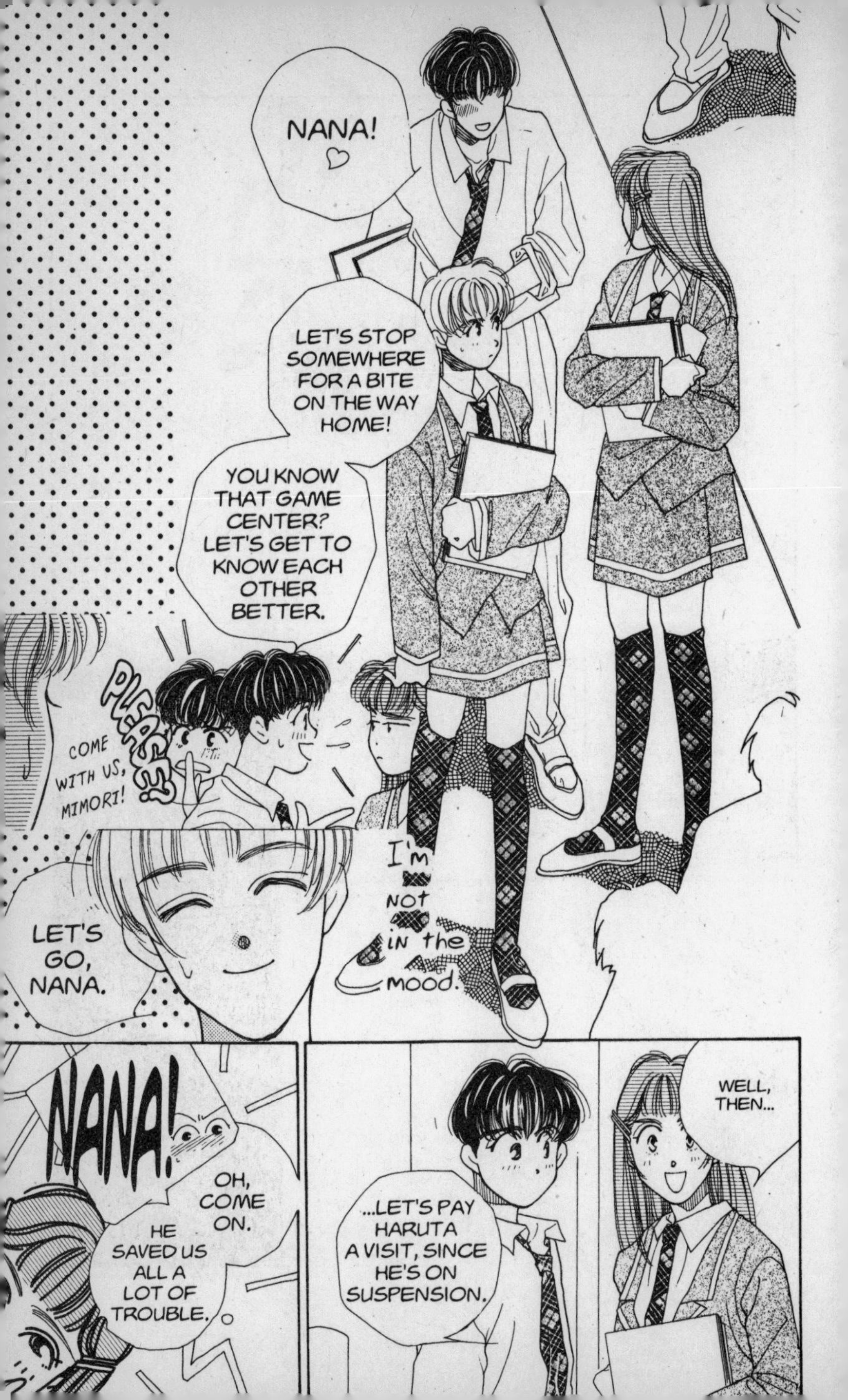

NANA! ♡
LET'S STOP SOMEWHERE FOR A BITE ON THE WAY HOME!
YOU KNOW THAT GAME CENTER? LET'S GET TO KNOW EACH OTHER BETTER.
I'm not in the mood.
PLEASE!
COME WITH US, MIMORI!
LET'S GO, NANA.
WELL, THEN...
...LET'S PAY HARUTA A VISIT, SINCE HE'S ON SUSPENSION.
NANA!
OH, COME ON.
HE SAVED US ALL A LOT OF TROUBLE.

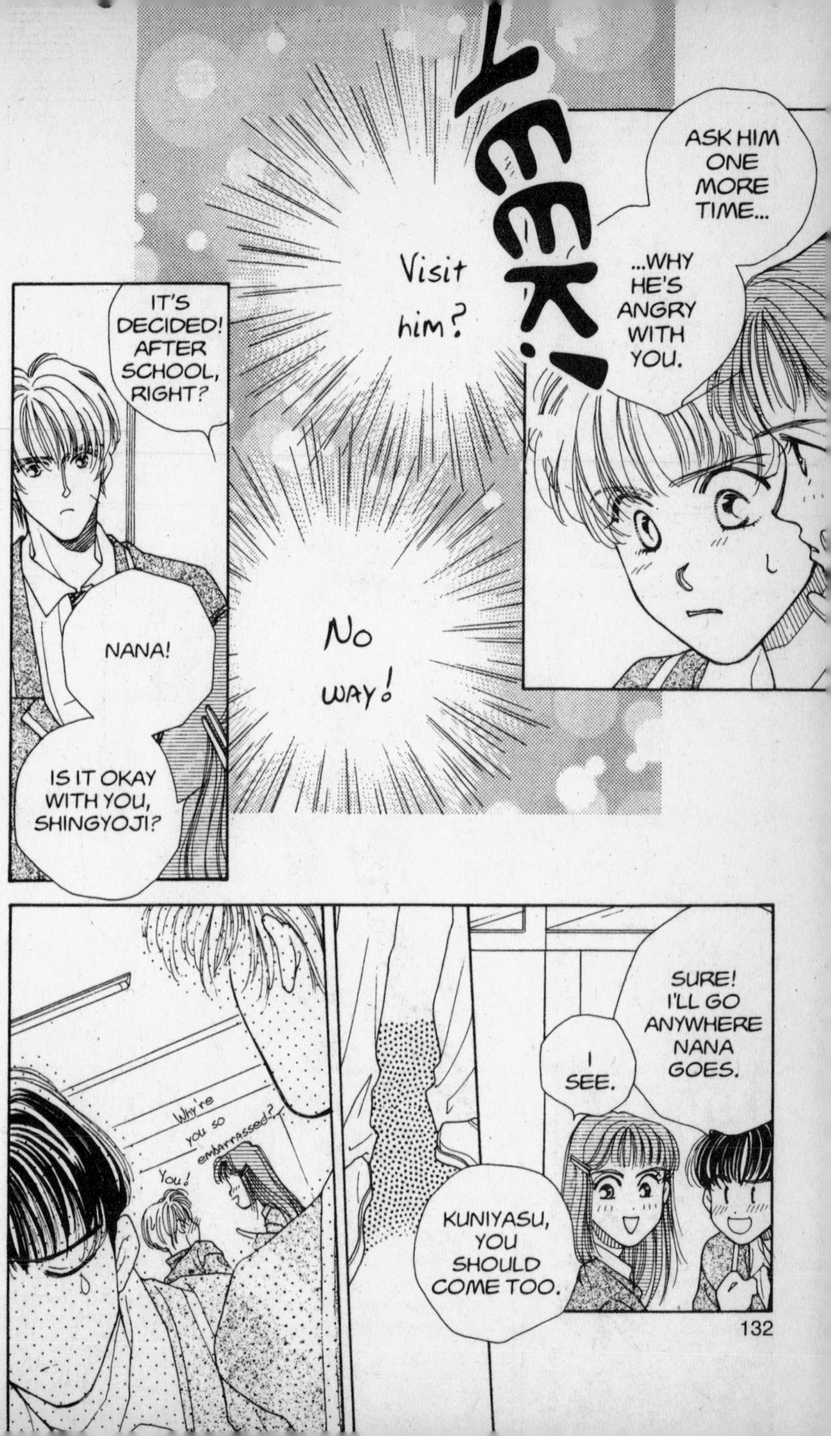
ASK HIM ONE MORE TIME...
...WHY HE'S ANGRY WITH YOU.
YEEK!
Visit him?
No way!
IT'S DECIDED! AFTER SCHOOL, RIGHT?
NANA!
IS IT OKAY WITH YOU, SHINGYOJI?
SURE! I'LL GO ANYWHERE NANA GOES.
I SEE.
KUNIYASU, YOU SHOULD COME TOO.
Why're you so embarrassed?
You!

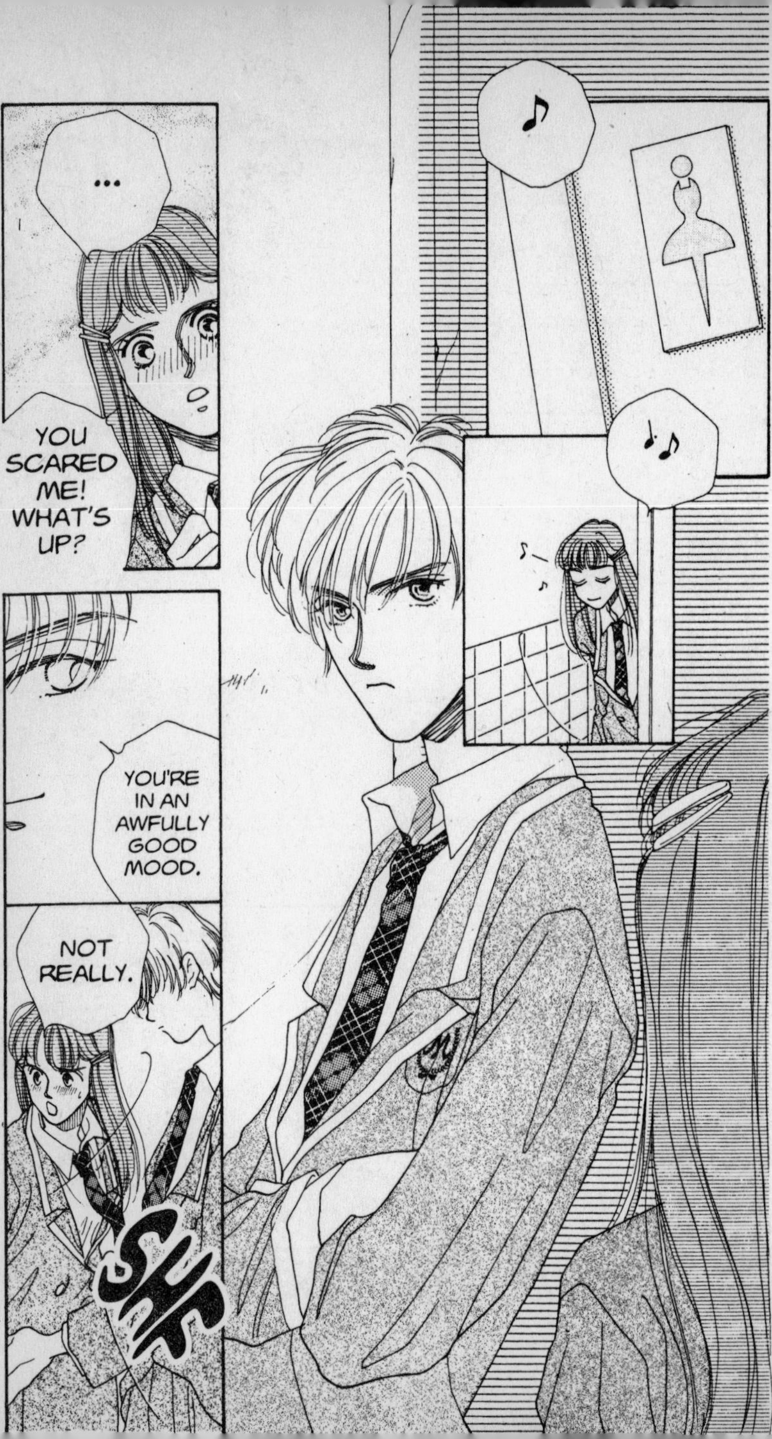
♪
♪♪
...
YOU SCARED ME! WHAT'S UP?
YOU'RE IN AN AWFULLY GOOD MOOD.
NOT REALLY.
SHF

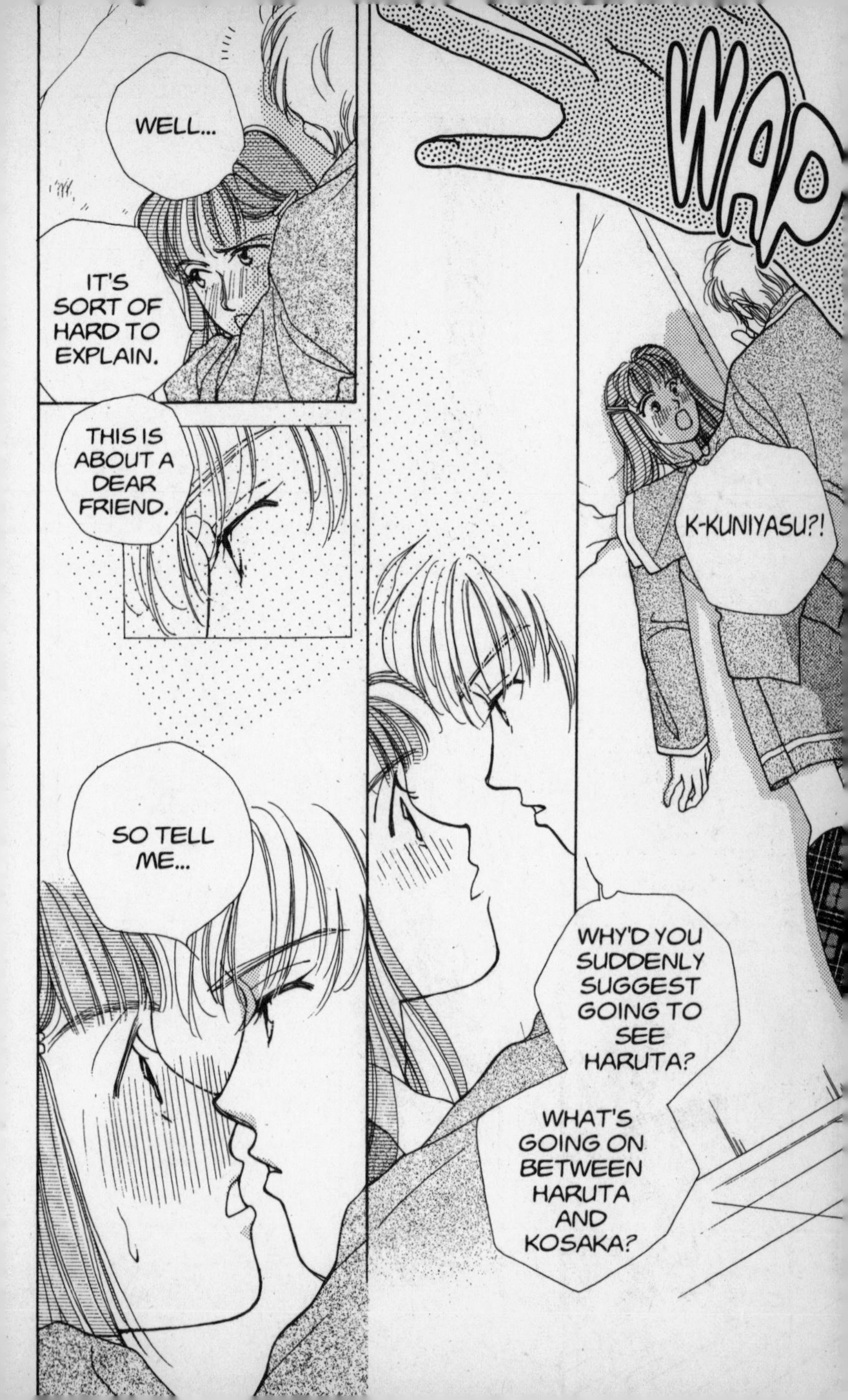
WAP
K-KUNIYASU?!
WHY'D YOU SUDDENLY SUGGEST GOING TO SEE HARUTA?
WHAT'S GOING ON BETWEEN HARUTA AND KOSAKA?
WELL...
IT'S SORT OF HARD TO EXPLAIN.
THIS IS ABOUT A DEAR FRIEND.
SO TELL ME...

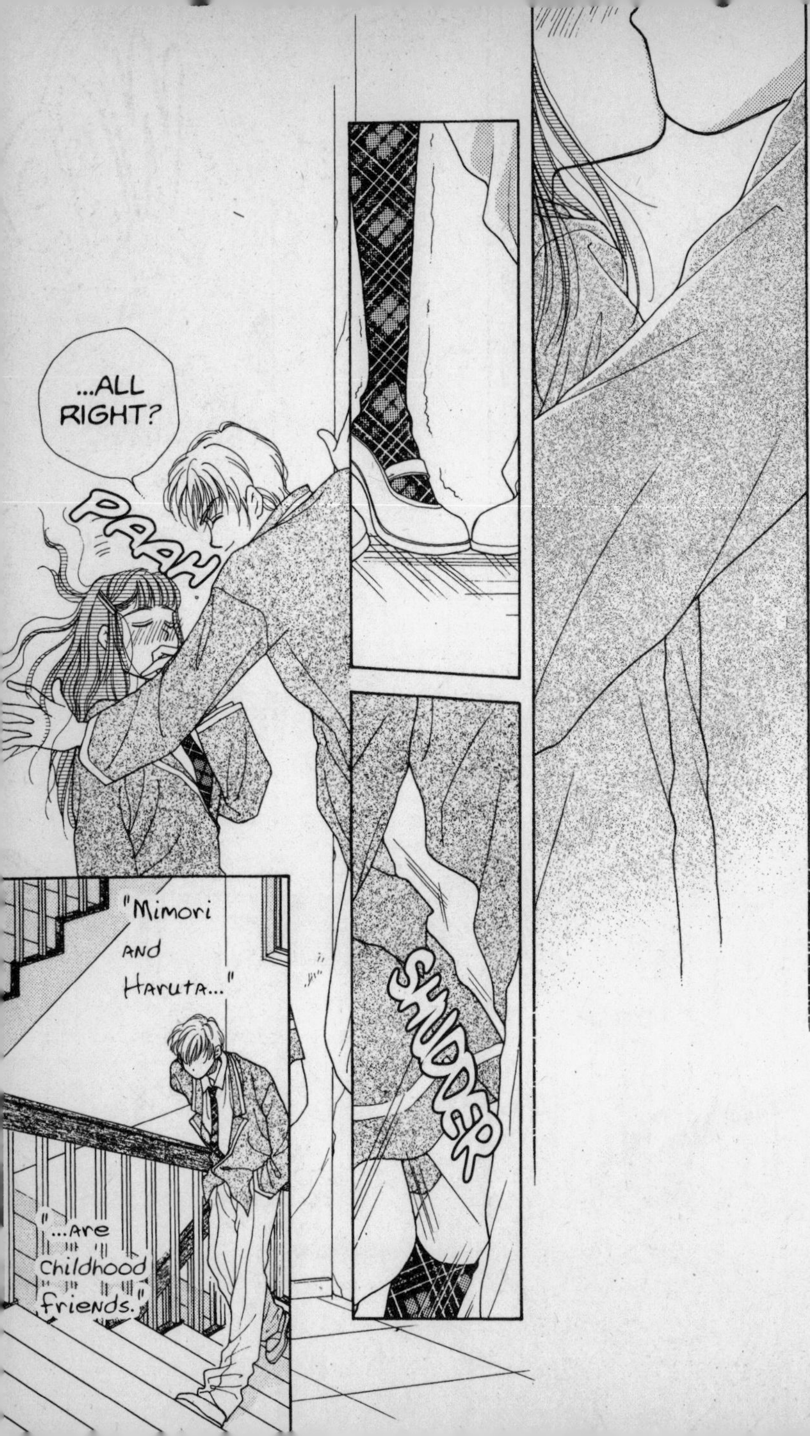
SHUDDER
...ALL RIGHT?
PAAH
"Mimori and Haruta..."
"...are childhood friends."

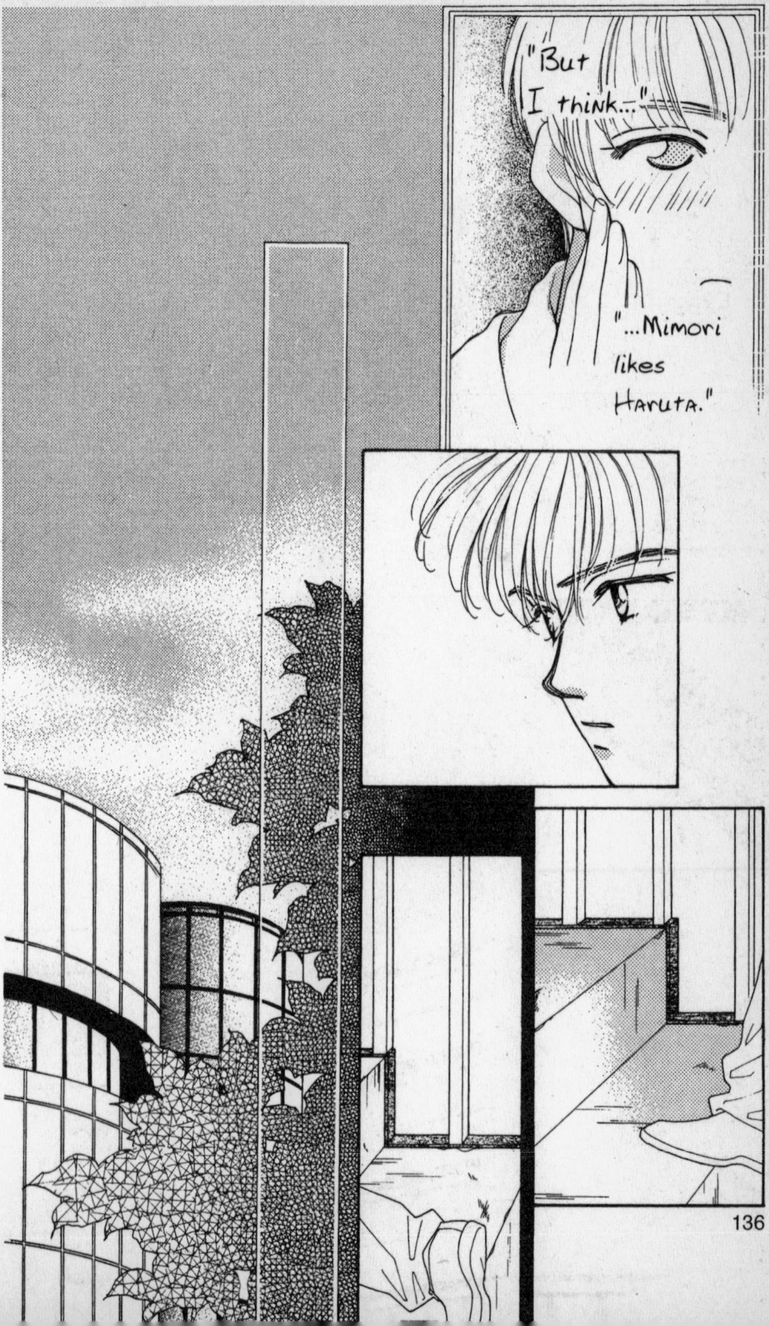
"But I think..."
"...Mimori likes Haruta."

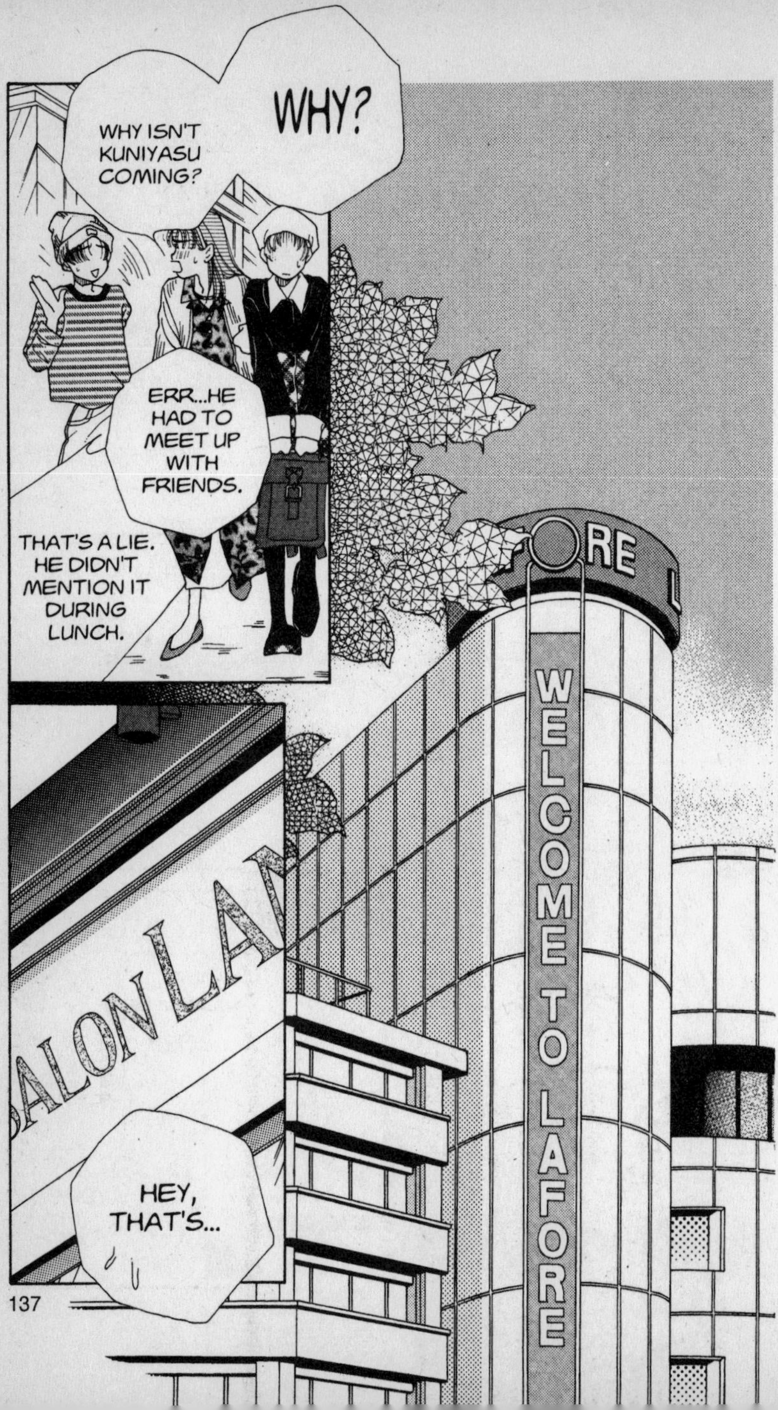
WHY?
WHY ISN'T KUNIYASU COMING?
ERR...HE HAD TO MEET UP WITH FRIENDS.
THAT'S A LIE. HE DIDN'T MENTION IT DURING LUNCH.
WELCOME TO LAFORE
SALON LA
HEY, THAT'S...

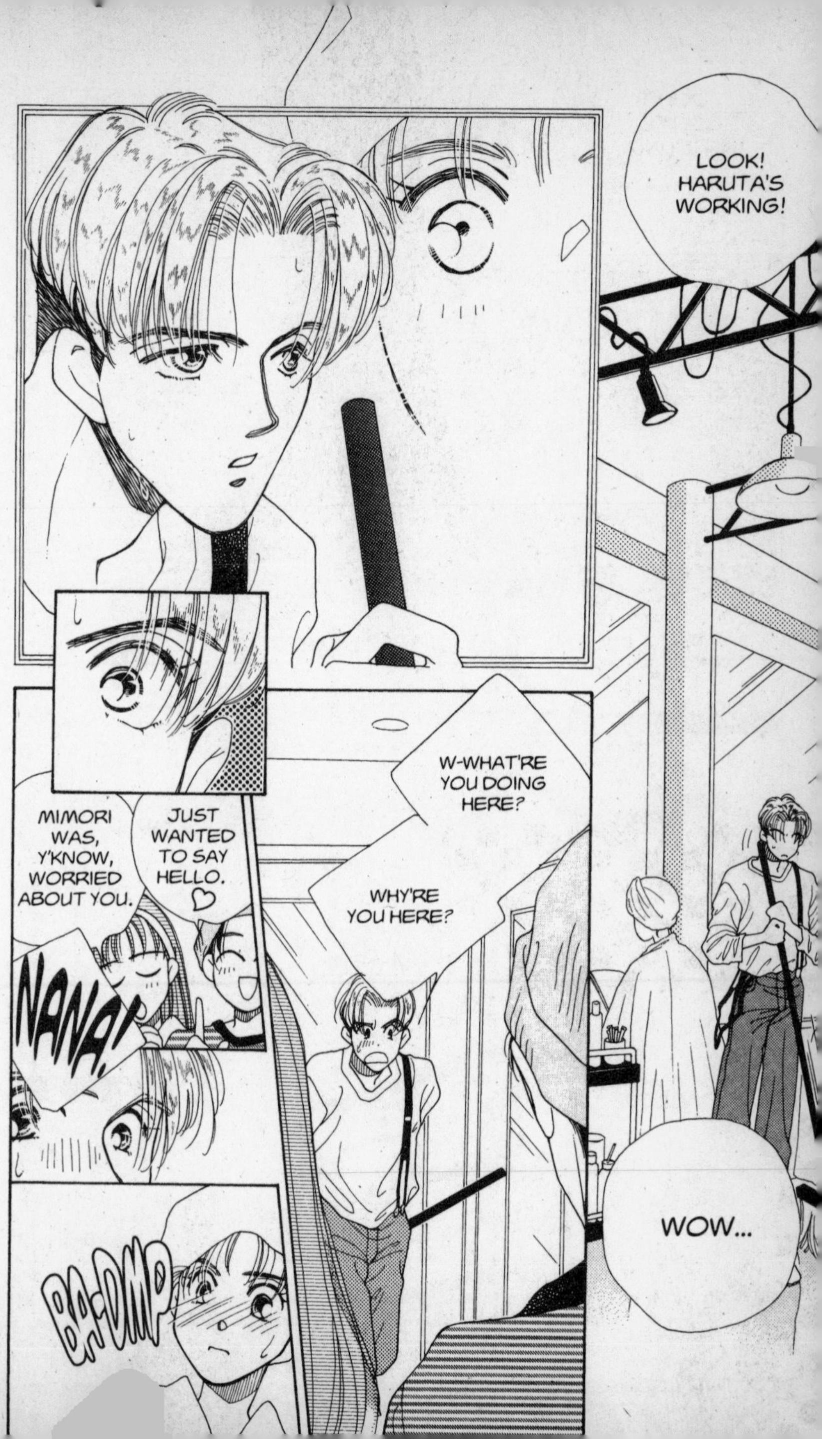
LOOK! HARUTA'S WORKING!
WOW...
W-WHAT'RE YOU DOING HERE?
WHY'RE YOU HERE?
JUST WANTED TO SAY HELLO. ♡
MIMORI WAS, Y'KNOW, WORRIED ABOUT YOU.
NANA!
BA-DMP

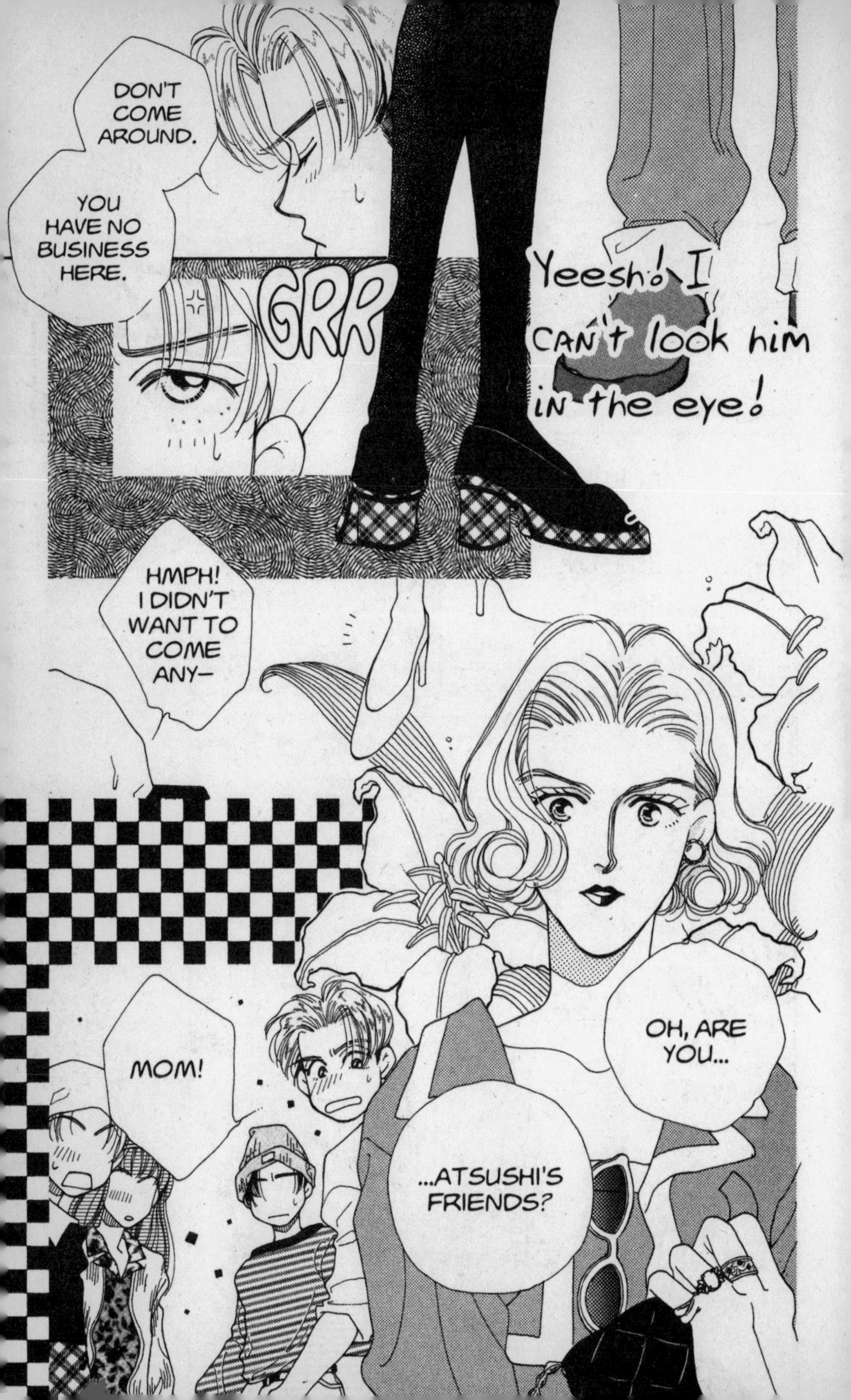
DON'T COME AROUND.
YOU HAVE NO BUSINESS HERE.
Yeesh! I CAN'T look him in the eye!
GRR
HMPH! I DIDN'T WANT TO COME ANY-
OH, ARE YOU...
...ATSUSHI'S FRIENDS?
MOM!

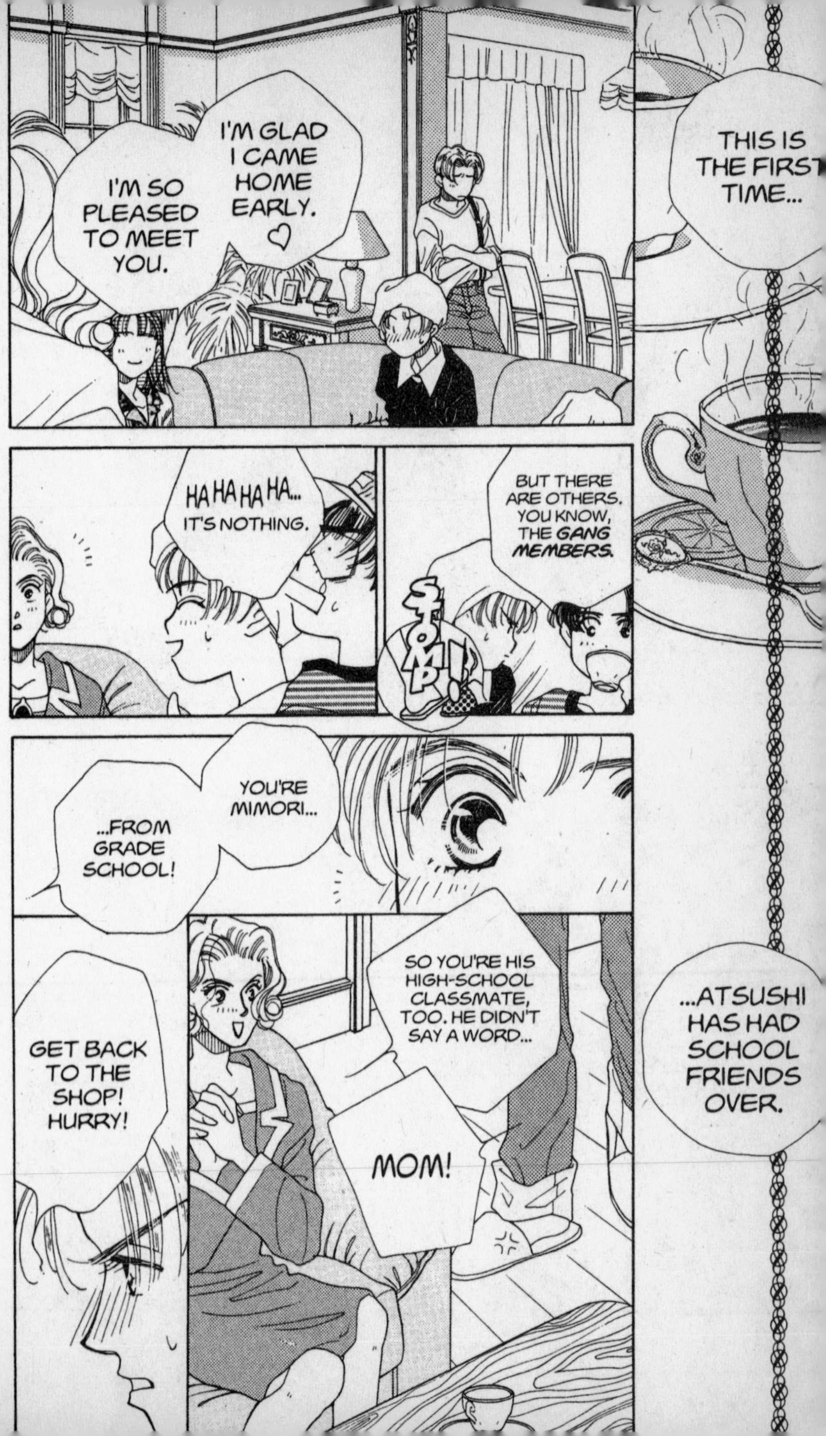
THIS IS THE FIRST TIME...
...ATSUSHI HAS HAD SCHOOL FRIENDS OVER.
I'M GLAD I CAME HOME EARLY. ♡
I'M SO PLEASED TO MEET YOU.
BUT THERE ARE OTHERS. YOU KNOW, THE GANG MEMBERS.
STOMP!
HA HA HA HA... IT'S NOTHING.
YOU'RE MIMORI...
...FROM GRADE SCHOOL!
SO YOU'RE HIS HIGH-SCHOOL CLASSMATE, TOO. HE DIDN'T SAY A WORD...
MOM!
GET BACK TO THE SHOP! HURRY!

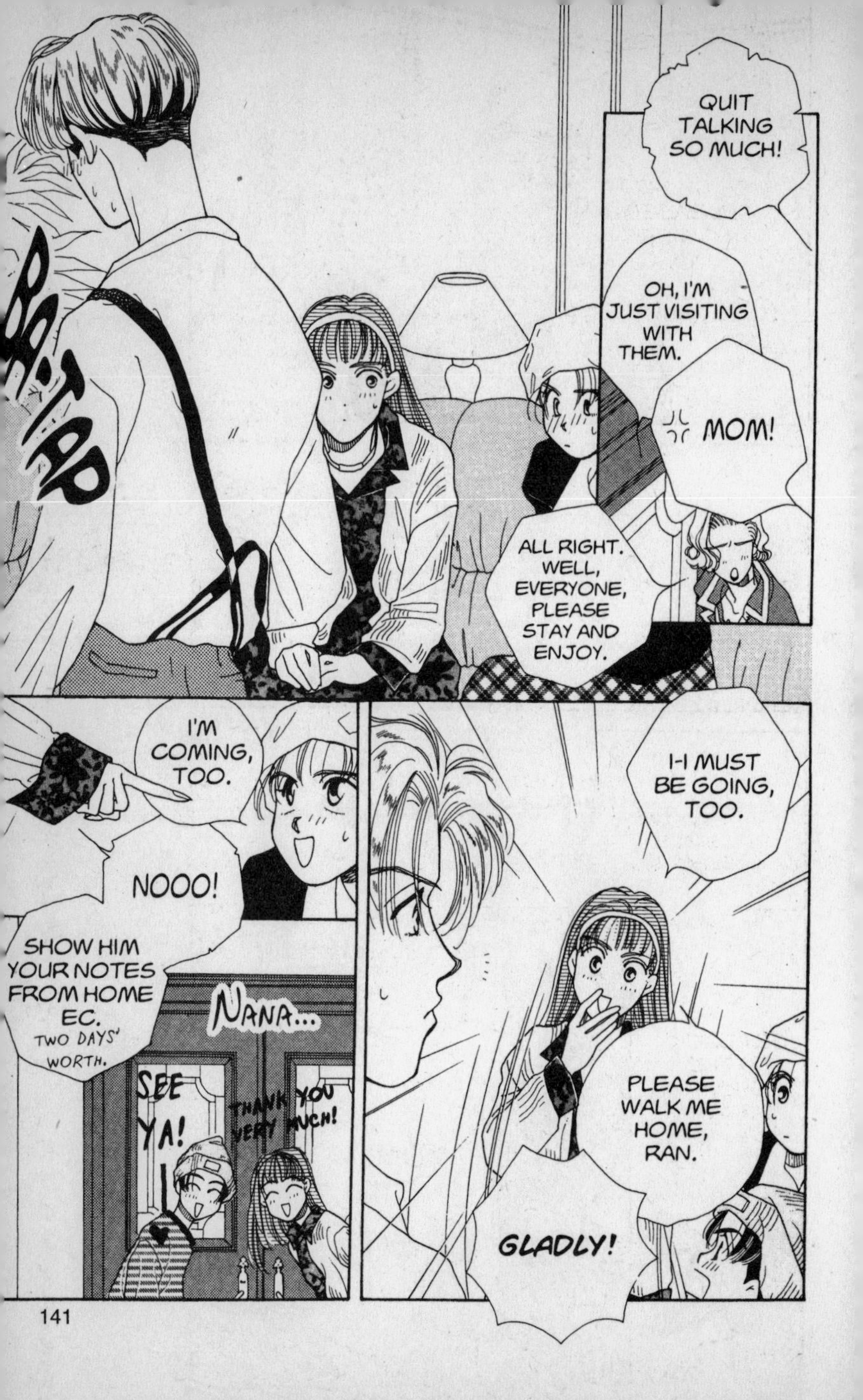
QUIT TALKING SO MUCH!
OH, I'M JUST VISITING WITH THEM.
MOM!
ALL RIGHT. WELL, EVERYONE, PLEASE STAY AND ENJOY.
BAP-TAP
I-I MUST BE GOING, TOO.
PLEASE WALK ME HOME, RAN.
GLADLY!
I'M COMING, TOO.
NOOO!
SHOW HIM YOUR NOTES FROM HOME EC. TWO DAYS' WORTH.
NANA...
THANK YOU VERY MUCH!
SEE YA!

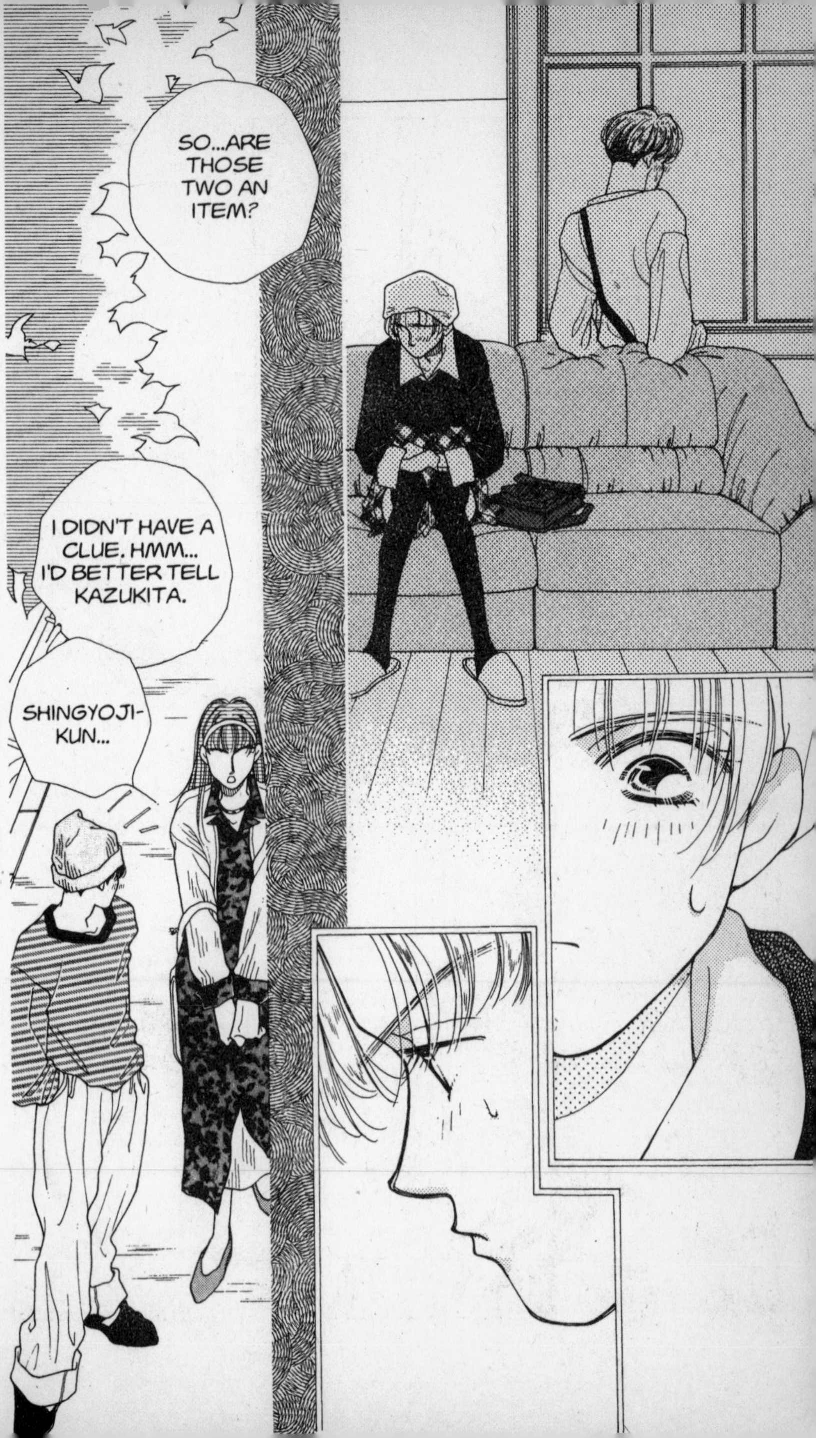
SO...ARE THOSE TWO AN ITEM?
I DIDN'T HAVE A CLUE. HMM... I'D BETTER TELL KAZUKITA.
SHINGYOJI-KUN...

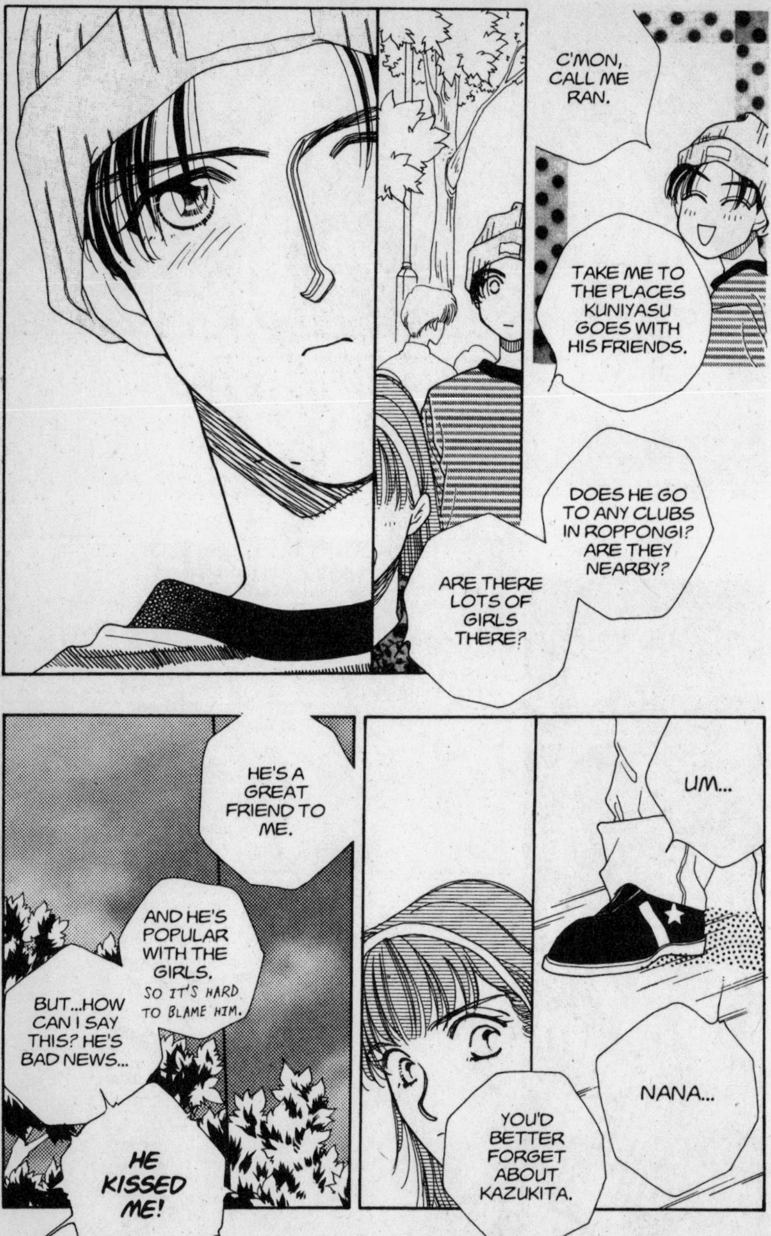
C'MON, CALL ME RAN.
TAKE ME TO THE PLACES KUNIYASU GOES WITH HIS FRIENDS.
DOES HE GO TO ANY CLUBS IN ROPPONGI? ARE THEY NEARBY?
ARE THERE LOTS OF GIRLS THERE?
UM...
NANA...
YOU'D BETTER FORGET ABOUT KAZUKITA.
HE'S A GREAT FRIEND TO ME.
AND HE'S POPULAR WITH THE GIRLS.
SO IT'S HARD TO BLAME HIM.
BUT...HOW CAN I SAY THIS? HE'S BAD NEWS...
HE KISSED ME!

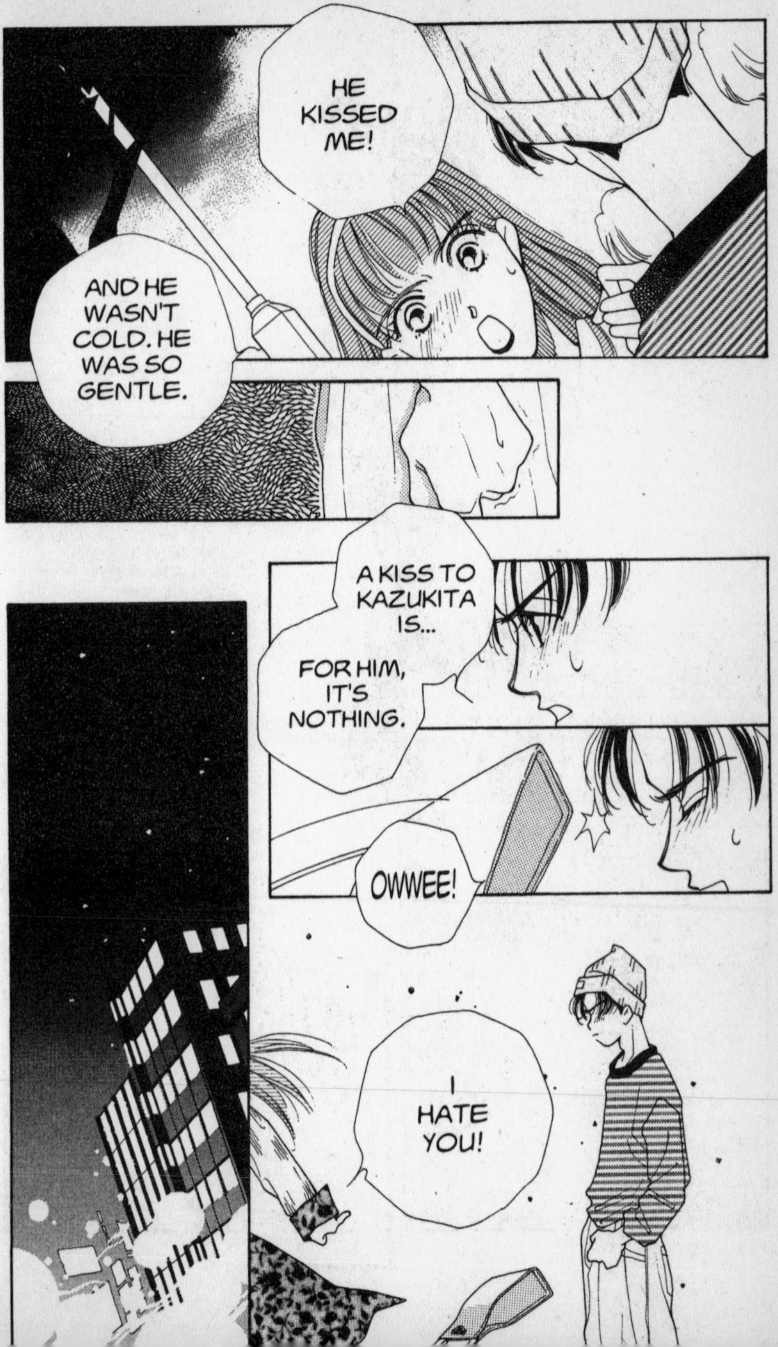
HE KISSED ME!
AND HE WASN'T COLD. HE WAS SO GENTLE.
A KISS TO KAZUKITA IS...
FOR HIM, IT'S NOTHING.
OWWEE!
I HATE YOU!

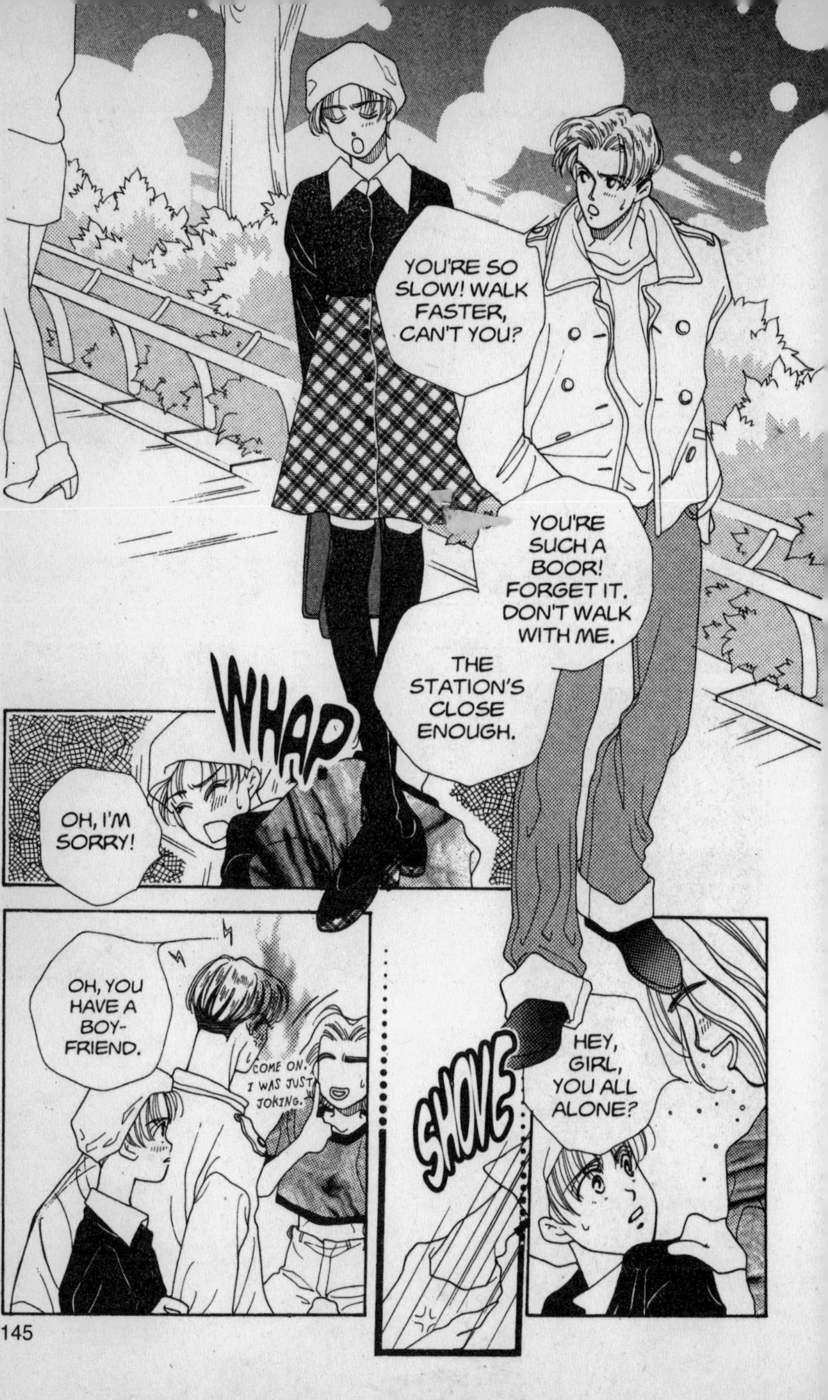
YOU'RE SO SLOW! WALK FASTER, CAN'T YOU?
YOU'RE SUCH A BOOR! FORGET IT. DON'T WALK WITH ME.
THE STATION'S CLOSE ENOUGH.
WHAP
OH, I'M SORRY!
HEY, GIRL, YOU ALL ALONE?
SHOVE
OH, YOU HAVE A BOY-FRIEND.
COME ON. I WAS JUST JOKING.

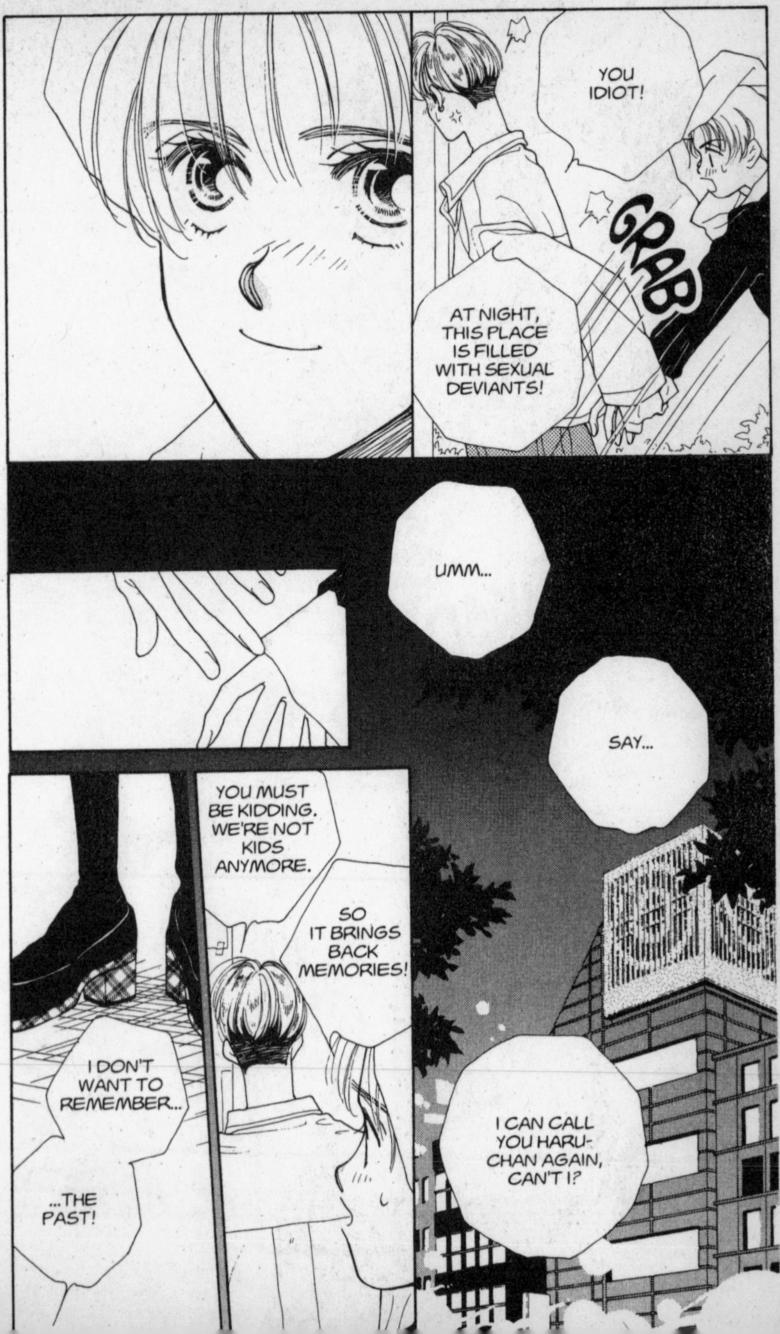
YOU IDIOT!
GRAB
AT NIGHT, THIS PLACE IS FILLED WITH SEXUAL DEVIANTS!
UMM...
SAY...
I CAN CALL YOU HARU-CHAN AGAIN, CAN'T I?
YOU MUST BE KIDDING. WE'RE NOT KIDS ANYMORE.
SO IT BRINGS BACK MEMORIES!
I DON'T WANT TO REMEMBER...
...THE PAST!

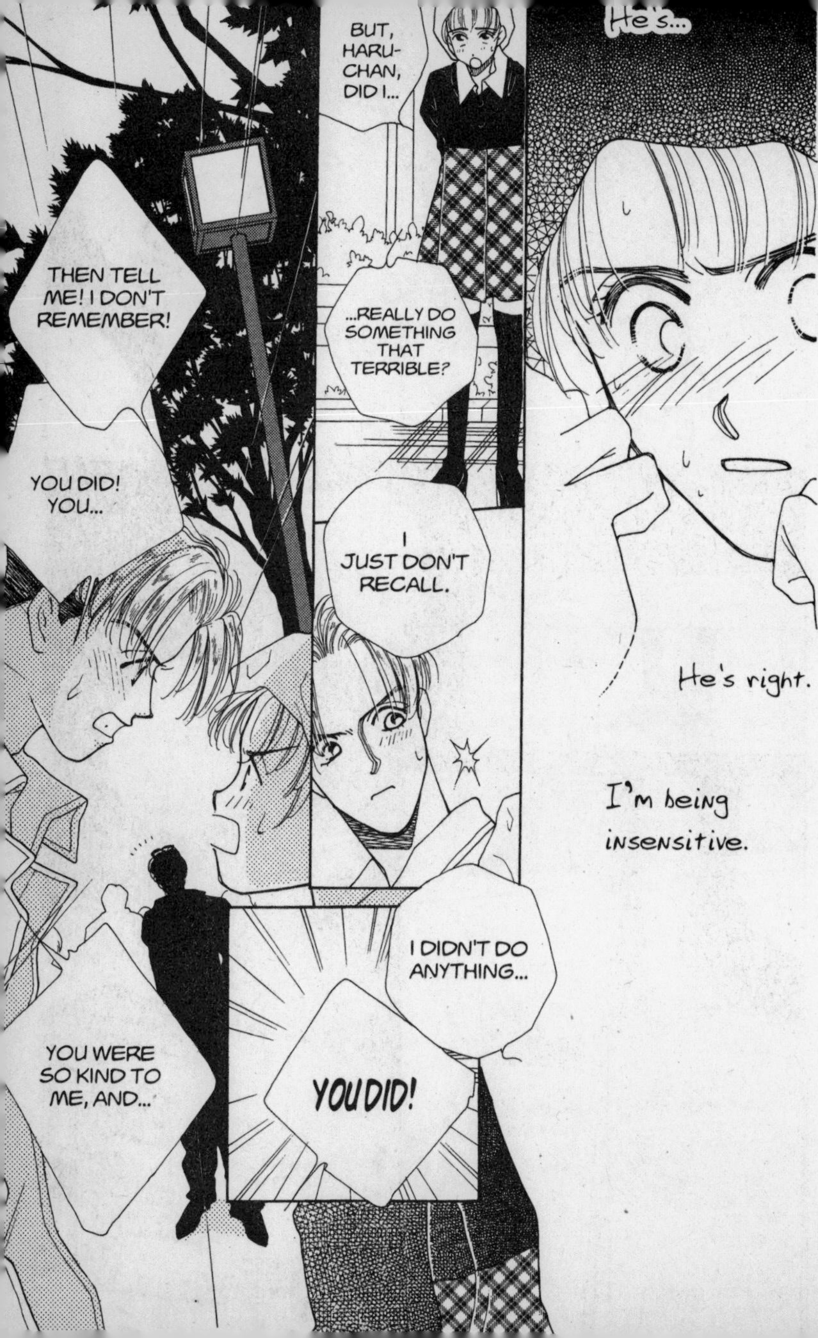

He's...
He's right.
I'm being insensitive.
BUT, HARU-CHAN, DID I...
...REALLY DO SOMETHING THAT TERRIBLE?
THEN TELL ME! I DON'T REMEMBER!
I JUST DON'T RECALL.
YOU DID! YOU...
I DIDN'T DO ANYTHING...
YOU DID!
YOU WERE SO KIND TO ME, AND...

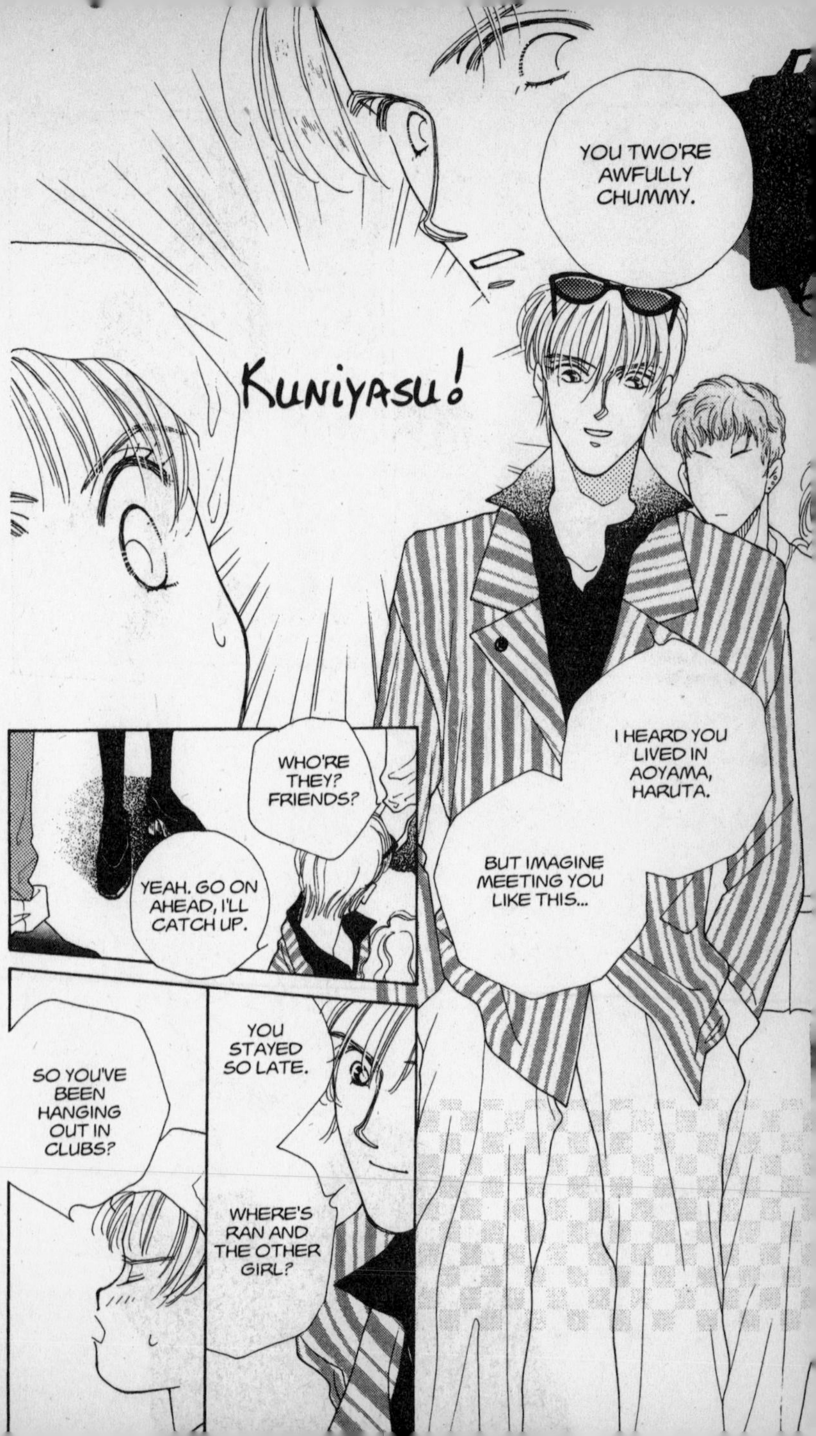
YOU TWO'RE AWFULLY CHUMMY.
KUNIYASU!
I HEARD YOU LIVED IN AOYAMA, HARUTA.
BUT IMAGINE MEETING YOU LIKE THIS...
WHO'RE THEY? FRIENDS?
YEAH. GO ON AHEAD, I'LL CATCH UP.
YOU STAYED SO LATE.
WHERE'S RAN AND THE OTHER GIRL?
SO YOU'VE BEEN HANGING OUT IN CLUBS?

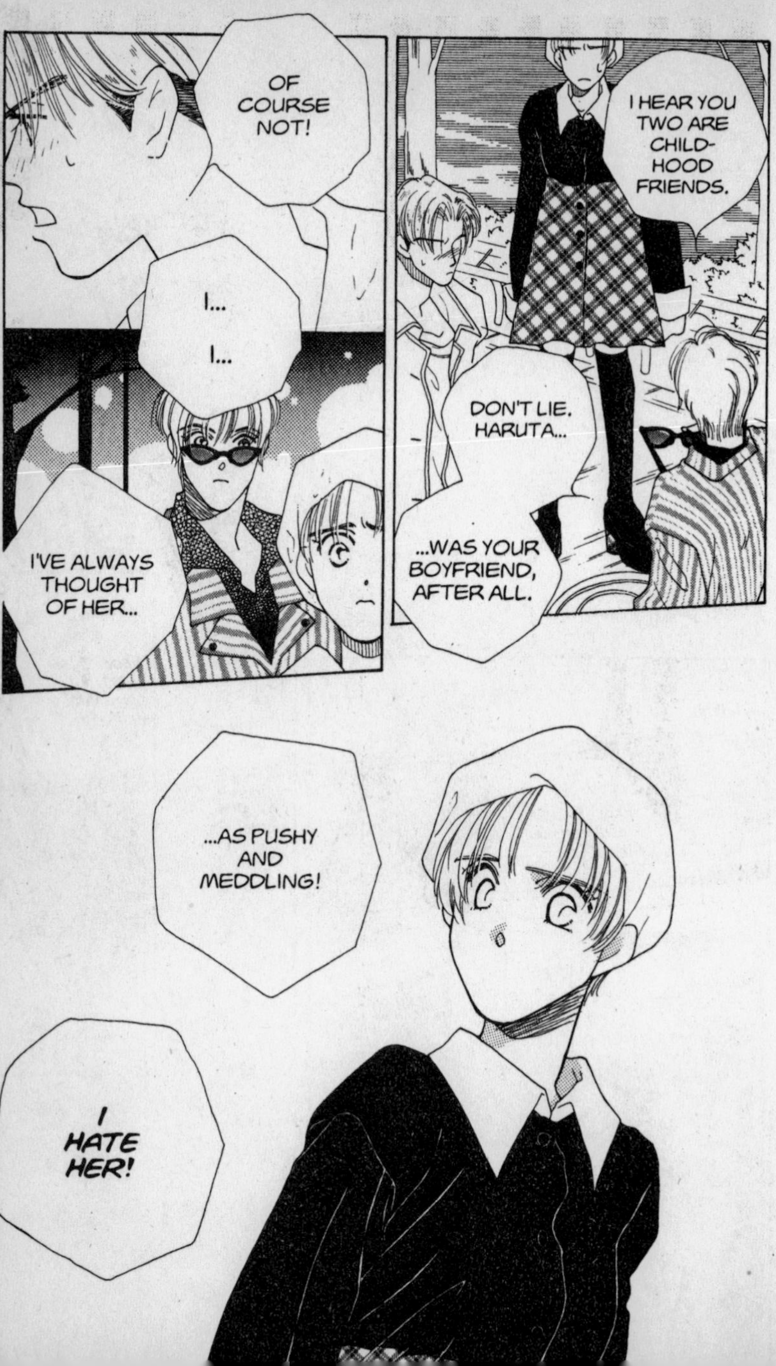
I HEAR YOU TWO ARE CHILDHOOD FRIENDS.
DON'T LIE. HARUTA...
...WAS YOUR BOYFRIEND, AFTER ALL.
OF COURSE NOT!
I... I...
I'VE ALWAYS THOUGHT OF HER...
...AS PUSHY AND MEDDLING!
I HATE HER!

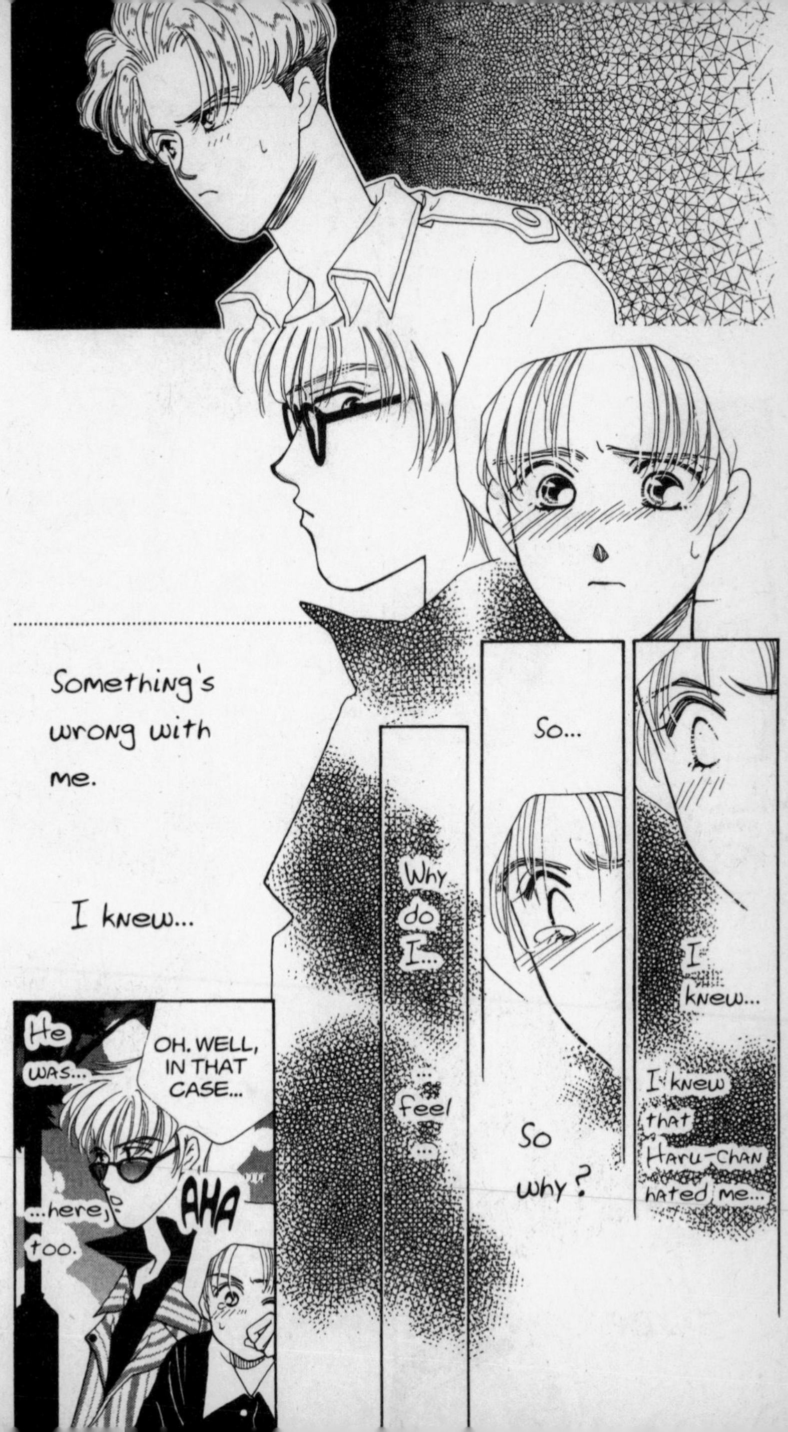

I knew...
I knew that Haru-chan hated me...
So...
So why?
Why do I...
...feel...
Something's wrong with me.
I knew...
OH. WELL, IN THAT CASE...
He was...
AHA
...here, too.

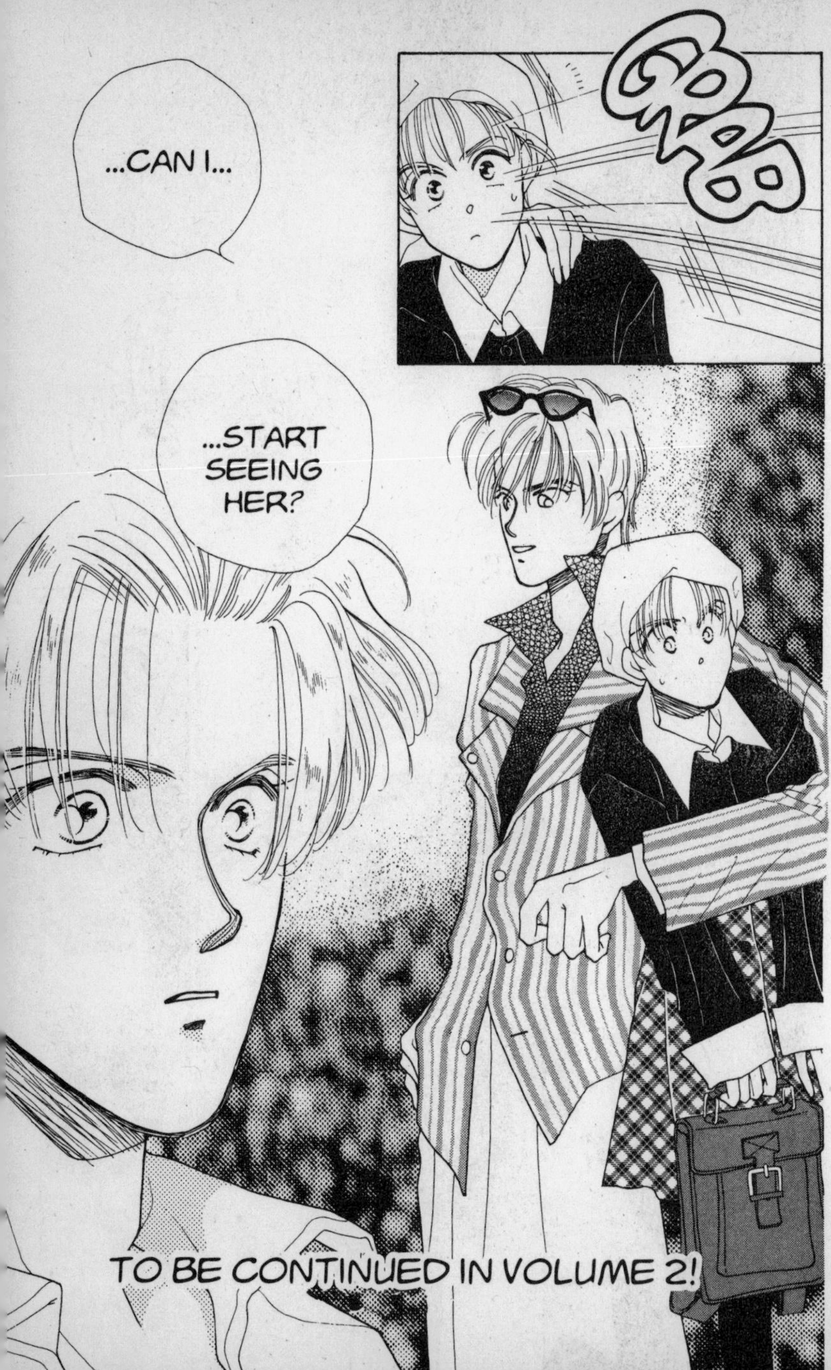
GRAB
...CAN I...
...START SEEING HER?
TO BE CONTINUED IN VOLUME 2!

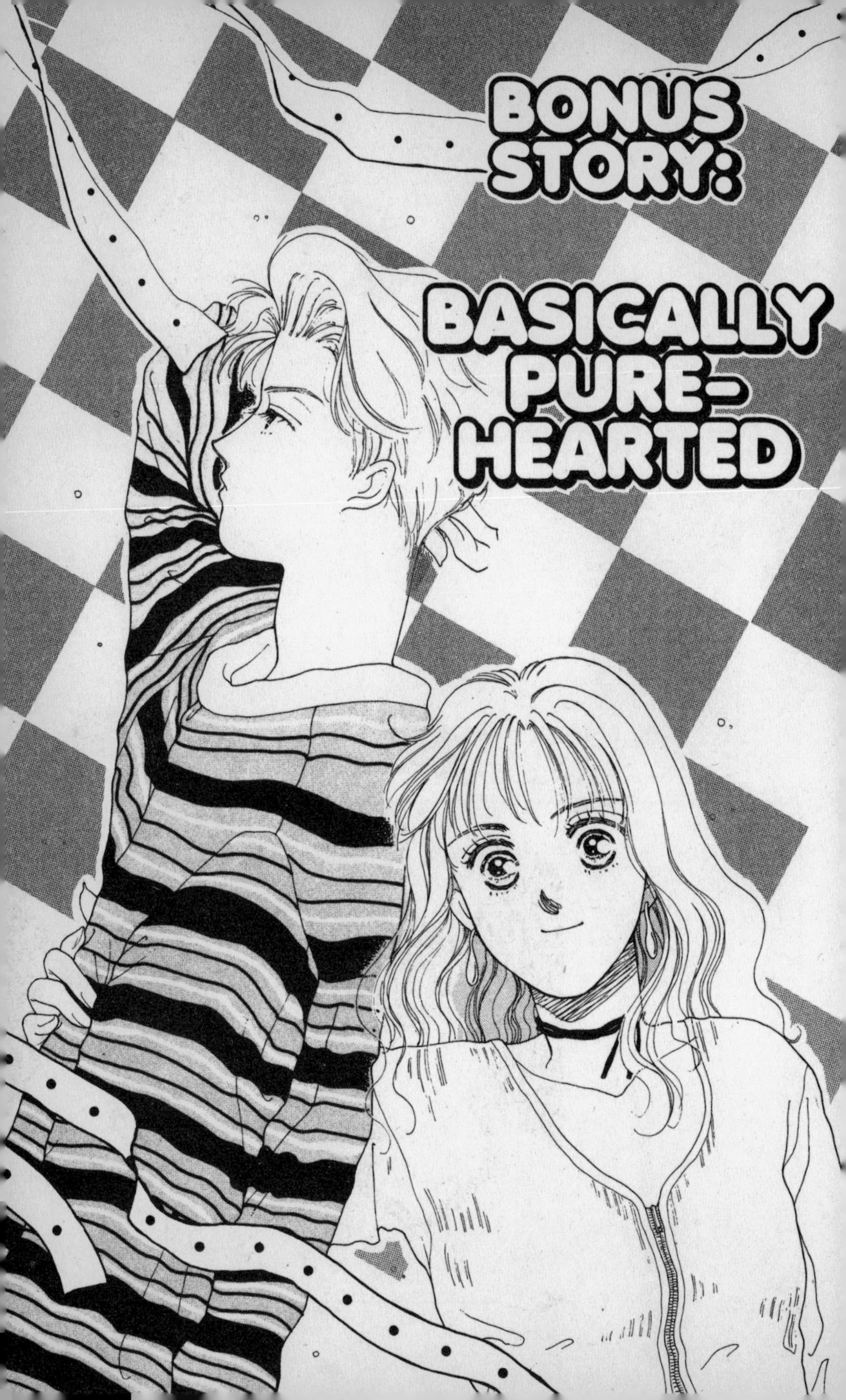
BONUS STORY:
BASICALLY PURE-HEARTED

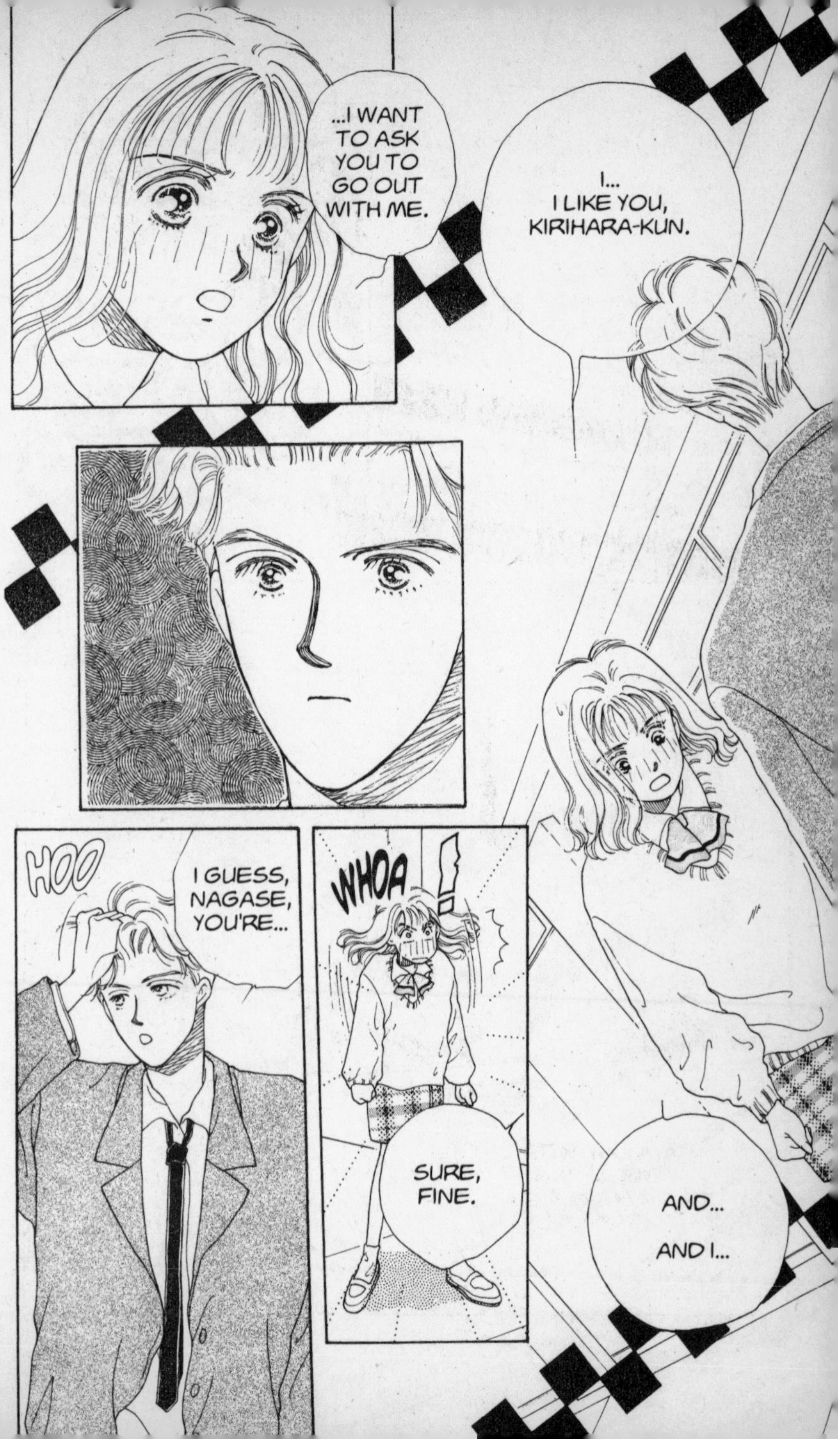
I... I LIKE YOU, KIRIHARA-KUN.
AND... AND I...
...I WANT TO ASK YOU TO GO OUT WITH ME.
WHOA
!
SURE, FINE.
HOO
I GUESS, NAGASE, YOU'RE...

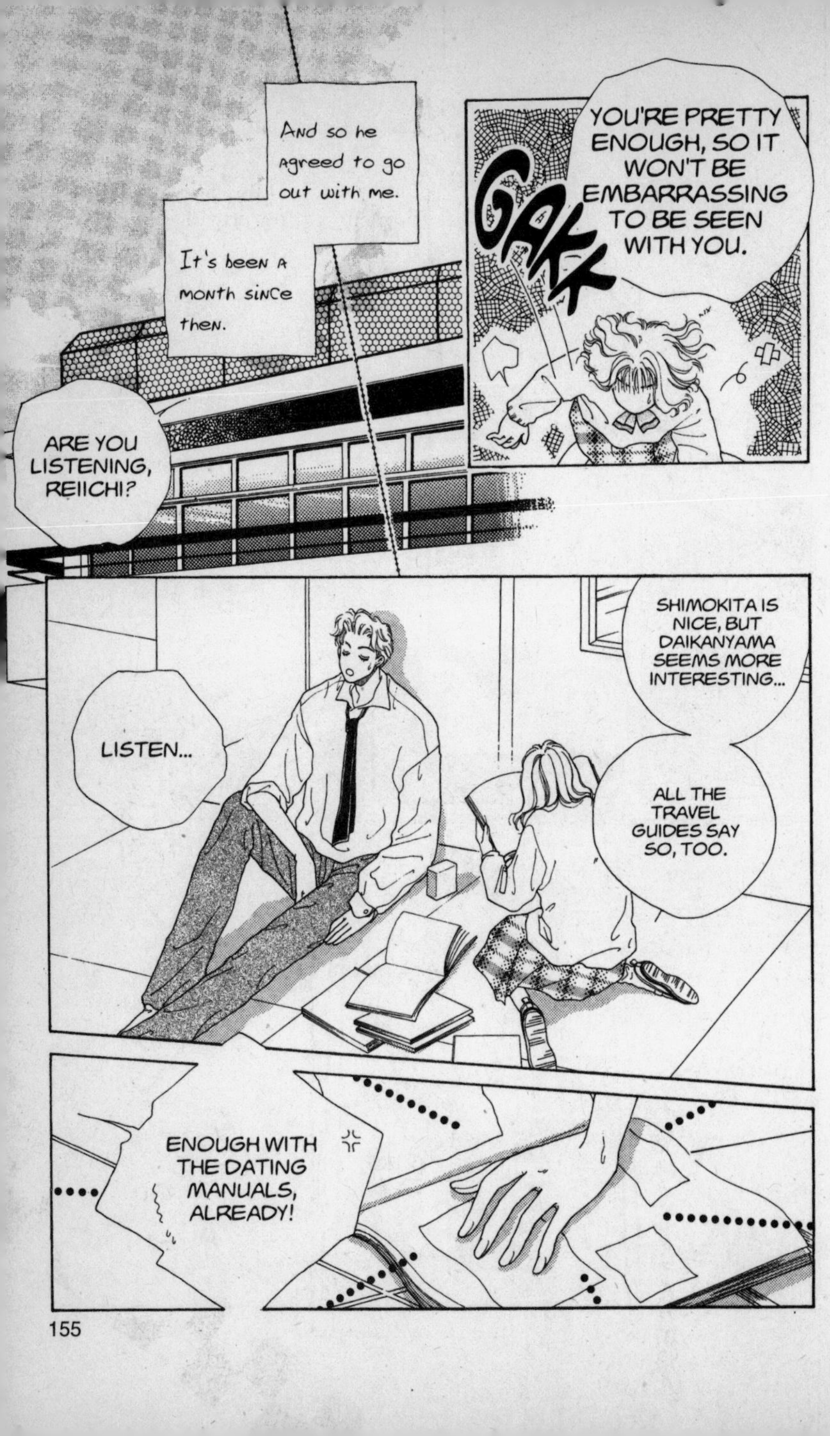
YOU'RE PRETTY ENOUGH, SO IT WON'T BE EMBARRASSING TO BE SEEN WITH YOU.
GAKK
And so he agreed to go out with me.
It's been a month since then.
ARE YOU LISTENING, REIICHI?
SHIMOKITA IS NICE, BUT DAIKANYAMA SEEMS MORE INTERESTING...
ALL THE TRAVEL GUIDES SAY SO, TOO.
LISTEN...
ENOUGH WITH THE DATING MANUALS, ALREADY!

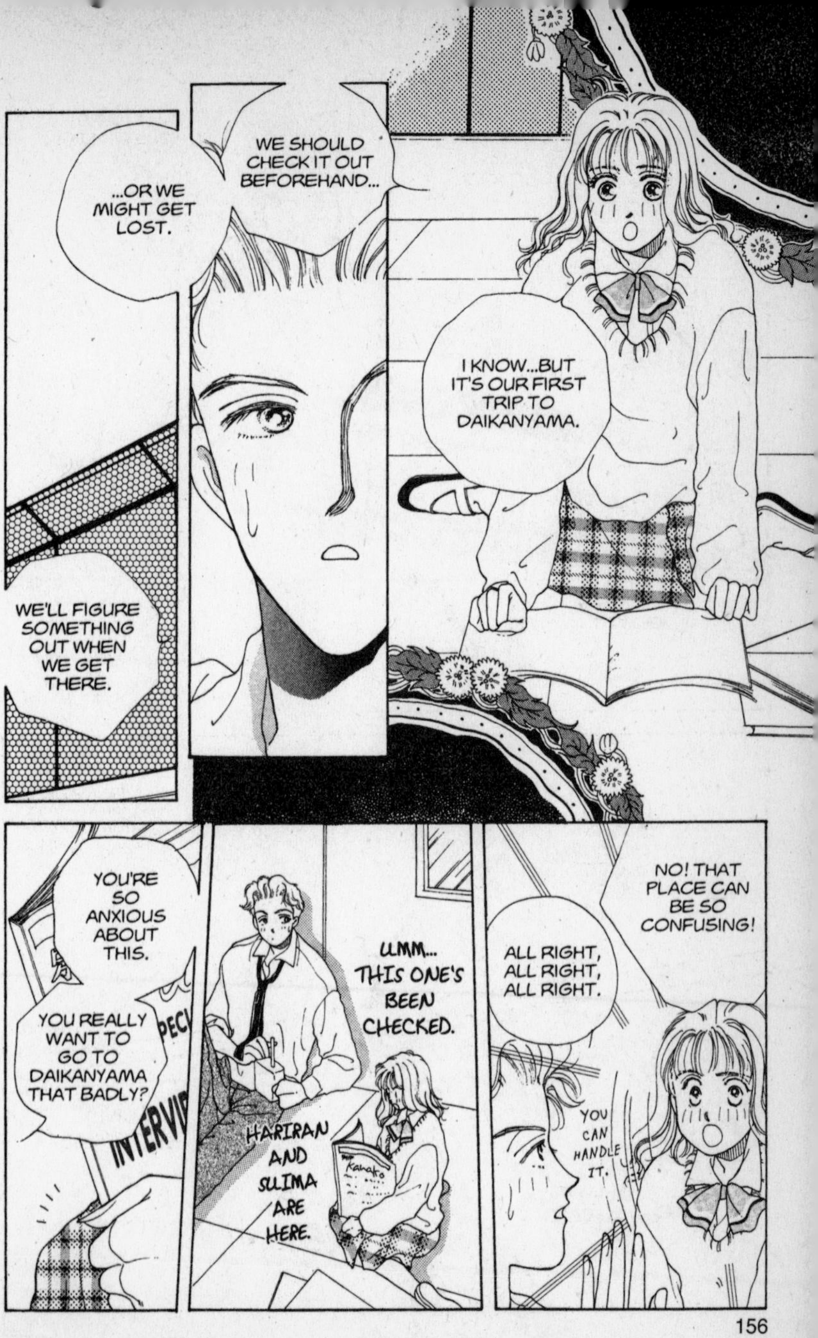
I KNOW...BUT IT'S OUR FIRST TRIP TO DAIKANYAMA.
WE SHOULD CHECK IT OUT BEFOREHAND...
...OR WE MIGHT GET LOST.
WE'LL FIGURE SOMETHING OUT WHEN WE GET THERE.
NO! THAT PLACE CAN BE SO CONFUSING!
ALL RIGHT, ALL RIGHT, ALL RIGHT.
YOU CAN HANDLE IT.
UMM... THIS ONE'S BEEN CHECKED.
HARIRAN AND SUIMA ARE HERE.
Kanako
YOU'RE SO ANXIOUS ABOUT THIS.
YOU REALLY WANT TO GO TO DAIKANYAMA THAT BADLY?

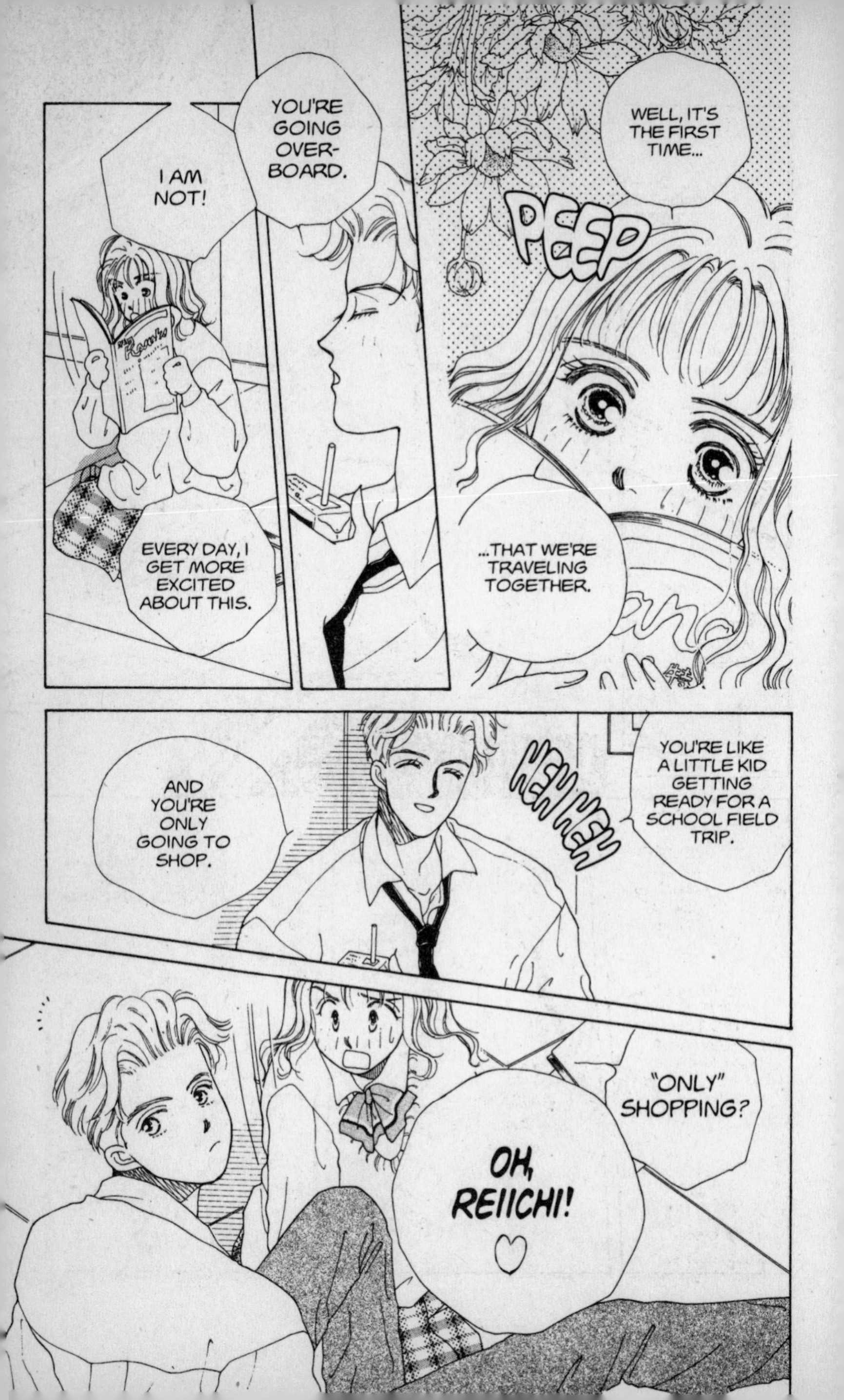
WELL, IT'S THE FIRST TIME...
PEEP
...THAT WE'RE TRAVELING TOGETHER.
YOU'RE GOING OVER-BOARD.
I AM NOT!
EVERY DAY, I GET MORE EXCITED ABOUT THIS.
YOU'RE LIKE A LITTLE KID GETTING READY FOR A SCHOOL FIELD TRIP.
HEH HEH
AND YOU'RE ONLY GOING TO SHOP.
"ONLY" SHOPPING?
OH, REIICHI! ♡

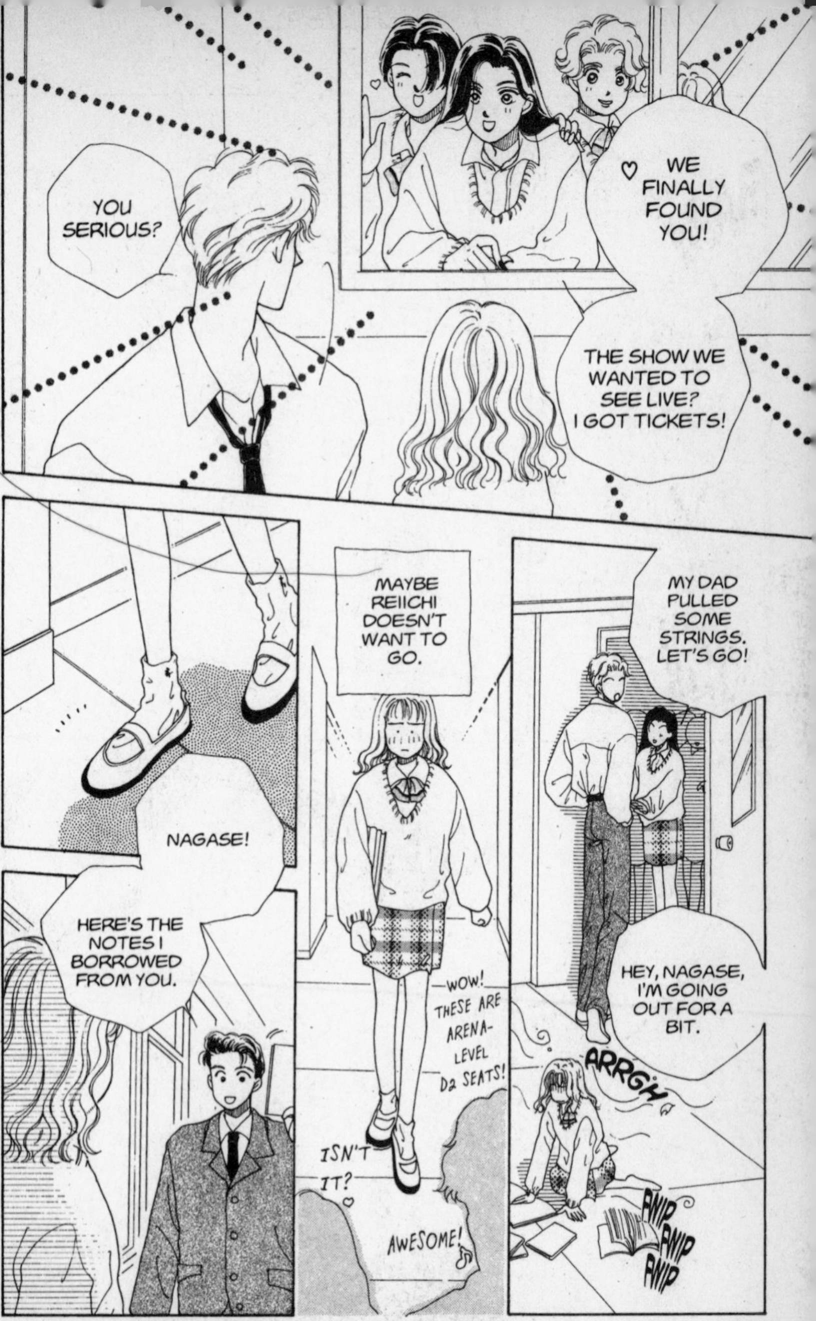
♡ WE FINALLY FOUND YOU!
THE SHOW WE WANTED TO SEE LIVE? I GOT TICKETS!
YOU SERIOUS?
MY DAD PULLED SOME STRINGS. LET'S GO!
HEY, NAGASE, I'M GOING OUT FOR A BIT.
ARRGH
AWIP AWIP AWIP
MAYBE REIICHI DOESN'T WANT TO GO.
WOW! THESE ARE ARENA-LEVEL D2 SEATS!
ISN'T IT?
AWESOME!
NAGASE!
HERE'S THE NOTES I BORROWED FROM YOU.

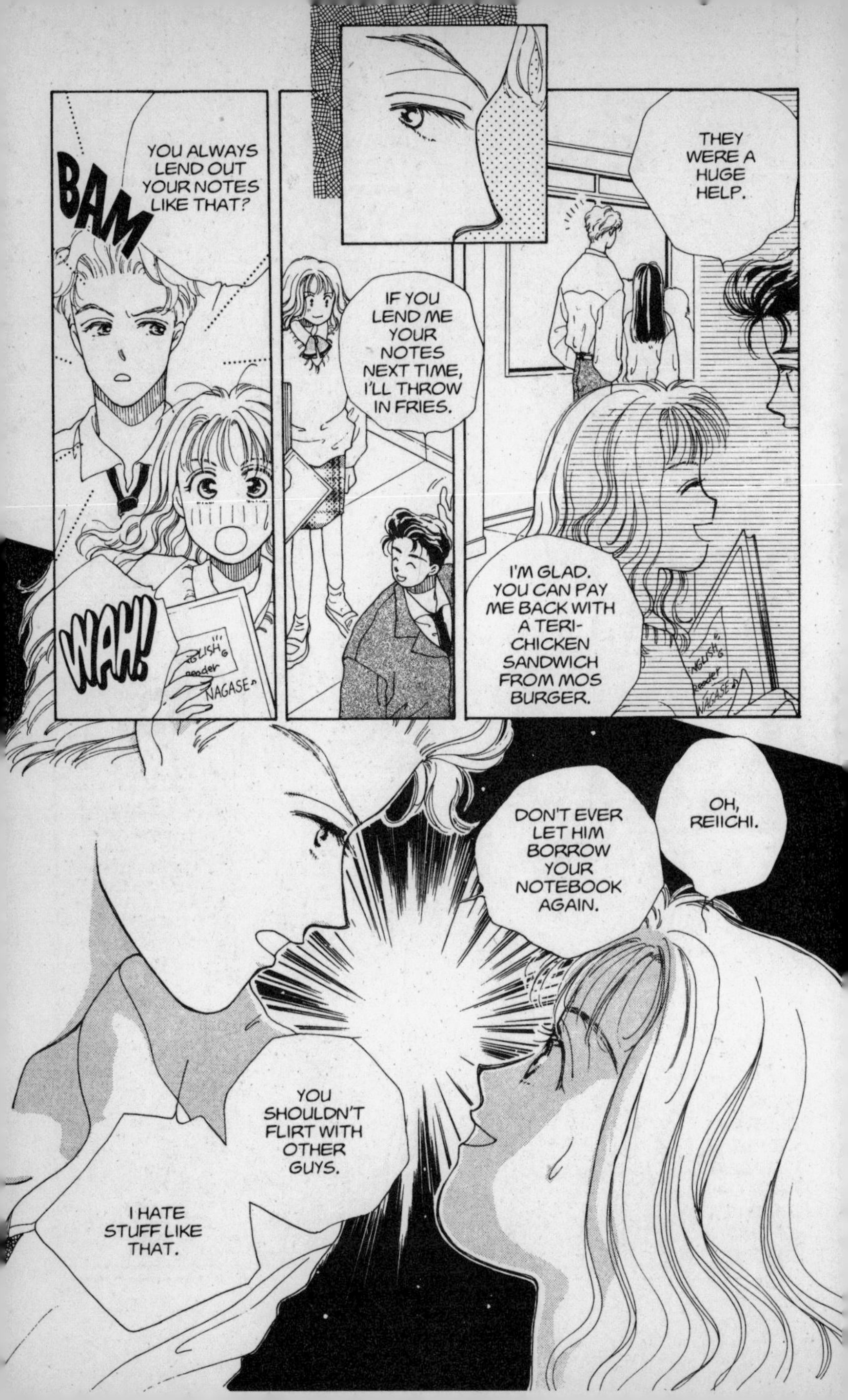
THEY WERE A HUGE HELP.
I'M GLAD. YOU CAN PAY ME BACK WITH A TERI-CHICKEN SANDWICH FROM MOS BURGER.
IF YOU LEND ME YOUR NOTES NEXT TIME, I'LL THROW IN FRIES.
BAM
YOU ALWAYS LEND OUT YOUR NOTES LIKE THAT?
WAH!
OH, REIICHI.
DON'T EVER LET HIM BORROW YOUR NOTEBOOK AGAIN.
YOU SHOULDN'T FLIRT WITH OTHER GUYS.
I HATE STUFF LIKE THAT.

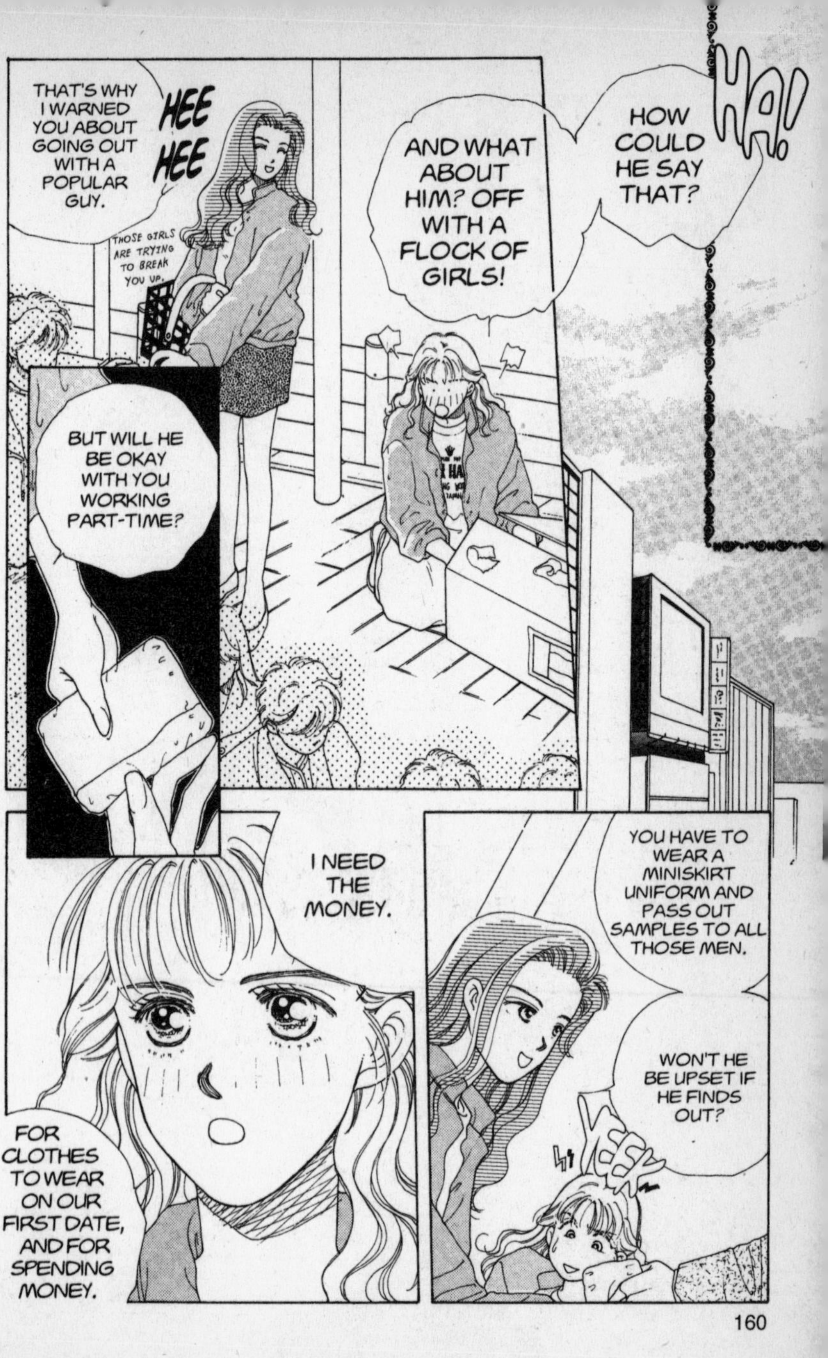
HA!
HOW COULD HE SAY THAT?
AND WHAT ABOUT HIM? OFF WITH A FLOCK OF GIRLS!
THAT'S WHY I WARNED YOU ABOUT GOING OUT WITH A POPULAR GUY.
HEE HEE
THOSE GIRLS ARE TRYING TO BREAK YOU UP.
BUT WILL HE BE OKAY WITH YOU WORKING PART-TIME?
YOU HAVE TO WEAR A MINISKIRT UNIFORM AND PASS OUT SAMPLES TO ALL THOSE MEN.
WON'T HE BE UPSET IF HE FINDS OUT?
I NEED THE MONEY.
FOR CLOTHES TO WEAR ON OUR FIRST DATE, AND FOR SPENDING MONEY.

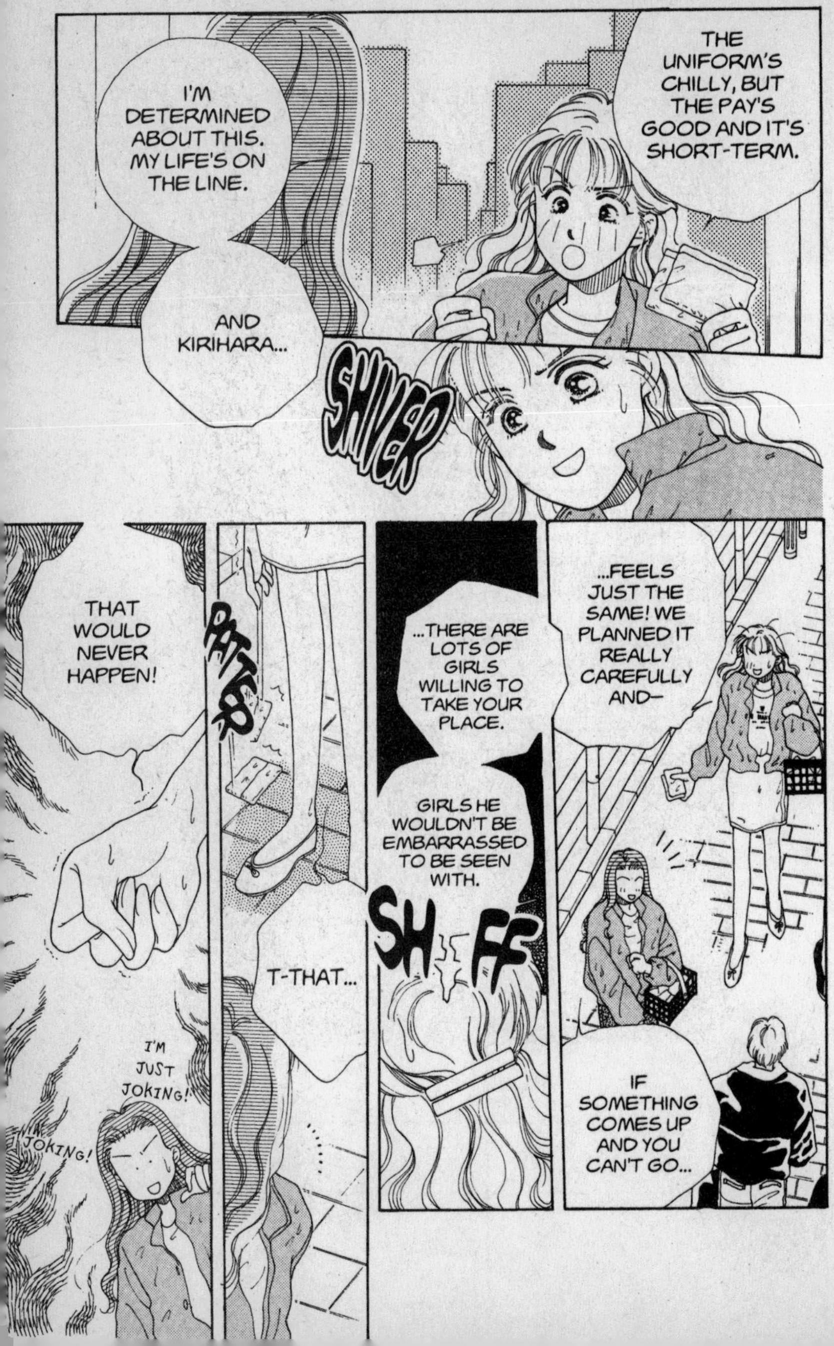
THE UNIFORM'S CHILLY, BUT THE PAY'S GOOD AND IT'S SHORT-TERM.
I'M DETERMINED ABOUT THIS. MY LIFE'S ON THE LINE.
AND KIRIHARA...
SHIVER
...FEELS JUST THE SAME! WE PLANNED IT REALLY CAREFULLY AND—
IF SOMETHING COMES UP AND YOU CAN'T GO...
...THERE ARE LOTS OF GIRLS WILLING TO TAKE YOUR PLACE.
GIRLS HE WOULDN'T BE EMBARRASSED TO BE SEEN WITH.
SHFF
PATTER
T-THAT...
THAT WOULD NEVER HAPPEN!
I'M JUST JOKING!
JOKING!

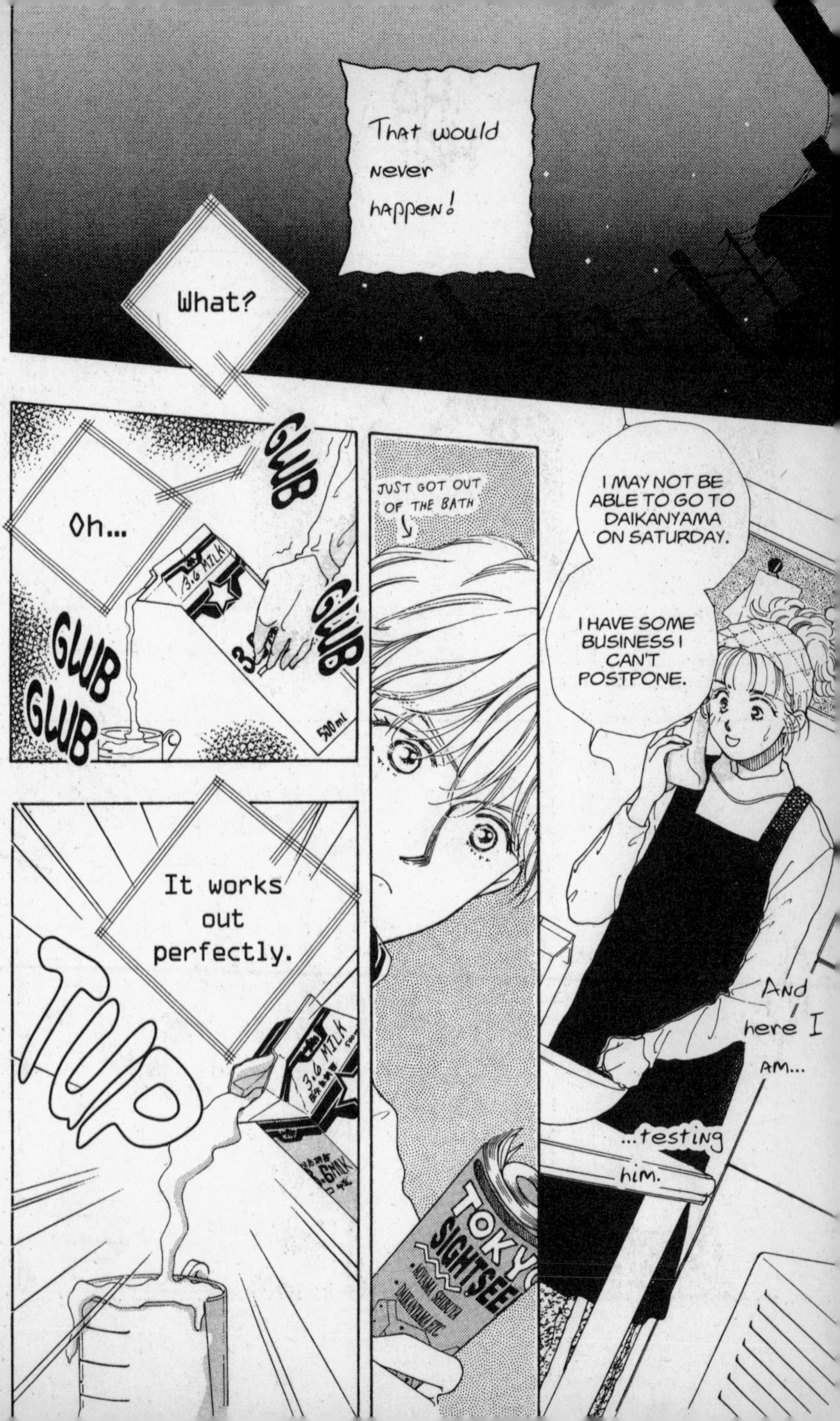
That would never happen!
What?
I MAY NOT BE ABLE TO GO TO DAIKANYAMA ON SATURDAY.
I HAVE SOME BUSINESS I CAN'T POSTPONE.
And here I am...
...testing him.
JUST GOT OUT OF THE BATH
SIGHTSEE
Oh...
GLUB
GLUB
GLUB GLUB
3.6 MILK
500ml
It works out perfectly.
TUP

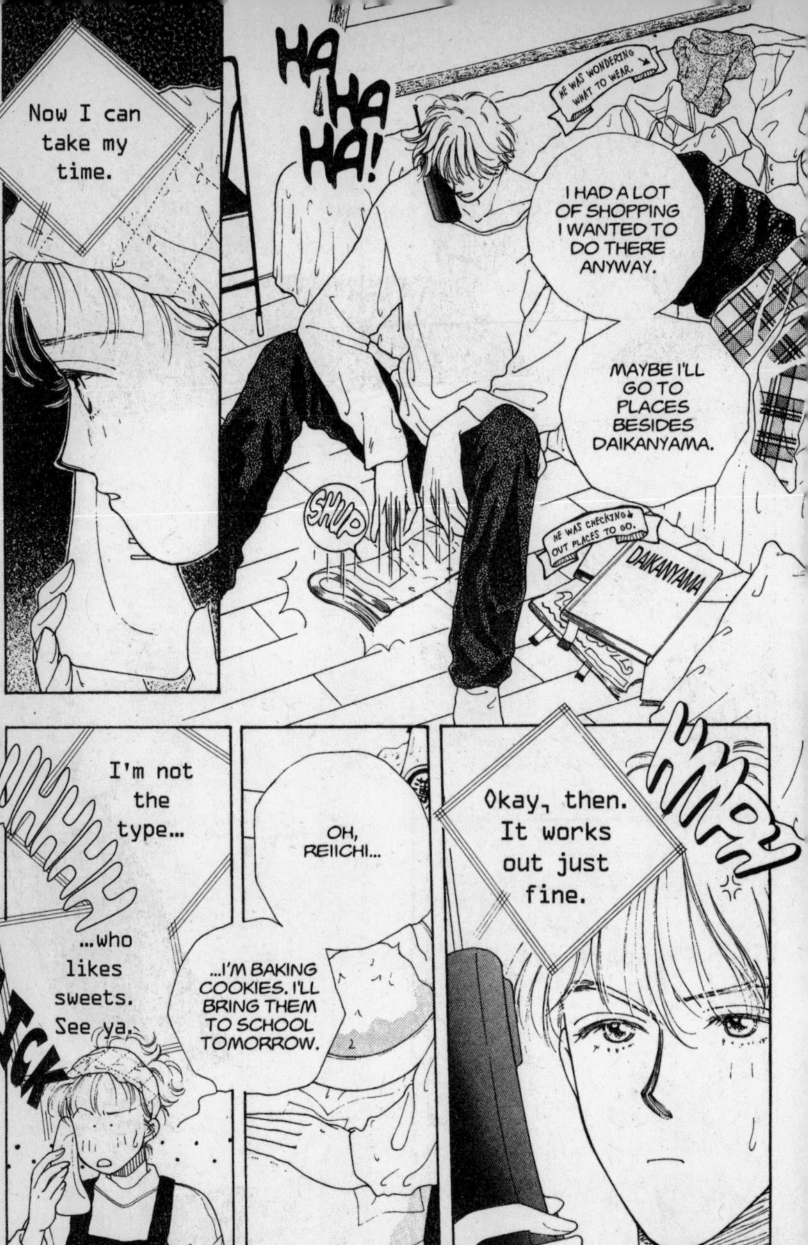
HA HA HA!
HE WAS WONDERING WHAT TO WEAR.
I HAD A LOT OF SHOPPING I WANTED TO DO THERE ANYWAY.
MAYBE I'LL GO TO PLACES BESIDES DAIKANYAMA.
SHUP
HE WAS CHECKING OUT PLACES TO GO.
DAIKANYAMA
Now I can take my time.
HMPH
Okay, then. It works out just fine.
OH, REIICHI...
...I'M BAKING COOKIES. I'LL BRING THEM TO SCHOOL TOMORROW.
I'm not the type...
...who likes sweets. See ya.
CLICK

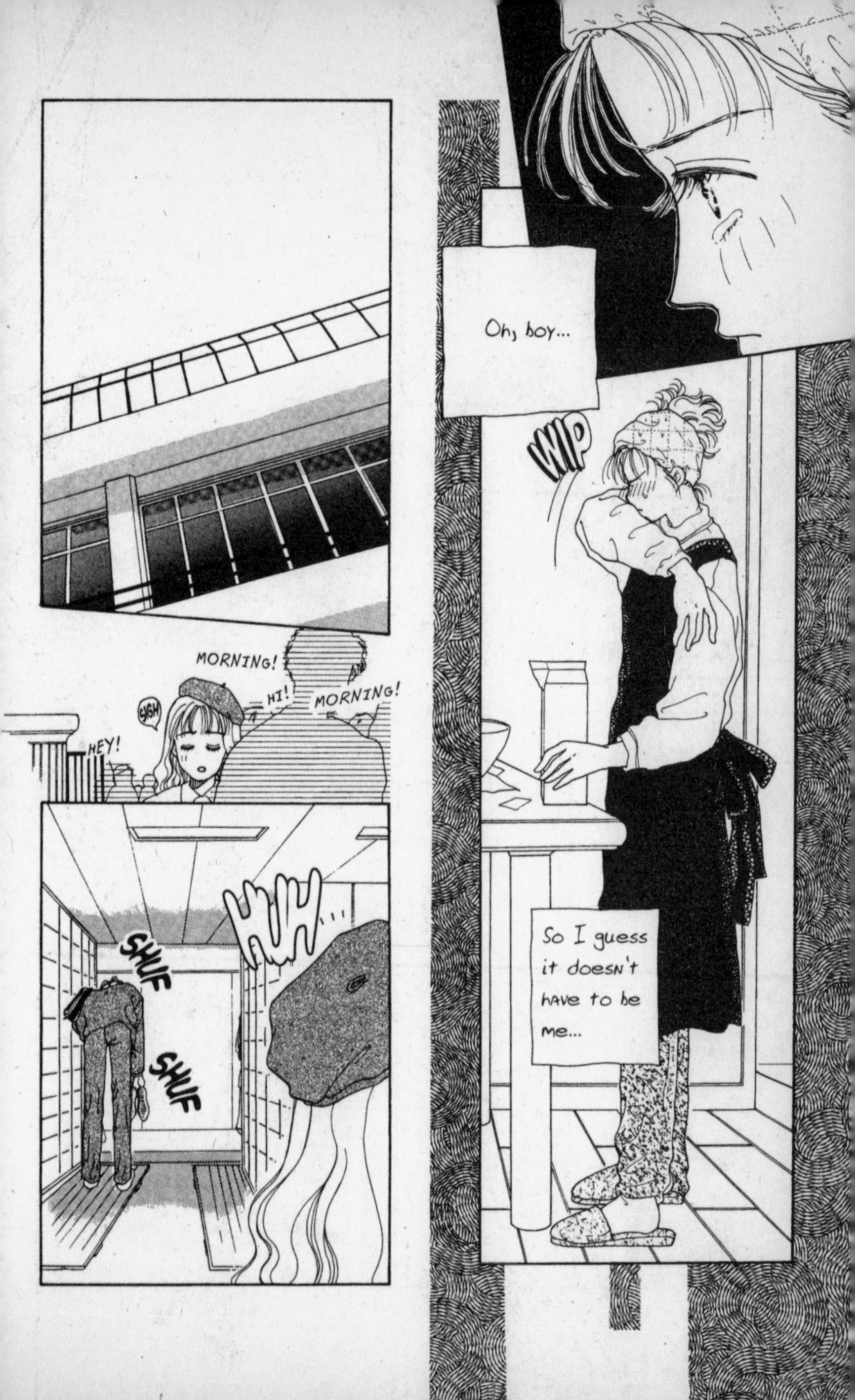
Oh, boy...
WHIP
So I guess it doesn't have to be me...
MORNING!
MORNING!
HI!
SIGH
HEY!
HUH...
SHUF
SHUF

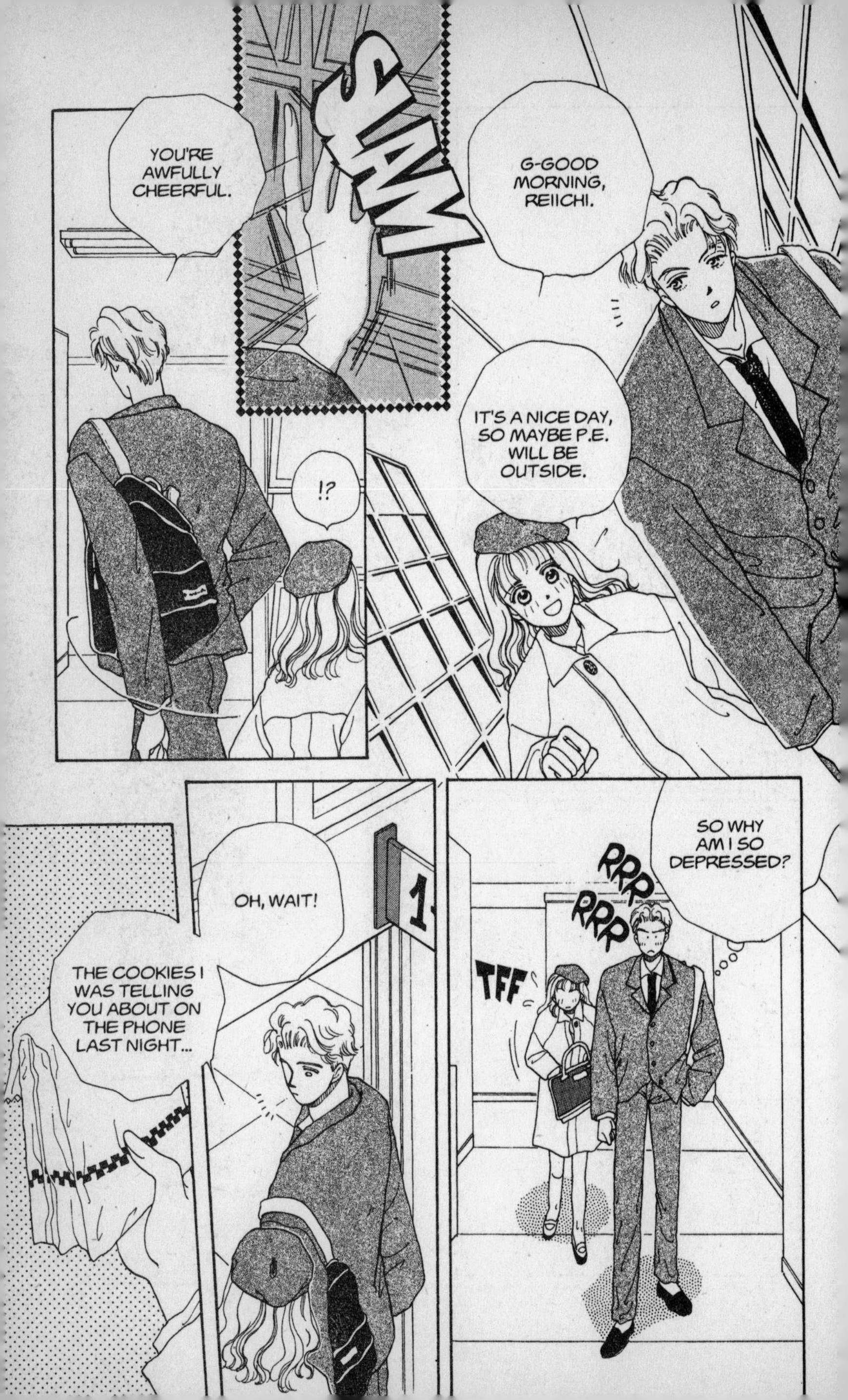
G-GOOD MORNING, REIICHI.
IT'S A NICE DAY, SO MAYBE P.E. WILL BE OUTSIDE.
SLAM
!?
YOU'RE AWFULLY CHEERFUL.
SO WHY AM I SO DEPRESSED?
RRR RRR
TFF
1-
OH, WAIT!
THE COOKIES I WAS TELLING YOU ABOUT ON THE PHONE LAST NIGHT...

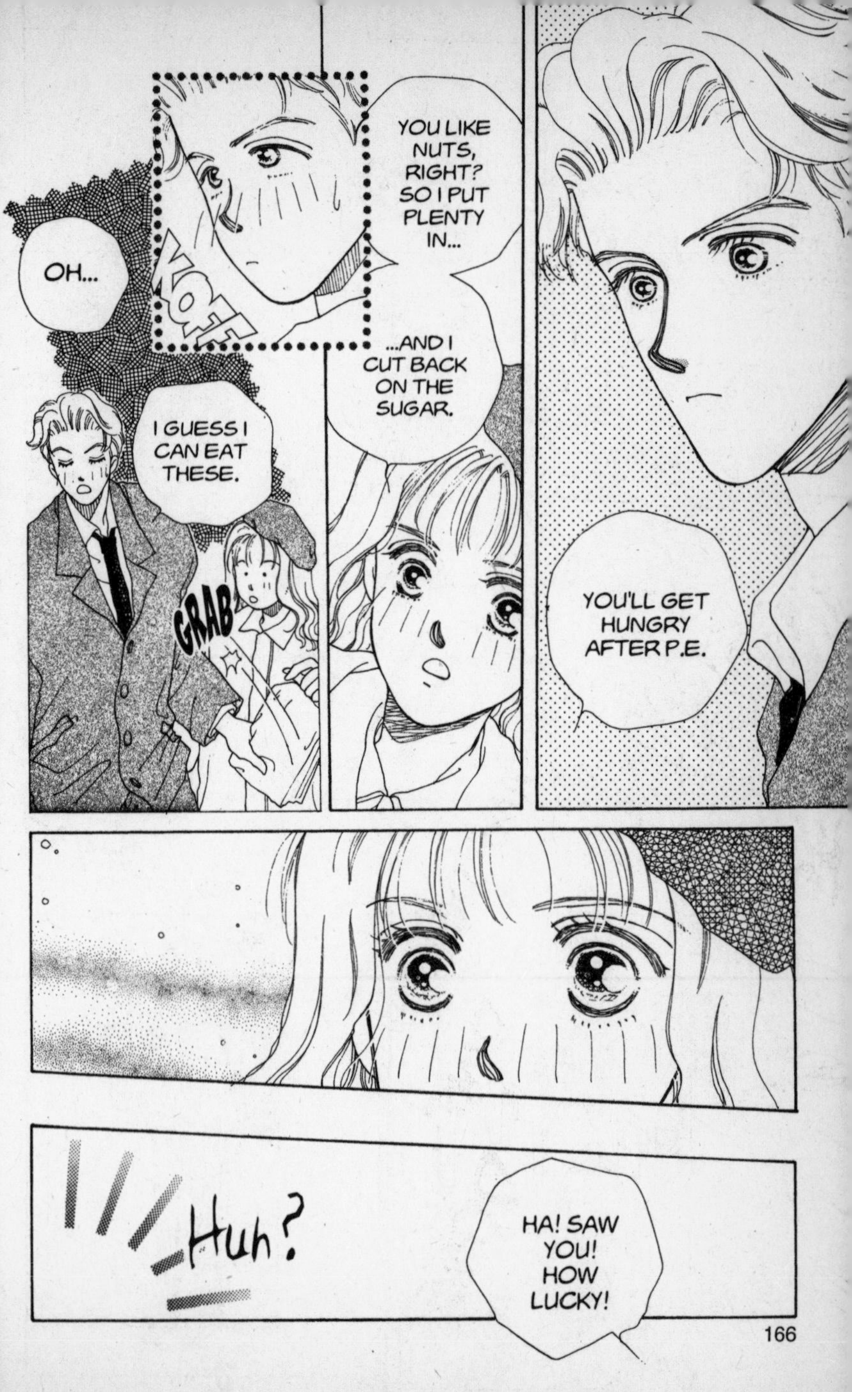

YOU'LL GET HUNGRY AFTER P.E.
YOU LIKE NUTS, RIGHT? SO I PUT PLENTY IN...
...AND I CUT BACK ON THE SUGAR.
KOFF
OH...
I GUESS I CAN EAT THESE.
GRAB
HA! SAW YOU! HOW LUCKY!
Huh?

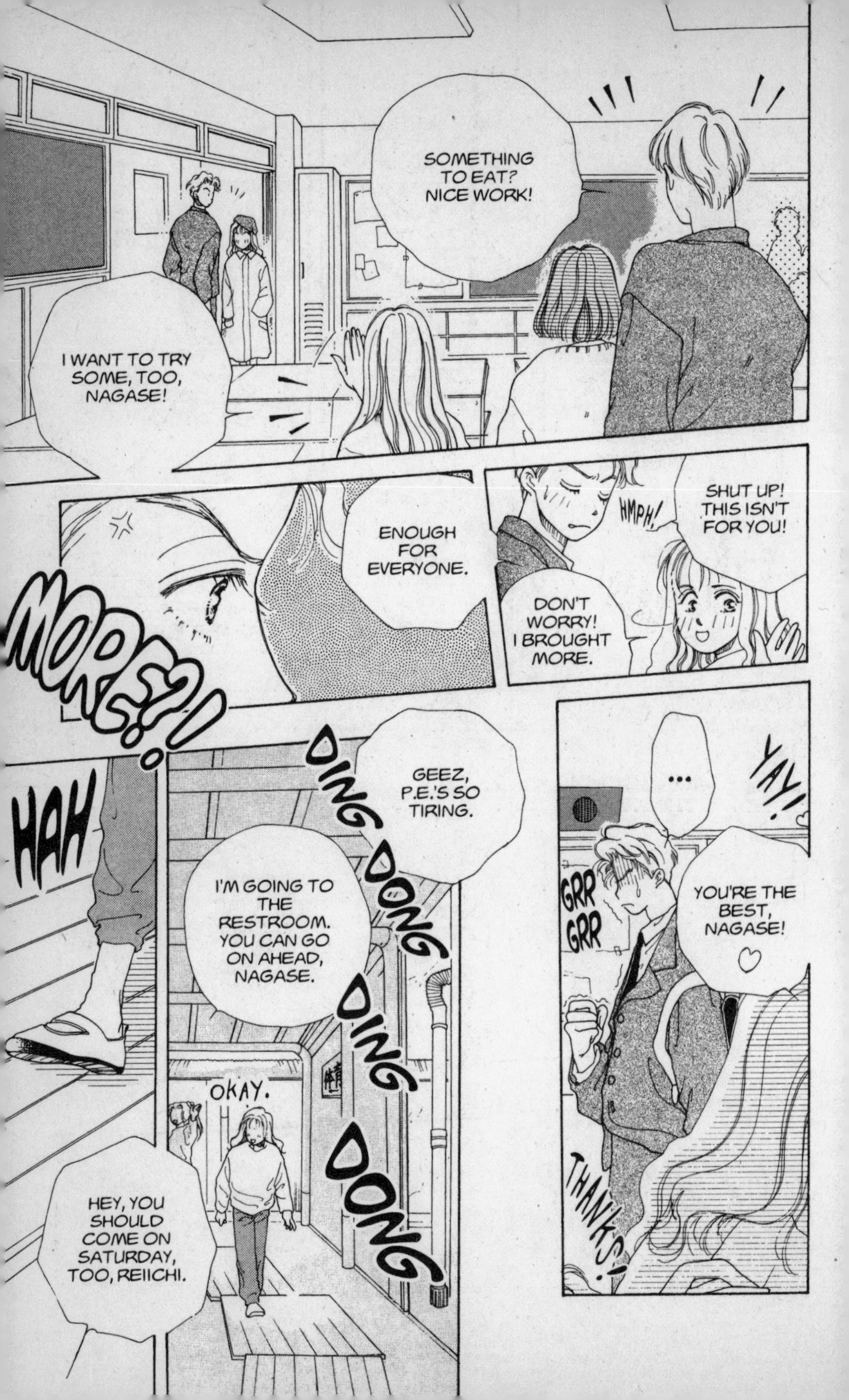
SOMETHING TO EAT? NICE WORK!
I WANT TO TRY SOME, TOO, NAGASE!
SHUT UP! THIS ISN'T FOR YOU!
HMPH!
DON'T WORRY! I BROUGHT MORE.
ENOUGH FOR EVERYONE.
MORE?!!
YAY!
...
GRR GRR
YOU'RE THE BEST, NAGASE!
THANKS!
GEEZ, P.E.'S SO TIRING.
DING DONG DING DONG
I'M GOING TO THE RESTROOM. YOU CAN GO ON AHEAD, NAGASE.
OKAY.
HEY, YOU SHOULD COME ON SATURDAY, TOO, REIICHI.
HAH

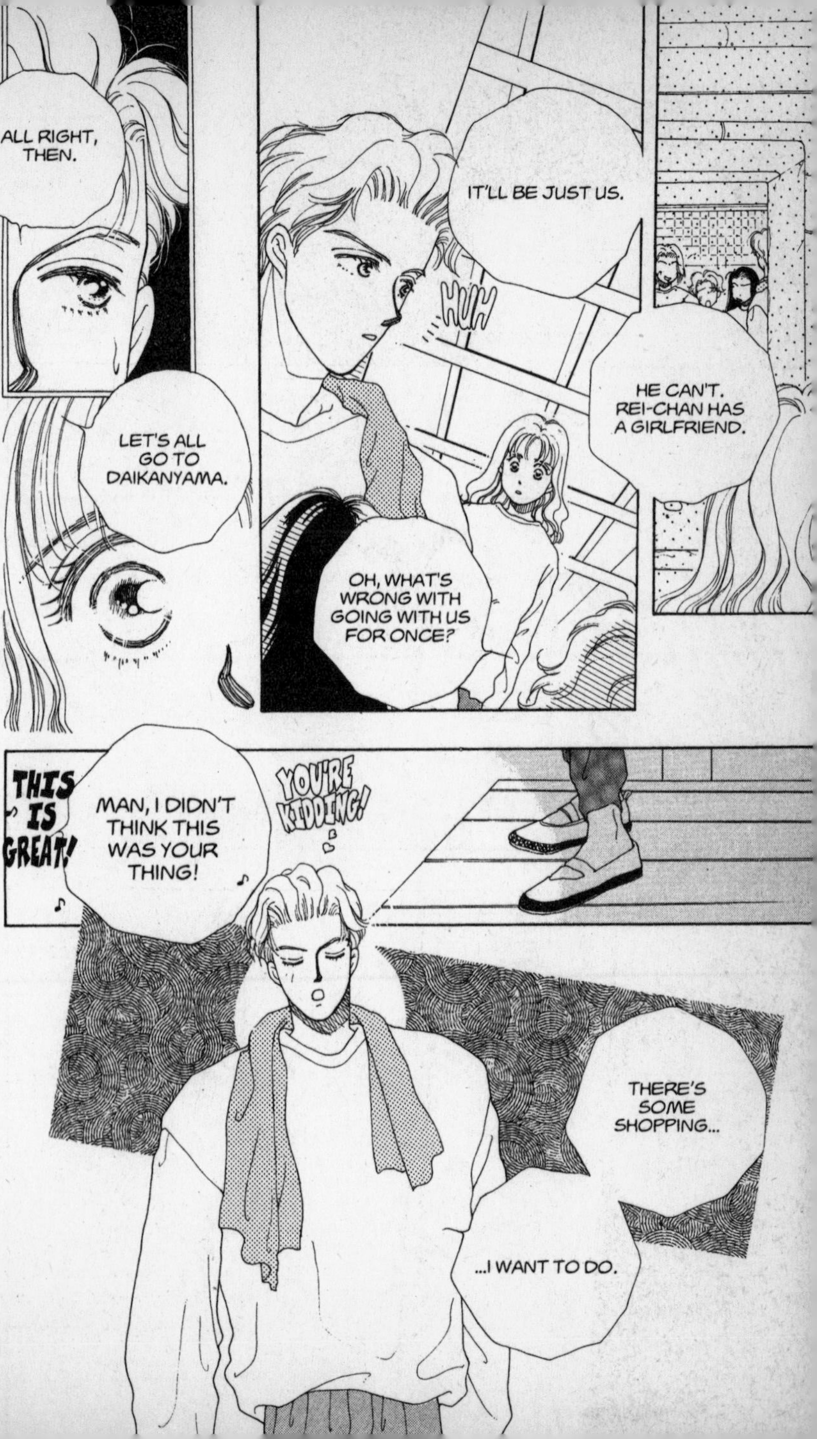
HE CAN'T. REI-CHAN HAS A GIRLFRIEND.
IT'LL BE JUST US.
HUH
OH, WHAT'S WRONG WITH GOING WITH US FOR ONCE?
ALL RIGHT, THEN.
LET'S ALL GO TO DAIKANYAMA.
THERE'S SOME SHOPPING...
...I WANT TO DO.
YOU'RE KIDDING!
MAN, I DIDN'T THINK THIS WAS YOUR THING!
THIS IS GREAT!

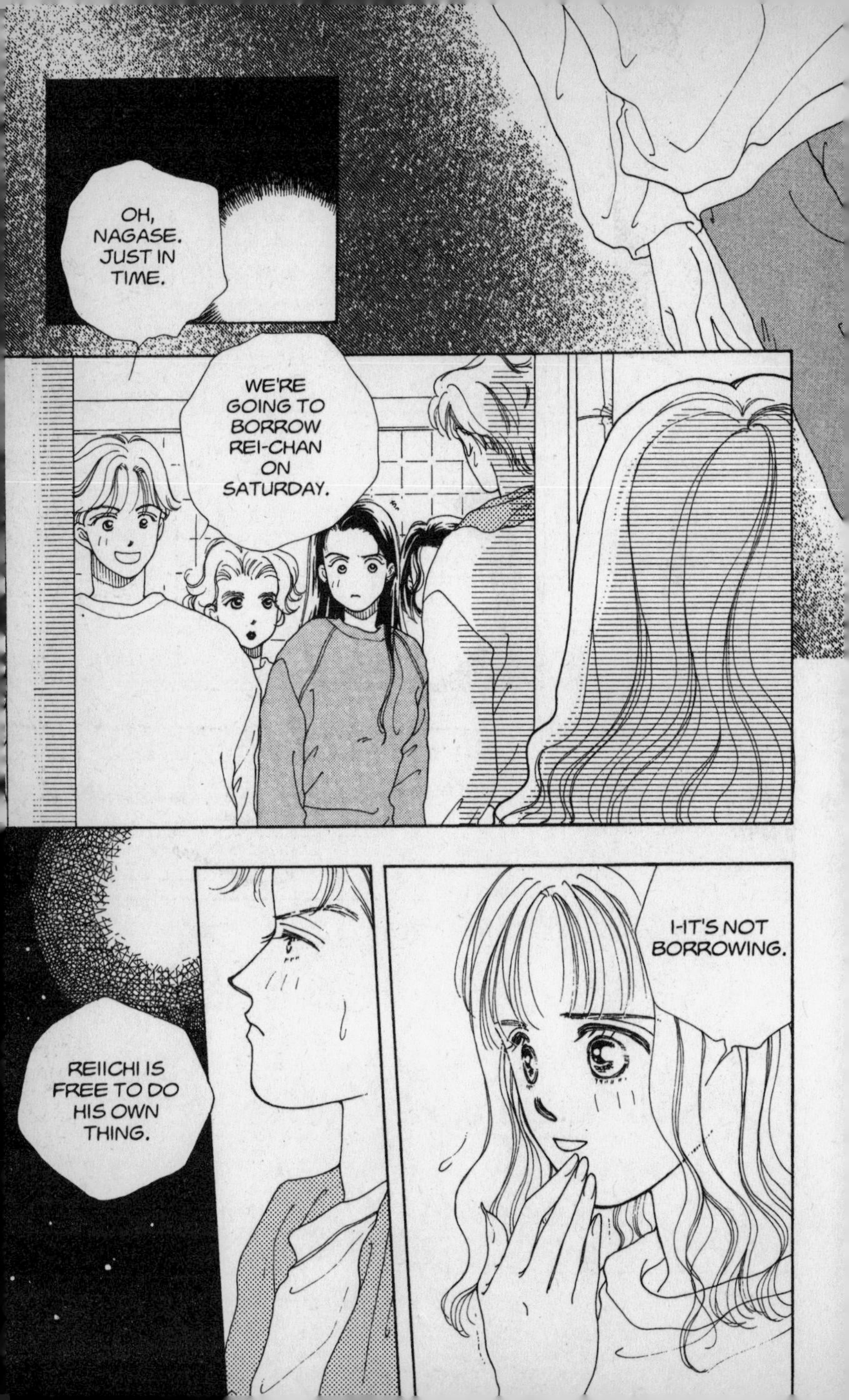
OH, NAGASE. JUST IN TIME.
WE'RE GOING TO BORROW REI-CHAN ON SATURDAY.
I-IT'S NOT BORROWING.
REIICHI IS FREE TO DO HIS OWN THING.

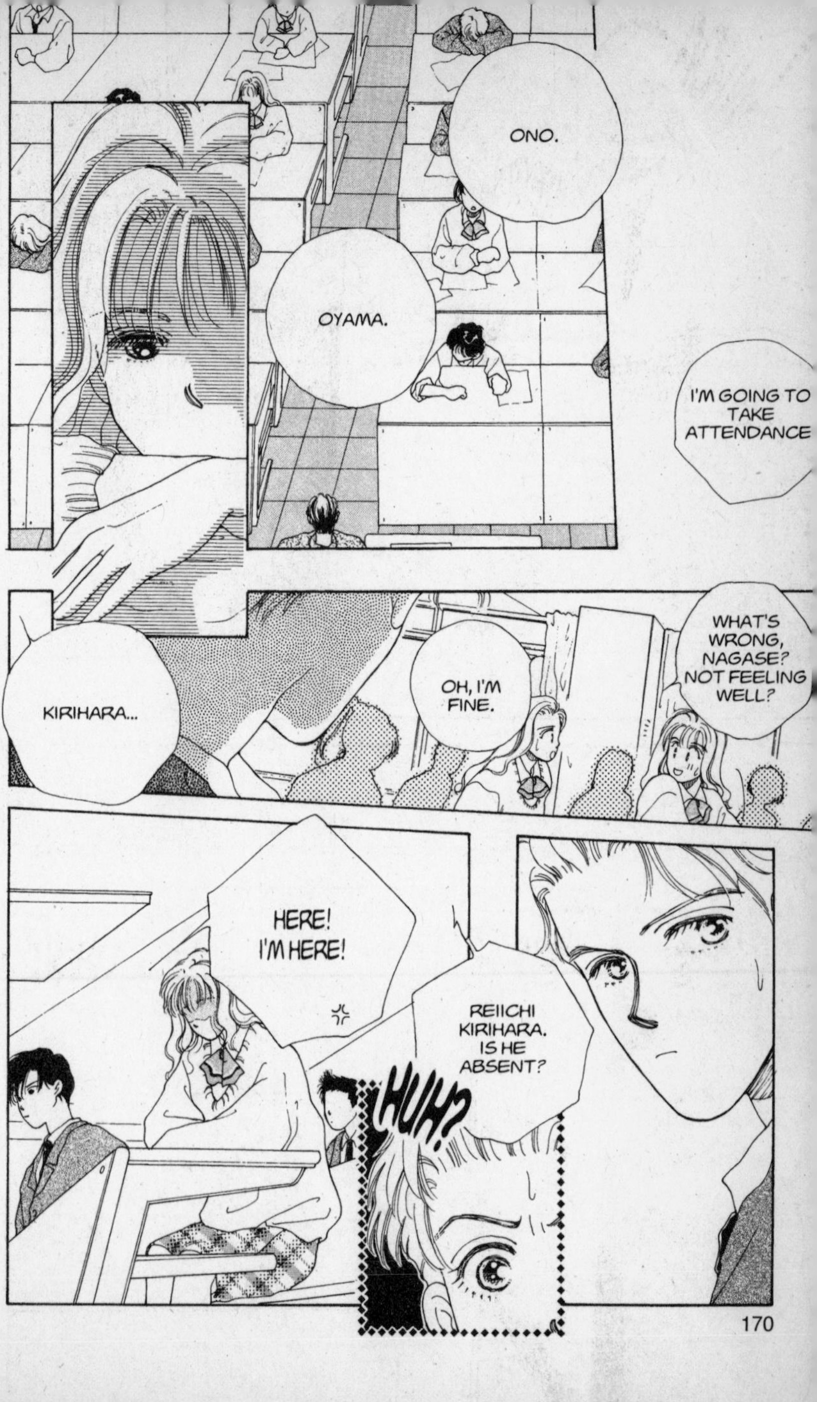
I'M GOING TO TAKE ATTENDANCE
ONO.
OYAMA.
WHAT'S WRONG, NAGASE? NOT FEELING WELL?
OH, I'M FINE.
KIRIHARA...
REIICHI KIRIHARA. IS HE ABSENT?
HUH?
HERE! I'M HERE!

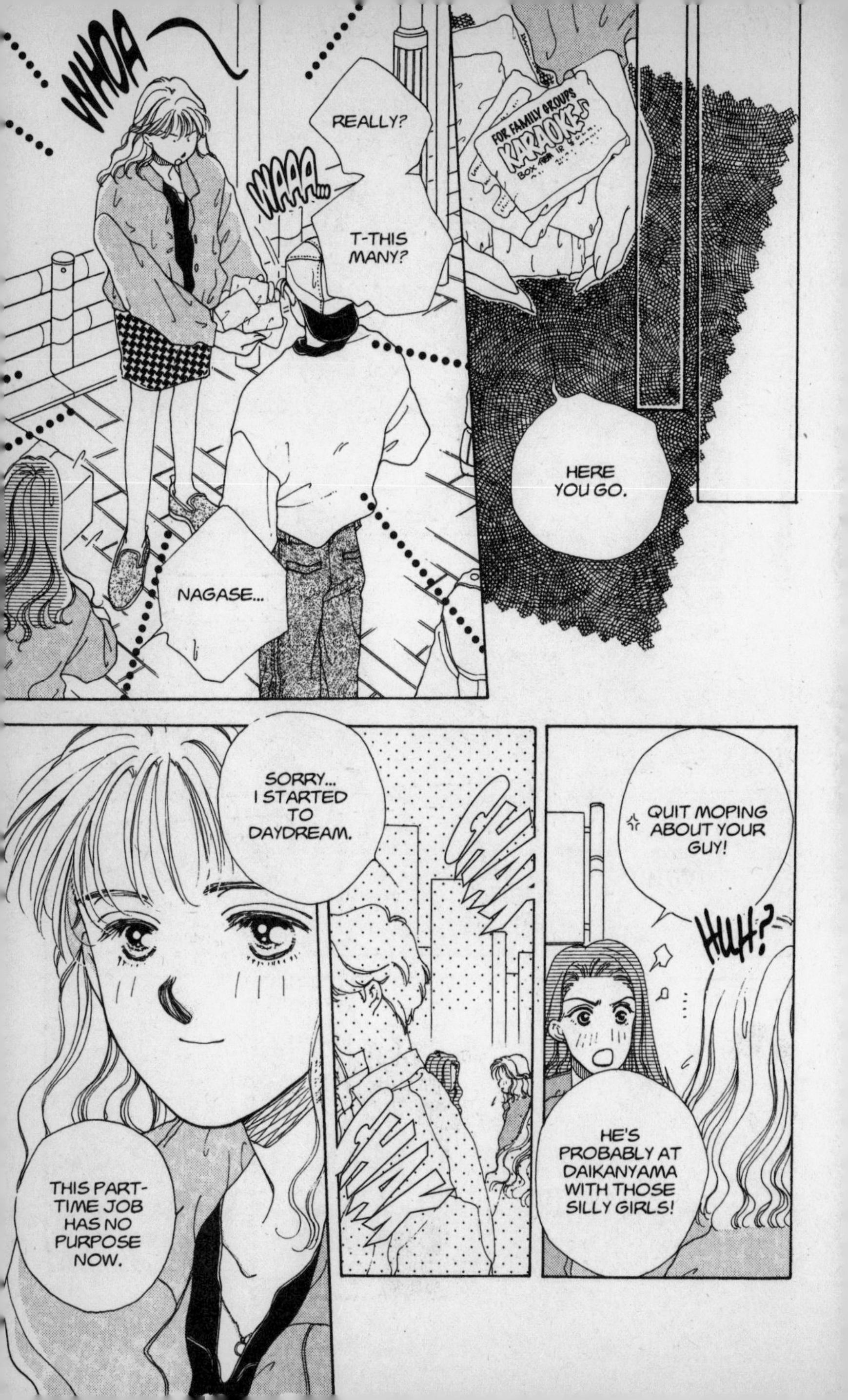
FOR FAMILY GROUPS
KARAOKE
HERE YOU GO.
REALLY?
T-THIS MANY?
WAAA...
WHOA
NAGASE...
QUIT MOPING ABOUT YOUR GUY!
HUH?
HE'S PROBABLY AT DAIKANYAMA WITH THOSE SILLY GIRLS!
SORRY... I STARTED TO DAYDREAM.
THIS PART-TIME JOB HAS NO PURPOSE NOW.

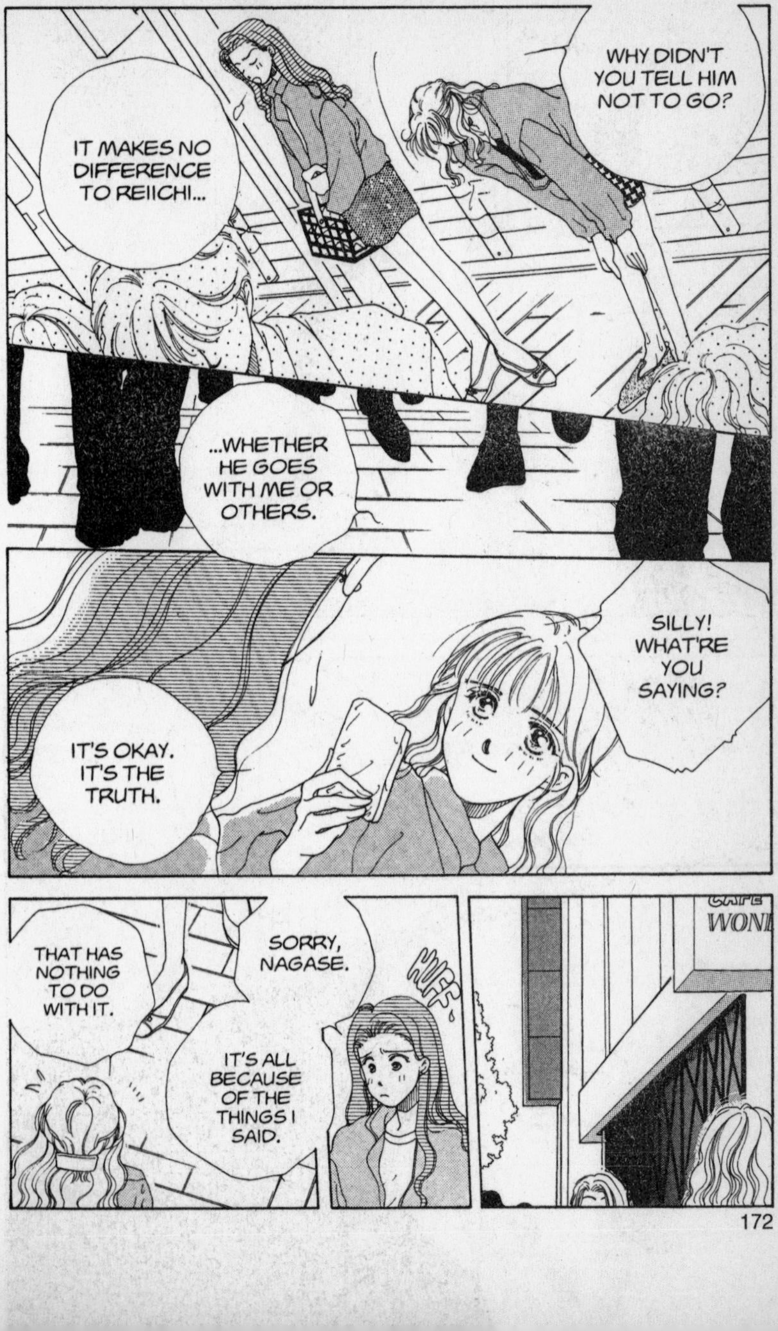
WHY DIDN'T YOU TELL HIM NOT TO GO?
IT MAKES NO DIFFERENCE TO REIICHI...
...WHETHER HE GOES WITH ME OR OTHERS.
SILLY! WHAT'RE YOU SAYING?
IT'S OKAY. IT'S THE TRUTH.
SORRY, NAGASE.
HUFF
IT'S ALL BECAUSE OF THE THINGS I SAID.
THAT HAS NOTHING TO DO WITH IT.

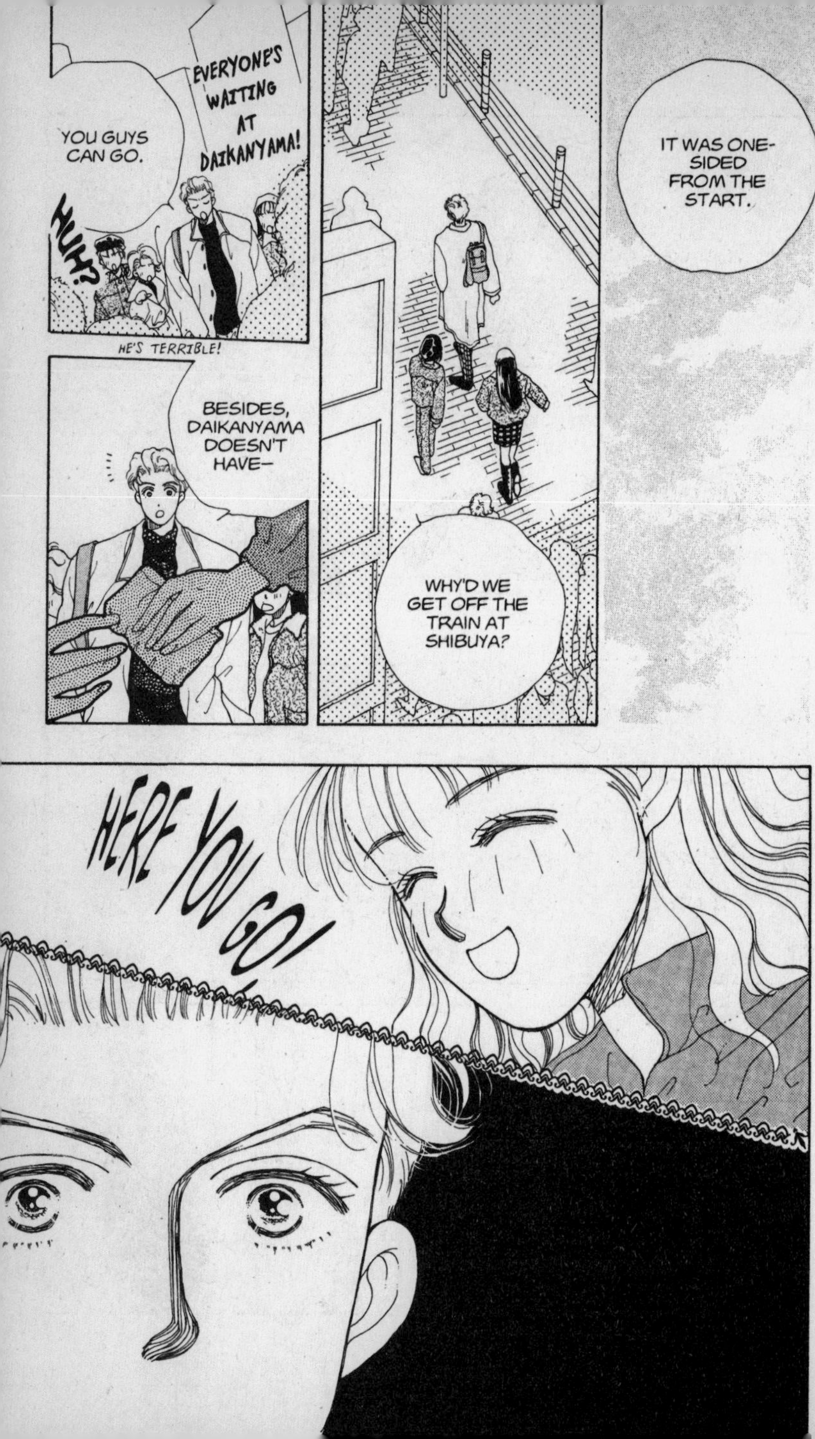
IT WAS ONE-SIDED FROM THE START.
WHY'D WE GET OFF THE TRAIN AT SHIBUYA?
EVERYONE'S WAITING AT DAIKANYAMA!
YOU GUYS CAN GO.
HUH?
HE'S TERRIBLE!
BESIDES, DAIKANYAMA DOESN'T HAVE—
HERE YOU GO!

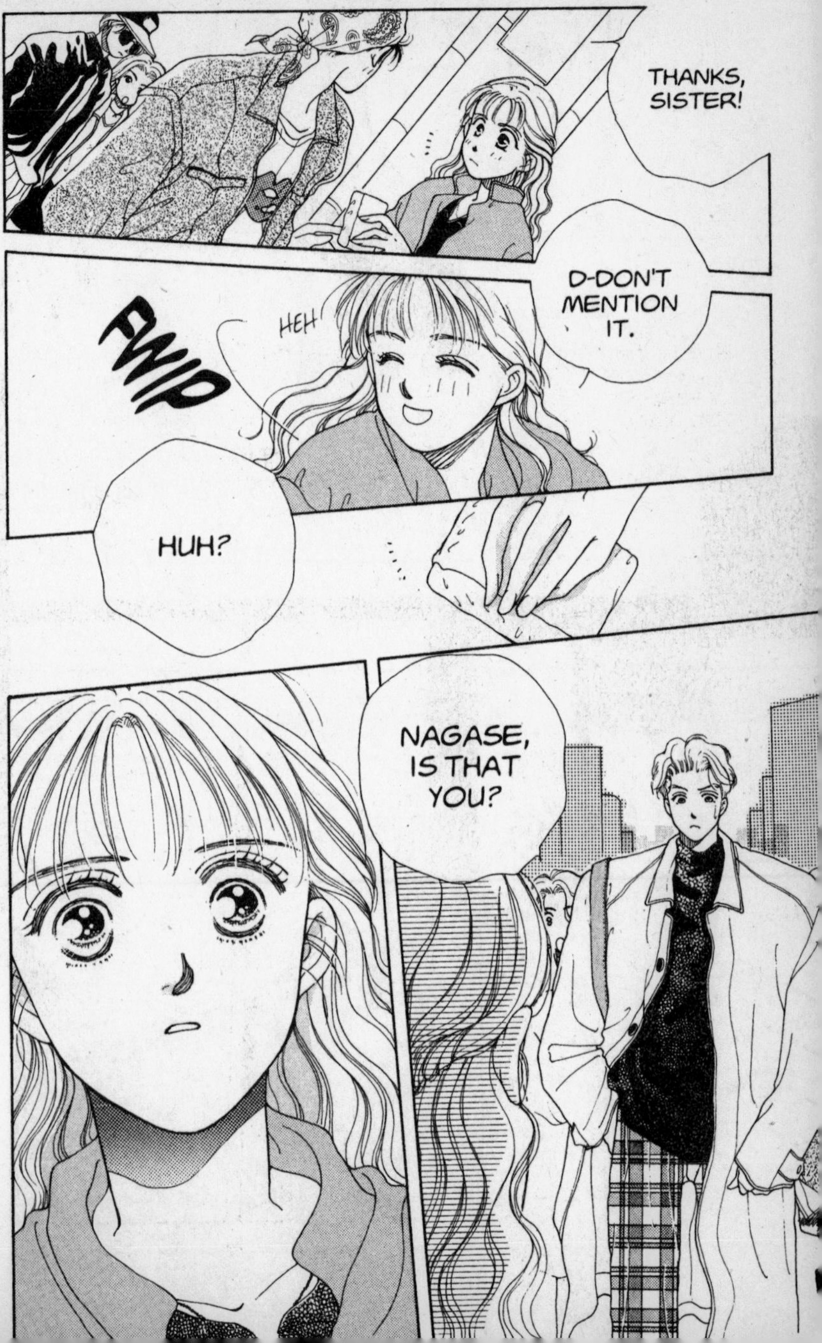
THANKS, SISTER!
D-DON'T MENTION IT.
HEH
FWIP
HUH?
NAGASE, IS THAT YOU?

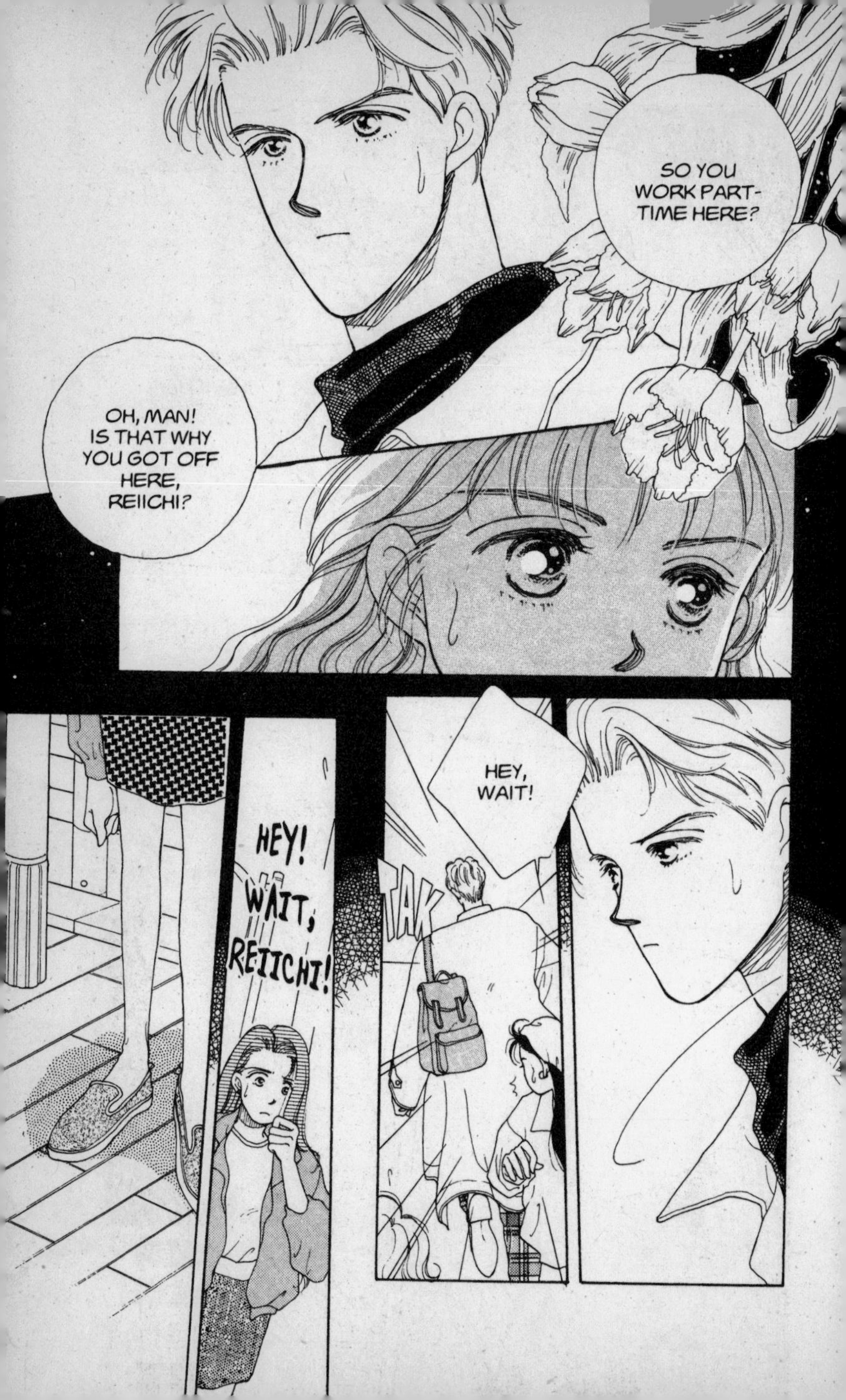
SO YOU WORK PART-TIME HERE?
OH, MAN! IS THAT WHY YOU GOT OFF HERE, REIICHI?
HEY, WAIT!
TAK
HEY! WAIT, REIICHI!

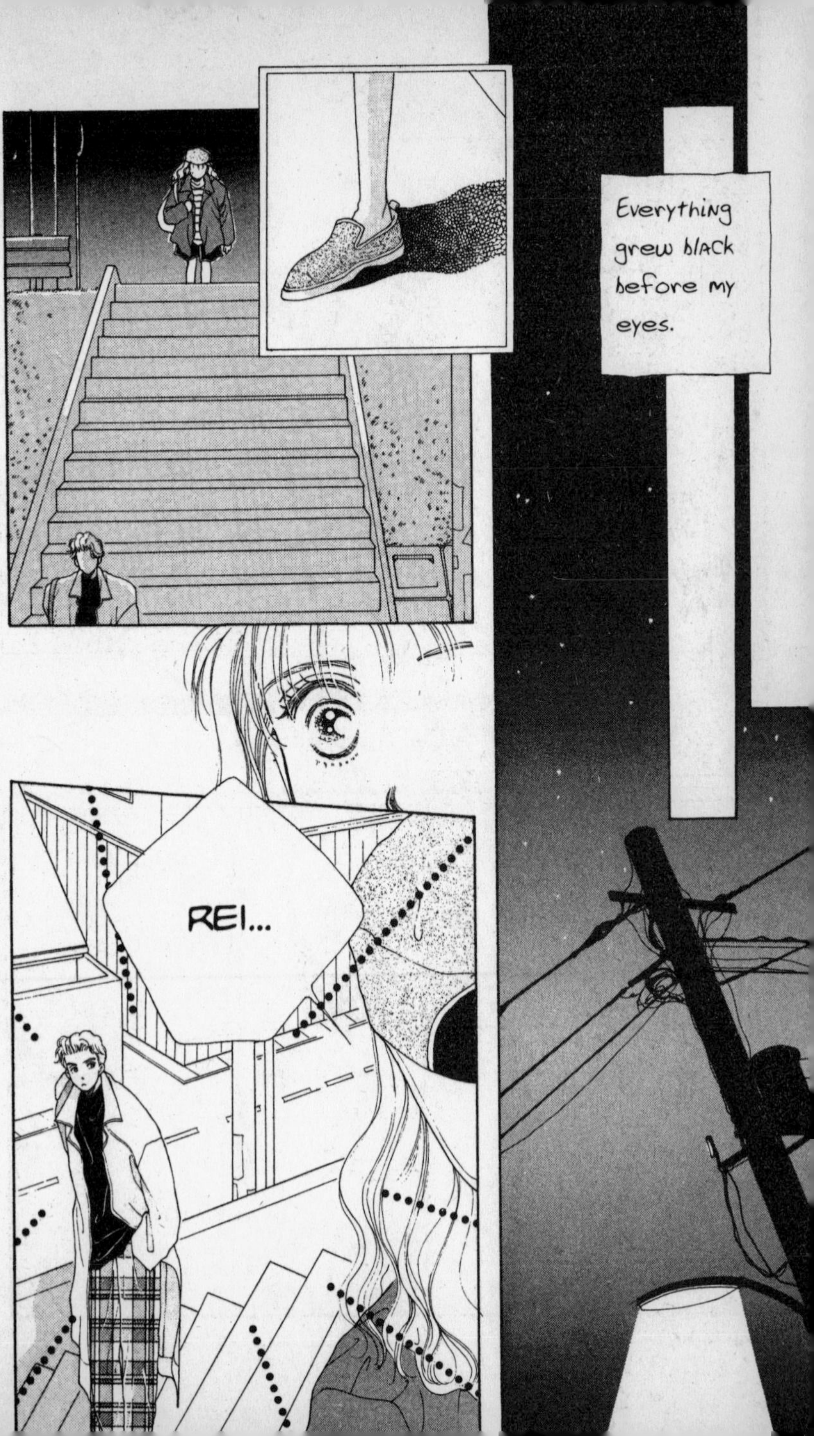
Everything grew black before my eyes.
REI...

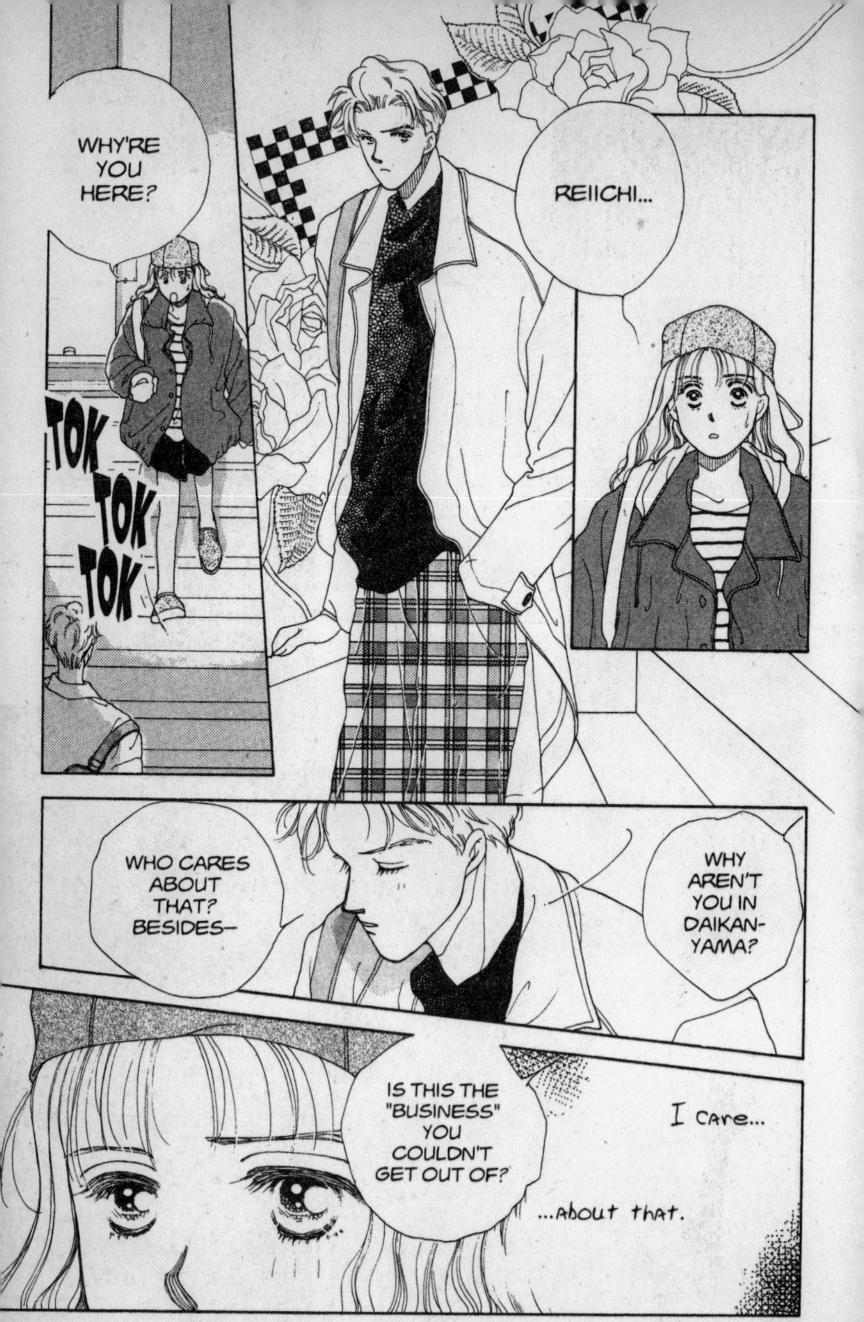
REIICHI...
WHY'RE YOU HERE?
TOK TOK TOK
WHY AREN'T YOU IN DAIKAN-YAMA?
WHO CARES ABOUT THAT? BESIDES—
IS THIS THE "BUSINESS" YOU COULDN'T GET OUT OF?
I care...
...about that.

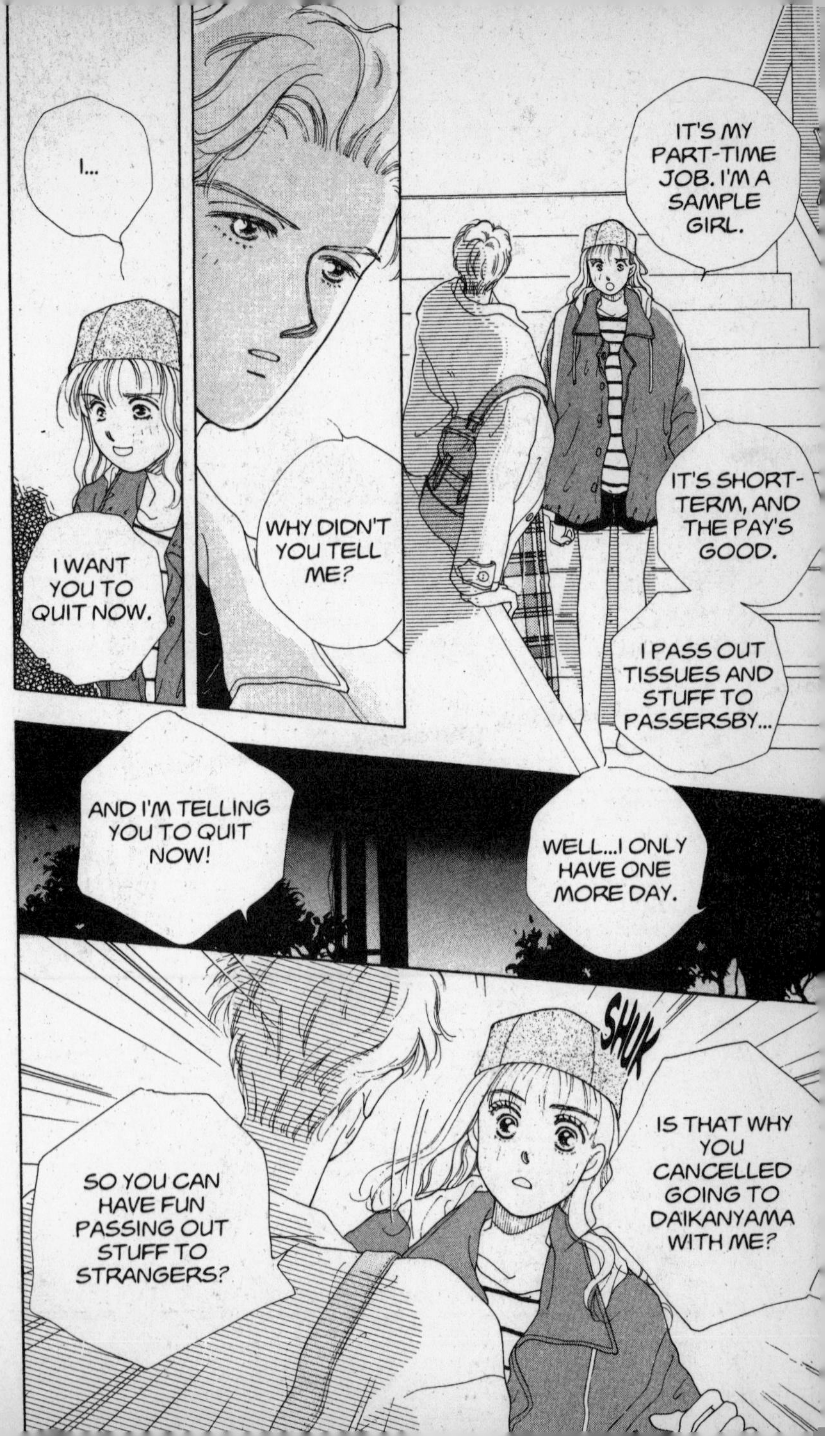
IT'S MY PART-TIME JOB. I'M A SAMPLE GIRL.
IT'S SHORT-TERM, AND THE PAY'S GOOD.
I PASS OUT TISSUES AND STUFF TO PASSERSBY...
WHY DIDN'T YOU TELL ME?
I...
I WANT YOU TO QUIT NOW.
WELL...I ONLY HAVE ONE MORE DAY.
AND I'M TELLING YOU TO QUIT NOW!
SHUK
IS THAT WHY YOU CANCELLED GOING TO DAIKANYAMA WITH ME?
SO YOU CAN HAVE FUN PASSING OUT STUFF TO STRANGERS?

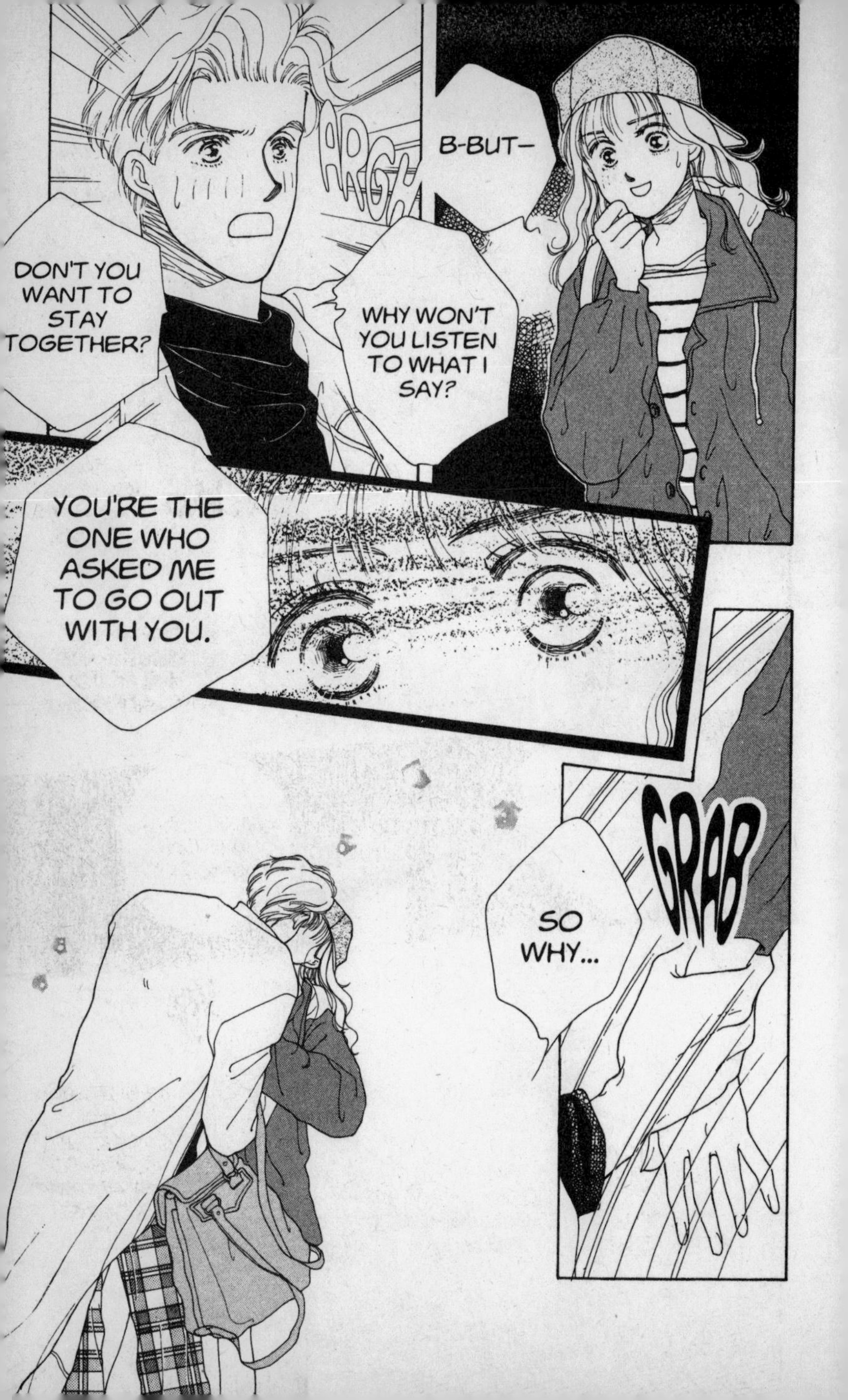
B-BUT—
ARGH
WHY WON'T YOU LISTEN TO WHAT I SAY?
DON'T YOU WANT TO STAY TOGETHER?
YOU'RE THE ONE WHO ASKED ME TO GO OUT WITH YOU.
GRAB
SO WHY...

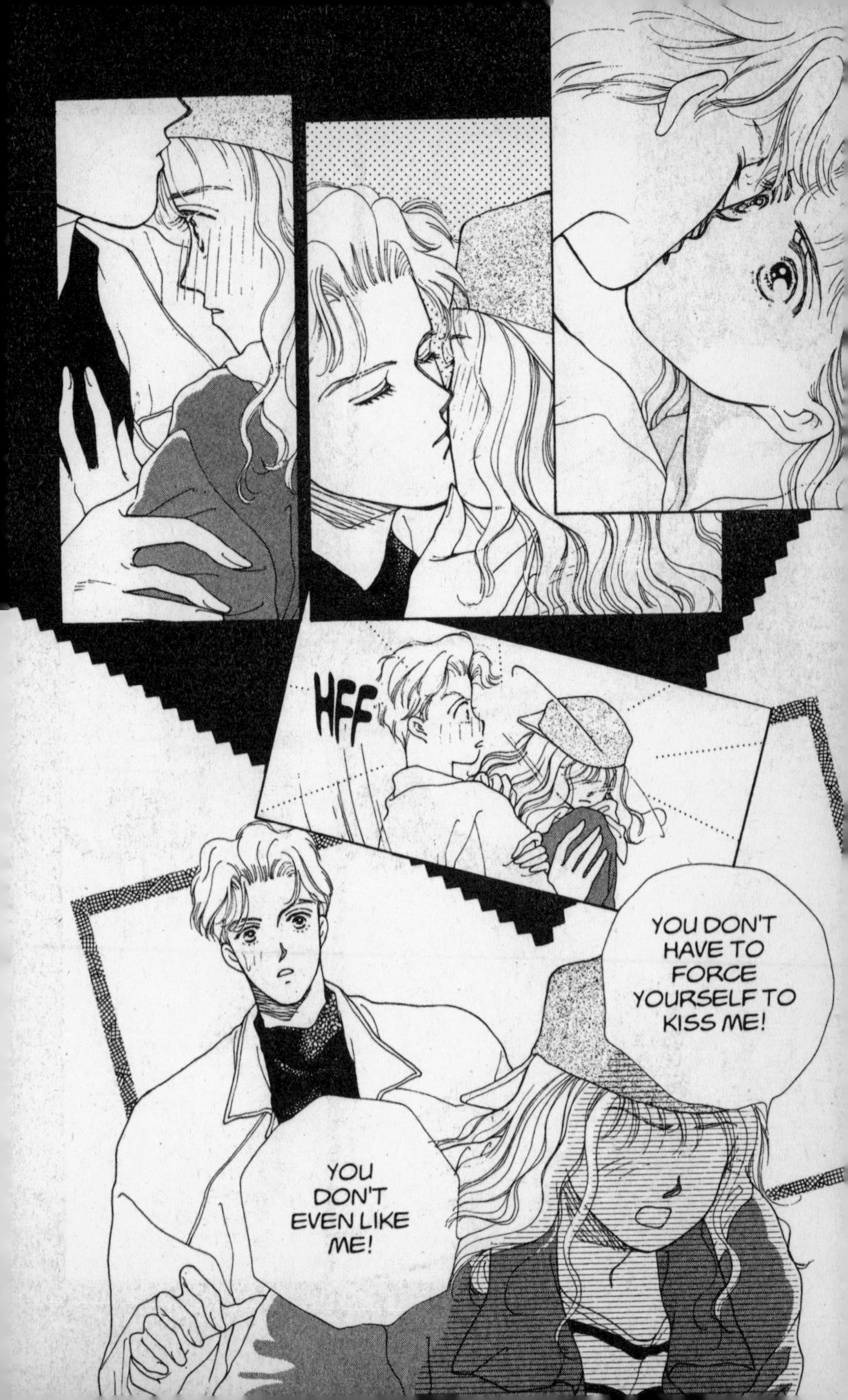
HFF
YOU DON'T HAVE TO FORCE YOURSELF TO KISS ME!
YOU DON'T EVEN LIKE ME!

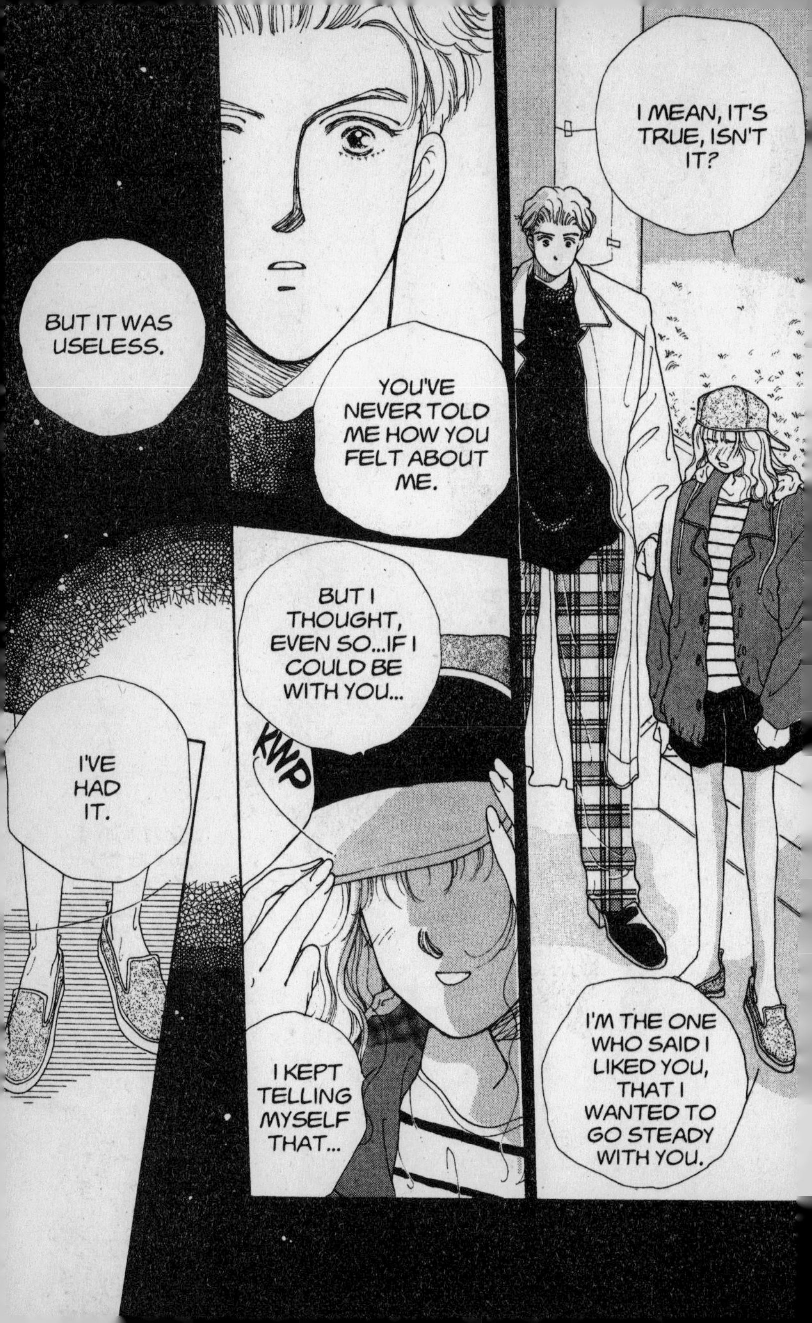
I MEAN, IT'S TRUE, ISN'T IT?
I'M THE ONE WHO SAID I LIKED YOU, THAT I WANTED TO GO STEADY WITH YOU.
YOU'VE NEVER TOLD ME HOW YOU FELT ABOUT ME.
BUT I THOUGHT, EVEN SO...IF I COULD BE WITH YOU...
KWP
I KEPT TELLING MYSELF THAT...
BUT IT WAS USELESS.
I'VE HAD IT.

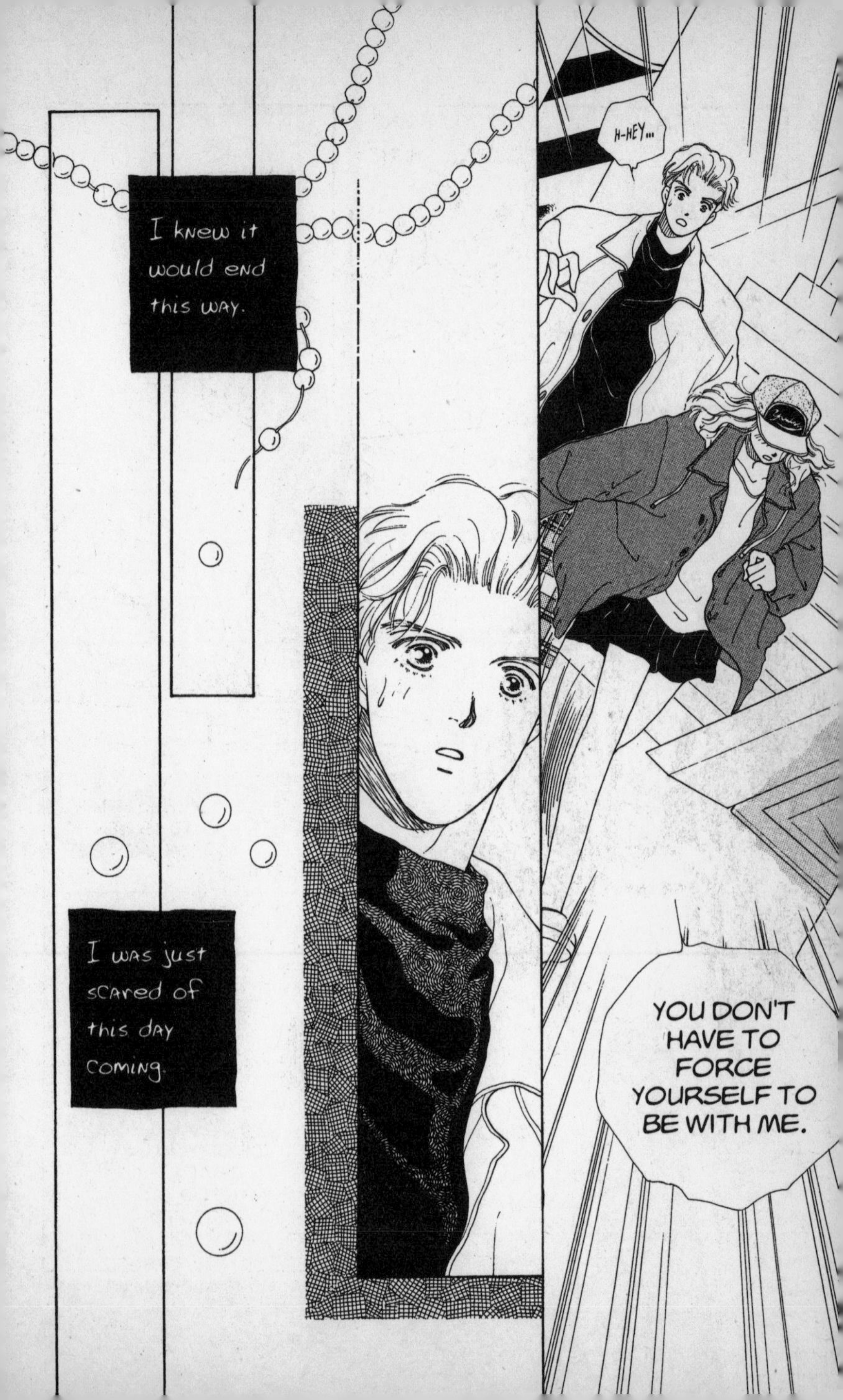
H-HEY...
YOU DON'T HAVE TO FORCE YOURSELF TO BE WITH ME.
I knew it would end this way.
I was just scared of this day coming.

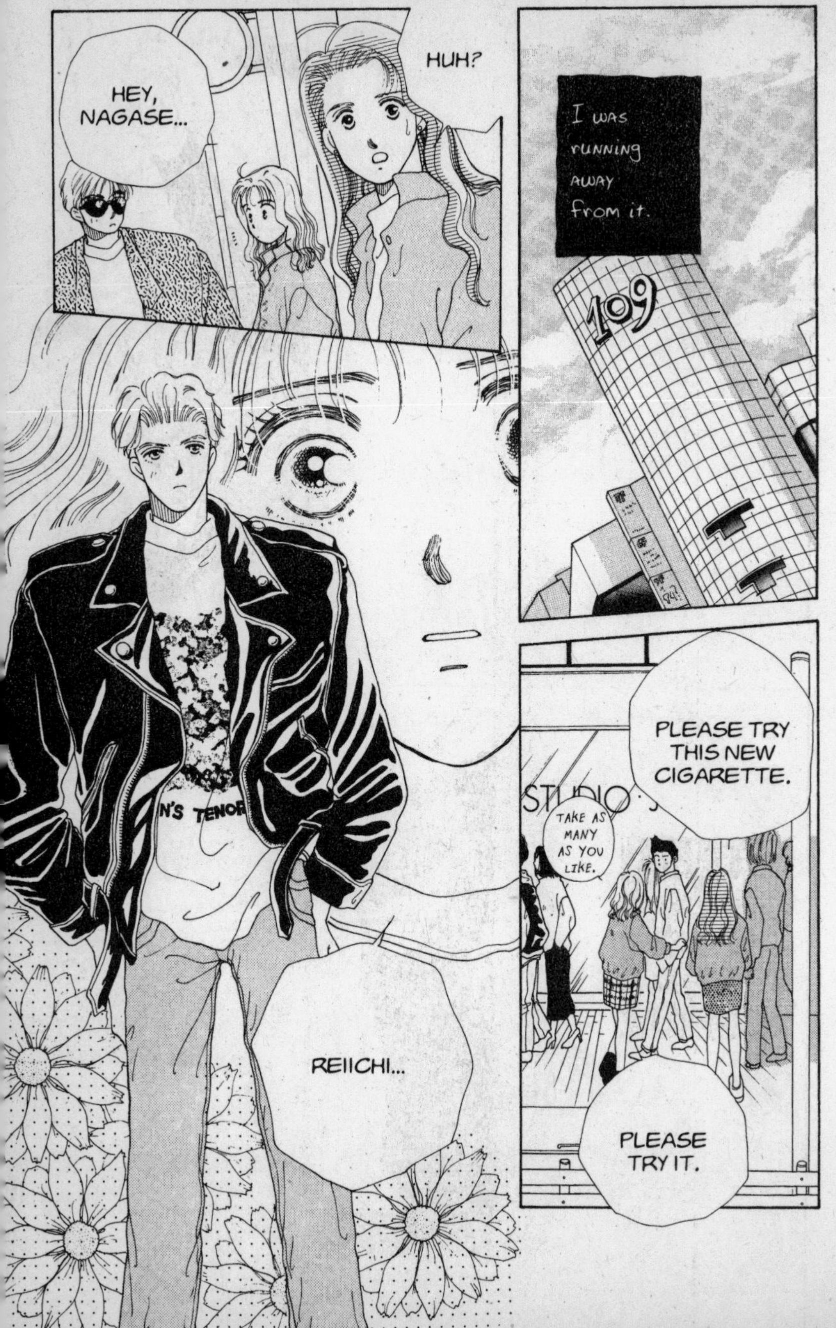
I was running away from it.
109
HEY, NAGASE...
HUH?
PLEASE TRY THIS NEW CIGARETTE.
STUDIO
TAKE AS MANY AS YOU LIKE.
PLEASE TRY IT.
N'S TENOR
REIICHI...

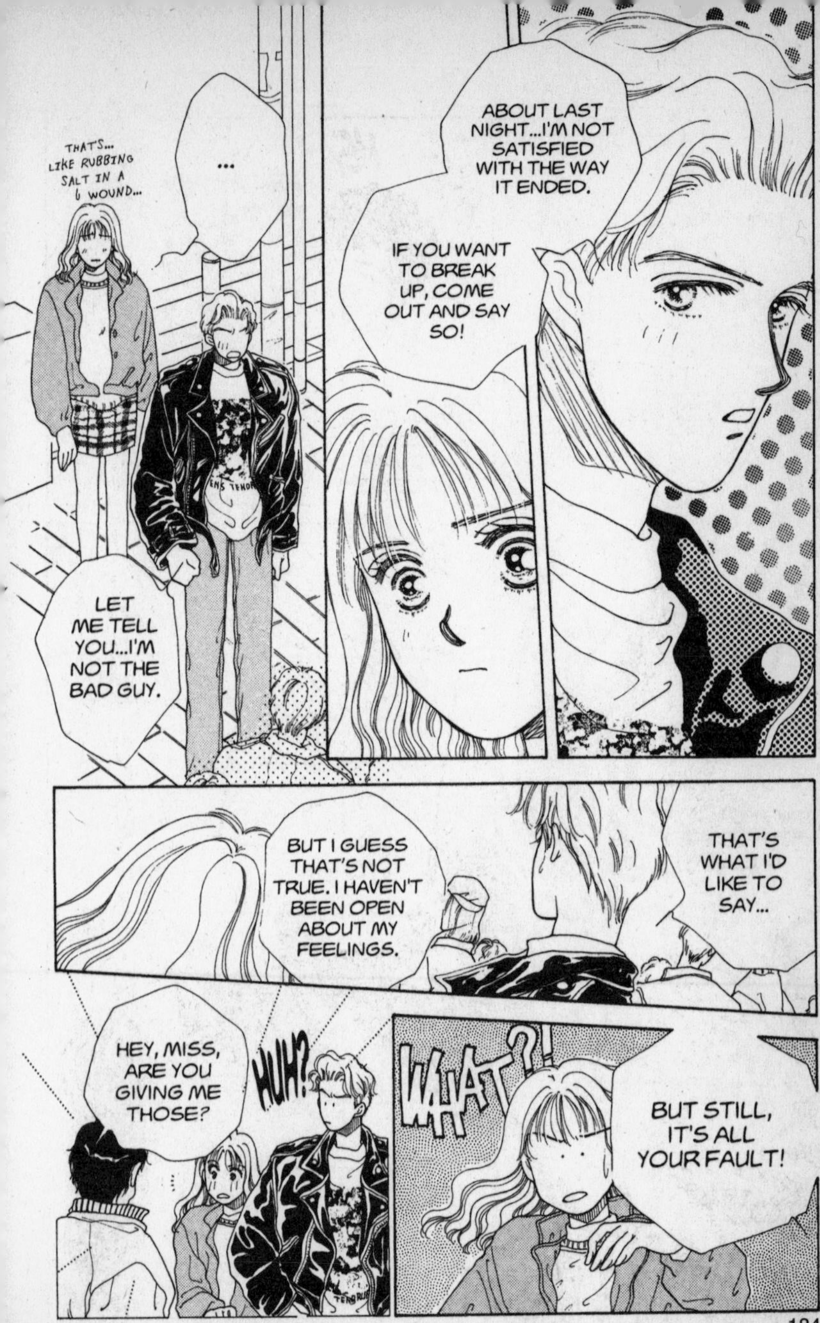
ABOUT LAST NIGHT...I'M NOT SATISFIED WITH THE WAY IT ENDED.
IF YOU WANT TO BREAK UP, COME OUT AND SAY SO!
...
THAT'S... LIKE RUBBING SALT IN A WOUND...
LET ME TELL YOU...I'M NOT THE BAD GUY.
THAT'S WHAT I'D LIKE TO SAY...
BUT I GUESS THAT'S NOT TRUE. I HAVEN'T BEEN OPEN ABOUT MY FEELINGS.
WHAT?
BUT STILL, IT'S ALL YOUR FAULT!
HUH?
HEY, MISS, ARE YOU GIVING ME THOSE?

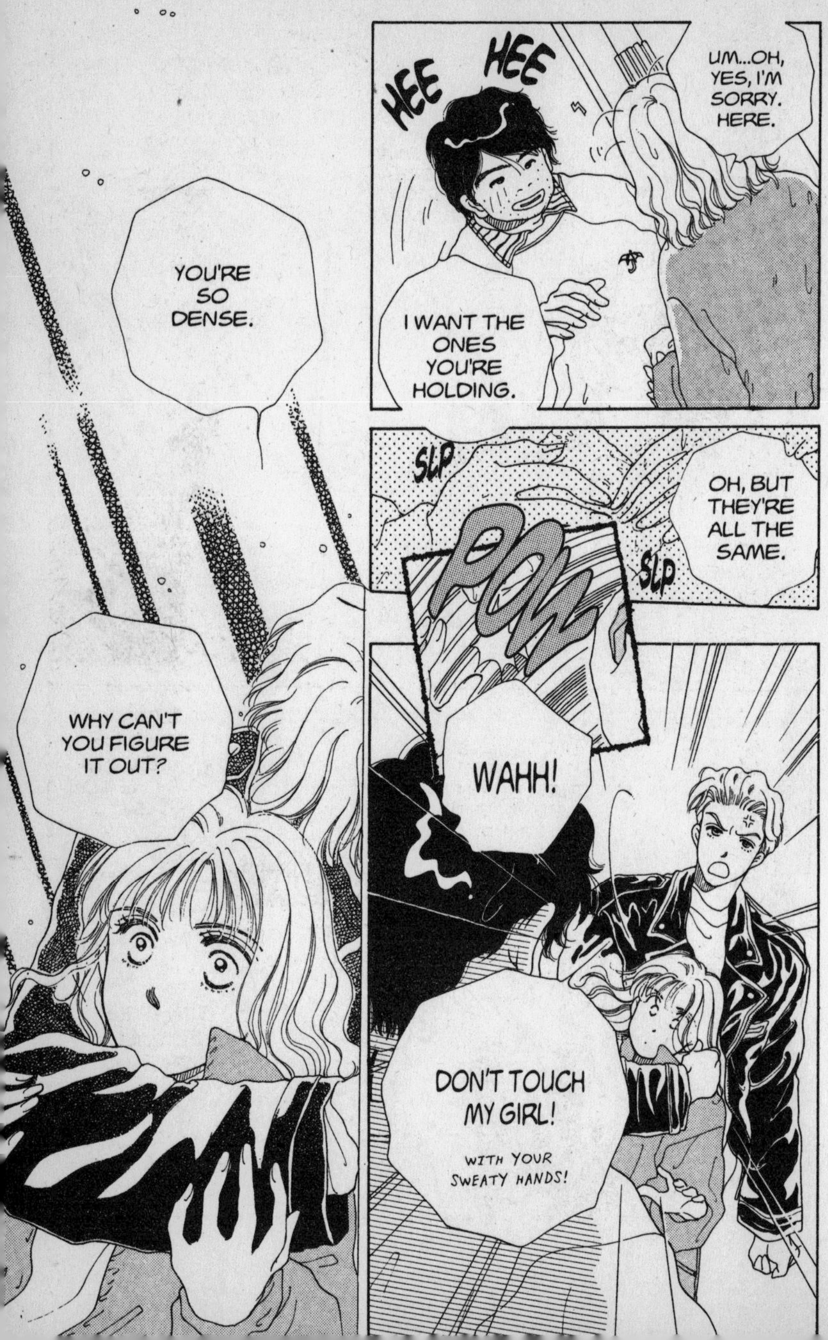
UM...OH, YES, I'M SORRY. HERE.
HEE HEE
I WANT THE ONES YOU'RE HOLDING.
OH, BUT THEY'RE ALL THE SAME.
SLP
SLP
POW
WAHH!
DON'T TOUCH MY GIRL!
WITH YOUR SWEATY HANDS!
YOU'RE SO DENSE.
WHY CAN'T YOU FIGURE IT OUT?

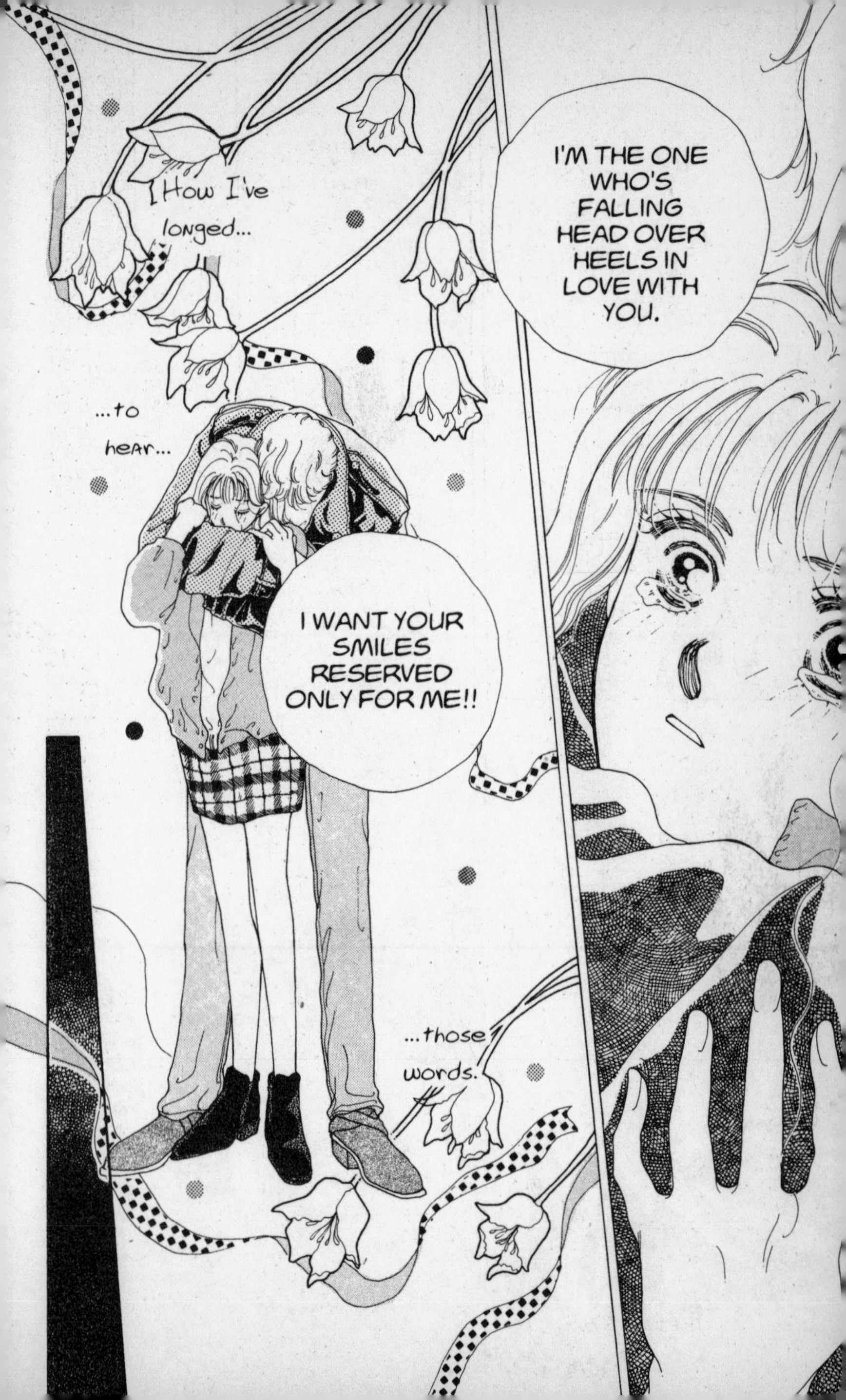
I'M THE ONE WHO'S FALLING HEAD OVER HEELS IN LOVE WITH YOU.
How I've longed...
...to hear...
I WANT YOUR SMILES RESERVED ONLY FOR ME!!
...those words.

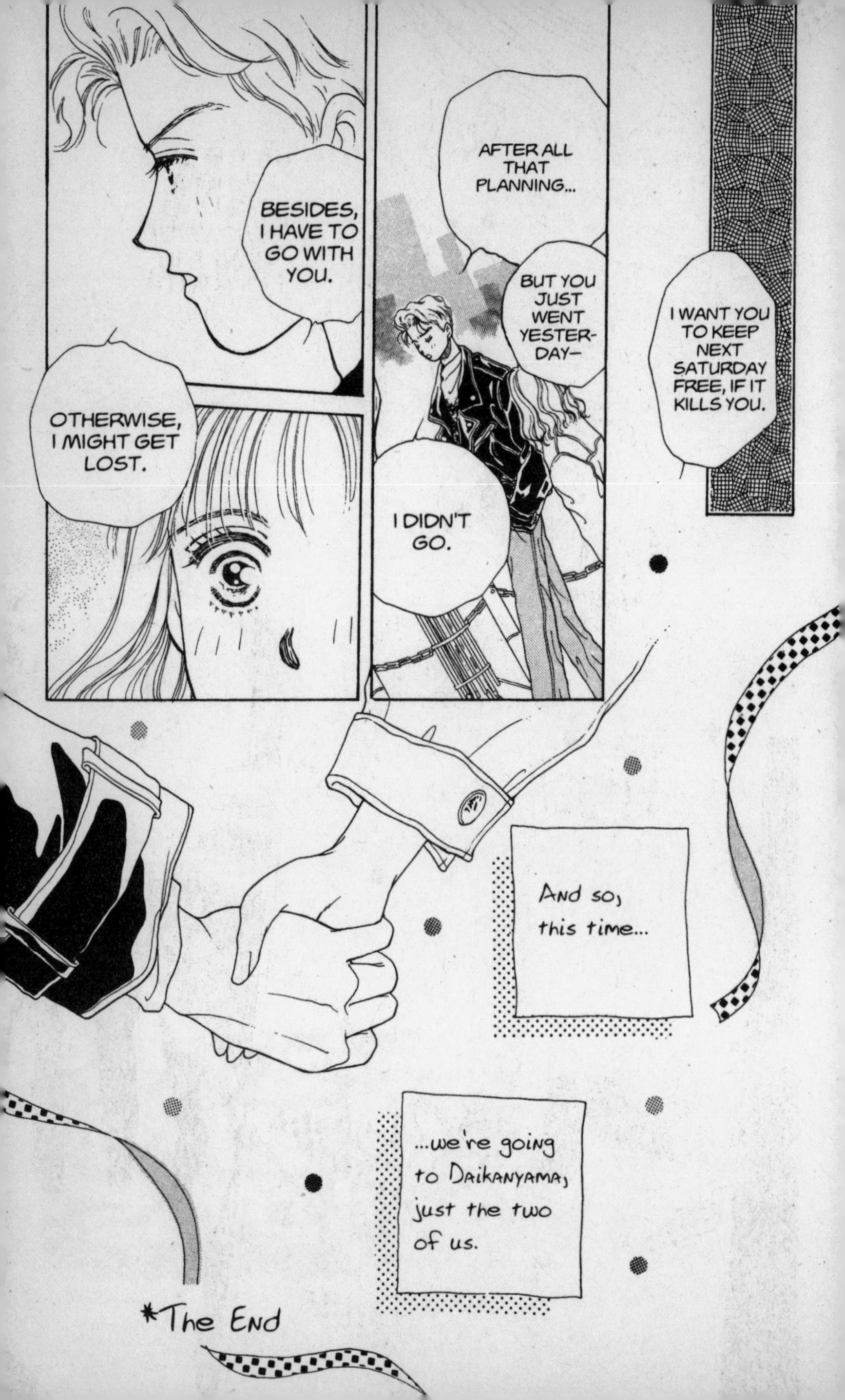
I WANT YOU TO KEEP NEXT SATURDAY FREE, IF IT KILLS YOU.
AFTER ALL THAT PLANNING...
BUT YOU JUST WENT YESTER-DAY—
I DIDN'T GO.
BESIDES, I HAVE TO GO WITH YOU.
OTHERWISE, I MIGHT GET LOST.
And so, this time...
...we're going to Daikanyama, just the two of us.
*The End

TOKYO BOYS GIRLS

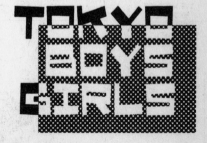

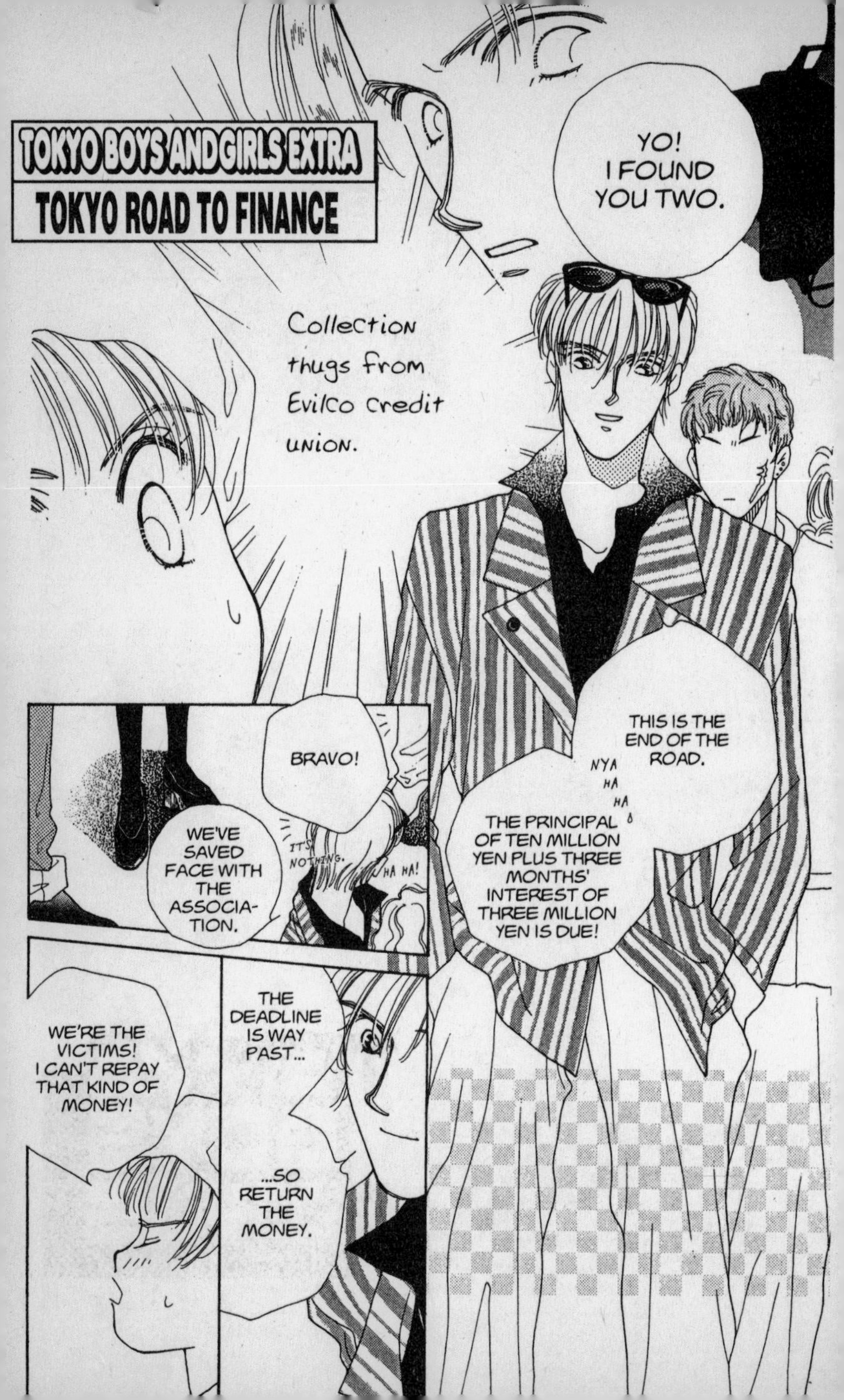
TOKYO BOYS ANDGIRLS EXTRA
TOKYO ROAD TO FINANCE
YO! I FOUND YOU TWO.
Collection thugs from Evilco credit union.
THIS IS THE END OF THE ROAD.
NYA HA HA
THE PRINCIPAL OF TEN MILLION YEN PLUS THREE MONTHS' INTEREST OF THREE MILLION YEN IS DUE!
BRAVO!
WE'VE SAVED FACE WITH THE ASSOCIATION.
IT'S NOTHING.
HA HA!
THE DEADLINE IS WAY PAST...
...SO RETURN THE MONEY.
WE'RE THE VICTIMS! I CAN'T REPAY THAT KIND OF MONEY!

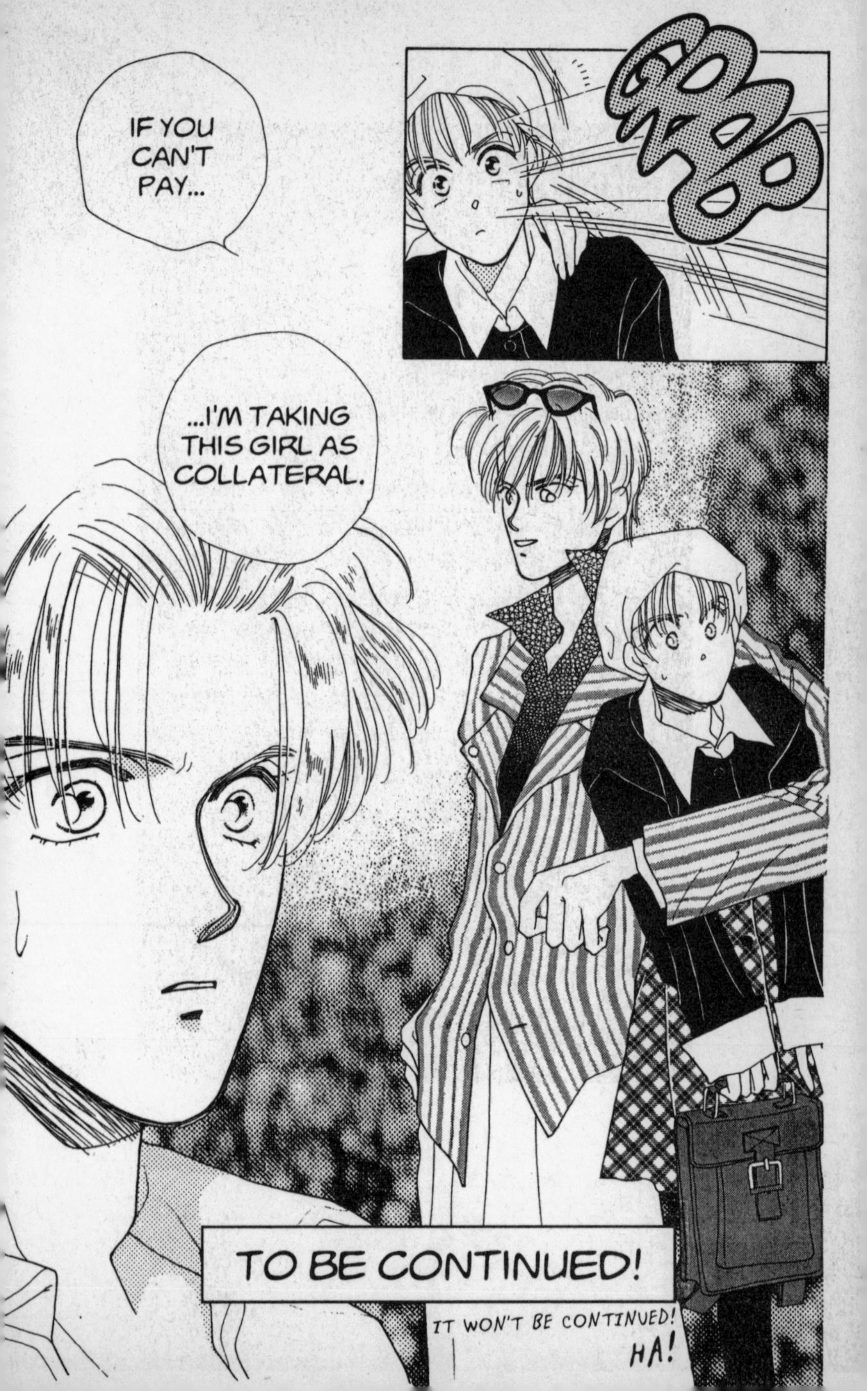
GRAB
IF YOU CAN'T PAY...
...I'M TAKING THIS GIRL AS COLLATERAL.
TO BE CONTINUED!
IT WON'T BE CONTINUED! HA!

Miki Aihara was born in the Shizuoka prefecture of Japan and currently lives in Tokyo. She made her debut in 1991 with *Lip Conscious!*, published in *Bessatsu Shoujo* Comic. Her immensely popular manga *Hot Gimmick* is published in English by VIZ Media. Aihara moves houses frequently, and loves to go to movies and shop for clothes. One of her hobbies is keeping tropical fish.

Shojo Beat

TOKYO BOYS & GIRLS VOLUME 1
The Shojo Beat Manga Edition

STORY AND ART BY
MIKI AIHARA

English Adaptation/Shaenon Garrity
Translation/JN Productions
Touch-up Art & Lettering/Bill Schuch
Design/Courtney Utt
Editor/Ian Robertson

Managing Editor/Megan Bates
Director of Production/Noboru Watanabe
Vice President of Publishing/Alvin Lu
Vice President & Editor in Chief/Yumi Hoashi
Sr. Director of Acquisitions/Rika Inouye
Vice President of Sales & Marketing/Liza Coppola
Publisher/Hyoe Narita

Printed in the U.S.A.

Published by VIZ Media, LLC
P.O. Box 77010
San Francisco, CA 94107

Shojo Beat Manga Edition
10 9 8 7 6 5 4 3 2 1
First printing, June 2005

viz media

PARENTAL ADVISORY
TOKYO BOYS & GIRLS is rated T+ for Teen Plus. Contains strong language, sexual themes. Recommended for older teens (16 and up).

RATED T+ FOR OLDER TEENS

store.viz.com